P9-ECJ-471

The Eternal Ethernet

Second edition

Data Communications and Networks Series

Consulting Editor: Dr C. Smythe, University of Sheffield

Selected titles

Other related Addison Wesley Longman titles

The Eternal Ethernet

Second edition

Alexis Ferrero

Addison-Wesley

Harlow, England • Reading, Massachusetts • Menlo Park, California • New York
Don Mills, Ontario • Amsterdam • Bonn • Sydney • Singapore • Tokyo • Madrid
San Juan • Milan • Mexico City • Seoul • Taipei

© Addison Wesley Longman 1999

Addison Wesley Longman Limited
Edinburgh Gate
Harlow
Essex
CM20 2JE
England

and Associated Companies throughout the world.

Original edition translated by Stephen S. Wilson
Updates translated by the Book Production Company
Typeset by 35 in 10/12pt Times
Cover designed by ODB Design & Illustration, Reading
Printed and bound in Great Britain by Biddles Ltd., Guildford and King's Lynn.

First published 1996
Second edition 1999

ISBN 0-201-36056-X

British Library Cataloguing-in-Publication Data
A catalogue record for this book is available from the British Library.

Library of Congress Cataloging-in-Publication Data
Ferrero, Alexis.
    The eternal ethernet / Alexis Ferrero ; translated by Stephen S.
Wilson. — 2nd ed.
      p.   cm.
    Includes bibliographical references and index.
    ISBN 0-201-36056-X
    1. Ethernet (Local area network system)   I. Title.
TK5105.8.E83F4713   1999
004.67′8—DC21   98- 41596
                                                    CIP

To my wife Elisabeth
and my children Baptiste & Clelia

Contents

Trademark notice

Apple, Macintosh, Apple Talk, Apple Share, Local Talk and Token Talk are registered trademarks of Apple Computer, Inc.

DECnet, VMS and ULTRIX are trademarks of Digital Equipment Corporation

DOS, LAN Manager and Windows are trademarks of Microsoft Corporation

ETHERNET and ISO ETHERNET are trademarks of DEC, Intel and Xerox

ISMOS is a registered trademark of NEC

NFS and Sun Net Manager are trademarks of Sun Microsystems, Inc.

Token Ring and SNA are trademarks, and LAN Server and NetView are registered trademarks of International Business Machines Corporation

Unix and NetWare are registered trademarks of Novell, Inc.

XNS is a trademark of Xerox Corporation

XWindows is a trademark of Massachusetts Institute of Technology

Introduction

- How to read this book

- The requirement

- The main characteristics of Ethernet

- The components

- Operation

- Commercial position

- Evolution

How to read this book

This book is divided into three parts, each with a different aim.

- Part I is an introduction to the technical framework with which we shall be concerned throughout the book. It contains an explanation of the basic notions of telecommunications and networks, which will be useful to an understanding of the following chapters.
- Part II provides a detailed technical description of the Ethernet standard and the characteristics of the hardware components of a network.
- Finally, Part III describes specific methods and tools to be used at different stages in the design, development and maintenance of an Ethernet local area network.

Thus, this book is addressed towards anyone faced with the management of one or more networks at any stage; he or she will find theoretical data, information and practical advice here.

Parts II and III may be read separately from each other; however, Part III requires some knowledge of the technical environment of Ethernet. After reading the whole book, the engineer who wishes to know even more will be able to get to grips with the relevant standards and norms more easily.

A list of contents is given at the beginning of each of the three parts. The book ends with a fairly complete glossary of technical terms, whose brief explanations provide readers with an introduction to connected areas.

The requirement

The technology of Ethernet local area networks was developed at the beginning of the 1980s by a grouping of computer-industry companies who perceived a need for high-speed (at least for the period) data communications between relatively close computers.

The aim of these manufacturers was to define a communications standard which was capable of guaranteeing the interconnectability of machines at the level of a building or an industrial site (Figure I.1).

They wanted their product to permit rapid data transfer, and to be easy to install, evolve and maintain. They were ready to conform to a layered architecture such as that recommended by the standardization bodies. Moreover, they intended to publish the definition and the characteristics of the elements of this network. Thus, up until the differences in proprietary solutions, they were able to open the market for hardware adapted to Ethernet networks to all manufacturers.

Today, Ethernet is the most common local area network standard. It still provides an adequate performance for the large majority of applications and its cost,

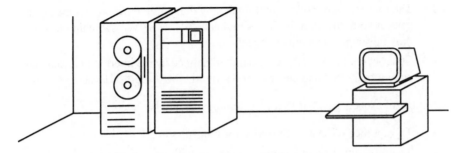

Figure I.1 Elementary aim: to enable two machines to intercommunicate.

given its popularity, continues to decrease. The equipment which constitutes the network (that which effectively carries out the data transfer) is constantly improving and increasing in capacity and security.

The main characteristics of Ethernet

The fundamental technical characteristics of Ethernet can be summarized using a number of phrases which follow. All these specific points will be discussed in detail elsewhere in the book.

- Ethernet has become a 'universal' network, in the sense that interfaces have been developed for all types of machine (from the smallest portable to the mainframe).
- The maximum distance between two stations connected to the same network is 4 km at 10 Mbps (using fiber links).
- Up to 1024 machines can be connected to a shared Ethernet network.
- It is possible to connect or disconnect a machine from the network without disturbing the operation of the whole network.
- The original global speed is 10 Mbps in serial mode (or approximately 10^6 characters per second) on the network as a whole, where this capacity is shared between all the stations. With the latest developments, this speed can be multiplied by 10 (namely 100 Mbps) or even 100 (1 Gbps).
- It permits short waiting-time delays prior to emission, in normal situations.
- Ethernet uses a distributed access method for all the machines connected. All stations are equal as far as the network is concerned, and there is no master station which controls the network. However, the recent dynamic packet switching technology provides for a considerable improvement in this operation by dedicating the entire bandwidth to each access.

- The transmission mode is half duplex by default, in other words, the signals pass in both direction, but not simultaneously. However, switching also permits full duplex machine connection.

- Ethernet conforms to the OSI standard defined by the international standardization body ISO and covers layer 1 and the MAC part of layer 2.

A number of aspects peculiar to this technology should be noted:

- The absence of levels of priority for transmission.

- The difficulty of implementing a system with privacy protection (since the data circulating in the network is accessible to all stations) and a relative vulnerability to malicious acts.

- The recovery of packets when numerous successive errors have occurred is left to the communication system.

The components

In a simplified view, an Ethernet network consists of stations interconnected as shown in Figure I.2.

The following components are indispensable to the operation of an Ethernet network:

- The medium or physical carrier of the signals, which may be coaxial or twisted pair cable for electrical signals, or fiber optic cable for optical signals.

- The transceiver, a unit responsible for emitting and receiving signals on the medium.

- The repeater, a device capable of interconnecting several cable segments.

- The Ethernet controller, usually in the form of a slot-in card for the machine to be attached. This implements the link between the computer backplane and the transceiver.

- A cable segment may be several hundred meters long (up to 100 meters for twisted pair and 2 km for optical fiber).

- The transceiver is located on the medium; it is the point at which the machine is connected to the network.

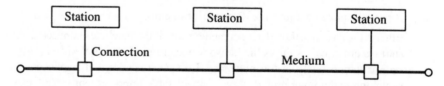

Figure I.2   Schematic view of an Ethernet network with three stations.

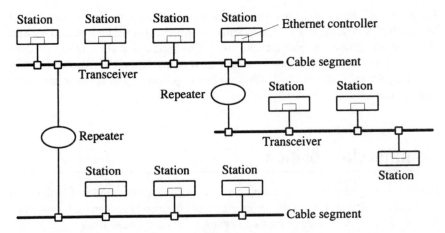

Figure I.3 Schematic diagram of an Ethernet network consisting of three interconnected cable segments.

- The repeaters shown in Figure I.3 have many ports, integrating one transceiver per port; they are called hubs.
- The link between the Ethernet controller and the transceiver is often implemented by quite a short cable (few meters).

Finally, one should not forget the human component, which constitutes a resource that is all too often hidden. Clearly, a network of several tens of machines inevitably requires management tasks to manage the communication facilities as a whole (network equipment, software, resource sharing). A procedure to plan and organize the resources, both material and human, should be provided for in conjunction with any important installation.

Operation

The logical operation of an Ethernet network may, in turn, be summarized as follows:

- It is based on a fair distributed access method, in which each item of equipment is always capable of deciding on its own whether it can occupy the medium with its emission.
- It transports the data within packets (or frames) emitted on the medium. These frames necessarily have a length between 64 and 1518 8-bit bytes (with a data field of between 46 and 1500 bytes).
- It requires an interface for the computer to be connected; this interface manages the MAC functions inherent to Ethernet and communicates with the level 2 entity above it.

The global efficiency of the network is quite high, although it is sometimes difficult to quantify. In fact, the overall bandwidth can only be utilized for a shared network with a small number of machines attached. This means that for a fairly extensive network including a large number (several tens) of machines, the speed of 10 Mbps is no longer totally accessible. This phenomenon is normal and is due to the access method used.

Commercial position

Ethernet is a type of network dating from some fifteen years ago and is thus well tried and tested. It represents the technology most frequently used in business-related local area networks, followed by its competitor network: Token Ring.

The current cost of an Ethernet network has become relatively low, thanks to the large amount of hardware already installed. Moreover, since Ethernet is the most common technology in terms of the different types of machine that may be attached, it is equally applicable to PC, PS/2 and Apple Macintosh microcomputers and workstations of all kinds, and to supercomputers (using their front-end interface).

The division of market shares analyzed by the Dell Oro Group provides evidence of the dominance of Ethernet among local area network architectures (Figure I.4).

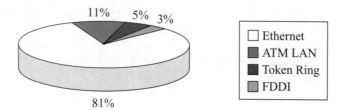

Figure I.4 Market shares of local area network switching in the world in 1997.

Evolution

Finally, the recent evolutions of Ethernet give a new impetus to this technology as we reach the last years of the millenium. Thus, it is now possible to double the bandwidth with a full duplex operation, to work at 100 Mbps, or even at 1 Gbps, instead of 10 Mbps based on the same infrastructures with the extension of the standards, 1000BaseT, or to dedicate the entire bandwidth to each network connection, at the same time eliminating the limitations of the access method, with dynamic packet switching. The integration of Ethernet data traffic with voice and video communications is also possible through ATM transport using LAN_Emulation capabilities.

PART I

The world of telecommunications

Chapter 1

The standardization bodies

- Aims

- The main bodies

- The stages of standard documents

Several standardization bodies are involved in the area of telecommunications and local area networks, and the documents they produce (standards) have an important impact on the industrial world and on the choices available to users.

Warning

As in the remainder of the book, we are principally interested here in digital data communications.

1.1 Aims

Historically, manufacturers of computer equipment have developed proprietary communication systems permitting the exchange of data between their machines. This service was a response to needs voiced by users who had an important set of machines, some of which were distant from others. The first solutions that were implemented resolved the problem for a few specific machines, but they were only rarely suitable for several types of configuration.

Moreover, in the best case, these hardware and software solutions were still adapted solely to the equipment of a single constructor. This meant that a specific gateway was needed to permit intercommunication between heterogeneous computer equipment.

With the enormous growth of computer hardware, the cost and complexity of developing these specific interconnection elements soon became prohibitive. This led to the definition, for certain types of hardware intended for general use, of detailed technical characteristics which were strongly recommended to developers and manufacturers. These specifications were then circulated widely, published or distributed free of charge (in electronic form, over networks). When they are laid down by the relevant competent bodies, these technical documents become standards or working standard documents. When they come from a manufacturer or private company, but have not been officially standardized, they are called *de facto standards*.

More generally, the role of these bodies is to provide a well-defined specification of all the characteristics and values, which can be used to develop hardware that will function in an identical manner or that will be mutually compatible.

1.2 The main bodies

- The International Organization for Standardization (ISO), as its name indicates, operates at an international level and is responsible for standardization in almost all areas.

- The ISO dates from 1947 and now has a membership of almost 100 standardization bodies. It is organized into technical committees, subcommittees and working groups. This is a body that cannot be ignored and its standards (denoted IS, for International Standard) are the result of a great deal of development work. ISO is not only involved in telecommunications; some of its standardization work in other areas covers the sensitivity of photographic films, programming languages, units of physical measurement, and so on.

- The Comité Consultatif International Télégraphique et Téléphonique (CCITT) is a body which brings together the network providers (PTTs of various countries) and which has a fundamental role in the standardization of telecommunications (principally in relation to technical operation-related aspects and to the fixing of price scales). The CCITT has been re-integrated in the ITU (International Telecommunication Union) in 1993 as the ITU-T. It publishes its recommendations or advice every four years (1984, 1988, 1992, 1996) in several volumes.

- The American National Standards Institute (ANSI) plays a similar role to that of the ISO but at the national level in the United States.

- The French equivalent of ANSI is the Association Française de Normalisation (AFNOR). Similarly, Germany has the Deutsches Institut für Normung (DIN) and Britain has the British Standards Institution (BSI).

- The Institute of Electrical and Electronics Engineers (IEEE, pronounced 'i triple e') is an American body which manages various research projects; it has international authority.

  The IEEE played a very active part in the standardization of the Ethernet and Token Ring local area network types, by evolving the manufacturers' standards (Xerox–Digital–Intel and IBM) into an ISO standard. The results of its standardization work in the area of local area networks are known by the number of the committee responsible for them (committee 802, since it was created in February 1980); thus, they are of type 802.X where X is the number that identifies the project more specifically. For example, IEEE 802.3 corresponds to the standardization of Ethernet, IEEE 802.5 to that of Token Ring and IEEE 802.6 to that of DQDB. The IEEE 802 committee is also referred to as the LMSC: LAN MAN Standard Committee.

  For information, we note that the IEEE standardized the HP-IB bus (frequently used to communicate with measuring instruments) in IEEE 488.

1.3 The stages of standard documents

In the standardization process the document produced by the standardizing body passes through several stages.

For example, for ISO, new subjects are first catalogued as NWI, for *New Work Item*. Then, the document produced may be accepted as a Committee Draft (CD, formerly Draft Proposal (DP)). It then becomes a Draft International Standard (DIS) and finally, an International Standard (IS).

Supplementary paragraphs may be added via Addenda, which may also pass through the stages of Proposed Draft Addendum (PDAD) and subsequently Draft Addendum (DAD). Similarly, corrections to a published standard may be issued in the form of Amendments (AM) which may pass through the stages of Proposed Draft Amendment (PDAM) and Draft Amendment (DAM).

We shall see later that certain specifications take several years to pass through all the stages that lead to effective standardization. In their impatience to market their solutions as quickly as possible, equipment manufacturers and software developers refer to draft versions of the future document. In this way, they try to place themselves as close as possible to the future standard, but do not respect the simple fact that drafts are clearly made to be commented on and should not be used to claim conformance to.

Moreover, these drafts evolve regularly, which implies that only the last one can be identical with the standard, being voted to be so, while the previous drafts differ from the final version in at least one respect, and possibly in several.

Conclusion

It should be borne in mind that the standardization bodies, be they national or international, have become increasingly useful to users by virtue of the strict rules which they lay down in each of the areas in which they operate.

Moreover, manufacturers should ultimately also benefit from this increasing tendency towards homogeneity.

Chapter 2

The layered models

- Introduction to the OSI model

- The lower layers

- The higher layers

- The TCP/IP model

- Other models

One of the most important ISO standards in the areas of data transmission and networks consists of a segmentation of the functions which a telecommunications system must perform (hardware and software).

This segmentation involves a breakdown into layers and is used to divide the work as a whole into modules, each having its own well-defined task. The interfaces between the layers are clearly standardized, and the signals passing through these are called services or indications, depending on their direction (the lower layer provides services to the higher layer which, in return, transmits indications).

2.1 Introduction to the OSI model

ISO was led to define a standard partitioning of the functions of a telecommunications system, going from the physical transmission medium to the applied software for use on the system. This partitioning gave rise to the Open Systems Interconnection (OSI) model, known as ISO standard IS 7498 (15 November 1984) (Figure 2.1).

The first document defining the OSI model dates back to 1984, but the definition work in ISO began as early as 1977. The proposed standard was accepted in 1978, but amendments have also been made since then.

It should be understood that, as in the case of programming languages, for which only the functionality is standardized (and not the compilation or interpretation procedures), the standards relating to telecommunication technologies forming part of open systems define the exchanges with the outside world, but not the internal operation.

A terminology was chosen to denote messages passing from one layer to another. Accordingly, if layer N transmits a request to the layer below, the latter

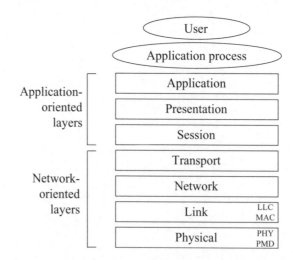

Figure 2.1 The seven layers of the ISO OSI reference model.

replies with a confirmation. On the contrary, if layer N emits towards the layer above, this is an indication, and the latter will return a response. In all cases, these messages pass through the service access points (SAPs) of each layer. The multilayer reference model had its origins in a desire to create standards that were more homogeneous and easier to apply. The subdivision of the functions of an arbitrary telecommunications system into layers with well-defined tasks results in an overall description which is necessarily more structured and better organized.

Thus, the OSI model constitutes a point of reference with which one should seek to make the system to be developed coincide. This makes it possible to determine the specifications of each layer of the technology in question, and to make each layer compatible with existing higher and lower layers from the design stage on.

Encapsulation

When a data packet passes from a layer N to the layer below, $(N - 1)$, it is supplemented by the addition of extra fields to its beginning and/or end. In the first case, the extra field is referred to as a header; in the second case it is a trailer (postfix or suffix). This added information supplements the frame at the level of the layer at which it was emitted (N here). Thus, when received by the layer of the same level (N) of the destination station, these fields are used in the processing which the latter must carry out. These fields may include the source and destination addresses (of level N), a parity check, the packet length, priority bits, identification of the protocol in the layer above $(N + 1)$ for decoding purposes, acknowledgment numbers, and so on.

This process of gradual enrichment of the message is called encapsulation, since the data arriving from the higher layer is incorporated in a more complete structure (Figure 2.2).

As an inverse to encapsulation, which takes place when data passes downwards through the communications model of the emitting machine, the receiving station applies a decapsulation (upwards movement).

It will have become apparent that the layers of the same level of each machine intercommunicate in some way (Figure 2.3). The information contained in the level N header is only of significance to level N of the target machine. This is made possible by the contribution of all the lower layers used.

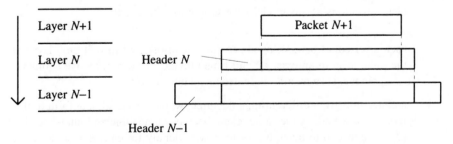

Figure 2.2 Process of encapsulation with passage through successive layers.

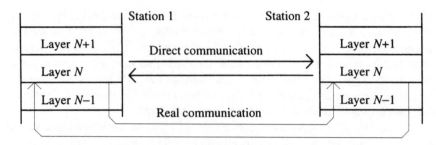

Figure 2.3   Virtual communication between equivalent layers.

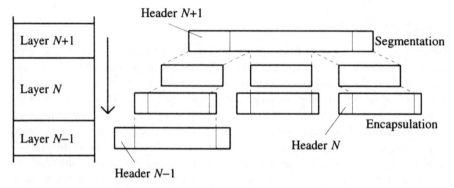

Figure 2.4   Segmentation, followed by the encapsulation of each resulting packet.

Segmentation

The packets reaching the layer of level N may have a length greater than that which may be handled by layer $N - 1$; layer N must then split up the original packet. This operation, called segmentation, must be performed in such a way that layer N of the receiving station is advised that it must reconstitute the original packet before transmitting it to layer $N + 1$ of the receiver, and so that it is able to perform this reassembly without difficulty (Figure 2.4).

Generalizations of this model have sought to ensure that:

- each layer could be developed separately and inserted to replace a layer of the same level in an existing unit (this provides for a progressive evolution of a complex system and facilitates its maintenance);

- architectures from different manufacturers would eventually conform to this model and would, by the same token, become compatible and inter-operable (this is intended to make the system user friendly for end users and reduce the need for interconnection gateways).

2.2 The lower layers

In this study of Ethernet local area networks, the layers with which we are concerned are the lowest ones, namely layers 1 and 2. In fact, Ethernet covers level 1 and only part of level 2.

The functionality of Ethernet ends at the interface between the Medium Access Control (MAC) and Logical Link Control (LLC) layers, as is the case for other local area networks such as Token Ring or the FDDI.

The physical layer

It falls to the lowest layer of a telecommunications system to emit and receive the data in the form of physical signals on the transmission medium. This requires the definition of the mechanical, electrical or optical characteristics of the medium, the type of coding and the signal shape and levels in the standard for this layer. At this level, one thus finds a description of the medium, including the type of coaxial cable, the characteristics of optical fibers, the attenuation of twisted pairs as a function of frequency, and so on. Each medium is associated with a particular type of connection, the structural details of which must also be known in full. In addition, associated with each of these physical media, there will also be a description of the element responsible for emission and receipt, its effect on the medium (for example, possible perturbation of the characteristic impedance), the levels it should generate, its detection thresholds, its internal operational delays and the effect it may have on the network through its links.

Finally, there are restrictions (length of cable segments, number of connections, strength of background interference) which vary as a function of the medium and are inherent to each network technology.

The MAC layer

The MAC layer represents the lower half of layer 2, the other half being constituted by the LLC layer (Figure 2.5).

The role of layer 2 is to permit the transfer of data between the connected systems and to detect transmission errors. Thus, it is responsible for formatting the data into frames, establishing the physical communications, and releasing them, using the access procedures.

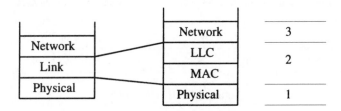

Figure 2.5   Subdivision of level 2.

The MAC layer itself controls the sharing of the medium using an access method. The choice of this sublayer is associated with that of the topology (the physical architecture), since the same method cannot be implemented on arbitrary topologies. In addition, the MAC layer determines a number of qualities of the network such as the reliability, the effect of inserting a machine or the behavior under heavy loads.

The LLC layer

As mentioned earlier, in the framework of local area networks, layer 2 or the Link layer, is divided into an inferior MAC layer and a superior LLC layer. Since the LLC sublayer is by default the layer that interfaces with the underlying LAN technology, this paragraph is dedicated to it. Please note, however, that in practice LANs interface just as frequently directly with a network layer (such as IP or IPX). Furthermore, we will see that the original Ethernet frame format was not designed to be followed by an LLC header.

LLC provides 3 types of services:

- Type 1: connectionless service without acknowledgment, the most frequent in LANs, and typically the one to be found for IP or IPX on Token Ring or FDDI;

- Type 2: connection-oriented service, must be seen as an equivalent of SDLC in LANs, employed for NetBEUI or MS-LAN Manager (as illustrated in Figure 2.6);

- Type 3: connectionless service with acknowledgment.

Please note that LLC is strongly inspired by the HDLC protocol (High level Data Link Control), with some slight differences (balanced asynchronous operation mode only, possible multiplexing via SAPs (Service Access Points), and so on).

Figure 2.6   Logical links established between two LLC layers.

1 byte		1 byte		1 or 2 bytes
I/G	DSAP	C/R	SSAP	Control

Figure 2.7   Header LLC.

For the SAPs, the least significant bit has a special meaning:

Individual/Group for the Destination SAP

Command/Response for the Source SAP

The three LLC frame categories differ in their control fields (least significant bit on the left-hand side):

Unnumbered (U): 1 1 M M P/F M M M   the M bits define the function

Supervisory (S):   1 0 S S 0 0 0 0 P/F N(R) the S bits define the function

Information (I):   0 N(S) P/F N(R)

where the P/F (Poll/Final) bit indicates polling (interrogation) in an LPDU command, and the end in an LPDU response.

N(S) is the sequence number of the sender and N(R) of the receiver, always in 7 bits.

U frames

1111_101   XID   Exchange Identification

Issued to obtain information on the remote node (supported LLC classes, maximum window size in reception) and to find the route to reach it (Source Routing).

1100_111   TEST

Sent to the remote node to verify whether it is still accessible, or to find a route to reach it (Source Routing).

1100_000   UI   Unnumbered Information

Simple datagram, used in LLC Type 1.

1111_110   SABME   Set Asynchronous Balanced Mode Extended

Sent by one side to establish a connection with another LLC.

1111_000   DM   Disconnected Mode

Issued by an LLC when it considers the connection to be terminated.

1100_010   DISC   Disconnect

Sent by an LLC to close a connection.

1100_110   UA   Unnumbered Acknowledge

Sent back as acknowledgment of a SABME frame or a DISC received.

1110_001   FRMR   Frame Reject Response

Issued by an LLC when it considers the received frame to be incorrect.

I frames

Information frames convey data, and are part of a connection. They contain the sequence number of the sender, corresponding to the transmitted frame, and the sequence number of the receiver which serves to acknowledge the frames received from the remote node.

S frames

1000 0000   RR   Receiver Ready

Issued by an LLC to indicate that it is ready to receive data (I frames) and to acknowledge the preceding I frames. The receiver sequence number of the control field indicates the number of the next I frame expected and acknowledges the preceding frames.

1010 0000   RNR   Receiver Not Ready

The LLC indicates that it is present, but not ready to receive, to slow down or suspend the transmission from the remote node. The sequence number has the same meaning as before, bearing in mind that all frames issued by the partner following the indicated number are considered to be lost.

1001 0000   REJ   Reject

The LLC demands retransmission of the frames starting with the specified sequence number (the preceding frames are implicitly acknowledged)

Table 2.1 Correspondence Command/Response.

	Command	Response
Type 1	UI	
	XID	XID
	TEST	TEST
Type 2	I	I
	RR	RR
	RNR	RNR
	REJ	REJ
	SABME	UA
	DISC	DM
		FRMR

LLC Type 1

In Type 1 mode (connectionless), the service provided is a simple datagram forwarding, without guarantee of delivery nor sequencing at arrival. This is the type of LLC usually employed by IP and IPX.

LLC Type 1 only uses UI, XID and TEST frames.

LLC Type 2

In Type 2 mode (connection-oriented), LLC provides capabilities of retransmission, respect of ordering (via sequence numbers), and buffer management with sliding window for flow control.

This type of LLC is employed for NetBIOS, SNA and LAN Network Manager. LLC Type 2 uses all types of frames except UI frames.

In the operation of a Type 2 connection, three phases can be distinguished: establishment of a link between two stations (TEST, XID, SABME-UA, RR), sending and receiving of data via this link (I frames, RR), and closure of the link (DISC-UA, DM).

Flow control by means of a sliding window allows provision of a 'burst mode' where N frames (maximum 8) can be sent in succession before having to wait for their acknowledgment in return.

Table 2.2 SAP numbers assigned by the IEEE.

0x00	Null SAP	IEEE
0x02	Indiv LLC Sublayer Management	IEEE
0x03	Group LLC Sublayer Management	IEEE
0x04	SNA Path Control Individual	
0x05	SNA Path Control Group	addresses all SNA SAPs
0x06	DoD IP	IP (v4) of the TCP/IP model
0x08	SNA Management	
0x0C	SNA Management	
0x0E	PROWAY 2B	
0x10	NetWare	
0x42	STAP BPDU IEEE 802.1D	IEEE bridging
0x4E	EIA RS-511	message service
0x5E	ISI IP	
0x7E	ISO 8202 (X.25)	
0x80	XNS (3Com)	
0x86	LLC	
0x8E	PROWAY-LAN	
0xAA	SNAP	SubNetwork Access Protocol
0xBC	VINES IP (VIP)	
0xD4	LAN Station Manager	
0xE0	NetWare (IPX)	
0xF0	NetBIOS	
0xF4	LAN Network Manager Individual	LM functions at LLC Level
0xF5	LAN Network Manager Group	
0xF8	default for IMPL	Initial Micro-Program Load
0xFA	Ungermann-Bass	
0xFC	Discovery	for dynamic address determination
0xFD	RPL (Remote Program Load)	
0xFE	ISO CLNS IS 8473	for ISO connectionless Network layer
0xFF	Global DSAP	

The Null and Global SAPs are opened automatically. The Null SAP allows answering a remote node before a SAP has been activated.

SNAP

As the LLC header has only a limited capacity for indicating the type of the next (higher) protocol, a complementary header has been devised. This LLC 'extension' also allows reproduction of an indication similar to that supplied by the Ethernet V 2.0 frames format, which has served as a basis for the development of a large number of protocols.

The SNAP (Sub-Network Access Protocol), indicated by the SSAP and DSAP = 0xAA, is composed of two complementary fields of a total of five bytes, the OUI (Organizationally Unique Identifier) and the Type or EtherType. The minimum LLC service is of Class I, the LLC default type is Type 1, and the field control is 3, that is, Unnumbered Information.

RFC 1042 explains how to exploit this header to make use of address research protocols, such as ARP and its derivatives, on IEEE 802.X LANs. Here, the OUI is 0, and not the three bytes assigned by the IEEE to the manufacturers. The Type field takes the values previously defined for Ethernet and specified by RFC 1700 on Assigned Numbers.

	1 byte	1 byte	1 byte	3 bytes	2 bytes
MAC header	DSAP = 0xAA	SSAP = 0xAA	Control = 03	OUI	EtherType

Figure 2.8 LLC and SNAP headers.

The cases where the OUI is not 0 (with a value of 00-00-F8) correspond to encapsulation (bridge tunneling) of protocols that have no equivalent on Ethernet, and to the utilization of an LLC Type 2. See chapter 13.2 for more details.

As the LLC and SNAP headers correspond to eight supplementary bytes between MAC and Network header, the maximum length of the data field of the MAC frame is reduced accordingly. Thus, in Ethernet the data field passes from 1500 to 1492 bytes maximum.

2.3 The higher layers

In the context of Ethernet networks, the higher layers are those above and including the network layer.

Table 2.3 EtherType in hexadecimal.

0000-05DC	IEEE802.3 Length Field	8013	SGI diagnostics
0101-01FF	Experimental	8014	SGI network games
0200	Xerox PUP (see 0A00)	8015	SGI reserved
0201	PUP Addr Trans (see 0A01)	8016	SGI bounce server
0400	Nixdorf	8019	Apollo Computers
0600	Xerox NS IDP	802E	Tymshare
0660-0661	DLOG	802F	Tigan, Inc.
0800	Internet IP (IPv4)	8035	Reverse ARP
0801	X.75 Internet	8036	Aeonic Systems
0802	NBS Internet	8038	DEC LANBridge
0803	ECMA Internet	8039-803C	DEC Unassigned
0804	Chaosnet	803D	DEC Ethernet Encryption
0805	X.25 Level 3	803E	DEC Unassigned
0806	ARP	803F	DEC LAN Traffic Monitor
0807	XNS Compatibility	8040-8042	DEC Unassigned
081C	Symbolics Private	8044	Planning Research Corp.
0888-088A	Xyplex	8046-8047	AT&T
0900	Ungermann-Bass net debugr	8049	ExperData
0A00	Xerox IEEE802.3 PUP	805B	Stanford V Kernel exp.
0A01	PUP Addr Trans	805C	Stanford V Kernel prod.
0BAD	Banyan Systems	805D	Evans & Sutherland
1000	Berkeley Trailer nego	8060	Little Machines
1001-100F	Berkeley Trailer encap/IP	8062	Counterpoint Computers
1600	Valid Systems	8065-8066	Univ. of Mass. @ Amherst
4242	PCS Basic Block Protocol	8067	Veeco Integrated Auto.
5208	BBN Simnet	8068	General Dynamics
6000	DEC Unassigned (Exp.)	8069	AT&T
6001	DEC MOP Dump/Load	806A	Autophon
6002	DEC MOP Remote Console	806C	ComDesign
6003	DECNET Phase IV Route	806D	Computgraphic Corp.
6004	DEC LAT	806E-8077	Landmark Graphics Corp.
6005	DEC Diagnostic Protocol	807A	Matra
6006	DEC Customer Protocol	807B	Dansk Data Elektronik
6007	DEC LAVC, SCA	807C	Merit Internodal
6008-6009	DEC Unassigned	807D-807F	Vitalink Communications
6010-6014	3Com Corporation	8080	Vitalink TransLAN III
7000	Ungermann-Bass download	8081-8083	Counterpoint Computers
7002	Ungermann-Bass dia/loop	809B	Appletalk
7020-7029	LRT	809C-809E	Datability
7030	Proteon	809F	Spider Systems Ltd.
7034	Cabletron	80A3	Nixdorf Computers
8003	Cronus VLN	80A4-80B3	Siemens Gammasonics Inc.
8004	Cronus Direct	80C0-80C3	DCA Data Exchange Cluster
8005	HP Probe	80C4-80C5	Banyan Systems
8006	Nestar	80C6	Pacer Software
8008	AT&T	80C7	Applitek Corporation
8010	Excelan	80C8-80CC	Intergraph Corporation

Table 2.3 (cont'd)

80CD-80CE	Harris Corporation	81A5-81AE	RAD Network Devices
80CF-80D2	Taylor Instrument	81B7-81B9	Xyplex
80D3-80D4	Rosemount Corporation	81CC-81D5	Apricot Computers
80D5	IBM SNA Service on Ether	81D6-81DD	Artisoft
80DD	Varian Associates	81E6-81EF	Polygon
80DE-80DF	Integrated Solutions TRFS	81F0-81F2	Comsat Labs
80E0-80E3	Allen-Bradley	81F3-81F5	SAIC
80E4-80F0	Datability	81F6-81F8	VG Analytical
80F2	Retix	8203-8205	Quantum Software
80F3	AppleTalk AARP (Kinetics)	8221-8222	Ascom Banking Systems
80F4-80F5	Kinetics	823E-8240	Advanced Encryption Syste
80F7	Apollo Computer	827F-8282	Athena Programming
80FF-8103	Wellfleet Communications	8263-826A	Charles River Data System
8100	Tag TPID 802.1Q	829A-829B	Inst Ind Info Tech
8107-8109	Symbolics Private	829C-82AB	Taurus Controls
8130	Hayes Microcomputers	82AC-8693	Walker Richer & Quinn
8131	VG Laboratory Systems	8694-869D	Idea Courier
8132-8136	Bridge Communications	869E-86A1	Computer Network Tech
8137-8138	Novell, Inc.	86A3-86AC	Gateway Communications
8139-813D	KTI	86DB	SECTRA
8148	Logicraft	86DD	IPv6
8149	Network Computing Devices	86DE	Delta Controls
814A	Alpha Micro	86DF	ATOMIC
814C	SNMP	86E0-86EF	Landis & Gyr Powers
814D-814E	BIIN	8700-8710	Motorola
814F	Technically Elite Concept	8821	CIF
8150	Rational Corp	8A96-8A97	Invisible Software
8151-8153	Qualcomm	9000	Loopback
815C-815E	Computer Protocol Pty Ltd	9001	3Com(Bridge) XNS Sys Mgmt
8164-8166	Charles River Data System	9002	3Com(Bridge) TCP-IP Sys
817D-818C	Protocol Engines	9003	3Com(Bridge) loop detect
818D	Motorola Computer	FF00	BBN VITAL-LanBridge cache
819A-81A3	Qualcomm	FF00-FF0F	ISC Bunker Ramo
81A4	ARAI Bunkichi		

The network layer

The network layer is responsible for processing the switching and routing information associated with a packet, establishing the logical link to the remote machine and providing connection indications. However, different, more or less complete, services may be offered. For example, the network layer may implement an error check or a monitoring of the flow associated with actions in the event of failure. This layer may also be responsible for multiplexing, if that takes place. We shall also see that protocols specific to routing equipment (for exchanges between routers) are found at this level.

Three types of service are defined to quantify the quality of the network layer:

- Type A. Reliable service: an acceptable (low) rate of notified errors, an acceptable rate of unnotified errors.

- Type B. An unacceptable (high) rate of notified errors, an acceptable rate of unnotified errors (requires a restart procedure on errors notified at the transport level).

- Type C. An unacceptable rate of notified and unnotified errors (requires detection procedures and procedures for restarting on errors, sequencing correction procedures and procedures to eliminate duplicates).

According to the properties of level 3, layer 4 may or may not be released from certain control tasks.

The following are to be found at this level (or the equivalent for other models): the ISO 8473 network layer; CLNP; the DoD protocols IP and ICMP; Digital Equipment Corporation's (DEC) DRP protocol, and certain routing protocols such as RIP, OSPF, IS–IS and ES–IS (ISO 9542).

Outside the area of local area networks, one may find, for example, the X.25 layer 3 (IS 8208), and the network protocol of ISDN channel D (CCITT I.451) or the ATM Adaptation Layer (AAL) of the ATM model.

Each of these protocols belongs to a particular structure, the OSI model being the only one which respects the standard completely. However, the blocks which constitute it appeared after the non-conforming protocols, which were already proven. Thus, there exist certain similarities. For example, the qualities of ISO's Connectionless Network Protocol (CLNP), and the DoD's Internet Protocol (IP) are fairly similar. The ISO/CLNS header, which is illustrated in Figure 2.9, could be compared

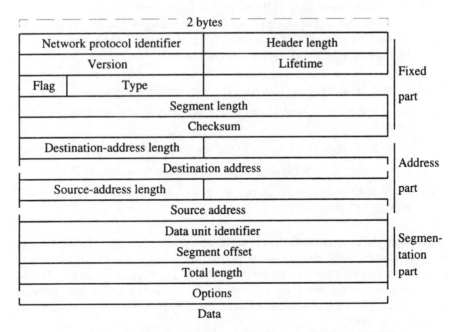

Figure 2.9   Header for ISO's connectionless network layer (CLNS).

with that of the DoD's Internet Protocol, described a little later in the section on TCP/IP (see Figure 13.28).

The information of this layer 3 includes items which are useful for the routing of datagrams, such as logical source and destination addresses and the maximum number of hops (via routers) that may be taken to reach the target station. If the message from the layer above has been segmented, data which can be used to reconstitute it from the fragments emitted by the network layer of the correspondent will be found. This data comprises the data unit identifier, which actually corresponds to a sequence number, the offset (or displacement) of the segment in the complete packet and the total length of the packet before fragmentation.

Globally, layer 3 enables two transport-layer modules to exchange data. Finally, it should be stressed that the network level addresses are defined by the user, that they incorporate the logical sub-network or domain concept and can be used to denote a station with the group to which it belongs, and that they are not defined by the manufacturer.

The transport layer

This layer controls the transparent transfer of data between end systems over the network. It checks the inherent properties of the network and may have to re-order (sequence) packets reaching it, to control the flow (for example, by informing the remote machine that it should slow down its emissions) if the selected layer below does not implement this service. Similarly, the transport layer may have to detect errors, losses, and duplicates and recover the correct information when these events occur, to provide, if necessary, a reliable service to the layer above.

The transport level is responsible for establishing a link on behalf of the higher layer (5), managing the data transfer and then releasing the connection.

ISO has defined five classes of transport layer:

- Class 0. Basic class, no restart on error, no multiplexing, no flow control.
- Class 1. Basic class with restart on notified errors, no multiplexing, no flow control.
- Class 2. No restart on error, multiplexing with or without flow control.
- Class 3. Restart on notified errors, multiplexing with or without flow control.
- Class 4. Error detection, restart on errors whether notified or not, multiplexing with flow control.

The transport-level class should be chosen as a function of the type of network layer available (see the previous section on the Network layer). The possible (network layer type, transport layer class) pairs are (A,0), (A,2), (B,1), (B,3), and (C,4). The reasons for these associations are linked to the distribution of certain tasks between levels 3 and 4, given that the transport layer should be able to provide a service which is of practical use.

Moreover, ISO has standardized a class 4 transport protocol called TP4 (IS 8072 and 8073, service and protocol), which is identical to CCITT's X.224.

The upper layers

The application-oriented layers begin with level 5. Thus, these protocols are more concerned with the formatting of the information exchanged between the application layers than with the connection and communication processes on networks (which are the responsibility of layers 1 to 4).

Thus, there exist standard notations such as ASN.1, which defines the format of all data types, whether numerical (integers, long integers, floating point) or alphanumeric.

At the very top of the model are those protocols which have a function of an applied level that is directly linked to the network capabilities such as virtual (remote) terminal emulation, messaging, file transfer, the sharing of peripherals, access to shared databases, and the use of distributed applications.

For example, one easily comprehensible level 7 application is *electronic mail* (or *e-mail*). This is used to send messages or transmit files to one or more users quickly and, with the generalization of network interconnections, almost anywhere in the world. Intermediate equipment interprets the name of the addressee and routes the packet to the target station to deposit it in the appropriate mailbox. A true two-way communication, with real-time questions and answers, can only be envisaged if the transmission delays are acceptable (for example, on a local area network). These messaging applications may be associated with directory management protocols.

In the ISO world, electronic mail is implemented by the MHS X.400 layer (message handling service), standardized by CCITT, while in the DARPA world, we have the Simple Mail Transfer Protocol (SMTP, RFC 821) over TCP/IP. Note that the directory system relies on the X.500 standard in the ISO world and DNS in the DARPA world.

The protocol stacks of certain manufacturers conform approximately with OSI and may be represented in parallel with the seven layers. For example, Xerox has defined Xerox Network System (XNS), Apple has developed AppleTalk and Digital Equipment has developed DECnet. Each system is modular and includes functionalities which can also be found in the seven layers standardized by IS 7498.

XNS

XNS was used in Xerox's architecture and also in the protocol stack Net/One defined by Ungermann Bass, in that of 3Com and, with slight modifications, in Novell's IPX. In Xerox's case, XNS includes the modules shown in Figure 2.10.

The logical addresses of XNS consist of a physical network number (in 32 bits, represented in decimal) and the number of the machine (in 48 bits, represented in hexadecimal, usually taken from the MAC address).

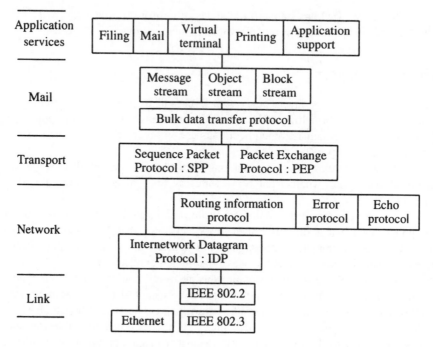

Figure 2.10   Protocols of the XNS layer structure.

Apple Talk

Similarly, AppleTalk has the following layers:

- Level 7: Application (utility- and application-oriented network).
  AppleShare, file and print servers
- Level 6: Presentation (representation, format conversion).
  Apple Filing Protocol (AFP), PostScript
- Level 5: Session (synchronization of dialogue).
  AppleTalk Data Stream Protocol (ADSP), Printer Access Protocol (PAP)
  AppleTalk Session Protocol (ASP), Zone Information Protocol (ZIP)
- Level 4: Transport (transport, splitting of messages into packets).
  AppleTalk Transaction Protocol (ATP), Name Binding Protocol (NBP)
  Routing Table Maintenance Protocol (RTMP)
  AppleTalk Echo Protocol (AEP), TCP, UDP
- Level 3: Network (routing of packets).
  Datagram Delivery Protocol (DDP), Internet Protocol (IP)
- Level 2: Link (data transfer, error detection).
  AppleTalk Link Access Protocol (ALAP):
  LocalTalk (LLAP), EtherTalk (ELAP), TokenTalk (TLAP)
- Level 1: Physical (transmission medium, electrical interface).
  LocalTalk, Ethernet, Token Ring

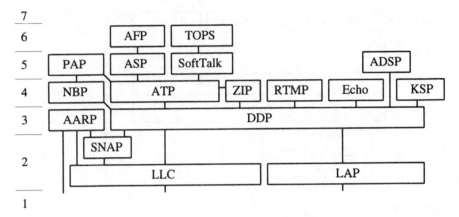

Figure 2.11   AppleTalk protocol family.

AppleTalk's logical addresses have 24 bits, comprising a network number in 16 bits and a node number in 8 bits (hence the limitation on the number of machines per network inherent in this technology). This address is usually represented by two decimal digits separated by a full stop. We note that value 0 in one of these fields corresponds to the notion of unspecified (this applies to all networks or nodes).

The AppleTalk routing protocols (Figure 2.11) such as DDP are simple but not very reliable. By propagating erroneous data they can cause a large network to crash. They have evolved with the introduction of the AppleTalk, Update-based Routing Protocol (AURP), which also reduces the bandwidth consumption in its routing exchanges by sending only the modified data. The AppleTalk Phase 2 routers are therefore less talkative than in Phase 1.

DECnet

DECnet is the architecture used in all Digital's machines with the VMS or Ultrix operating system. Like its competitors, it permits exchanges between applications, file management, resource sharing, remote virtual terminals, and network management. DECnet cohabits with TCP/IP in certain Unix stations.

Since Digital was one of the creators of the initial Ethernet technology, with Xerox and Intel, as far as its hardware is concerned, Ethernet may be considered as the *de facto* local area network. On Ethernet, the physical addresses of machines implementing DECnet consist of the manufacturer's prefix AA-00-04 and two bytes of the level 3 logical address. This is a special case for Ethernet, where the physical address cannot generally be parametrized. The logical address comprises the area number in 6 bits, followed by the node number in 10 bits.

One of the main innovations in DECnet Phase V is the replacement of the architecture by the OSI model (Figure 2.12). Thus, the management protocol becomes CMIP/CMIS and other proprietary modules are replaced by blocks conforming to ISO: HDLC replaces DDCMP for exchanges over wide area networks,

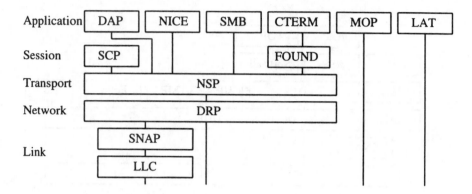

DAP: Data Access Protocol
MOP: Maintenance Operation Protocol
LAT: Local Area Transport
SCP: Session Control Protocol
NSP: Network Services Protocol

Figure 2.12   DECnet protocol stack.

and X.400 is chosen as the messaging system. Similarly, the IS–IS and ES–IS rout-ing protocols are supported. The addresses are of the NSAP (network service access point) type with a (variable-length) prefix, an area number (in 2 bytes, but which must lie between 0 and 63), a station identifier (in 6 bytes, beginning with AA-00-04), and a selector field (in one byte).

The MOP protocol is used for maintenance operations and may be used for the remote loading of a remote machine or to test a station by exchanging a packet.

The LAT protocol, which is used to manage terminal server exchanges, does not have a network layer and thus cannot be routed. Moreover, any significant delay in the routing of packets may lead to their elimination. Thus, one might envisage reserving a special priority for traffic of this type.

ISO

Finally, returning to the layers of the OSI model, we shall describe a number of modules already standardized by the ISO (Figure 2.13). There exists a terminology for information structures at every level. This is not necessarily always used properly, or even respected, even in this book. Thus, the data passing through the layers is referred to as shown in Table 2.4.

In addition, well-defined abbreviations are used to identify the level from which a communication unit (or PDU, Protocol Data Unit) comes. For example, a frame may be denoted LPDU (for Link Protocol Data Unit), a message from the transport level by TPDU (for Transport Protocol Data Unit), and so on.

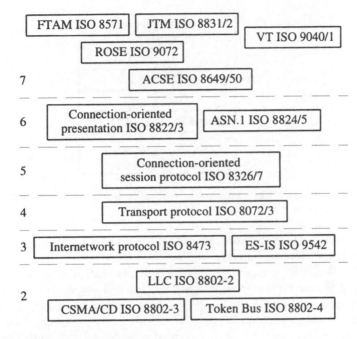

FTAM: File Transfer Access and Management
JTM: Job Transfer and Manipulation
VT: Virtual Terminal
ROSE: Remote Operation Service Element
ACSE: Association Control Service Element
ASN.1: Abstract Syntax Notation 1
ES–IS: End System to Intermediate System

Figure 2.13   Examples of protocols standardized by ISO at each level.

Table 2.4   Terminology for information structures at every level.

Physical level	1	Bit sequence
Link level	2	Frame
Network level	3	Packet
Transport level	4	Message
Session level	5	Transaction

Network Operating Systems

Finally, we shall attempt to describe the position of Network Operating Systems (NOS) for local area networks, such as Novell's NetWare, Microsoft's Windows NT, IBM's OS/2 WARP and Banyan's VINES. The main function of this software, which

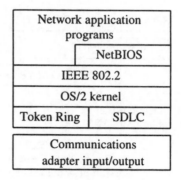

Figure 2.14 Position of NetBIOS in the IBM protocol stack.

was developed in the microcomputer world, is to make the resources of one or more servers available to a collection of PCs.

Originally, these programs provided for the sharing of printers or disks; however, they have evolved considerably since then and now constitute proper systems offering various services (sharing of peripherals or applications, distributed databases, security by duplication of disks, electronic mail, division of the set of users into hierarchical domains, password-based access protection, routing, and gateways between different interfaces). In response to processing needs, the servers have become multiprocessor micros or true workstations (with high-performance CPU, multiprocessor architecture, and so on).

However, this essentially software environment, which is often wrongly referred to as a local area network, consists of a set of specific protocols. In the OSI architecture, it essentially comprises proprietary layers, from the application to the network layer.

We mention NetBIOS (Network Basic Input Output System), which may be positioned between level 3 and the session level, and which serves as an interface between level 6 (presentation); for example, in the form of the server message block protocol and the MS-Windows software at the application level on the one hand, and the LLC or the controller card (direct interface) on the other (Figure 2.14). NetBIOS was originally produced by IBM, but this interface has become a fundamental building block in the systems of other manufacturers.

The NOS are intrinsically related to the technologies of local area networks, since they exploit the facility for establishing communication between several workstations (principally of the PC type) within a building, which usually corresponds to the area covered by local area networks. However, they are fundamentally powerful software packages, which give added value to a collection of microcomputers by improving the global context (common resources, centralized updating) and not simply by describing communication layers. Thus, they have to be properly positioned in relation to the local area network technologies which they use.

These management systems should be referred to as NOS. The distribution of market shares in the United States shows that a major part of client–server environments is attributed to Microsoft's Windows NT, followed by Novell's Net-Ware and Unix with NFS.

2.4 The TCP/IP model

In parallel with the ISO efforts, and slightly ahead in time, the Department of Defense (DoD) of the United States began to develop a modular protocol family for its own needs. This is commonly known as TCP/IP, with reference to its Transport and Basic Network protocols. These technologies were developed within the framework of DARPA, the Defense Advanced Research Project Agency.

This family of protocols is constituted of four layers: Technology (Network Hardware), Network (Internet), Transport, Application. The two lower layers on which it was initially based were Ethernet and X.25. The Network protocol is usually IP, completed by ARP (and its derivatives) and ICMP (which is built over IP). Since then, IP has been ported to the vast majority of current (and past) LAN, HSLAN, MAN, or WAN technologies.

The (partially unforeseen) success of this protocol family is due to two things: first of all, the systematic implementation of all base protocols of the model on all Unix machines, and second, the specific (but particularly flexible and responsive) standardization method.

In fact, the specifications of the IP world are developed under the responsibility of the IETF (Internet Engineering Task Force), an organism depending on the IAB (Internet Activities Board). The IAB, initially (1983) constituted by the DARPA and restructured in 1989, bears the responsibility of coordinating the efforts of the IETF and the IRTF, and of supervising the architecture and development of the technologies for this environment. The IRTF (Internet Research Task Force), on a superior level, deals with ambitious and mostly long-term projects which require research effort and scientific expertise.

IETF

The IETF is responsible for the specification of new protocols, for their modification, and for guaranteeing their cross-compatibility. It leads the way towards standardization by providing freely accessible working documents (including drafts) mainly via the Internet. Everybody can thus submit a specification proposal. These documents, called RFC (Request For Comments), go through various stages of referencing: Informational (or opinion paper), Experimental Protocol, Proposed Standard, Draft Standard, Standard. Finally, an RFC can also become Historical when it has lost its validity. In parallel to this State, the protocols also possess a Status: Limited Use, Elective, Recommended, Required. For obsolete technologies, the status is Not Recommended.

Few protocols have effectively become standards (RFC 2400), but many are sufficiently stabilized to be currently employed.

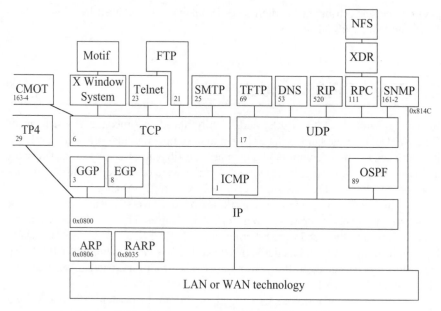

Figure 2.15   Main protocols of the TCP/IP world.

Addressing

IP addressing (or IPv4) is characterized by three principal address classes (Figure 2.16), always coded in four bytes and expressed in decimal (see Figure 2.16). These classes are still sufficient to satisfy the requirements of enterprises of different sizes. A complementary level of division can be introduced by means of subnetting, allowing the enterprise to segment its domain space into IP subnetworks. IPv6 addressing, which will eventually replace the current IP, is coded with 16 bytes.

Developments

After several catastrophic announcements regarding the capacity to manage the rapidly growing park of IP machines worldwide, and the revival of the big question on the capability of this environment to satisfy the requirements of the future, methods have been devised and applied to prolong the use of IP for several years to come, while waiting for current implementations of its successor IPv6 (ex IPng), such as CIDR (Classless Inter-Domain Routing), or address translation between private and public networks.

To conclude, we would like to remind you that TCP/IP has been the principal player against the ISO family of protocols and that, once again, the installed base has not allowed a massive and costly migration to begin without a foreseeable benefit. In fact, TCP/IP, because of its universality, could already appear as the 'standard' solution sought for, guaranteeing its functional capacity by its large number of large-scale installations.

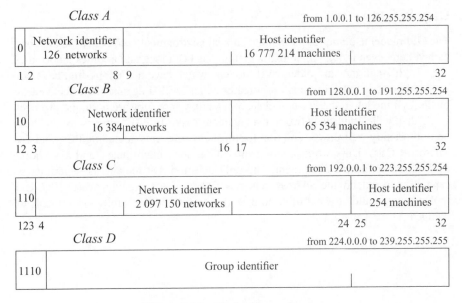

Figure 2.16   IPv4 address classes.

2.5 **Other models**

In parallel with the model developed by ISO, other models have been implemented in global network solutions offered by the major manufacturers. We mention the most important of these. Some others have also been described earlier in the higher layers paragraph.

SNA

IBM has defined a layer model associated with its communications architecture SNA (System Network Architecture) which can be used to link all IBM hardware, from large systems to PCs.

SNA has evolved since 1974 to offer increasingly rich functions, permitting more global hardware configurations and providing more extensive software capabilities.

Since IBM is the most important computer manufacturer on the world scale, the number of machines connected by SNA links is considerable and communications in SNA format represent the majority of data transfers.

Similarly, other manufacturers such as Bull and DEC, have their own architecture models (Distributed System Architecture (DSA) and Digital Network Architecture (DNA), respectively). However, we note that the recent evolution of Digital's DNA system has made it similar to that of ISO.

Conclusion

The OSI model is omnipresent in the technical environment with which we are concerned here, even though its implementation has been long and at times laborious.

Although they are older, rival models, which have had a long life, have not yet disappeared, and criticisms are already being leveled against the effectiveness of the OSI model. Today we can observe a healthy move toward a unique protocol stack that will simplify network management task. TCP/IP appears as the best non-proprietary well-proven solution for most environments, including PCs (and the Microsoft OSs), Unix workstations from all vendors, mainframes, and any short-term future connected equipment. The only question that remains is regarding its capability to extend the address scheme further in the coming years. IPv6, its replacement, could at worst offer an opportunity for another family of protocols to compete.

Chapter 3

Data communication networks

- Machine bus

- LAN

- MAN

- HSLAN

- WAN

For a long time, the main objective of telecommunications was voice transport (using the telephone). However, now, image transport (by video) and digital data transfer represent a considerable part of the exchanges.

Voice and video have the analog nature of their signals in common and do not generally form part of the area of digital communications; thus, we shall often leave them aside in the remainder of this book.

In the closing years of this century, the arrival of information technology has generated a real need for communication between computers. As machines dedicated to digital data processing became increasingly numerous and grew to be indispensable in almost all areas, it often appeared advantageous to make them 'talk' to each other. For them to work in a cooperative manner, sharing the same files (applications or data) or the same peripherals (storage units, printers, terminals), it is of course preferable to provide rapid and efficient communications. Solutions have been found and implemented for all requirements, whether between two buildings, two towns or two continents. However, these solutions must also evolve as machines progress in terms of speed and processing capability.

There are several main categories of network, classified according to the distances they cover. From the largest down, these are machine buses, LANs, MANs and WANs (Figure 3.1).

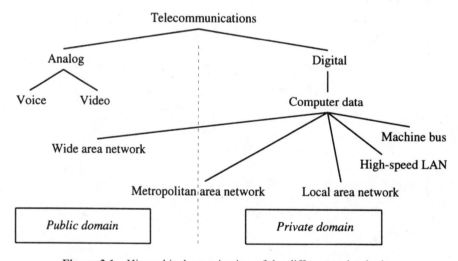

Figure 3.1 Hierarchical organization of the different technologies.

Remark The network technologies to be discussed here are located at levels 1 and 2 of the OSI model and are therefore comparable.

3.1 Machine bus

The machine bus, or backplane, is presented here more as an example than as a true network.

This is an old technology, since it dates from the modular design of electronic systems. The machine bus comprises all the wires and connectors which are generally found inside the computer and which enable the various cards (CPU, FPU, graphics processor, input/output, disk manager) to intercommunicate. This set often consists of passive elements (conductors) and has a bus, or sometimes a chain topology. The binary data circulates in parallel on the 8, 16, 32 or 64 wires, depending on the capability of the microprocessor. The speed on the backplane is a performance criterion for the machine.

Despite its apparent simplicity, this network needs rules concerning the right to emit, which, at the end of the day, simply comprise the protocol associated with the physical carrier.

For information, we mention the best known buses: Industry Standard Architecture (ISA), Extended ISA (EISA), Micro Channel Architecture (MCA), and the more recent Vesa and Peripheral Component Interconnect (PCI) in the microcomputer world; Small Computer Systems Interface (SCSI) and Versa Module Eurocard (VME) in the world of minicomputers.

3.2 LAN

LAN stands for local area network. Local area networks first appeared at the beginning of the 1980s and thus correspond to the multiplication of 'small' computers – workstations and microcomputers.

To be precise, we note that there are two classes of local area network: enterprise local area networks and industrial local area networks. The first category brings together the technology and hardware which may be found in an enterprise, while the second category corresponds to local area networks which are able to support industrial environments (more severe robustness and reliability constraints, resistance to electromagnetic interference). We must immediately point out that enterprise local area networks are far more numerous and that their standardization is more complete. The introduction of industrial networks is generally linked to the manufacturer who produces and therefore promotes them. In fact Ethernet, the local area network which we shall study here, is an enterprise local area network, as are Token Ring, LocalTalk and ARCnet.

In practice, local area networks are always controlled by the user; thus, they are part of the private domain of telecommunications. As their name indicates, their extent is limited to a few kilometers (from 1 to 10 km), their speed ranges from several hundred kilobits per second (kbps) to several megabits per second (Mbps) (say, 250 kbps to 20 Mbps, or, more recently, 100 Mbps, and even 1 Gbps).

Local area networks are often easy to install and implement, particularly for small configurations. They are also fairly reliable and certainly very economical.

However, the niche originally occupied by local area networks, which was limited to departmental needs, has tended to expand towards an organized structure relevant to the whole enterprise.

Networks installed in production structures sometimes use enterprise network technologies such as Ethernet. However, standards also exist for industrial networks, for example MAP (Manufacturing Automation Protocol) from General Motors (which is based on the IEEE 802.4 Token Bus standard, IEEE 802.2, and other protocol modules standardized by ISO). Since these networks have to connect automata, robots, sensors, calculating machines, and workstations (to collect and process the measurements), the constraints on industrial LANs are quite different from those on enterprise LANs. A high speed is not indispensable (some industrial LANs rely on RS 232 links); however, the network technology should be oriented towards real-time operation with an access method that guarantees, if possible, an upper limit for the delay for access to the medium and transmission. Since the exchanges are sometimes rudimentary (sequence of digital data) the seven OSI layers are not always indispensable. Moreover, the exchanges are predefined (return of measurements, programming of automata) and the set of elements in communication changes little.

The category of industrial LANs includes, for example, FACTOR, MODBUS (from Gould), BITBUS (from Intel), and the field bus FIP (Factory Instrumentation Protocol).

3.3 MAN

MAN stands for Metropolitan Area Network. This is a category which has appeared in the last ten years with the advent of products which were difficult to classify in any other way, since they were clearly superior to conventional LANs.

The MAN is characterized by connection capabilities over greater distances than the LAN, namely of the order of several kilometers. However, by virtue of their recent appearance, these technologies also have higher speeds than those of LANs, of the order of 100 Mbps. The best known representatives of this category are FDDI and DQDB.

FDDI

Fiber Distributed Data Interface (FDDI) was developed by former members of the Sperry Corporation in 1982. It was put forward to the ANSI X3T9.5 committee (which became X3T12) and then standardized by ISO in IS 9314 (except for a number of parts, including SMT management, which are still pending). In this sense, FDDI, as a local area network, has, exceptionally, always been manufacturer independent (Ethernet was a product of Xerox–DEC–Intel, Token Ring was a product of IBM). ANSI's X3T9 committee, which is responsible for interfaces and input/output, among other things, has dealt with the SCSI bus (X3T9.2) and the Fiber Channel (X3T9.3).

FDDI was introduced several years ago on the market place; but found only limited acceptance as Ethernet has significantly improve since, and as ATM propose to fulfil more ambitious needs. Possible media include single-mode and multimode optical fibers and (shielded and unshielded) twisted pairs, together with media which are not standardized, such as coaxial cable and laser links. Interface cards are available for a full range of machines, down to the PC, even though in the latter case an FDDI card is not justified in terms of proportional cost and potential performance.

A derivative of FDDI, capable of transporting synchronous traffic, has been defined, FDDI-II. However, this technology, which is more general as it is able to transport voice and data, has an uncertain future, given that it is overshadowed by the relative success of the MAN from which it stems and that FDDI-II hardware is essentially non-existent. Moreover, with the advent of ATM, FDDI-II has lost most chance to ever gain interest from the market.

DQDB

Queued Packet and Synchronous Exchange (QPSX) originated in Australia and was taken up by IEEE 802.6 as Distributed Queue Dual Bus (DQDB). This network uses a (possibly looped) double unidirectional bus and, in addition to data signals, also supports voice or video by virtue of its synchronous capabilities.

The speed is a function of the physical layer chosen and may, for example, be 45 Mbps (ANSI DS3) or 139 Mbps (CCITT G.703). The access method is based on relatively complex distributed queue management, whose fairness it has been difficult to obtain.

The use of cells compatible with those of Asynchronous Transfer Mode (ATM) potentially provides for an easy integration of DQDB metropolitan area networks into the ATM architectures of service providers in the future.

Except for FDDI, very few products are currently available; however, there appears to be a tendency towards the belief that ATM should be the only viable MAN solution in the future.

3.4 HSLAN

High Speed Local Area Network (HSLAN) is a technology which aims to offer an even greater bandwidth, in response to the requirements of heavy applications such as graphical transfers (real-time synthesized moving images, saving of whole disk units, and so on).

Existing solutions on the market are directed solely towards these demanding gaps, and used to be proprietary products in the past (since there is no need for standardization).

We mention HyperChannel from Network Systems Corporation (NSC), which was a network based on 75 Ohm CATV coaxial cable, offering a speed of 50 Mbps per channel and using a CSMA/CD access method. Four channels may be grouped together to form 200 Mbps links between at most 16 machines.

At the beginning of the 1990s the UltraNet product from Ultra (purchased by CNT) has appeared. This had a star topology and offered a speed of 1 Gbps (gigabit per second) on optical fiber or coaxial cable. It could be used to link the most important machines of a computing center over quite short distances (several tens of meters).

But the two major HSLAN are HiPPI (High Performance Parallel Interface) and Fiber Channel. We will describe Fiber Channel here as it has been used as the basis of Gigabit Ethernet. HiPPI was developed by the Los Alamos National Laboratory, which is being studied by ANSI working group X3T9.3. This defines a network operating at 100 or 200 Mbytes/s (32- or 64-bit bus) based on wound copper twisted pairs, over distances up to 25 m and, later, on optical fiber (up to 10 km) or coaxial cable (36 m), when the signal is transmitted in serial mode.

Fiber Channel

In 1988, the ANSI X3T9.3 (now X3T11) created the Fiber Channel working group with the aim of elaborating a simple, efficient and powerful data transfer method for fast exchange of large amounts of information between workstations, mainframes, supercomputers, backup systems and graphics terminals. The result is a standardized technology working in serial mode with a more or less high throughput, even over long distances, and exploiting circuit or packet switching.

Even if the original motivations still recall the needs FDDI was supposed to meet from its very conception, today's competing Fiber Channel technologies are HiPPI, SCSI and IPI.

It should be noted that the three IT manufacturers HP, IBM and Sun were the originators of the development of this new technology.

Fiber Channel is defined by a layered model (of five layers), but it must be seen as a Link level technology in the same way as the local and metropolitan networks described up to now.

The edge devices are called nodes, and their port is of N_Port type, as opposed to the ports of the switches constituting the network, which are of F_Port type (F for Fabric). The topology can theoretically accommodate up to 16 million nodes (2^{24}) because the addresses are coded in 24 bits.

Besides the strictly point-to-point topology (two devices), there is a way of functioning of bandwidth sharing on the basis of an arbitrated loop (FC-AL: Arbitrated Loop) where one of the accesses takes the responsibility of arbitrating the operation. Then, the port nodes are of NL_port type, and the limit is of 127 accesses per loop. The loop can be attached to a Fiber Channel switch via an FL_Port port. Obviously, communication takes place sequentially by couples of ports.

The Physical level standard of Fiber Channel is FC-PH which comprises the description of FC-0, FC-1 and FC-2.

	Channels				Networks		
FC-4	IPI	SCSI	HIPPI	SBCCS	802.2	IP	ATM
FC-3	Common services						
FC-2	Framing protocol / Flow control						
FC-1	Coding / Decoding						
FC-0	133 Mbps	266 Mbps		531 Mbps	1 Gbps	Higher rates	
	Optical fiber single mode	Optical fiber multimode		Coaxial cable		Twisted pair	

FC-PH spans FC-2, FC-1, and FC-0 on the right side.

Figure 3.2 Details of Fiber Channel specifications.

FC-0

FC-0, the lowest layer, defines the physical characteristics of the interface, that is of media, connectors, sending and receiving components and effective transmission throughput. Thus, the following throughputs are described (from highest to lowest):

1 Gbps	precisely	1062.5 Mbps	or	100 Mbyte/s
531 Mbps	precisely	531.25 Mbps	or	50 Mbyte/s
266 Mbps	precisely	265.625 Mbps	or	25 Mbyte/s
133 Mbps	precisely	132.8125 Mbps	or	12.5 Mbyte/s

The effective throughput in Mbyte/s is due to the 8B/10B coding.

Multiple media are supported, from the most powerful to the most widely used: single-mode optical fiber 9/125 μm and multi-mode optical fibers 50/125 and 62.5/125 μm, all equipped with SC duplex connectors, coaxial cables (video and miniature) with TNC and BNC connections, and shielded twisted pair (150 Ohm) with DB9 connectors.

FC-1

FC-1 is responsible for online coding and decoding, and for integration and synchronization with the clock of the physical signal. Transmission is always carried out in serial mode.

The code used is of type 8B/10B (that is, the code registered by IBM for its ESCON 200 Mbps devices) which is responsible for the difference between payload and binary throughput (only four fifths of the bandwidth are used for data transfer).

Table 3.1 List of media and lengths supported in Fiber Channel.

Media type	Maximum distance	Throughput (Mbyte/s)	Type of sender
Single-mode optical fiber	10 km	100 (max)	Long-wave laser
Multi-mode optical fiber 50 μm	1 km 2 km	50 25	Short-wave laser
Multi-mode optical fiber 62.5 μm	500 m 1 km	25 12.5	Long-wave LED
Coaxial video cable	25 m 50 m 75 m 100 m	100 50 25 12.5	ECL
Miniature coaxial cable	10 m 20 m 30 m 40 m	100 50 25 12.5	ECL
Shielded twisted pair	50 m 100 m	25 12.5	ECL

This code is composed of a 5B/6B function applied to the first five bits of each byte and a 3B/4B function which together provide an efficient error detection capacity.

Furthermore, this is a well-balanced (dc-balanced) code which presents a transition density that allows simplified clock recovery.

FC-2

The FC-2 layer is the transport mechnanism of Fiber Channel. It describes the signaling protocol and the data framing protocol, and defines three distinct service classes: Class 1, 2 and 3.

Class 1 corresponds to circuit switching, allowing a pair of devices to communicate with each other (obtaining the equivalent of a point-to-point connection) for the duration of a transfer. This type of communication has an advantage in terms of efficiency of information exchange because, once the connection is established, the dialog cannot be disturbed. Indeed, while communication is being established, the two ends can theoretically no longer communicate with anyone except their unique interlocutor.

Class 2 is a connectionless packet switching service, however, with guaranteed delivery by means of acknowledgments of receipt. It does therefore not need a preparatory phase as with class 1, and if necessary allows several distinct routes in the network to be followed, thus optimizing the use of available capacities.

Intermix is an optional mode which corresponds to a mixture of the features of classes 1 and 2, authorizing the use of the free bandwidth of a class 1 operation by connectionless communications.

Class 3 provides a diffusion (one to many) type service, connectionless and without acknowledgment. In cases where the return delay of a packet is not neglectable (several kilometers of distance), class 3 can provide a noticeable improvement in performance at the expense of security.

In cases where the order of data is not respected (which is possible because packets can take different routes), correct sequencing is assured at reception, by means of the frame control fields.

FC-3

The FC-3 layer aims at offering Common Services for advanced features, such as the following:

Striping which achieves a higher throughput by transmitting information on several ports (and links) simultaneously in parallel

Hunt Group which correspond to a group of node ports which are associated an identifier alias which allows a frame addressed to this group to be sent to any of the free (non busy) nodes of the group.

Multicast which correspond to the capacity to retransmit simultaneously to multiple destination, in broadcast (to all N_Port) or in multicast (to a subset).

FC-4

The FC-4 offers flexible integration of the existing standards and other data communication protocols with Fiber Channel through application interfaces.

This way IPI, SCSI, HiPPI, SBCCS (Single Byte Command Code of IBM), IEEE 802.2, IP and ATM (AAL5) have a standard mode to be interfaced to Fiber Channel.

4 bytes	24 bytes	0/8 bytes	0 to 2048 bytes	4 bytes	4 bytes
Start of frame	Frame header	Optional header	Data	CRC	End of frame

Figure 3.3   Structure of the Fiber Channel frame.

The justification for HSLAN resides on two needs: higher bandwidth connection for demanding stations or servers, but also a backbone link between powerful switches.

A simple calculation of the bandwidth needed to display a moving image with high resolution in real time gives an idea of the enormous requirements in this area: 24 images per second with a definition of 1024×1024 points and 24 color planes (16 million possible shades) ~ 600 Mbps. It becomes clear that a rate in gigabits per second is justified for this type of application.

Finally, for information, we note that the propagation delay for a packet on a link in a network is independent of the speed, and that it depends solely on the

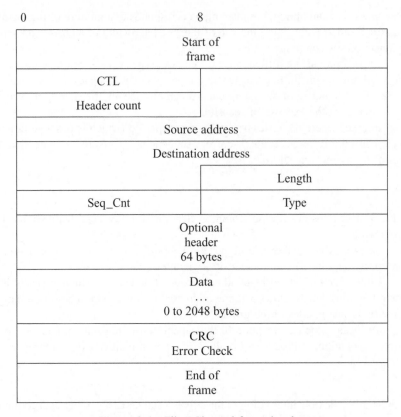

Figure 3.4   Fiber Channel frame header.

speed of the physical signal on the medium. This factor should be taken into account when one increases the speed offered by virtue of the new technologies, for example, by providing for adapted acknowledgment methods or longer messages.

3.5 WAN

Wide Area Network (WAN) is a vast category of networks which covers almost all capabilities for transmission of digital data over large distances. These distances may amount to several kilometers or several tens of thousands of kilometers.

Wide area networks are distinguished from the networks described previously by the fact that they are provided by national service providers and generally represent a public service. In fact, the great majority of local area networks, metropolitan area networks and machine buses are located within an enterprise and are therefore private (even if they borrow public lines for some of their sections).

The physical carriers that may be used for WANs include twisted pairs, coaxial cables, fiber optic cables, radio links, and satellite links. The transmission modes are also quite varied and may include:

- dedicated leased lines with speeds from 9600 bps to 1.5 or 2 Mbps, and 34 or 45 Mbps more recently;
- Frame Relay, simple and efficient frame switching technology for speeds up to 2 or even 8 Mbps;
- X.25 packet-switching circuits with speeds from 9.6 to 512 kbps and above;
- Integrated Services Digital Networks (ISDN) with speeds of 56 or 64 kbps for basic access (BRI) and 1.5 or 2 Mbps for primary access (PRI);
- Sonet and SDH (Synchronous Optical Network and Synchronous Data Hierarchy) physical layer protocol offering throughput of multiples of 51.8 or 155.5 Mbps, and up to 10 Gbps and more;
- ATM as the unifying cell switching technology, relying on Sonet/SDH for all types of traffic and uses (LAN, MAN and WAN).

We note that broadband ISDN services will be offered on top of the ATM technology which most carriers have selected for their internal infrastructure.

Conclusion

We have seen that all potential niches in data communications are occupied by technologies of various ages, associated with hardware which is evolving at different rates.

On the one hand public wide area networks are old, but increasing in performance, while on the other hand private local area networks are more recent and are evolving more rapidly; at the same time, other categories have come to respond to needs lying between the limits of LANs and WANs.

Standardization is undoubtedly proceeding in all areas, and in time will provide homogeneity and a long-awaited greater interoperability. Finally, to summarize the relative positions of each class, Figure 3.5 shows the hierarchy of class types.

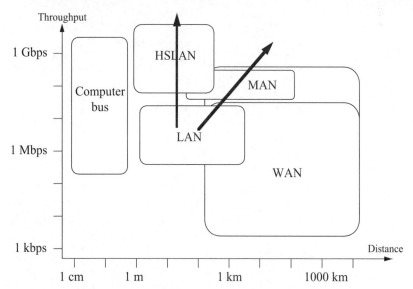

Figure 3.5   Relative positions of networks.

Chapter 4

Local area networks

- Definition of local area networks

- The physical media

- The topologies

- Multiplexing

- Access methods

- Encoding and transmission

- Local area network rivals to Ethernet

- The place of local area networks in telecommunications

4.1 Definition of local area networks

As we have seen above, local area networks form part of the world of telecommunications and, to be precise, concern the requirements for the exchange of data communications within an enterprise.

Thus, they permit the transfer of digital data between computers and allow users of computer applications to copy files or share certain resources via the network.

4.2 The physical media

The communication bearer is part of the first layer of the model. Thus, it should be described in the document which standardizes the type of technology used for the lower layers.

Coaxial and twisted pair cables transport electrical signals, optical fiber transports optical signals, the air transports electromagnetic waves.

We note that the attenuation induced by the medium is measured in dB (decibel, tenth of the unit called a Bel) which is a relative (rather than absolute) unit corresponding to $10 \times \log_{10}$ (signal power/reference power). Thus, the dBm corresponds to a measurement with respect to a reference signal of 1 mW and 1 mW = 0 dBm.

Coaxial cable

Coaxial cable is a cylindrical cable consisting of two concentric electrical conductors (which are different and said to be asymmetric). The first, solid cable, constitutes the core, while the second external conductor, which is cylindrical and hollow, is placed around the first, but insulated from it (Figure 4.1).

Electrical signals are emitted using the external conductor (often braided) for a reference potential. The two conductors are separated by an insulating dielectric and, in addition, the external conductor is surrounded by a layer providing mechanical and electrical protection.

To obtain a minimal attenuation, calculations show that the optimal ratio between the diameters of the two conductors is 3.6.

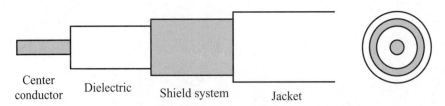

Center conductor   Dielectric   Shield system   Jacket

Figure 4.1   Sideways and face on views of a bare coaxial cable.

The advantages of coaxial cable are:

- Its good transmission properties (high propagation speed, low attenuation, wide bandwidth, limited RF emission).
- Its high immunity to electromagnetic interference.
- The ease with which it can be manipulated (connector crimping, laying in cable run) and its general robustness.

Its disadvantages are:

- Its relatively high cost, since it is a quality component.
- Its bulk, due to its large diameter for a single physical link (in comparison with other media) and its rigidity.

Optical fiber

Optical fiber is a conductor of optical signals which is made from silica (pure and doped) or from plastic.

Plastic Optical Fibers (POF) are more recent, and although they are currently evolving rapidly, they do not have the performance of silica fibers. Their attenuation remains very high and, even though their robustness and low price are very attractive, they are, for the present, restricted to a number of atypical applications.

Thus, we shall concentrate on silica optical fibers, which may be of different types according to the diameter of the fiber core and the curve of variation of the (refractive) index as a function of the distance from the center of the fiber. If the core has a very small diameter, of the order of ten microns or less, the fiber only permits a single rectilinear optical path without reflection from the walls of the silica cylinder and the transmission performance is then of a high level (very large bandwidth, very low dispersion, low attenuation).

Optical fiber of this type is called single mode (or unimode) and, given its capabilities, it is primarily used for high speeds and large distances, and, in particular, for international connections. Of course, the disadvantages of this type of fiber are the cost (due to the quality requirements on its production) and assembly difficulties (laying of connectors, cable splicing). Thus, single-mode optical fibers are rare in local area networks since the distances and the speeds are not sufficiently restrictive.

If the fiber core has a diameter of several tens of microns, there are several optical paths between the two ends and the fiber is called multimode. There are two categories of multimode fiber: stepped-index fibers and graded-index fibers.

These categories are distinguished by the curve of the index of the core as a function of the distance from the center (Figure 4.2). In the former case, the index jumps abruptly from the value for the core to the value for the sheath (we note that single-mode fiber is also stepped index), while in the latter case, the index changes gradually from the maximum value (at the center) to the value for the sheath on the outside.

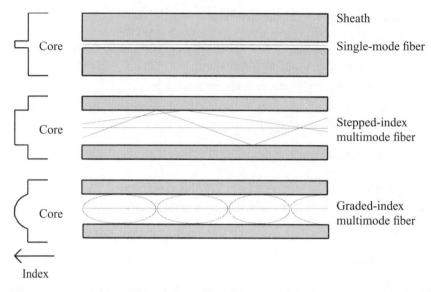

Figure 4.2   Cross sections of three types of optical fiber and trajectories of the light rays.

Stepped-index fiber thus has several possible paths for the light rays, since these are reflected from the walls when the index changes. Graded-index fiber deflects rays moving away from the core by its variation of the index, which brings them back towards the center.

Stepped-index fiber performs less well than graded-index fiber, which is explained, with some simplification, by the fact that the total difference in length between the shortest path and the longest path is greater, so the dispersion is greater for light rays in broken lines. Thus, graded-index fiber is often preferred, and is the fiber type most commonly used in computer networks.

In each category, the diameters of the core and the sheath may take several standard values. For example, for local area networks, the 62.5/125 μm graded-index fiber has become the most common optical fiber. However there are also other fibers, which are described in Table 4.1.

The ICE has listed certain optical fibers together with their properties, such as the 50/125 μm fiber as described in Table 4.2 which carries the number IEC 793-2 type A1a; similarly, the 62.5/125 μm fiber corresponds to IEC 793-2 type A1b, the 85/125 μm fiber to IEC 793-2 type A1c and the 100/140 μm fiber to IEC 793-2 type A1d.

At high throughput (1 Gbps, for example), multi-mode optical fibers with graded index can present an additional limitation. This is due to the DMD (Differential Mode Delay) which appears with LED lasers, which are particularly directional. It is the result of the superposition of several radial modes which are shifted at arrival and reduce the accessible distances (further than the attenuation constraint). The importance of the DMD phenomenon is increased by the fact that the elliptic curve of the graded index presents in practice a slight incline at its peak.

Table 4.1   The characteristics of different optical fibers.

Conductor material	Type	Diameters	Attenuation (in dB/km)	Bandwidth (in MHz.km)	Numerical aperture
Silica	Single mode	8 to 10/125 μm	< 0.5 @ 1300 nm < 0.3 @ 1550 nm		
	Multi-mode graded index	50/125 μm IEC 793-2 type A1a	2 to 4 @ 850 nm 0.5 to 2 @ 1300 nm	200–1000 @ 850 nm 200–2000 @ 1300 nm	0.2 to 0.3
		62.5/125 μm IEC 793-2 type A1b	< 3.5 @ 850 nm < 1 @ 1300 nm	> 200 @ 850 nm > 500 @ 1300 nm	0.275
		85/125 μm IEC 793-2 type A1c	2 to 4 @ 850 nm 0.5 to 2 @ 1300 nm	200–1000 @ 850 nm 200–2000 @ 1300 nm	0.26
		100/140 μm IEC 793-2 type A1d	3 to 4 @ 850 nm 1 to 2 @ 1300 nm	100–300 @ 850 nm 100–500 @ 1300 nm	0.29
	Multi-mode	200/280 μm	< 5 @ 850 nm	> 20 @ 850 nm	0.29
		200/380 μm	< 6 @ 850 nm	> 20 @ 850 nm	0.22
Plastic	stepped index	1000 μm ICE 793-2 type A4d	< 180 @ 650 nm < 100 @ 570 nm	10–20 @ 650 nm	

Silica is a material with an attenuation which is a function of the signal frequency. Developers have always sought to work with the least attenuated frequencies, such as the most common frequency at 1.17 MHz (850 nm). However, over time, improvements in the manufacturing process for silica fibers have reduced the attenuation at the frequencies used, but other wavelengths offering a greater performance, such as 1300 nm, then 1550 nm, have appeared (Figure 4.3).

These wavelengths require fibers of higher quality, but provide a clearly superior performance. For example, at 1300 nm, the 62.5/125 μm fiber has an attenuation of less than 0.8 dB/km, while at 1550 nm the single-mode fiber has an attenuation of less than 0.2 dB/km.

One additional factor is the Numerical Aperture (NA) of the fiber. The NA corresponds to the maximum angle at which a ray may be incident on the fiber core on entry and be guided by it. The wider the NA is, the greater the fraction of light from the optical energy source which finds a path across the fiber will be. The numerical aperture is directly associated with the idea of the cone of acceptance, which is the angular delimitation between the rays reaching the fiber which will be led to the interior of it by refraction and those which will not enter the fiber (by reflection) or will leave it immediately.

The aperture is a fundamental parameter in the evaluation of the amount of light produced by the emitter which will effectively enter the fiber. Since electronic components emit within a well-defined angle, the larger the angle is, the greater the signal strength at point zero will be and the greater the distance traveled before reaching the minimum detection threshold of the receiver will be.

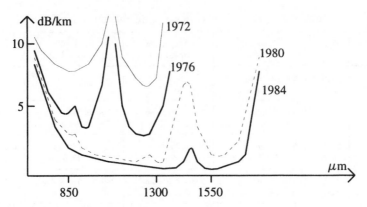

Figure 4.3 Improvement in the attenuation of silica fibers as a function of the wavelength.

Table 4.2 Table of loss on the signal passing between two different types of fiber.

Receiving fiber	Emitting fiber				
	Diameters, μm	50/125	50/125	62.5/125	85/125	100/140
Diameters, μm	NA	0.2	0.22	0.275	0.26	0.29
50/125	0.2	0 dB	0.4 dB	2.2 dB	3.8 dB	5.7 dB
50/125	0.22	0 dB	0 dB	1.6 dB	3.2 dB	4.9 dB
62.5/125	0.275	0 dB	0 dB	0 dB	1 dB	2.3 dB
85/125	0.26	0 dB	0 dB	0.1 dB	0 dB	0.8 dB
100/140	0.29	0 dB	0 dB	0 dB	0 dB	0 dB

Connection of two fibers of different types results in an additional loss over and above the losses incurred due to the connectors themselves. In fact, changes in the diameter and numerical aperture are generally responsible for substantial attenuation. Thus, the FDDIPMD standard gives a table of the additional attenuations (apart from connectors) due to the connection of two different types of fiber.

We note that if the diameter and the numerical aperture (corresponding to the cone of acceptance) of the receiving fiber are larger than those of the emitting fiber, the loss is zero, since no light rays are lost.

Optical connection is an area rich in diverse solutions. The criteria for quality are a low attenuation, high reproducibility of this attenuation (on successive connections), robustness to numerous manipulations, and a mechanical resistance relatively independent of the movements of the fiber. There is a great variety of connector types (ST, SMA, MFO, PFO, FC, SC) with characteristics generally linked to the cost. In fact, these are expensive and fragile elements whose criticality is inversely proportional to the diameter of the fiber. For example, the typical insertion losses of these connectors on the 62.5/125 μm fiber are 0.5 dB for ST, 1.5 dB for SMA and 0.35 dB for MFO and PFO. The locking resistance varies from 100 to 250 N.

In practice, an optical cable contains several fibers (from two to more than ten) which are all arranged in a protective tube or in grooves. Through its structure, the cable guarantees the necessary mechanical protection by limiting the torsion, elongation, and flattening of the whole.

It should not be forgotten that the implementation of the corresponding emitters has also become more complex with these developments. The delivery of sufficient power for an increasing cable-segment length inevitably leads to the use of lasers instead of Light-Emitting Diodes (LED). When single-mode fiber with a very thin core is used, lasers become mandatory because of the emitted power. Moreover, LEDs have a relatively broad spectrum of emission in comparison with lasers, which have a narrow spectrum consisting of a few rays only. However, one should also bear in mind that LEDs are now reliable and inexpensive, while lasers are more complex and have a greater variation with temperature.

In all cases, these emitters are getting old and their characteristics may change. Thus, an acceptable range of variation between the initial operation of a component and the end of its life may be defined in a standard (it is 1 dB in 10BaseF).

Optical receivers may be PIN photodiodes, avalanche photodiodes or integrated detector/amplifiers, the first type being the most common. These receivers each have a range of operational frequencies (usually from ~500 to ~1000 nm for silicon photodiodes) depending on their sensitivity. However, generally, they can be dazzled by excessively powerful light signals. Thus, care should be taken to insert at least a minimum length of optical fiber or jumper cable between an emitter and a receiver (from 1 to 5 meters). This is also sufficient to ensure that rays passing through the sheath are definitely lost.

The twisted pair

The medium based on the twisted pair consists of two conductor wires wound around each other. In the majority of cases, several pairs are grouped together inside the same cable. This is an inexpensive medium, but one which also has a limited capacity.

There are different types of twisted pair (Table 4.3), which vary according to the diameter of the conductors, the number of twists per meter, the periodic variation of the twist length, the shielding (per pair, per group of pairs, per cable) or the absence of shielding (Figure 4.4). The electrical performance depends upon these construction parameters.

Figure 4.4   A twisted pair of electrical conductors (unshielded).

Table 4.3 Standard characteristics of twisted pair cables.

	UTP 100 and 120 Ohm	STP 150 Ohm
Conductor diameter	0.4–0.65 mm	0.6–0.66 mm
Diameter over insulated conductor	≤ 1.4 mm	≤ 2.6 mm
Shield around cable unit	No	Yes
Outer diameter of cable	≤ 20 mm	≤ 11 mm
Minimum bending radius for pulling during installation	8 times outer cable diameter	7.5 cm
Minimum bending radius installed	4 times outer cable diameter	
One-time bend radius		20 mm
Pulling strength	≥ 50 N/mm² × Cu_{min}	

Electrical signals are emitted in a symmetrical manner, in other words, by applying a voltage $V(t)$ to one conductor and $-V(t)$ to the other.

The main computer manufacturers each had their own range, which they originated themselves. This enabled them to base all the physical interconnection facilities of their equipment on a given type of medium and to propose homogeneous solutions. For example, IBM has a complete range of media and connectors adapted to its needs, namely the ICS (IBM Cabling System).

The ICS defines several cable types (types 1 to 9) each with particular characteristics and adapted to a given use. The most common cable is that of type 1, which consists of two twisted pairs shielded individually and globally (the screening consists of an aluminum ribbon). The copper conductors have diameters of 0.64 mm (22 AWG). The colors are red and green for one pair and orange and black for the other. The screening consists of aluminized polyester ribbons. The braiding consists of electroplated copper wires and the external sheath is made of supple PVC (generally black). ICS type 1 cable has a characteristic impedance of 150 ± 15 Ohm, from 3 to 20 MHz (and 270 Ohm at 9.6 kHz). The signal speed is of the order of 0.75 c. The DC resistance is 57.5 Ohm/km (115 Ohm/km in loop). Finally, the attenuation is less than 11 dB/km at 1 MHz, 36 dB/km at 10 MHz and 45 dB/km at 16 MHz. IBM refers to this cable type as 'data grade media' and associates it with a general hermaphrodite connector type (wall socket and patching). It pushes this for its Token Ring installations at both 4 and 16 Mbps.

Similarly, AT&T has its Systimax Premise Distribution System (PDS) which consists of a cable with four unshielded twisted pairs, where each conductor has a diameter of 24 AWG (0.5 mm). The cable has a characteristic impedance of 100 Ohm and an attenuation of 7.5 dB at 10 MHz and 10 dB at 16 MHz over 100 meters.

Table 4.4 Standard electrical characteristics of different twisted pair cables.

	100 Ohm			120 Ohm			150 Ohm
Category	3	4	5	3	4	5	
Characteristic impedance	100 ± 15 Ohm (> 1 MHz) 125 ± 25 (64 kHz)			120 ± 15 Ohm (> 1 MHz) 125 ± 45 (64 kHz)			150 ± 15 (> 1 MHz)
Maximum DC loop resistance	19.2 Ohm/100 m						12 Ohm/100 m
Minimum phase velocity of propagation (1–100 MHz)	0.4 c	0.6 c		0.4 c	0.6 c		0.6 c
Minimum DC insulation resistance	150 MOhm km						1 GOhm km
Attenuation (dB/100 m)							
at 64 kHz	0.9	0.8			0.8		
at 256 kHz	1.3	1.1			1.1		
at 512 kHz	1.8	1.5			1.5		
at 772 kHz	2.2	1.9	1.8		1.5	1.7	
at 1 MHz	2.6	2.1			2	1.8	
at 4 MHz	5.6	4.3			4	3.6	2.2
at 10 MHz	9.8	7.2	6.6		6.7	5.2	3.6
at 16 MHz	13.1	8.9	8.2		8.1	6.2	4.4
at 20 MHz	NA	10.2	9.2	NA	9.2	7	4.9
at 31.25 MHz	NA	NA	11.8	NA	NA	8.8	6.9
at 62.5 MHz	NA	NA	17.1	NA	NA	12.5	9.8
at 100 MHz	NA	NA	22	NA	NA	17	12.3

Finally, in France, Bull used to offer a cable called Bull A 2 and a patching system (modules and patch panel arrangement) which constituted the Bull Cabling System (BCS). The Bull A 2 cable was available in the form of 4 to 112 twisted pairs encased in a global shielding and a synthetic layer for mechanical protection. This cable is said to be screened. The copper conductors have a diameter of 0.6 mm, the insulation is heavy colored polyethylene. The order of the four pairs (wires 1 to 8) is as follows: white–gray, blue–colorless, yellow–orange, brown–violet. The screening is an aluminized ribbon. The exterior sheath consists of fireproof PVC (generally yellow). Bull A 2 has a characteristic impedance of 100 ± 15 Ohm at 1 MHz. The in loop DC resistance is bounded above by 130 Ohm/km. Finally, the attenuation is less than 1.4 dB/km at 1 kHz, 25 dB/km at 1 MHz, and 72 dB/km at 10 MHz. Within the BCS, this cable is associated with RJ45 connectors in the form of wall sockets and plugs and modules for patching purposes.

Carriers similar to the twisted pair may also be developed based on four twisted wires (quads); CNET's L120 (France Télécom) is an example of this. This is available in the form of 8, 16, 24, 64 or 256 wires, the whole being screened. The conductors of annealed copper have a diameter of 0.6 mm, and the insulator is a double layer of polyethylene. The screening is a ribbon of aluminized polyester with a thickness of 0.04 mm and the sheath consists of a thermoplastic halogen-free material (with an ivory color). The minimum bend radius supported without deformation is five times the external diameter of the cable. The L120 has a characteristic impedance of 120 ± 10 Ohm from 1 to 16 MHz (or 100 MHz) and 110 ± 10 Ohm at 100 kHz. The in loop resistance is less than 133 Ohm/km. The propagation speed is greater than or equal to 0.75 c. Finally, the attenuation is less than 5.5 dB/km at 100 kHz, 18 dB/km at 1 MHz, 52 dB/km at 10 MHz, 60 dB/km at 16 MHz, and 150 dB/km at 100 MHz. The cable with two quads (or four pairs) of 6 mm wires is designated by L120 4 6.

This last medium, with characteristic impedance and performance between those of ICS type 1 cables and unshielded cables or those which are only screened, could be standardized at the European level and would be useful in an international homogenization of installations.

Other manufacturers also have their own, more or less original, cabling ranges, some of which (for example, that of DECnet) include a modular connection system (borrowed from AMP) with easily interchangeable sockets, which can be used to adapt a fixed cable to various uses, incorporating baluns if necessary (small connection elements placed between two cables which can adapt the impedances from one to the other).

Finally, we note that the first solution implementing FDDI on shielded twisted pairs (150 Ohm characteristic impedance) requires an attenuation less than 12 dB over 100 meters at a frequency of 62.5 MHz. This solution, called CDDI, has made way for the future TP-PMD standard, which operates at 31.25 MHz on shielded and unshielded twisted pairs (category 5).

Table 4.5   Approximate attenuation (dB/100 m) at high frequency (MHz) for UTP5 'enhanced'.

Frequency	120	140	150	155	160	180	200	255	300	400	500
Attenuation	24	26	27	27.6	28	30	32	36	39	46	56

The air

The atmosphere, in other words, the ambient air over short distances, can be used as a transmission medium for electromagnetic waves.

The frequency of these waves causes variations in their transmission quality, in terms of the distance covered, the permeability of buildings, reflection by certain materials, and so on.

Of course, all these radio links pass through the Earth's atmosphere, like satellite links which use this medium on part of their path.

However, as far as local area networks are concerned, the constraints are different and the applications more recent. Emitters should not be dangerous for people working in associated buildings, and the length of the links should preferably be limited to several hundred meters. The radio waves of the communication system should not interfere with electronic and computer equipment in the vicinity and should not suffer interference from these. Transmission should support a speed of the order of megabits per second at least.

Wireless local area networks are very easy to install as far as the integration of a machine into the network is concerned, since it is sufficient to direct the antenna for connection purposes. They are also financially advantageous, since, even though they may sometimes be more expensive initially, they prove to be very economical when machines are moved frequently.

Other technologies, such as microwave transmission, transmission by laser beam over 1 km and infrared transmission, have been applied to local area networks, as we shall see in the next chapter.

4.3 The topologies

The topology of a network defines the structure of its logical layout; in other words, how the elements of the network are interconnected.

Like the medium, the topology forms part of the physical layer of the model. Thus, the rules for installation and connection are given in the standard associated with this level. We shall see later that there is a difference between the logical topology and the physical layout.

There are two main categories of elementary topologies:

- topologies based on point-to-point links (the star, the ring, the chain, the mesh);
- topologies which allow more than two physical accesses to the carrier (the bus).

Other, more complex topologies, such as tree structures, may be obtained by combining the elementary topologies (these will be described later).

The mesh

If all the machines of the network are linked together in pairs they form a fully meshed topology. If only some of these connections exist the topology is meshed, but not fully (Figure 4.5).

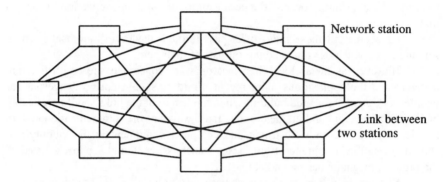

Figure 4.5 Example of a meshed topology (not fully meshed).

Historically, this was the first topology implemented, which is easily understandable, since it stems from the evolution of a set of machines with point-to-point links.

The main advantage of such a topology follows from the fact that there is a direct link between two machines which it is desired to bring into communication with each other and thus the whole bandwidth is accessible. However, the meshed topology has the disadvantage that its evolution is fraught with difficulty as the number of attached machines increases. Moreover, the cost of such a technology is strongly linked to the number of machines and rapidly becomes prohibitive. For N machines, the number of links needed for a fully meshed topology is $N(N-1)/2$, which is of the order of $N^2/2$.

The star

If all the machines in the network are attached to a single element, which is then the heart of the network, the topology is that of the star (Figure 4.6).

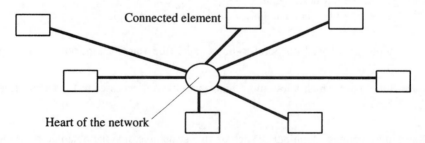

Figure 4.6 Star configuration.

One of the main advantages of this topology is that each medium segment is used as a point-to-point link, so it is possible to operate it at its maximum speed. However, this network as a whole is very vulnerable, since it depends entirely upon the operational state of the central node. We also note that at the physical level, the central element does not have the same characteristics as the peripheral elements.

The chain

The chain consists of a set of machines which are interconnected in pairs. Although it resembles the bus, the chain differs in the fact that the network communication bearer is not just a single medium segment but also includes the intermediate elements which propagate the signal (Figure 4.7).

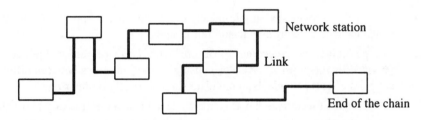

Figure 4.7   Network of several machines in a chain.

The connection points are thus not totally passive; even when they are not involved in a communication, they serve as repeaters. When a machine wishes to withdraw from the network, it has to replace its attachment by a direct connection (a bypass), which may be done using a relay. This constraint is identical in the case of a ring topology, and care should also be taken not to exceed the maximum permissible distance between two active connections.

The chain can be installed with a very short total medium length and, together with the bus, is the most economical topology in this respect. However, high reliability of the network cannot be guaranteed, since the communication between two stations may be interfered with by malfunctioning of any one of the elements between these.

We note that LocalTalk used a topology of this type, a daisy chain on a twisted pair.

The ring

The concept of the ring arises when one thinks of a loop in which each machine is only connected to each of its two nearest neighbors (Figure 4.8).

The ring is the only topology which does not require a bidirectional link between the connection points. In fact, if the ring has a direction in which the information circulates, the unidirectional link does not prevent any exchanges, but the path followed is not always the shortest.

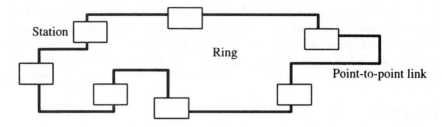

Figure 4.8 Simple ring linking seven stations.

We note that the ring can be constructed using a unidirectional chain topology looped back on itself.

The advantages of the ring topology are:

- A loop that provides a simple means of giving access opportunity to all machines with a deterministic and fair process;
- The possibility of exceeding 100% efficiency (with respect to the speed provided by the physical layer) by causing several messages between different pairs of correspondents to circulate simultaneously on the ring;
- A high level of security and management due to the fact that it is easy to list all the machines present (each has ready knowledge of its nearest neighbor(s)).

The disadvantages of the ring are:

- An implicit order in information flow which imposes a fixed delay in all communications;
- A vulnerability to machines suffering chronic failures (repetitive and short duration) which cause reinitialization of the ring whenever the problem occurs;
- A physical topology which is in general very different from a ring, because of the structure of the prewiring.

The bus

If the elements are connected alongside each other (in parallel) on the same medium, the topology used is called the bus (Figure 4.9).

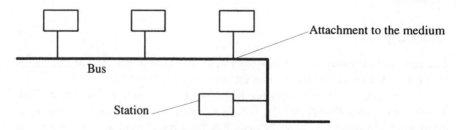

Figure 4.9 Bus configuration.

In general, the data propagates along the medium from the point of connection of the emitting station in both directions. When an emission takes place the receiving stations have no influence over the signal and their presence or absence is therefore transparent.

The advantages of this topology are:

- A transparency to the presence or absence of machines not implicated in the exchange (this is also linked to the fact that the machines all have the same status – no machine is indispensable to the operation of the network as a whole);
- A relatively short length of medium is needed to connect all the elements;
- The bus topology may be associated with a simple, distributed access method.

The disadvantages of the bus topology are:

- The management of the right to emit is vulnerable to ill-intentioned actions;
- The network is relatively insecure, due to the shared medium giving a global visibility of all exchanges.

Examples of existing technologies which use this topology include Ethernet, MAP and LocalTalk in certain configurations.

Finally, we note that all the technologies which use the air as a physical media of electromagnetic waves shared between several emitters are equivalent to buses (except for techniques based on narrow directed beams).

The tree

The previous topologies are, in some way, basic topologies from which more complex configurations can be developed. Thus, it is possible to construct a tree-like topology from buses or stars (Figure 4.10).

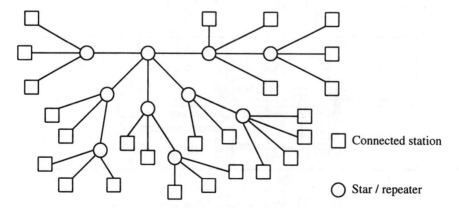

☐ Connected station

◯ Star / repeater

Figure 4.10   Tree-like structure based on cascaded stars.

Table 4.6 Characteristics of the various topologies.

	Star	Ring	Bus	Chain	Tree	Mesh
Symmetry	No	Yes	Yes	No	No	Yes
Order	No	Yes	No	Yes	No	No
Directional	No	*A priori*	No	No	No	No
Number of segments	$N-1$	N	1	$N-1$	$N-1$	$N(N-1)/2$
Privacy	Yes	No	No	No	Possible	Yes

In fact, these examples are closer to reality than the basic topologies, since by virtue of their numerous evolutions, local area networks have adopted different topologies which can be found gathered together in certain heterogeneous configurations. Ethernet on coaxial cable uses a bus-based tree-like structure, as described in Chapter 1.

Table 4.6 summarizes a number of the major characteristics of each topology.

The physical topology

Once the logical topology has been chosen, it remains to install the network in the building. At this stage, a certain number of practical questions arise (see Chapter 15 for more details), which almost inevitably lead to media segments being laid in a star structure. The heart of the star is the plant room which contains the patch cabinet serving an office at each end. Thus, the chain, ring or logical bus is reconstructed by jumper connections at the level of the patch panel, based on the physical star structure (Figure 4.11).

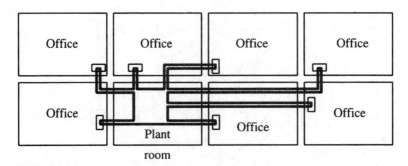

Figure 4.11 Star-cabled ring.

We end by recalling that the bus topology is the only one in which the presence or absence of other attached machines is transparent to all stations. This characteristic may be viewed as a desirable quality if one has to manage a network in a very dynamic way. On the other hand, the ring (which may be viewed as a looped chain) requires the cooperation of all the connected elements in order to pass messages. This has the advantageous result that it is easy to monitor the state of each machine. Finally, the evolution to tree-like topologies is inevitable, with the use of interconnection hardware interlinking different networks.

4.4 Multiplexing

Readers will have realized that for most of the topologies described up to this point (except the fully meshed topology), the medium, or the physical media of the network, is shared between all the connected machines. Thus, there is a need to determine how the machines will behave when several of them wish to emit data at the same time. This leads to the choice of a type of multiplexing: in time or in frequency.

Time-Division Multiplexing (TDM) involves letting the machines have full use of the medium, but sequentially. Frequency-Division Multiplexing (FDM) corresponds to a simultaneous sharing of the medium with the assignment of distinct and separate frequency ranges.

Time-division multiplexing

Time-division multiplexing is simpler to implement at the physical level, since all the machines emit in a similar way and only the method governing the contention for and assignment of the right to emit must follow a logical procedure (Figure 4.12). Thus, the data items emitted by each station follow consecutively on the same transmission medium and have similar characteristics (physical size, encoding, structure). There are several methods for managing and allocating the right to emit, which will be described in the following section.

This form of multiplexing has the advantage of a certain homogeneity, but remains generally limited as far as the use of the bandwidth is concerned. In fact, to increase the total speed (and thus the frequency of the signals), one needs to be able to manage the packet scheduling even more rapidly.

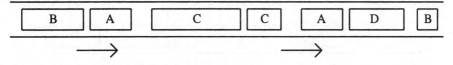

Figure 4.12 Packets from different sources sharing the same transmission channel.

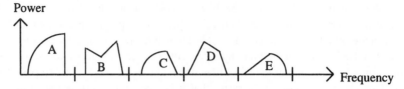

Figure 4.13 Five dedicated frequency channels sharing the spectrum.

Frequency-division multiplexing

Frequency-division multiplexing involves dedicating a specific frequency channel to each type of exchange (Figure 4.13). To establish diverse or multiple communication, several windows have to be individually managed by the connected stations. Frequency-division multiplexing is complicated to implement on a network of machines which must all be able to intercommunicate. In fact, the number of frequency bands available is always limited and the distribution of the links to be established is not necessarily self-evident.

An important application of frequency-division multiplexing is found in the world of voice transport. Telecommunications providers concatenate several thousand telephone communications on a single broadband link by frequency-division multiplexing. However, frequency-division multiplexing also exists for local area networks.

The global efficiency of frequency-division multiplexing is not always optimal, since the logical channels are each reserved for a single communication (at least while that is taking place).

Finally, the assembly of several physical communication links between two entities for a single transmission requirement may be referred to as space-division multiplexing (Figure 4.14). In this case, it must be physically possible to share the traffic between the different channels available; and not have each line dedicated to a particular use. Otherwise, one link might remain unused while another was overloaded.

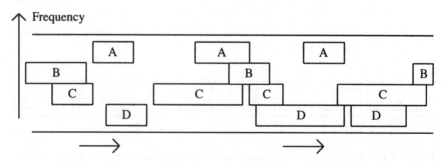

Figure 4.14 Packets from different sources sharing the same transmission channel.

4.5 Access methods

The access method is the method used to manage the right of access to the medium. It is a layer 2 attribute and, more precisely, an attribute of the MAC sublayer when that is separated from the LLC.

The access method corresponds to the protocol for managing the transmissions, which is indispensable to the proper operation of the whole and is responsible for the merits and shortcomings of the network technology. Thus, the behavior of Ethernet or Token Ring as a function of the number of active machines, their respective positions and their qualities in transmission, is determined by the choice of access method.

Master–slave

This is the easiest method conceivable. A single element is the master, which is responsible for successively interrogating all the machines which it believes are likely to wish to emit in order to grant them the right to occupy the media in response.

This technique, also called polling, implies that one machine is responsible for ensuring the operation of the whole network. Thus, it is a relatively easy method to implement and is reliable as far as the distribution of emission times is concerned, since the element which takes the decision knows all the connected machines, is aware of all the previous exchanges and may recall the priorities of each. On the other hand, this technique depends entirely upon the availability and trouble-free operation of the master, which makes it vulnerable to faults and bugs.

Finally, we note that the topology most naturally associated with this access method is the star, although other topologies may also be used.

Slot

The slot method is easy to understand. This method, which should preferably be implemented on a ring, but may be implemented on a double bus (unidirectional), uses an entity responsible for generating and continuously transmitting empty cells of a fixed size (slot) consecutively on the medium (Figure 4.15).

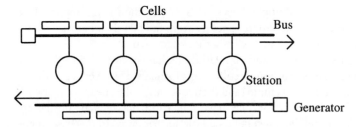

Figure 4.15   Example of a double unidirectional bus with slots.

These cells have a bit which indicates whether or not they are occupied by data. When a station wishing to transmit sees a free slot pass it, it places data there and sets the bit to the value corresponding to 'occupied'. Then, in the case of a ring topology, a station is responsible for releasing the cell by deactivating the occupation bit; this will be either the emitting station or the destination station. In the case of a bus, the cells are lost at the ends of the bus; moreover, they have to be reserved using a relatively complex procedure.

Aloha

Aloha is the expression of greeting in the Hawaiian language. It is also a multiple access technique in stars (where the center is a satellite) proposed in 1969 by the American University of Hawaii.

This access method can be used to share a single radio channel (possibly high speed) between several unsynchronized emitters and receivers. Each is authorized to emit when it has a message to communicate and its addressee, the central node, operating on the same channel, will be able to capture these emissions. If all goes well, the stations transmit their messages one after the other and the central station stores these to pass them to protocols which are capable of decoding them. On the other hand, if two or more stations decide to emit almost simultaneously, the signals emitted are superposed and become jumbled (producing a collision) and all the messages transmitted at the same time are lost. In this case, the upper layers have to salvage the process and try to retransmit the lost packet.

One clear advantage of this method is its simplicity, together with the fact that it is perfectly distributed. Its most restrictive shortcoming is the rapid degradation in its performance under heavy load. In fact, if a large number of machines seek to communicate on the channel, the losses due to collisions are more numerous and the system tends to a state of complete blockage, since each lost frame requires a retransmission attempt (and thus additional traffic).

A version exists in which all the machines are synchronized (this is not always easy to implement) and only attempt to emit at well-defined time intervals; this is slotted Aloha. These periodic gaps, corresponding to possible transmissions of packets, reduce the probability of contention.

CSMA/CD

The Carrier Sense Multiple Access (CSMA) method is an improved derivative of the Aloha method. The progress comes from the fact that, before emitting, a station senses the medium to detect whether it is occupied.

If a signal is already circulating, the emission is deferred, which considerably reduces the proportion of collisions of signals. However, since the transmission speed on the medium is finite (and even less than c, the speed of light in the vacuum) it is possible that a station may have failed to detect signals on the channel even though an emission had just begun a little further away. In this case, there will again be a collision.

Ethernet has the advantage over CSMA of being able to detect these colli-sions (Collision Detection – CD) and then attempting to retransmit in cases of loss. This considerably increases the reliability of layers 1 and 2. The detection of colli-sions during transmission involves a comparison of the message seen on the medium with that which it wishes to emit.

There are several different CSMA/CD methods, whose differences relate to the way in which the transmission is managed after the wait for the channel to become free. If a retransmission attempt is not made at the end of the packet but only after a random delay, the method is said to be non-persistent. If the attempt is always triggered immediately after the packet has passed (as soon as the channel is free), the method is said to be persistent or 1-persistent. On the other hand, if the attempt is only initiated with a probability P (less than 1), the method is said to be P-persistent. If the machine waits (complementary probability $1 - P$) it reloops on the same procedure of sensing the channel, waiting for it to become free and then transmitting (immediate, with probability P).

We note that CSMA/CD is very effective for low loads, although this method cannot guarantee a speed proportional to the load and is not adapted to the manage-ment of levels of priority.

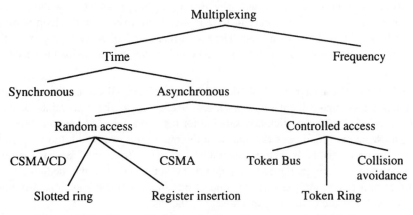

Figure 4.16   Hierarchical organization of access-control techniques.

Token

In the token method, the station possessing the token has the right to emit. The token is unique and must then circulate among all the machine controllers to ensure that each has the possibility of transmitting the messages confided to it.

The token-passing method thus requires the existence of an order among all the machines; the token must circulate in a precise direction. Thus, each item of equipment must at least know its predecessor in the chain, and sometimes its successor. Therefore, it seems that there must be an initial discussion stage in which

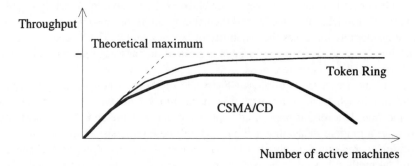

Figure 4.17 Graphs showing the relative efficiency of two access methods, in terms of actual speed.

the machines get to know each other and position themselves in the virtual loop. Thus, the efficiency of the system is not optimal for low loads.

This access method has the advantage of being reliable, since, as we have just seen, each machine is guaranteed a regular right to emit (in a deterministic manner, once for each passage of the token around the loop). However, it has the disadvantage of complexity. In fact, whenever a machine is added or withdrawn, or whenever the token is lost, a certain time is inevitably lost while the loop is reinitialized by an agreement of all the elements. Moreover, the delay in accessing the medium does not tend to zero, but remains bounded even when the load is very low.

Conclusion   The access methods described above have all the merits and shortcomings which make them more-or-less well adapted to the constraints of each network. CSMA/CD is particularly suitable for networks subject to continual evolution, on which the load does not approach the maximum bandwidth too frequently (since the performance is then considerably degraded). Token passing has a higher performance and can guarantee a bounded delay in the access to the medium, but is more complex and more sensitive to connections and disconnections; it is also more limited as far as the number of machines is concerned.

Finally, in summary, we present the interdependences of these methods in the form of a diagram (Figure 4.16).

Some of the asynchronous access methods (that is, those which are not based on a set of synchronized elements and cannot guarantee a minimum speed and a given minimum transmission delay under all conditions), such as token passing or register insertion, may be adapted to synchronous communications without too much difficulty. Others, such as CSMA/CD, are not readily suitable for transporting signals requiring synchronous multiplexing (essentially voice and video).

A comparison of the behavior of Token Ring and CSMA/CD shows that the performance may degrade quite drastically as the load increases when a random access technique is used (Figure 4.17).

4.6 Encoding and transmission

Encoding and transmission form part of level 1 and are thus defined in the standardization documents for that layer.

The transmission may be carried out with amplitude, frequency or phase modulation, which is still found in analog domains. In the digital domain, we essentially speak of encoding, although these methods of processing signals before their emission on the medium are sometimes similar. The aim is the same: to facilitate transmissions by improving the signal quality after it has travelled. Various encoding methods exist, each with qualities of simplicity or immunity to certain degradations (noise, attenuation, distortion) which make them appropriate for a given technology. One major constraint still remains, namely the suitability for the binary world; for example, a very high-performance encoding method adapted to the transport of data with 3, 5, 6 or 7 bits will not be easy to use.

The NRZ code

Non-Return to Zero (NRZ) code is one of the simplest, since it consists of a sequence of two possible electrical levels, V and $-V$, where V corresponds to the binary value 1 and $-V$ to 0. This code tends to minimize the continuous component of the transmitted signal. Thus, if 1s and 0s are present in approximately equal numbers and well distributed, the average level of the electrical signal is close to zero. However, the spectrum of the NRZ code has a large part of its power around the frequency 0, which is sometimes a hindrance.

The NRZI code

In Non-Return to Zero Inverted (NRZI) code, the number 1 is encoded by a change of state (rising or descending edge) after the clock pulse, 0 is encoded by an absence of a change in state. Thus, this code does not have a polarity.

A comparison of signals encoded using the NRZ and NRZI codes is shown in Figure 4.18.

The Manchester code

This is a code in which 1 is represented by a rising edge and 0 by a descending edge. Thus, it cannot be read correctly by inverting the direction. The Manchester code guarantees one transition (rising or descending edge) per clock pulse, which is equivalent to transporting a synchronization signal. The continuous component is always constant and may therefore be chosen to be zero. The signal spectrum is bunched between $1/2T$ and $1/T$ with zero power at frequency zero, but it has a total width twice that of the NRZ. The code has an efficiency of 50% since two levels are used to encode one bit of data.

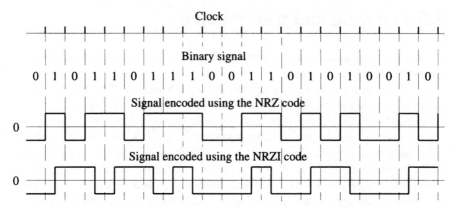

Figure 4.18 Comparison of signals encoded using the NRZ and NRZI codes.

This is the code used for Ethernet local area networks at 10 Mbps. Finally, we note that this code may be viewed as a code in phase $(-\pi/2, \pi/2)$ of the signals to be transmitted, which also explains why it is called a biphase code.

The differential Manchester code

The differential Manchester or biphase differential code consists of two signals with a binary significance and two non-data symbols. A 0 is encoded by a change in level (rising or descending edge) at the start and in the middle of an interval, while a 1 is encoded by a simple change of level in the middle of an interval. If no edge is present between two clock pulses, the signal is neither 0 nor 1 and therefore does not constitute data; however, despite this it can be used as a flag. Two non-data symbols are defined, one with a change of level on the clock pulse and the other without a change of level (called K and J). These may be used to identify certain MAC level fields within the frame and to delimit the data field.

Readers will have noted that the encoding is only defined in terms of changes of level and is thus independent of the polarity. Moreover, it does not have a continuous component and thus capacitance or inductance coupling is easy. Finally, the regular transition in the middle of a clock pulse transports inherent synchronization information. This code, which, like the Manchester code, has an efficiency of 50%, is used in the Token Ring technology at 4 and 16 Mbps.

A comparison of signals encoded with the Manchester and differential Manchester codes is shown in Figure 4.19.

The 4B/5B code

The 4B/5B code is a code which uses 5 bits to encode 16 possible values (whence the equivalent of 4 bits) by adding a built-in check. This coding is used for the FDDI and Fast Ethernet technologies in conjunction with an NRZI coding for the 5 bits

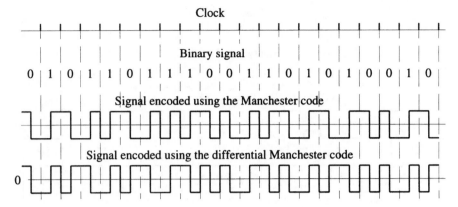

Figure 4.19   Comparison of signals encoded using the Manchester and differential Manchester codes.

produced. Of the 32 possible states, 2^4 are used for significant numerical values, eight are used for start- and end-of-frame indications, and eight are code violations. This code has the advantage over the previous two codes of having an intrinsic efficiency of 80%, since 16 numbers are effectively encoded with 5 bits.

8B/10B

8B/10B is a code employed by Fiber Channel (and originally by IBM) which has the advantage of handling one byte at a time. It makes use of (rather large) conversion tables, integrates a character that controls alignment, and has the additional advantage of being well-balanced. Since 256 data combinations are coded with 10 bits, the code possesses a very useful integrity check.

The FM-0 code

FM-0 (also referred to as biphase space) is the code used by LocalTalk. This code is fairly similar to the Manchester codes in the sense that the clock frequency is transported explicitly by the signal: there is one transition for each bit transmitted, but at the beginning and the end of the period (instead of in the middle, as in the Manchester codes). A bit at 0 requires an additional transition in the middle of the period, while a bit at 1 retains the same level throughout the period.

A comparison of signals encoded using MLT-3 and FM-0 is given in Figure 4.20.

Subsequently, we find codes with more than two levels, but whose edges are still synchronized on a fixed clock. The use of several levels generally allows a significant reduction of the frequency spectrum used, by means of less 'brutal' variations.

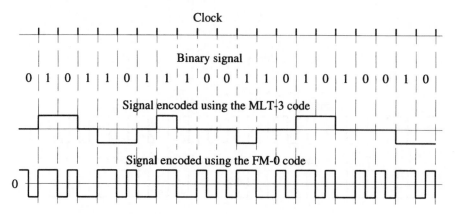

Figure 4.20 Comparison of signals encoded using MLT-3 and FM-0.

The MLT-3 code

MLT-3 stands for Three Levels MultiLine Transmission, and is a code which permits a reduction in the emitted frequency spectrum by using more than two states. This code is very similar to NRZI; it has three possible levels –1, 0, and 1. The transmission of a bit at 0 does not require a change of level, while the transmission of a bit at 1 does require a change of level. The levels follow the four-state period: 0, 1, 0, –1.

The standard which adapts FDDI technology to the Shielded or Unshielded Twisted Pair (UTP category 5), referred to as Twisted Pair – Physical Media Dependent (TP-PMD), uses this type of encoding. Similarly, the 100BaseTX Ethernet Addendum to IEEE 802.3 covers this mode of emission.

8B/6T

The 8B/6T code has been introduced by Ethernet 100BaseT4. It converts a byte into 6 codes of three levels (256 combinations are coded by means of 729 possibilities). Thus, the integrity of the signal is checked, and the frequency spectrum usage nevertheless reduced by more than 60% (in comparison to NRZ, for example).

Finally, the last most powerful and most complex codes use multiple physical levels, but also exploit the position of the edge to convey information. They are amplitude and phase modulated, or coded by means of a mesh. Obviously, these codes can also work on words or sequences of bits, and include an intrinsic consistency check.

PAM5

Five-level Pulse Amplitude Modulation employs pulse emission at five levels (–2, –1, 0, 1, 2) which, in the case of Ethernet at 100 Mbps (100BaseT2) to 1 Gbps, is exploited by a four-state mesh coding which is significantly immune against noise. This proposition also emerges from work on ADSL and HDSL.

4.7 Local area network rivals to Ethernet

Setting aside Ethernet, we have seen that other enterprise local area networks are commercially available, each with its own merits and shortcomings. In what follows, we review their main characteristics, leaving readers to judge them for themselves.

Token Ring

This local area network was developed by IBM and, like Ethernet, was ultimately standardized by the IEEE (in IEEE 802.5), then by ISO in 1992 in IS 8802.5.

It is based on a logical ring topology (with a physical implementation based on a star and a capacity for redundancy on inter-concentrator links). It uses a token-passing access method and has a speed of 1 Mbps (historically) or, more generally, 4 or 16 Mbps. The medium used comprises two individually shielded or unshielded twisted pairs (such as ICS type 1) and optical fiber for certain extensions. Communication is carried out in synchronous serial mode (at the physical level) with a baseband signal. Differential Manchester coding is used with a binary big-endian order of emission (highest-order bit of the byte sent first). The original connector technology was of an hermaphrodite type (but more commonly RJ45) on the network elements (MAU, for example) and of type DB9 on the NIC connector interfaces. The data is emitted in the form of frames (with a structure similar to that of Ethernet) whose minimum length is 21 bytes and whose maximum length is dependent on the capabilities of the set of attached machines, but may extend to 4450 bytes (at 4 Mbps) or 17 800 bytes (at 16 Mbps).

The restrictions are a maximum of 260 connections per ring (250 according to ISO) and a recommended length of 100 meters or less for lobes between the station and the MAU (750 meters being theoretically acceptable on STP with two repeaters).

Following the early release of the 16 Mbps Token Ring, more recent developments have made it possible to exceed the capabilities of the technology, whether by increasing the speed using 100VG-AnyLAN at 100 Mbps (which will be discussed later), or by using dynamic packet switching which makes it possible to dedicate the whole bandwidth to each pair of ports when a packet is exchanged. This switching may also be associated with a full duplex operation which would then offer 32 Mbps for each access, this mode being called Dedicated Token Ring (DTR).

Table 4.7 Number of different elements in a Token Ring network.

	Type of	STP IBM type 1		UTP categ. 4 or 5		UTP IBM type 3	
Speed (Mbps)	MAU	4	16	4	16	4	16
Number of machines	Passive	250	250	144	250	144	72
	Active	144	180	72			

We note that Token Ring was, in the first instance, essentially a manufacturer's proprietary product, which explains why it has interfaces for all IBM machines, although this is not necessarily true for the market as a whole.

The lack of openness of Token Ring is, with its intrinsic richness and complexity, the reason why it took so long for the technology to evolve toward higher speed. The full-duplex mode (DTR: Dedicated Token Ring) and the 100 Mbps Token Ring (HSTR: High Speed Token Ring) will only be standardised at best in 1998, impeding the ability of Token Ring products to fight fairly against their Ethernet counterpart.

LocalTalk

LocalTalk is a local area network developed by Apple for its Macintosh range, although it has never been standardized.

It is a technology with modest capabilities, which is practical and very easy to implement. The access method is CSMA/CA (CA for collision avoidance, which corresponds to a phase of exchange of indications before the emission of the packet), the speed is 230.4 kbps, the original topology is the chain and the medium is a twisted pair with characteristic impedance 120 Ohm (the diameter of the conductors may range from 0.4 to 0.6 mm). Originally, at most 32 nodes could be linked on a single segment over a total distance of less than 300 meters, but the evolution of compatible and rival products has led to support for two other topologies (bus and star, with passive or active hardware) and the raising of the maximum distance to 1.5 km in certain configurations. The maximum number of machines per network is 254. Connectors are of the RJ11 or 3-pin mini-DIN type.

We note that all Macintoshes and all Apple printers used to have a native LocalTalk interface.

Finally, we must distinguish between AppleTalk and LocalTalk: the former brings together the whole area of Apple network communication, and thus covers the seven layers, with different possible network technologies (EtherTalk, TokenTalk), while the latter defines a specific LAN technology (lower layers).

ARCnet

ARCnet was developed by Datapoint Corporation, but has only recently been considered by one of the standardization bodies (ANSI 878.1 standard, for its latest extension). However, its capabilities were interesting and its market was not negligible. It was an inexpensive technology, focused on the world of microcomputers.

The throughput offered is 2.5 Mbps and 20 Mbps (multiplication by a factor of 8) with the recent version of ARCnet plus, which is upwards compatible. The topology used is the star, the access method is based on token passing and the media are RG62 (93 Ohm) coaxial cable, fiber optic cable or twisted pair. The network can accommodate 255 machines and the frames contain up to 507 bytes of data.

FDDI

Although FDDI is not a LAN, it undeniably constitutes an alternative to Ethernet networks. FDDI was introduced as a replacement for top-of-the-range Ethernet since it provided a generally superior performance (in terms of length, speed, number of machines). We note that it was still considerably more expensive than Ethernet. However, FDDI was also viewed as a network for interconnecting several Ethernet networks, that is, as a backbone of the architecture. It was then no longer a direct competitor, but a complementary element in the construction of a global solution. We shall now describe some of the main technical characteristics of FDDI.

The network uses a token-passing method with early release, on a (basic) topology comprising a contra-rotating double ring. In case of failure of a link or a machine, the secondary ring is used to ensure the continuity of the ring by looping (or wrapping) back to the primary ring. FDDI offers a speed of 100 Mbps and uses mainly fiber optic cable. Its restrictions include a maximum of 500 stations (doubly attached) per network and a circumference of 100 km. The distance between two stations may extend to 2 km (62.5/125 μm fiber recommended) for multimode fibers and 35 to 58 km for single-mode fibers (according to the category of the emitters and receivers). The FDDI frames have a structure similar to those of Token Ring and may contain up to 4500 bytes of data. The encoding is of the 4B/5B type and requires only 125 Mbaud. The connector technology comprises a pair of connectors: ST duplex.

The concentrator is an important element which can be used to create branches of a tree-like topology, while retaining the redundancy of the links by dual homing. Simple attachments in a master–slave configuration are also available, but at the logical level the overall network topology remains a single ring.

Finally, since FDDI was developed according to the OSI model, the highest layer is naturally the LLC IS 8802-2.

Conclusion   In an attempt to provide impartial advice, we now give a rapid comparative review of the local area networks discussed above.

Ethernet has the advantage of being a standardized, manufacturer-independent network, which is very common, easy to modify, broadly extensible, and relatively inexpensive (medium and active elements). Its disadvantage is that it does not cope well with new requirements in terms of security and Quality of Service.

Token Ring is a fairly common standardized network, which has a high performance and retains its capabilities under all loads. Its disadvantage is that it is more expensive (active elements) and sometimes not available for certain computers (workstations, mainframes). It retains a strong link with its original manufacturer (IBM).

LocalTalk was a network which focuses on the interconnection of Apple microcomputers. It was very practical, very user-friendly and simple to implement. However, it was limited in terms of speed and the total number of machines supported.

ARCnet is a network which was standardized belatedly. Its capabilities were often sufficient, it was easy to use and very user-friendly but had an uneven distribution.

Table 4.8   Characteristics of the most common local area networks.

Technology	Ethernet	Token Ring	LocalTalk	ARCnet	FDDI
Standard	IEEE 802.3 ISO 8802-3	IEEE 802.5 ISO 8802-5	–	ANSI 878.1	ANSI X3T9.5 ISO 9314
Maximum speed	1/10/100 Mbps 1 Gbps	4 & 16 Mbps	230 kbps	2.5 & 20 Mbps	100 Mbps
Code	Manchester 4B/5B, 8B/10B	Differential Manchester	FM-0	Miller	4B/5B (+ NRZI/MLT-3)
Max frame in bytes	1518	4450 & 17800	605	514 & 4231	4500
Min frame	64 (512 at 1 Gbps)	21 bytes	7 bytes	7 bytes	22 bytes
Throughput in pps	14880 at 10 Mbps	21739 & 68965	3200	26600 & 204100	446429
Medium	Coaxial cable Optical fiber Twisted pair	Twisted pair Optical fiber	Twisted pair	Coaxial cable Optical fiber Twisted pair	Optical fiber (multi/mono-) Twisted pair
Topologies	bus star	ring	chain	bus star	ring of trees
Access method	CSMA/CD	Token passing	CSMA/CA	Token passing	Timed token passing
Connection per network	1024	250 (IBM: 260)	32 (254 possible)	255 & 2047	500 DAS
Network dimension	4 km at 10 Mbps 412 m 100 Mbps	variable	300 m (1.5 km)	6.5 km	100 km
between node	2.5 m min	800 & 400 max		610 m max	MMF: 2 km max UTP: 100 m

FDDI is not a true local area network, but has been perceived as a top-of-the range challenger. It is a standardized, manufacturer-independent, high-performance network whose principal disadvantage is still its price (medium and active materials).

The main characteristics of the most common local area networks are summarized in Table 4.8.

4.8 The place of local area networks in telecommunications

Local area networks are relatively recent in the world of telecommunications. They have a high performance in terms of speed and transmission quality and have led users to consume large bandwidths, which partly explains why the providers are now offering higher speeds. For example, after 256 and 512 kbps, Frame Relay is now moving towards T1/E1 (1.544/2 Mbps) and leased lines at E3/T3 (34/45 Mbps), then 140 or 155 Mbps in response to the requirements for exchanges between research centers.

Thus, in summary, local area networks provide communication facilities on the scale of a building or a site which are now almost always owned by the enterprise; they are of a high quality without always being expensive and provide support for the evolution of long-distance digital telecommunications.

Chapter 5

Current trends

- Hubs

- Telephony

- Model

- Architecture

User requirements are evolving with the increase in consumer-based telecommunications-related information technology, and there is an incontestable demand for higher speeds, both at the local level (between the supercomputers in a computing center or simply between the servers) and at a distance (between remote sites), and on a unitary scale (in terms of access) or a global scale (for the infrastructure). The United States still retains a slight lead in the WAN area, which, for example, explains why what ISDN has to offer in terms of basic access is of less interest in the US.

The bandwidth has become the main criterion, given that the transmission quality has improved to a sufficient extent that the protocols of certain layers are capable of reducing the quality controls they implement.

Thus, a certain number of new technologies will respond to these demands in the short or long term. These principally include LAN frame switching, Fast Ethernet and Gigabit Ethernet, ATM, Frame Relay and Sonet. Some will be stages leading to a more homogeneous architecture. Several providers have thus embarked on important research and development work relating to ATM technology which provides a fast cell-switching technique (a packet may have a variable length, while a cell has a fixed size). A rapid review of these new arrivals in the WAN arena is given in Figure 5.1.

All LAN technologies have taken a very significant benefit from frame switching. In fact all the limitations due to the MAC process itself can be almost completely eliminated by switching each frame depending on its effective destination. Switches (or fast multiport bridges), as opposed to hubs, offer to aggregate the bandwidth of each port, instead of sharing it among all users. This appears to be the most powerful way to leverage existing network capacities, by replacing only some core network equipment without any changes on the workstation, NICs, cabling, NOS, etc. Moreover, switching goes naturally very well with multiple speeds, like the diversity given by Ethernet 10/100/1000 Mbps.

Frame Relay is a technique for relaying frames at level 2, which is already well established in the USA, as a higher-performance substitute for conventional packet switching (X.25). This standard provides an interface between private network and the service providers for all data communications but also more recently for voice type traffic, and allows one to keep the architectures in place. The current speeds are now generally of the order of T1/E1 (T1/E1 denotes the throughput in

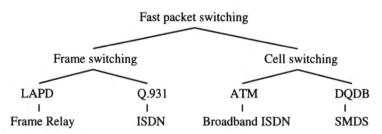

Figure 5.1 The four levels of the broadband world: concept, technologies, standards and services.

USA/Europe: 1.5/2 Mbps) and the price/performance ratio is less than that for existing technologies. In fact, the simplification of the protocol considerably reduces the checks on exchanges and thus avoids all the time lost in waiting for confirmation of receipt, which is particularly appropriate for irregular traffic (for example, in bursts).

Switched Multimegabit Data Services (SMDS) is a connectionless service provided for the interconnection of local area networks. Defined by Bellcore, it is based on the cell formatting of the IEEE 802.6 standard and was designed as a WAN. Unlike DQDB, it has no isochronous capabilities and thus does not offer voice or video transport. It currently operates at T1/E1 or T3/E3. Using a cell format similar to that of ATM, SMDS had the ambition to become a common service for access to trunk networks.

ATM as a broadband technology shows how to abandon time-division or frequency-division multiplexing in favor of fast cell switching, as is the case for ATM. The gain attributable to this service, which should soon be offered by telecommunication providers over large distances, will be even more perceptible for irregular traffic (such as that of local area networks) which, with ATM, will have access to a complete bandwidth when necessary (typically 1.5 or 2 Mbps and above) without the corresponding cost of fully dedicated leased lines or circuit switching. Moreover, this technology should be capable of handling all types of traffic, including digital data, voice, and video. Thus, use of ATM to link PABXs amongst themselves and to the public network may be envisaged. The ATM cell circulating on the virtual channels is short (53 bytes) and will result, if necessary, in the subdivision of frames. The speed of backbones may range from 51.8 Mbps to 155 Mbps, 622 Mbps, 2.4 Gbps, and above. Finally, ATM will form the main basic element of broadband ISDN associated with a whole range of service qualities. In the provider's network the physical layer supporting ATM is likely to be Synchronous Digital Hierarchy (SDH), and SONET in the USA. FDDI circuitry has also been proposed as a physical carrier for ATM (TAXI). Equipment in the form of patch panels, switches, brouters, and NIC cards is already commercially available.

Thus, it is foreseeable that users will install private ATM switches on their sites to interconnect the different distributed regional agencies. ATM would then have to find its place as a technology for the site backbone network, which, in addition to integrating the existing local area networks (by consistent connection of existing concentrators and interconnection devices to one or more ATM switches), would also permit direct connection of computers requiring various speeds and provide the privileged means of attachment to a WAN. Not many years ago ATM was perceived as the ultimate technology applicable at all levels, from PC connection to high-speed inter-site connection. However, even though ATM has a number of advantages, in terms of isochrony, quality of service, speed, congestion management and network management, the existing base of LAN equipment could not be suddenly called into question, and the migration would have to be quite gradual.

5.1 Hubs

Today's hubs are multiport, modular, multi LAN-technology repeaters (also referred to as multimedia) and multibus and multiring repeaters, to which additional functions have been added. We shall see later that active hubs or stars may already accommodate several technologies (Ethernet, Token Ring, LocalTalk, FDDI, serial links) in the same chassis. Consequently, the simple function of a repeater has been extended by dynamic switching, bridging and routing, and terminal server and gateway capabilities, with the subsequent implementation of network management facilities (device management and traffic monitoring by a standard protocol). These chassis have thus accumulated more and more resources, bringing together the equivalent of many boxes and combining various processing faculties. These hubs continue to improve incessantly, in terms of performance, modules implementing new technologies, higher internal speeds, and the sensitivity of observation or parametrization of each port. Thus, they have become vital nodes of the network, and henceforth will gradually integrate all networking functions into unique rich and powerful nodes. This can be seen in the increasing processing power required on those new hubs, and the manufacturers' efforts to implement more features in hardware to offer guaranteed high level performance.

5.2 Telephony

Another process, with its origin in a completely different field, involves the integration of these network level functions (above all, the repeater, bridge, switch, and router stages) with the PABX network. The main idea here is to reduce costs by merging LAN and telephone networks and servers (the PABX being perceived as a certain type of 'circuit server'). Clearly LANs have the bandwidth to easily transport voice channels and eventually video communication, but today they still lack most of the required synchronization capabilities. On the other hand, NOS servers could easily deal with call signaling (plus the security and accounting), and eventually bring a much better human interface through traditional graphical application and window menus. This trend is nevertheless quite a revolution, as it bring to the same market large vendors from different industries and with different technical cultures.

5.3 Model

As far as protocols are concerned, and although the OSI reference model was chosen by most government organizations a few years ago, the cost and difficulty encountered in porting it in all types of environments appear sufficiently restrictive to encourage moves towards a simplified or modified (and thus, partially non-standard) suite of protocols. The long-awaited 'all ISO' solution thus seems to be slightly compromised.

5.4 Architecture

After looking at recent developments, one might detect a tendency towards an increased stratification in the telecommunications world, comparable to that which is already in place in the world of electronics and information technology. Just like the complex software systems which are now being developed in a hierarchy of modules (beginning with the operating system and moving towards the application), or the memory of an electronic system which is divided into ever smaller and faster units (tape back-up, hard disk unit, disk cache, central memory, CPU cache memory, internal registers), communication systems will be constructed from the set of all commercially available technologies by placing these one above each other (see Figure 5.2).

Thus, we foresee that tomorrow, the computing center will have an HSLAN for its supercomputers, which will be interconnected with one or more backbone MANs to meet the connection needs of servers and powerful graphics stations, these networks being in turn connected to a multitude of small LANs, feeding all the

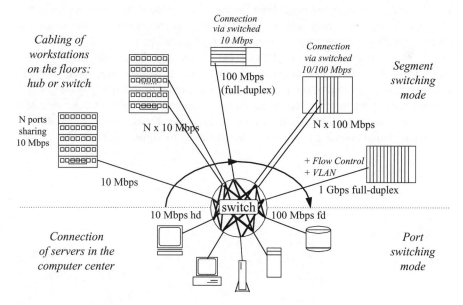

Figure 5.2 Structured data networks with two levels.

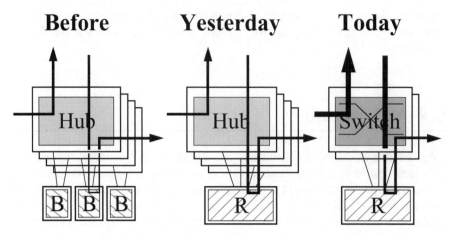

Figure 5.3   From hub to switch.

offices. Of course, ATM may act as a backbone technology before taking up a position similar to an HSLAN and ultimately becoming a commonplace LAN attachment.

LAN hardware is, therefore, becoming ever richer with concomitant overall performance benefits for all elements (repeaters, hubs and stars, switches, bridges, routers, gateways).

The increasing complexity of network architecture is intended to provide a better answer to each different need. The same type of technology or product cannot fulfill exactly the requirements at both the core and the edge of a network, in terms of global throughput, delay, number and type of ports, additional features (security, routing, filtering), management, and monitoring capabilities.

This subdivision of the global architecture with the development of new technologies forces manufacturers to integrate more powerful components in their equipment, but also to progressively increase the number of levels of the OSI model implemented in the interconnection product. As can be seen in Figure 5.3, what was once a concentrator in the LAN has become a high speed bridge (or switch), and the router will soon become a Layer 3 switch (as shown in Figure 13.21).

PART II

Ethernet

Chapter 6

History and evolution of the standard

- Ethernet

- The IEEE 802.3 standard

- The ISO 8802-3 standard

To provide the reader with a sound introduction to the current Ethernet specifications, we shall rapidly review the stages leading from the preliminary documents to the IEEE 802.3 standard, and then to the IS 8802-3 standard.

6.1 Ethernet

In the early 1970s, Xerox was working on open office automation systems and embryos of local area networks. It developed an experimental version of Ethernet operating at 3 Mbps on 75 Ohm coaxial cable which could cover up to one kilometer, but the technologies were still evolving. Robert Metcalf, who was working at Xerox at that time, is often considered as the father of the Ethernet.

In collaboration with the Digital Equipment Corporation (DEC) and Intel, Xerox published the blue book *The Ethernet* in September 1980. This was version 1.0. The name stood for network of the ether (the passive cable, in this case). The main features of Ethernet, including the method, the topology, the physical medium and the main constraints, were already present, and the modifications which followed later only amounted to improvements of the hardware components (Figure 6.1).

In November 1982, the developers published version 2.0 (AA-K759B-TK), which was fairly complete but partially incompatible with the previous version (for example, at the transceiver level). This document covered aspects of the MAC and physical layers and, unlike the IEEE and ISO standards, gave a relatively clear

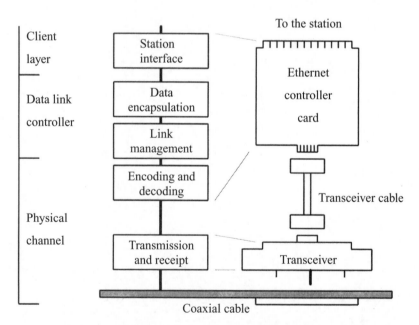

Figure 6.1   Ethernet architecture and typical implementation.

explanation of the operation of a whole network. The document contains few acronyms and its style and structure make it very readable. The MAC layer functionality (the access method, in fact) was written in Pascal. The conceivable media at that time were coaxial cable with 50 Ohm characteristic impedance and optical fiber (which was only intended for point-to-point links between two half repeaters). The largest network could have an extent of up to 2.8 km with, at most, two repeaters on a path between two stations (the repeater between the coaxial cable and the optical fiber was considered to be a half repeater), which corresponds to three 500 m cable segments, a 1 km optical link and six 50 m drop cables ($3 \times 500 + 1000 + 6 \times 50 = 2800$ m). These specifications included the description of a means of testing equipment at the level of the lower layers, the loopback mode, which used the type field value of 9000, which has disappeared in the standard documents.

As far as the available hardware was concerned, very few manufacturers were present, but DEC and Xerox already offered satisfactory solutions. The devices were cumbersome, the performance of the controller cards was even more modest, and only the basic elements of the construction kit for networks as we know them today (such as transceivers for monoport coaxial cable and biport repeaters) were available. There was little or no hardware for test, analysis or observation, and so at that time, any form of operation, without further detailed qualification, was acceptable.

6.2 The IEEE 802.3 standard

The IEEE took over the specifications for Ethernet and reformulated them in 1985 in a standard publication, ANSI/IEEE 802.3 (ISO/DIS 8802-3). Although this document was unprepossessing, and thus initially difficult to read, it was complete and left no ambiguity. The parallelism with the OSI model was established, and layer 2 was split in two to insert Ethernet in the MAC and physical layers (Figure 6.2).

A certain number of modifications were introduced, but the main features were retained and equipment conforming to IEEE 802.3 was to be interoperable with that conforming to Ethernet V 2.0. The drop cable was increased from 9 to 15 wires, the entire connector technology was redefined, and, in particular, the times were recalculated and the type field was replaced by a length field.

Remark   Since IEEE 802.3 is less meaningful than Ethernet, current networks – which almost all conform to the standard – have retained the original name. Similarly, in the rest of this book, we shall use IEEE 802.3 or Ethernet interchangeably when referring to current hardware, and specify Ethernet V 2.0 explicitly when referring to that particular standard.

In 1988, the IEEE published a collection of supplements to the IEEE 802.3 standard, which correspond to extensions, choices of other media, or other available speeds and technologies. As we shall see below, these complementary specifications were to become more or less important with time.

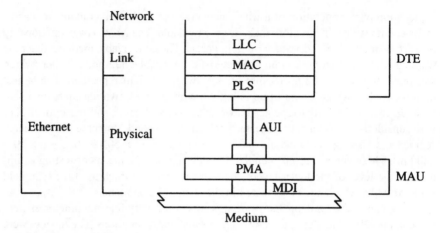

DTE: Data Terminal Equipment
LLC: Logical Link Control
MAC: Medium Access Control
PLS: Physical Layer Signaling
AUI: Attachment Unit Interface
MAU: Medium Attachment Unit
PMA: Physical Medium Attachment
MDI: Medium Dependent Interface

Figure 6.2   Decomposition of Ethernet into sublayers and relative positions in the OSI model.

Finally, ISO standardized the IEEE document in February 1989, incorporating thin coaxial cable (10Base2 or IEEE 802.3a) as the medium. Thus, Ethernet reached the end of its evolution, at least as far as the basic technical specifications with the standard media are concerned, despite the progress which had taken place since its conception which might have permitted regular improvements to the performance of such a network. This clearly illustrates the advantages and disadvantages of standardization, which ensures compatibility for the medium term, albeit based on a technology which is already aging.

The differences between Ethernet V 2.0 and IEEE 802.3

The transition from Ethernet to IEEE 802.3 required a number of modifications, which should be recorded, even though they were minor and do not hinder compatibility.

The main difference lies in the fact that the third MAC field of the frame, the type field, changed its meaning and became a length field. The addresses have a second special Individual/Universal bit following the Unicast/Multicast bit. Moreover, the addresses may theoretically have 16 or 48 bits, rather than just 48. The pin diagram for the drop cable is supplemented by an additional pair: Control Out (very rarely used) and by an individual screening per pair.

The maximum propagation time for a network was slightly increased, to be on the safe side and in order to impose weaker constraints on the hardware, and rose from a round-trip delay (RTD) of 46.38 μs to 49.9 μs. A test signal for the collision pair of the AUI cable was added, namely the SQE test which passes from the transceiver to the interface card. The transceiver is no longer necessarily connected to the cable by branching and may now be connected using type N screw connectors.

The supplements to IEEE 802.3

The IEEE 802 standards introduced a particular notation, whereby a technology is denoted by the maximum speed, the modulation type and the segment length. For example, Ethernet as we have described it above is denoted by 10Base5, signifying that it operates at 10 Mbps in baseband with segments of a maximum length of 500 m (5 × 100). Similarly, Ethernet on thin cable is denoted by 10Base2, signifying that the cable segments are limited to a length of 185 meters (~2 × 100).

Several supplements to IEEE 802.3 have been issued or are in hand (a, b, c, d, and so on). They are intended to supplement the basic document with implementations on other media or with special information. They are designed for insertion in the standard, to which they add certain paragraphs or replace certain chapters with new ones. The numbers of the sections (which correspond to chapters) are thus consistent with the IEEE 802.3 and IS 8802-3 documents. We shall review the main features of these supplements in order. We include technical details which readers may return to after reading the paragraphs describing the operation of each element.

Supplement IEEE 802.3a   Also called 10Base2, Thinnet, Thin Ethernet or Cheapernet. This adaptation was originally introduced by the InterLAN company.

The supplement describes the use of thin coaxial cable of the RG58 type with BNC connectors. The length of a thin cable is limited to 185 meters, and with these less cumbersome connectors the transceivers can be more easily incorporated in the connector interfaces. On its own, the 10Base2 type of medium retains all the main features of Ethernet 10Base5 (topology, number of segments, electrical levels, frame structures, and so on). However, the number of connections per segment decreases to 30 and the distance between these connections must be greater than 50 cm.

This technique is used widely, since it is very practical and reasonably priced; therefore, in what follows, the main constraints on Ethernet (10Base5) will also be given for 10Base2. Finally, we note that supplement IEEE 802.3a has been incorporated in the IS 8802-3 standard (section 10).

Supplement IEEE 802.3b   Also called 10Broad36, that is, 10 Mbps in broadband, with maximal distances of 3.6 km per segment.

The medium is CATV-type coaxial cable with 75 Ohm characteristic impedance. The code is Differential Phase-Shift Keying (DPSK). The topology uses single or double accesses to the cable (Figure 6.3). In the first case, a frequency converter is placed at the end, which requires emission and reception at different carrier frequencies at the point of access. In the second case, the cable is looped at one end

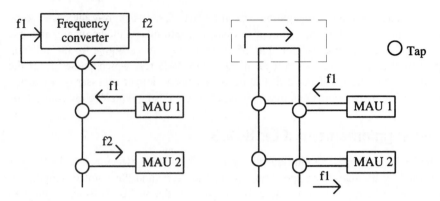

Figure 6.3 Example of emission on a system with broadband coaxial cable (single and double access).

and access is via the two segments with the same carrier frequency for a single MAU. In the first case, the carrier frequencies range from 43 MHz to 73 MHz with a spacing of 6 MHz and from 43 MHz to 265 MHz in the second case.

It is apparent that this is a (now rare) implementation of Ethernet which can be used to mix several data communication channels with serial links or video on a single cable, using frequency-division multiplexing.

Supplements IEEE 802.3c and d　These supplements give a more detailed specification of the characteristics of the repeater in a network of type 10Base5 or 10Base2 and of the characteristics of FOIRL-type optical links (fiber optic inter-repeater link).

The repeater interconnects the cable segments by regenerating the signals, extending the fragments (frame fragments of less than 96 bits may result from a collision), completing the preamble to 56 bits and propagating collisions by emitting Jam. It can also interrupt an excessively long emission or deactivate a port judged to be a regular source of faults. The repeater is called a repeater set when it incorporates the transceivers (of type 10Base5, 10Base2 or FOIRL). A full description of how it operates is given in Section 12.6.

The FOIRL link is a point-to-point optical link, preferably reserved for the interconnection of two repeaters. The recommended fiber is graded-index multimode silica fiber with a 62.5 ± 3 μm core and a 125 ± 3 μm sheath. The numerical aperture should be 0.275 ± 0.015 (corresponding to IEC 793-2 type Alb). The recommended connector technology was of the FSMA type (IEC 874-2) with an attenuation of at most 2.5 dB per connector pair. Other fiber types are also provided for, including the 50/125 μm, the 85/125 μm and the 100/140 μm. The wavelength at which these transceivers (called fiber optic media access units – FOMAU) operate is 850 nm (actually, between 790 nm and 860 nm). At this frequency, the attenuation of the fiber should be limited to 4 dB/km and to 8 dB over the whole link, where the bandwidth should be greater than 150 MHz per km. An optical power of 9 dB for a complete link is budgeted for, together with a maximum time of 500 ns (the longest link which can be implemented is less than or equal to 1 km). The optical transceiver has a crossing delay of 3.5 bit times in each direction for a valid signal and 3.5 bit times for collision detection. An idle signal (inactivity) is defined for the FOMAU, consisting of periodic pulses (short signals of one or two oscillations) with a frequency of 1 MHz (+25%, −15%), which is emitted when there is no traffic.

Supplement IEEE 802.3e Also called 1Base5, or StarLAN, this is a point-to-point method offering a speed of 1 Mbps on twisted pair. It currently uses a star topology (in which the multiport repeater is at the center; it is called the hub and incorporates built-in transceivers).

The unshielded twisted pair is of the telephone-pair type, comprising conductors with a diameter from 0.4 mm to 0.6 mm. It has a characteristic impedance of 100 ± 15 Ohm and a maximum attenuation of 6.5 dB at 1 Mhz. The physical copper link between the transceiver and hub (or multiport repeater) may extend to 250 meters (the 5 of 10Base5 is not very explicit here, because one has to consider the distance between two network attachment points, that is, two transceivers: 500 = 5 × 100 m), and the optical links may extend to 4 km. Five storeys of hubs may be installed in a cascade. The electrical levels lie between 2 and 3.65 V. There is an *idle* signal which occupies the line continuously during silences and alerts the hub to the presence of the transceiver. Manchester code violation signals (no change in level after the clock pulse) are used to transmit a notification of the presence of a collision or the idle signal. The connector technology is of the RJ45 type (ISO 8877) and only pins 1, 2, 3, and 6 are used (or two pairs) in unidirectional transmission (Figure 6.4).

This version of Ethernet, which was originally developed by AT&T, has now been abandoned in favor of 10BaseT. Since the rate in 1Base5 is a factor of ten less than that of Ethernet, there is no direct compatibility, but we shall see that there are (MAC level) bridges which can be used to link a 1Base5 network and a 10Base5 or 10Base2 network. The frame structure remains identical in all cases.

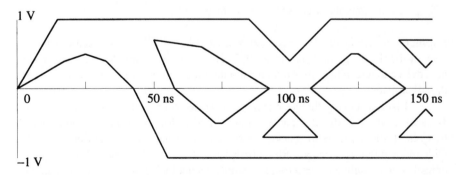

Figure 6.4 Approximate template of a Manchester signal on twisted pair.

Supplement IEEE 802.3h Supplement IEEE 802.3h, Layer Management, dates from 1991 and defines certain possibilities for monitoring or controlling the physical, MAC and LLC layers of a CSMA/CD network by adjoining a Layer Management Entity (LME) to each of these three functional blocks.

These entities correspond with the System Management Application Entity (SMAE) via Layer Management Interfaces (LMI). As far as the MAC level is concerned, signals such as the emission control (inhibition of all transmission), the change of MAC address, the acceptance of frames destined for another machine, the deactivation of the MAC layer, the management of recognized (and accepted), group addresses and the rejection (non reading) of multicast frames are defined there. This supplement replaces a part of Chapter 5 left empty in the IS 8802-3 standard.

Supplement IEEE 802.3i This fairly recent supplement defines the 10BaseT (T for twisted pair) part, that is, the possibility of constructing an Ethernet-type network on an unshielded twisted-pair medium.

Since the physical carrier is the same as that of 1Base5, 10BaseT is also commonly referred to as StarLAN 10 Mbps. Because the topology is a star, the accesses to the hub are made from point to point, and the links can be viewed as IRL. Thus, it is possible to cascade two levels of hubs. The cable segments have a maximum recommended length of 100 meters, a characteristic impedance of 85 to 111 Ohm between 5 and 10 MHz, a maximum delay of 1 μs and an attenuation of less than 11.5 dB from 5 to 10 MHz. The conductors may have a diameter from 0.4 to 0.6 mm (26 AWG to 22 AWG). The connector technology is still of type RJ45 (IS 8877 standardized by ISO) with the two pairs connected to the contacts: 1 and 2 for the transmission and 3 and 6 for receipt. Since the cabling is normally straight, crossover takes place inside the hub. The electrical data signals are between ±0.7 and 1 V. An idle signal is used to validate the receiving pair on each port of the hub and on each transceiver. This is called LinkIntegrityTest and consists of periodic pulses formed from a single oscillation. Supplement i adds Chapters 13 and 14 to IS 8802-3 (which originally only had 12 chapters).

We note that the limitation of the segment length to 100 meters is a recommendation, but is not in itself a criterion, since it has to be determined from a consideration of the time budget and the attenuation of the link. Some manufacturers offer solutions capable of covering 250 m or more.

Supplement IEEE 802.3j Better known as 10BaseF (F for fiber optic), this has been an IEEE 802.3 standard since 1993. This section is very detailed and readers are advised to return to it after reading about certain more recent aspects of Ethernet, described later.

10BaseF covers three subjects: passive asynchronous optical networks (or 10BaseFP, where P denotes passive star, Section 16); active synchronous optical networks (10BaseFB, B for backbone, Section 17), and the redefinition of FOIRL with more interesting capabilities (10BaseFL, Section 18). These three types of optical network define different, incompatible, technologies to meet different requirements. Given the range of aspects covered by this supplement to IEEE 802.3, the document includes the redefinition of several points relating to the operation of a network. Thus, it constitutes an important extension for Ethernet. The new Section 15 covers the elements common to the three applications of type 10BaseF, including the specification of the wavelength at which emitters operate at 850 nm (between 800 and 910 nm), the spectral width (less than 75 nm) and the templates of the optical signals for the synchronous and asynchronous cases. The recommended type of optical fiber is still the 62.5 μm, with a numerical aperture of 0.275. The attenuation is less than 3.75 dB/km (a value of 3.5 dB/km is still under discussion) and the bandwidth is at least 160 MHz per km. The connector technology is now of the ST type (IEC 86B, from AT&T) with a maximum insertion loss of 1 dB.

Fibers other than the 62.5/125 μm are authorized and the 10BaseF standard includes a table of the supplementary attenuations due to the use of these with the end machines specified for the 62.5/125 μm cable (see Table 6.1).

10BaseFP defines an optical network technology based on a star topology, with passive stars. We shall see later that the passive star consists solely of optical fibers fused together. For preference, the star consists of 62.5 μm fiber, but 50/125 μm fiber is also an alternative. It is connected to segments with transceivers at their ends. The cable segments from the transceivers to the star should not be longer than 500 m. The star may have up to 33 ports (each port includes a connector on input and a connector on output) or 17 ports for 50/125 μm. The attenuation due to a star between an input port and an output port should be between 16 dB and 20 dB. The attenuation on a link, from transceiver to transceiver, including the passive star, should be less than 26 dB, measured with a signal with a wavelength of 850 nm and a spectral width of 75 nm. The loss of power suffered by a signal on reflection on a connector should be greater than 25 dB. The crossing delays for a transceiver are 3.5 bit times for emission and 2.5 bit times for reception. The delay in detecting a collision is 3.5 bit times. Since the star has no electronic components (the signal is not processed there, only split), its crossing delay is essentially zero. Like the other supplements, 10BaseFP tends to standardize a technology which is already in the market place and, even, relatively old. The passive optical implementations have not always been very convincing to date, since they do not ensure exhaustive collision detection (provided for in CSMA/CD); the tendency has been to reserve them for

Table 6.1   Additional loss of optical power for different types of fiber.

Diameters μm Core/Sheath	Numerical aperture	Loss on emission dB	Loss on receipt dB	Total loss dB
50/125	0.2	5.7	0	5.7
50/125	0.21	5.2	0	5.2
50/125	0.22	4.8	0	4.8
85/125	0.26	1.6	2.6	5.2
100/140	0.29	0.5	4.5	5

situations in which only they are suitable, for example, in a very disturbed electro-magnetic environment, or when the star set-up has no electrical power.

10BaseFB (B for backbone), called 10BaseFA in earlier drafts, defines a new technology for Ethernet, namely synchronous communications. It is notable that this supplement goes beyond the usual framework, in that the transmission mode is no longer a simple adaptation of the original one specified for coaxial cable segments on point-to-point links.

Taking advantage of the point-to-point topology, the IEEE decided to choose a transmission mode which would ensure that no bits were lost at the start of reception. In asynchronous mode the receiver has no knowledge of the emitter's clock and has to begin by synchronizing itself on the received signal, which inevit-ably leads to the loss of a number of the leading bits; however, in synchronous mode the receiver is always synchronized with the only possible emitter, situated opposite it. This means that there is no longer any need for a clock signal preceding the frame (thus, the preamble loses its main function) and the receiver can read the message immediately with no bits lost. This gain gets around the constraint of the maximum number of repeaters on a path and the size of the network is only limited by the round-trip delay, which is unchanged. The transceiver then becomes the entry (or exit) point separating the asynchronous world (from the drop cable) and the synchron-ous world (the star or the group of synchronous stars).

More specifically, the medium is always occupied either by a signal denoting the state (wait, jabber, incorrect receipt) or by data (frames). Code violations of the Manchester code (code rule violation: CRV) are used to form the non-data signals. For example, the synchronous idle is a signal in the 2.5 MHz frequency slot and the remote fault (RF) has a frequency of 1.667 MHz. The remote fault signal covers the following three problems: jabber received, insufficient optical power, and invalid data. A link has a maximum length of 2 km and must have an end-to-end attenuation less than 12.5 dB. The maximum crossing delay for the transceiver is 2 bit times for emission and receipt; collision detection (presence of signals being emitted and received simultaneously) should be less than 3.5 bit times. However, the advantage of the synchronous mode accrues principally from the gains achieved at the level of the repetition stage. When the latter includes synchronous built-in transceivers, it is limited to 2 bit times plus the delay of 1 bit time on receipt and on emission in the transceivers.

Some drafts showed a desire to give the synchronous active star at least two ports compatible with the asynchronous FOIRL links. This should then avoid any communication in the case of improper connection of FOIRL transceivers on synchronous ports.

10BaseFL, called 10BaseFF in earlier drafts, is a new FOIRL with enhanced performance, which still uses active, asynchronous point-to-point links, but is upwards compatible. Like FOIRL, 10BaseFL can be used to enable two transceivers opposite each other to intercommunicate (see Figure 6.5) or to construct a star topo-logy around a multiport repeater, incorporating several optical transceivers. The optical power budget rises from 9 dB to 12.5 dB and the maximum length of a link increases to 2 km. On the other hand, the crossing delay for an optical transceiver is

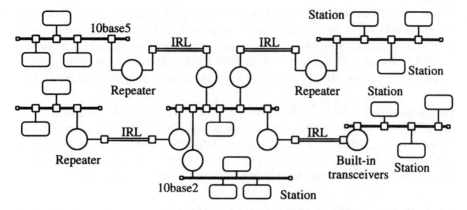

Figure 6.5 Example of an extensive Ethernet network incorporating coaxial cables and FOIRL links.

5 bit times (still identical in both directions), while the collision detection delay remains 3.5 bit times.

Supplements IEEE 802.3p and q Supplements IEEE 802.3p and q, defined in 1993, defined Guidelines for the Development of Managed Objects (GDMO), the format of managed objects, and the management layer for 10 Mbps transceivers, which corresponds to Sections 5 and 20 of the standard. These objects, or variables, belong to specific MIB, under the branches 'csmalayermgt' and 'mauMgt' defined for CMIP. These elements are also associated with the available types of action: Get and/or Set.

Supplements IEEE 802.3u Better known as 100BaseT or Fast Ethernet, this is a standard which describes a version of Ethernet on twisted pair and optical fiber operating at 100 Mbps. This technology is described in greater depth in Chapter 10. It covers Sections 21 to 30, which correspond to the following topics:

- Section 21: introduction to 100 Mbps networks.
- Section 22: reconciliation sublayer and MII.
- Section 23: 100BaseT4, which is based on four UTPs of category 3, 4 or 5.
- Section 24: 100BaseX, which uses the physical level of FDDI.
- Section 25: 100BaseTX which is based on two STPs or UTPs of category 5.
- Section 26: 100BaseFX which is based on two multimode optical fibers.
- Section 27: 100 Mbps repeater, specifications and functions.
- Section 28: Auto-negotiation at 10 and 100 Mbps.
- Section 29: 100 Mbps networks and characteristics.
- Section 30: Management at 10 and 100 Mbps.

Supplement IEEE 802.3x   The draft for full-duplex operation seems very late compared with the numerous existing solutions. Still, its current specifications have already been used to define full-duplex integration in the AutoNegotiation processes (at 100 Mbps and 1 Gbps), but also the Flow Control capabilities brought by new PAUSE MAC frames. This technology is described more thoroughly in Chapter 11.1.

Supplement IEEE 802.3y   This draft describes 100BaseT2, which is a Fast Ethernet technology capable of operating on only 2 twisted pairs of any category (3, 4 or 5). In addition, 100BaseT2 also supports the full-duplex mode. It appears to be the best theoretical physical layer for Ethernet at 100 Mbps, but it will probably suffer from the fact that the market has already adopted 100BaseTX since 1993.

Supplement IEEE 802.3z   These very important specifications allow the Ethernet speed to be multiplied by ten once again. With 1 Gbps throughput, Ethernet seems likely to remain a very satisfactory LAN solution for many more years.

- Section 34: Introduction to 1000 Mbps baseband networks.

- Section 35: Reconciliation Sublayer (RS) and Gigabit Media Independent Interface (GMII).

- Section 36: Physical Coding Sublayer (PCS) and Physical Medium Attachment (PMA) sublayer, type 1000BaseX.

- Section 37: Auto-Negotiation for 1000BaseX.

- Section 38: Physical Medium Dependent (PMD) sublayer and baseband medium, type 1000BaseLX and 1000BaseSX.

- Section 39: Physical Medium Dependent (PMD) sublayer and baseband medium, type 1000BaseCX.

- Section 41: Repeater for 1000 Mbps baseband networks.

- Section 42: System considerations for multi-segment 1000 Mbps baseband networks.

Supplement IEEE 802.3ab   This supplement completes the Gigabps Ethernet solution with the support of UTP (4 pairs of category 5).

- Section 40: Physical coding sublayer (PCS), physical medium attachment (PMA) sublayer and baseband medium, type 1000BaseT.

Supplement IEEE 802.3ad   A new field of study consists of multi-link connections between station and switch, or between switches. The goal here is to establish multiple physical links that would appear to be a unique connection with the aggregated bandwidth of its constituents. Moreover, the global trunk will also benefit from automatic fall-back capacity in case of failure of one of the physical links.

Table 6.2   IEEE 802.3 list of supplements.

	Title	Section	Date	Description
a	10BASE2	10	1992	Thin coaxial cable with BNC
b	10BROAD36	11	1985	Frequency multiplexing
c	10 Mbps repeater	9.1–9.8	1985	
d	FOIRL	9.9	1987	Inter-repeater optical link
e	1BASE5	12	1987	UTP 3/4/5 at 1 Mbps (StarLAN)
h	Management layer	5	1990	
i	10BaseT	14	1990	UTP 3/4/5 at 10 Mbps
j	10BaseF	15–18	1993	10BaseFL, 10BaseFB, 10BaseFP
k	Repeater management	19	1992	
l	PICS MAU 10BaseT	14.10	1992	Transceiver qualification method
m			1995	
n			1995	
p	10 Mbps MAU management	20	1993	
q	GDMO	5	1993	
r	PICS MAU 10BASE5	8.8	1996	Transceiver qualification method
s			1995	
t	120 Ohm cable in 10BaseT		1995	in addition to 100 Ohm
u	100BaseT (FX/TX/T4)	21–30	1995	Fast Ethernet over MMF & UTP/STP
v	150 Ohm cable in 10BaseT		1995	STP addition
w	MAC improvement			BLAM
x	Full-duplex (& flow control)	31	1998	at 10/100/1000 Mbps + autonegotiation
y	100BaseT2	32	1998	Fast Ethernet over 2 UTP3/4/5 pairs
z	1000BaseT (SX/LX/CX)	34–42	1998	Gigabit Ethernet MMF, SMF & STP
aa	100BaseT maintenance			Revision & correction 100BaseT
ab	1000BaseT	40		Giga Ethernet over UTP
ac	Frame format for VLAN			Alignment with 802.1Q Tagging
ad	Trunking			Link aggregation

The IEEE 802.1D standard

The IEEE 802.1D standard is not solely concerned with Ethernet networks, otherwise it would have been handled by the IEEE 802.3 working group, but also deals with the interconnection of local area networks of the IEEE 802 type by MAC level bridges.

As for the other standards, the hardware was already in existence before this document; this hardware was generally proprietary, but functioned without problems in a heterogeneous environment. The effect of the standard was to fix certain values and formats which had been freely implemented up to then. From then on, bridges conforming to IEEE 802.1D would work in cooperation and the automatic management of the set of all bridges interlinking the networks would be more consistent.

The IEEE 802.1D standard, which was taken up by the ISO in IS 10038 in 1993, therefore incorporates the description of Source-Routing-type bridging, which is inherent to Token Ring and, to a lesser extent, to FDDI.

Remark   For a better understanding of IEEE 802.1D, readers should try to read this paragraph is parallel with that on MAC bridges in Chapter 13.

The standard defines the content of the packets circulating between the bridge chosen as the root bridge and the other bridges (the packets are configuration or topology change BridgePDUs), and includes specifications relating to the behavior of bridges respecting the Spanning Tree Protocol (STP). The STP is the protocol that manages the global topology resulting from the interconnection of the networks, including loop detection and the choice of the fastest paths. The IEEE standard includes the lifetime of the entries in the learning table (5 minutes), the group address of the bridges (01-80-C2-00-00-00), the STP LSAP (01000010: 42 in hexa-decimal), and the maximum diameter in terms of bridges (maximum number of bridges between two stations: 7). It also includes the maximum delay in crossing a bridge (one second, with subsequent deletion of the frame), the maximum delay in the transmission of a BPDU (one second after detection of the requirement) and an overestimate of the increment in the maximum age of the message. In particular, as far as the operation of the STP is concerned, the standard includes the hello time (2 seconds), the maximum age attainable by a BPDU from its emission (20 seconds), the time in retransmission mode (15 seconds), and the minimum time a BPDU is retained. The priority of the bridge should be set between 0 and 65535, with 32768 as the default value; that of a bridge should be between 0 and 255 (default 128) and the cost of a path to the root should lie between 1 and 65535. We note that most numerical values have recommended or default values, accompanied by an indication of the absolute maximum acceptable value, which is often very much greater. The procedures for this standard are written in C (ANSI X3.159).

Supplement IEEE 802.1p   The draft 802.1p focuses on two needs: dealing with traffic of multiple priorities in bridges, and Multicast filtering. The first issue is addressed by using 2 to 8 queues on the retransmission side of each port. The second issue opens the door to a more complex mechanism consisting of a multicast registration protocol used by end-stations or bridges, that allow the propagation of certain multicast frames on the necessary bridge's port. IEEE 802.1p supplement has already been integrated in the latest IEEE 802.1D draft. This technology will be described more completely in Chapter 13.3.

Supplement IEEE 802.1Q   As the capital letter indicates, 802.1Q is not really a supplement but more a standard by itself. Still, as it is very closely related to bridging we will treat it as an extension to IEEE 802.1D. Briefly stated (it will be explained more thoroughly in Chapter 13.3) 802.1Q deals with VLAN logical segmentation of a bridged (switching) network, and with the transport of priority per frame. The first topic leads to a relatively complex process that has been derived from the multicast registration protocol designed for IEEE 802.1p.

The 802.1 committee is also working on a draft concerning remote bridges, which should become the standard IEEE 802.1G. This includes the definition of

Table 6.3   Description of the LAN type by the
SNAP fields.

Type of network	OUI	PID
IEEE 802.3 (CSMA/CD)	00-80-C2	00-01
IEEE 802.4 (Token Bus)	00-80-C2	00-02
IEEE 802.5 (Token Ring)	00-80-C2	00-03
ANSI X3T9.5 (FDDI)	00-80-C2	00-04
IEEE 802.6 (DQDB)	00-80-C2	00-05
IEEE 802.9	00-80-C2	00-06

certain values of the Organizationally Unique Identifier (OUI) and Protocol Identification (PID) fields of the SNAP. Thus, the OUI and PID, in hexadecimal, corresponding to different types of network can be seen in Table 6.3.

6.3 The ISO 8802-3 standard

The standardization dates from February 1989, which is some time after the appearance of Ethernet V 2.0, and which shows that an effective standardization may be belated and thus late in reaching an already very advanced market place. A new edition of IS 8802-3 was published in 1993 which integrates the IEEE 802.3 Supplements a, b, c, d, e, h and i. The 1996 edition integrates the supplements j, k, l, m, n, p, q, s, t and v (the most important one being 10BaseF). The latest editions date from 1998. It integrates in addition the supplements r, u, x, y, z and aa. The whole document representing now more than 1200 pages. It only lacks the technologies still under development, as 1000BaseT (GigaEthernet over UTP) and link aggregation. So it still lacks Fast Ethernet (supplement u), full-duplex (x) and GigaEthernet (z).

Furthermore, the original ISO document did not incorporate all the existing supplements at that time, since only 10Base2 occupies the relevant section (number 10), while other chapters remain open for study, untouched or incomplete. This is the case for Section 5 (network management), Section 9 (repeater and FOIRL), Section 11 (specification of broadband media), Section 12 (specification of 1Base5 type), and many others subsequently.

Chapter 7

Access method

- The CSMA/CD principle

- Operation of the MAC

The access method is the main procedure for which the MAC layer is responsible. Ethernet is based on CSMA/CS, which is described in Pascal in the standard and, as we shall see, is relatively simple.

7.1 The CSMA/CD principle

The CSMA/CD method is a particular version of the Aloha type method, in which every emitter is free to manage its emissions as a function of its needs and the availability of the medium.

When there is no traffic to transmit, the station remains silent and listens in to (or receives) the packets circulating on the cable. On a cable, this information may circulate in either direction and a machine has no way of determining this direction; however, that is not important.

When the machine needs to talk (that is, to emit one or more packets), it will act independently of the others because it knows nothing about them, except that when it senses a frame then one of them must be emitting. Since each machine has the possibility of beginning a transmission autonomously at any time, the access method is distributed and is said to be a Multiple Access (MA) method. Thus, the machine observes the medium in an attempt to detect a carrier (carrier sense, CS). If no frames are in transit it does not find the carrier. It then deduces that the medium is free and that it can therefore start to talk without interrupting anything. Thus, it sends its packets on the physical carrier, but continues to listen for the result of its emission for some time, in order to check that no other machine has behaved in the same way as itself at the same time.

In fact, two different stations may start to talk simultaneously, after each has checked immediately beforehand that no-one is talking. In this case, the signals interfere and are lost to everyone. For an access method with collision detection, a machine is able to detect a contention problem at the time it emits and to stop with the intention of resending its packet later when it again has the right to talk. To minimize the risk of encountering a second collision with the same machine, each waits for a random delay period before attempting to emit again. This reduces the probability of successive collisions between a pair of stations. However, so as not to saturate a network which is already heavily loaded, the machine will not attempt indefinitely to retransmit a packet if, on every attempt, it finds itself in collision with another. After a certain number of fruitless attempts, the packet is deleted, which means that it does not cause the network to collapse (by not overloading it further); this action tells the higher layers that there is a problem, since the exchange was perturbed by the loss of a message.

Readers will have noticed that this method has a weakness when the traffic is too heavy. The number of collisions increases with the load, and the effective bandwidth is correspondingly reduced further. Eventually, if the number of packets to be transmitted is actually too large, a state of compete blockage of the network, with a drastic fall in performance, might be reached.

7.2 Operation of the MAC

The function of the MAC layer is to manage the CSMA/CD and to communicate with the layer above to proffer its services. Thus, the MAC must be able to format the data packets into frames, recognize its address in the destination field and check the validity of frames received.

MAC encapsulates the information from the level above in a frame, by placing the packet that it is asked to transmit in the frame's data field. It fills the other MAC fields (which we shall discuss in detail later) using information accompanying the data. Thus, it adds the physical address of the destination station to the layer 3 information. This header includes the source address relative to the physical address of its own interface, the type (with an identification of the layer for which it is working) or the length (counting the number of bytes which are entrusted to it). Finally, it calculates the elaborate parity control field for the Cyclic Redundancy Check (CRC) and ends the frame.

Figure 7.1, which is taken from the standard, shows the main stages in the emission of a frame (but not how it is constituted). For a more complete description of all the states, readers should refer to Section 9.3 which explains the collision phenomenon in detail. Note that because the response to a test shown in a rounded rectangle (for example, Deferring on?) is binary (yes or no), sometimes only one option is shown, since the other can be deduced logically.

On receipt a check is made to verify that the bit sequence can form a correct frame. Several criteria are used for this. The total number of bits should not be too

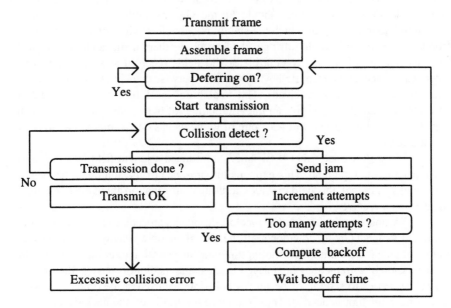

Figure 7.1   Block diagram of the emission of a frame.

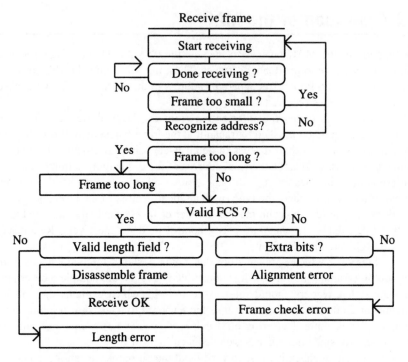

Figure 7.2 Block diagram of the receipt of a frame.

small, otherwise it would be impossible to reconstitute all the fields of a complete frame. The destination address should be the physical address of the station, or should relate to a group of which the station is a member. The frame should not be too long, otherwise it would infringe a basic rule of Ethernet and could not be valid. The calculation of the parity control for the fields received should give a result identical to the value transported by the frame, otherwise there is a bit error (wrongly transmitted or wrongly received). The total number of bits received should be divisible by eight, so as to give an integral number of bytes, otherwise the reconstituted frame is invalid, since at least one of its fields has one or more bits too many (or too few).

We shall see later that IEEE 802.3 introduced a length field into the frame by replacing the type field. This explains the presence of the additional test shown in Figure 7.2. In fact, this field provides additional information about the consistency of the frame received.

We note that the CSMA/CD method, despite its procedures for retrial on collision and its tendency to slow down all the emissions on a heavily loaded network, does not guarantee a minimum waiting time for the emission of a frame. In fact, the transmission of a frame may be delayed because the medium is busy at the time the MAC layer tries to send it, or because a collision occurred at the time of emission and a fresh attempt is needed. Thus, the more the traffic on the network increases, the more the average waiting time before the correct transmission of a frame increases (and this exponentially). The delay in emission may become unacceptable when the network is about to collapse. Other methods derived from CSMA, such as CSMA/DCR (deterministic collision resolution) can guarantee a limit on the delay prior to emission. In the case of CSMA/DCR, this is made possible by a deterministic, rather than probabilistic, conflict resolution procedure. The fact that the medium access time is not bounded for Ethernet may turn out to be very restrictive for real-time applications.

Chapter 8

Physical level

- Physical layer

- The main figures to remember

- Critical situations

8.1 Physical layer

The physical layer defines all the electrical and mechanical parameters relating to the communication medium. It also describes the elements responsible for the transmission, receipt, and regeneration of signals on the medium (transceivers and repeaters). For each type of element, a specification of its action, its effect, its encoding, and the procedures it uses is given.

For example, transceivers on coaxial cables should be able to read and write on a single pair of electrical conductors and detect the superposition of signals on the bus, while at the same time disturbing the impedance of the medium to which they are attached at little as possible. Other types of transceiver operating on point-to-point links are not subject to the same constraints, since the collision then corresponds to a situation of simultaneous emission and reception (easier to detect) and an imperfect adaptation does not necessarily harm the communication.

The code used by 10 Mbps baseband Ethernet is always of the Manchester type, whether on coaxial cable, twisted pair, fiber optic cable or the AUI cable. However, the electrical levels are different. In the first case, the continuous component is non-zero and the signal varies between 0 and −2 V, in the second case the signal is symmetric and varies between ±1 V.

As we have already seen, the Manchester code carries a polarity (the 1 and the 0 are distinguished by the direction of the edge), which implies that care must be taken not to invert the two conductors. This is easy when working on a coaxial cable (where the pair is naturally asymmetric), but is less straightforward for symmetric twisted pairs.

The characteristics of the electrical signals are defined later, together with the characteristics of transceivers, and the elements responsible for emission and receipt of the physical signals.

Generally, the power spectrum of 10 Mbps Ethernet signals has its main frequency peaks between 5 and 10 MHz (with harmonics on each side). The figures for the attenuation on the media are therefore given for the frequency range from 5 to 10 MHz.

On optical fiber, the signals are encoded using the Manchester code, but in the case of 10BaseFP (passive) and 10BaseFB (active synchronous), code violations are used to transmit certain fields. Thus, in passive technology, correct receipt of the start of a frame is unambiguously detected using a single clock time, without transition. In synchronous optical technology, waiting-state (idle, free) and remote-fault indications are communicated by periodic sequences of code violations over four or six clock periods.

Figure 8.1 shows the template of the optical signals. Note that the template for 10BaseFP signals is stricter, its margins being reduced by approximately one half.

A basic unit of time is often used in the Ethernet standards, namely the bit time, which represents the delay equivalent to the emission of a bit, or 0.1 μs = 100 ns (at 10 Mbps). Another time unit is the slot time, which is the minimum duration of a valid frame (512 bits). This is also used to measure other delays and timers (see the backoff algorithm in Section 9.3).

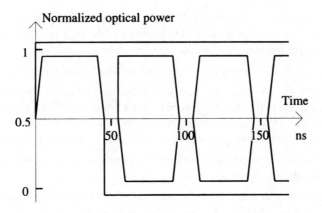

Figure 8.1   Template of optical signals for 10BaseFB and 10BaseFL.

8.2 The main figures to remember

Here is a recap of the main physical and numerical constraints associated with Ethernet together with a number of figures that can be deduced:

- A speed of 10 Mbps in serial mode (except for 1 Mbps in 1Base5 and 100 Mbps in 100BaseT).

- An emission time of 0.1 μs per bit (at 10 Mbps). On a standard coaxial cable, a bit occupies 23 meters and a short frame (counting all fields) would be 13.3 km long.

- A propagation speed ranging between 0.77 c (2.3×10^8 m/s) on standard coaxial cable and 0.59 c (1.77×10^8) on twisted pair.

- At most four repeaters (hence five segments) on the path between two stations.

- At most three non-IRL segments may be present on the path between two stations.

- On a path between two stations which includes four repeaters, each optical segment of the IRL type should be less than 500 meters long for FOIRL, 10BaseFB and 10BaseFL and less than 300 m long for 10BaseFP (when the segment corresponds to two links).

- On a path between two stations which includes three repeaters (hence four segments), no FOIRL segment should have a length greater than 1 km for 10BaseFL and 10BaseFB or 700 m for 10BaseFP. For terminal links (to DTE) these lengths are 400 m and 300 m, respectively. In the case of 10BaseFP, the segment again corresponds to two links, one on each side of the star.

- The AUI cables around a 10BaseFL or 10BaseFP segment should never exceed 25 m, so that the sum of the lengths of the AUI cables at the two ends of a single segment should never exceed 50 m.

- A length of 500 meters per segment of standard coaxial cable (yellow).

- A length of 185 meters per segment of thin coaxial cable. These two restrictions are due to the maximum permissible attenuation along a segment: 8.5 dB at 10 MHz and 6 dB at 5 MHz. Above these values, collision detection cannot be guaranteed as easily, since the signals may be too strongly attenuated.

- A distance of at least 2.5 m between each transceiver on the standard coaxial cable (yellow).

- A distance of at least 50 cm between each 'T' on the thin coaxial cable.

- At most 100 stations per segment of the standard coaxial cable (yellow).

- At most 30 stations per segment of the thin coaxial cable.

- At most 1024 stations per Ethernet network. This constraint does not derive from the previous two. In fact, a segment including 100 repeaters could feed 100 other segments, and hence $100 \times 99 = 9900$ stations. This limitation is intended to reduce the congestion probabilities on shared Ethernet networks.

- The frames have a length between 64 and 1518 bytes (60 and 1514 bytes excluding the CRC without VLAN tagging).

- A minimum interframe gap of 9.6 μs (at 10 Mbps).

- A maximum traffic of 14 880 short frames per second (at 10 Mbps).

- A maximum traffic of 812 long frames per second (at 10 Mbps). This is calculated as follows: $10^7/(64 + 8 \times N + 96)$ where N is the number of bytes in the frame, including CRC (thus N ranges from 64 to 1518).

- Up to 16 successive collisions for the transmission of a frame, with up to 10 increments of the delay interval.

- A crossing delay for a 10 Mbps transceiver of less than 3 bit times for emission and 6 bit times for receipt.

- A crossing delay for a 10 Mbps repeater of less than 7.5 bit times per frame.

Table 8.1 summarizes the various characteristics associated with each possible type of medium in Ethernet (we distinguish between two main categories: multi-access technologies and topologies with point-to-point links).

The number of connections on a 10BaseFP segment depends upon the number of ports the passive star has. The attenuation over a segment should not only be less than 26 dB (maximum) but also greater than 16 dB (minimum). Note that in 10BaseFP a segment includes two optical links and the star linking them, where the link with its connectors has an attenuation of less than 6 dB and the star has an attenuation of between 16 and 20 dB.

The length of a 10BaseT segment depends upon the cable capacity and may exceed 100 m.

Table 8.1   Summary of the restrictions according to medium type.

Type of medium	Number of connections	Segment length half/full-duplex	Propagation speed	Maximum attenuation per segment	Max delay per segment in half-duplex
10Base5	100	500 m	0.77 c	8.5 dB (10 MHz)	2 165 ns
10Base2	30	185 m	0.65 c	8.5 dB (10 MHz)	950 ns
10Broad36		3.6 km	0.87 c	36 at 52 dB	14 000 ns
10BaseFP	33	2 × 500 m	0.66 c	26 dB (850 nm)	5 000 ns
1Base5	2	250 m	0.59 c	6.5 dB (0.5–1 MHz)	4 000 ns
FOIRL	2	1 km	0.66 c	9 dB (850 nm)	5 000 ns
10BaseT	2	> 100 m	0.59 c	11.5 dB (5–10 MHz)	1 000 ns
10BaseFB	2	2 km	0.66 c	12.5 dB (850 nm)	10 000 ns
10BaseFL	2	2 km	0.66 c	12.5 dB (850 nm)	10 000 ns
100BaseT2	2	100 m	0.585 c	14.6 dB (2–16 MHz)	
100BaseT4	2	100 m	0.585 c	12.5 dB (2–12 MHz)	570 ns
100BaseTX	2	100 m	0.6 c	5.2/10 dB	556 ns
100BaseFX	2	0.412/2 km	0.66 c	11 dB (1300 nm)	2 040 ns
1000BaseT	2	100 m		24 dB (100 MHz)	
1000BaseSX	(62.5/125)	275 m	0.66 c	1.03 dB (850 nm)	
	(50/125)	316/550 m	0.66 c	1.92 dB (850 nm)	1 596 ns
1000BaseLX	(MMF)	316/550 m	0.66 c	0.825 dB (1300 nm)	1 596 ns
	(SMF)	0.32/5 km	0.66 c	2.5 dB (1300 nm)	1 596 ns
1000BaseCX	2	25 m		8.8 dB (625 MHz)	126.5 ns
AUI	DTE/MAU	50 m	0.65 c	3 dB (5–10 MHz)	257 ns
MII	DTE/PHY	0.5 m	0.65 c		2.5 ns
GMII					1 ns

Note that the physical size of an Ethernet element and the number of elements in it are limited, first, by the round-trip delay and, second, by the narrowing of the interframe gap. Any configuration should be validated against these two factors.

8.3 Critical situations

Ethernet technology has limits other than those described in the standard, in terms of traffic and efficiency. A network with several hundred truly active machines, each claiming of a fraction of several percent of the bandwidth, should be viewed as a large network. It will have load peaks, which will generally cause the communication performance to fall, and which are associated with high error and collision rates.

As the size of the network and the number of machines attached increase, a load which is sufficient to place the mode of operation beyond the preferred scope will be attained. It will then be necessary to consider inserting bridges in place of repeaters at the main interconnection nodes. A threshold of 40% is often cited as being the maximum load below which Ethernet operates well and above which problems become more frequent and bothersome. This is a global figure, which has no precise meaning if one does not know the configuration of the network in question. Another, more meaningful, indicator of how well the network is operating is the relative collision rate, in terms of occurrences per frame. This is normally less than 1/1000, but depends heavily upon the emission mode of the elements (regular, in slots, in bursts) and on their number and disposition (on the distance separating them). When the collision rate increases, the performance is degraded, retransmissions become more frequent and the timeouts of the higher protocols are put through their paces. Moreover, if a defective element (for example, one which fails to obey the Ethernet rules) disturbs the network, its action may translate into an increase in the collision probability and the faulty device may be detectable using an analyzer to monitor the collision counter.

It will have become evident that an assessment of the state of operation is no easy task and that the best indicator is necessarily relative to a previous state. Thus, regular, periodic observation accompanied by the generation of a number of statistical reports is recommended. The results may then be used as a reference to evaluate the health of the network in question at a given time.

In the great majority of cases, small Ethernet networks linked by bridges or switches may form a communication system which is sufficient for the whole enterprise. In fact, they form a chain, each link of which provides good working conditions (availability of almost the whole bandwidth). The requirements for exchange between these interconnected networks are theoretically less important than the local traffic in each network. This is a direct consequence of the division of the networks into coherent user groups. However, special situations may arise in which the Ethernet technology is under dimensioned. For example, a configuration consisting of a high-performance server feeding more than ten demanding client stations (for example, diskless) may generate peaks of almost 10 Mbps, placing the network in a stress zone in which all users suffer. Nevertheless, we stress that it is rare for the limitation to be due to the network rather than to the capabilities of the server.

Ignoring the problems inherent to Ethernet technology, such as collisions, short frames and misaligned frames, there exists a particularly awesome phenomenon known as a broadcast storm. This is triggered by the higher-level protocols (layer 3) and the associated routing functions, which, in certain partially inconsistent configurations (sometimes due to different implementations), propagate the same message from one machine to another by duplication. Each machine capable of understanding this message becomes involved in the movement and contributes to the useless loading of the network. These frames, whose destination address is a general broadcast address, cross the bridges (local and remote) and may rapidly saturate a whole network or all the networks.

These phenomena, which are difficult to control once they are triggered, can be combated, first, by limiting the number of machines with a dubious or illegal configuration (at the level of the higher protocols) and, second, by filtering broadcast frames when they cross bridges and, of course, when they cross routers. However, these incidents in which the network traffic becomes chaotic are very difficult to eliminate completely in large networks; at best they can be limited or confined.

Chapter 9

Packet formatting and errors

- The frame

- Defective frames

- Collision

- The idle signal

The data circulating on an Ethernet network is encapsulated in an entity called a frame. When various problems arise on the network (such as collisions), the resulting packet fragments may no longer possess the characteristics of a valid signal; these are errors.

9.1 The frame

The frame is the elementary structure used to circulate data on the network. It is defined at the MAC level and follows a number of rules. For example, the fields constituting it identify the emitting station, the destination station, and the type of data transported (indicated by the level 3 protocol) (Figure 9.1). It also has an elaborate parity control which is located in the last four bytes of the frame.

Finally, the minimum and maximum lengths are regulated, firstly by the need to always be able to detect collisions, and secondly, by the desire not to transfer power to a single machine for too long a period.

The transmission is in serial mode on the medium and the useful data, which is usually represented in the form of 8-bit bytes, has to be arranged in a bit sequence. The bytes are transmitted in order, that is, respecting the ordering used by the layer above. The bits of each byte are transmitted beginning with the least-significant bit (0 or 1) and ending with the most-significant bit (factor of $128 = 2^7$).

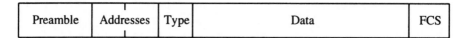

Preamble	Addresses	Type	Data	FCS

Figure 9.1   The different fields of the Ethernet frame.

The preamble

In reality, the preamble precedes the frame and allows the receiver's clock to synchronize itself with that of the emitter (do not forget that the transmission mode is asynchronous). It is sent to stabilize the decoding circuits and, therefore, it is envisaged that part of the preamble may be lost. Thus, it is considered normal for the first bits (up to 18 bits) not to reach the layer above (MAC layer).

The preamble may be considered to be at the physical level, while the other fields of the frame emanate from the MAC layer. The preamble consists of a sequence of successive 1s and 0s, and thus it does not contain any specific information. It can be decomposed into two subfields: a first of 56 bits in length, comprising alternating 1s and 0s, followed by a subfield called the Starting Frame Delimiter (SFD), which is eight bits long and continues the preceding sequence, except that the very last bit is set to 1. This double 1 tells the receiver that the actual frame is about to start and that the subsequent bits therefore comprise significant fields.

We note one further detail: if a collision is detected during the emission of the preamble, the emitting station should, nevertheless, continue to transmit the complete preamble.

In conclusion, a representation of the complete preamble, transmitted from left to right, is shown below:

10101010	10101010	10101010	10101010	10101010	10101010	10101010	10101011 SFD

MAC addresses

The frame includes two addresses: that of the addressee and the emitter. The destination address is transmitted first, followed by the source address (Figure 9.2). The Ethernet addresses are represented conventionally in hexadecimal, with a hyphen separating each of the six bytes.

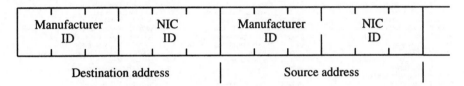

Figure 9.2 Position and partitioning of the two MAC addresses.

The reason for the existence of these addresses is, of course, to enable the machine targeted by the message to recognize itself as the addressee and to identify the machine which generated the frame circulating on the network. The two addresses have similar structures. They are six bytes long with, for IEEE 802.3, a possibility of using a two byte reduced format (which is very rare). The first three bytes identify the manufacturer of the connector card (and thus often of the machine) in a one-to-one fashion. The entries for these bytes are allocated to the manufacturers by a unique worldwide organization (in this case, the IEEE), which ensures the consistency of the system. The following three bytes give this manufacturer's number for the connector card ($256^3 = 16.78$ million possibilities). Thus, the whole forms a unique number for each interface card and, by the same token, for each machine with an Ethernet card.

In fact, what we have just seen is only really applicable when a frame has to be sent to a single machine, since Ethernet also allows one to reach several targets simultaneously, by what is known as diffusion. There is a choice of emitting to everyone (general diffusion or *broadcast*) or to a group of stations (*multicast*). The broadcast destination address is FF-FF-FF-FF-FF-FF in hexadecimal (which corresponds to a sequence of 1s in binary). The group address has the property that the first bit transmitted is set to 1 (or the first byte is odd), while the other bits of the first three bytes are able to retain the number of the manufacturer whose machines are targeted. Thus, a group may consist of machines from the same manufacturer.

We note that a source address corresponding to the exact address of the emitting connector card cannot logically have a group bit set to 1; thus, its first byte is necessarily even.

Table 9.1 contains a list of the first three bytes allocated to manufacturers.

Table 9.1   List of prefixes for different manufacturers.

Prefix	Manufacturer
00-00-0C	Cisco
00-00-0E	Fujitsu Ltd
00-00-0F	NeXT
00-00-10	Sytek
00-00-1B	Novell Inc
00-00-1D	Cabletron
00-00-20	DIAB (Data Industrier AB)
00-00-22	Visual Technology
00-00-23	ABB Automation AB, Dept.
00-00-2A	TRW
00-00-31	QPSX Communiocations PTY Ltd
00-00-32	GPT Ltd (ex GEC Computers Ltd)
00-00-37	Oxford Metrics Ltd
00-00-3C	Auspex Systems Inc
00-00-3F	Syntrex, Inc
00-00-46	Olivetti North America
00-00-49	Apricot Computers, Ltd
00-00-4C	NEC Corp
00-00-50	Radisys Corp
00-00-51	HOB Electronic Gmbh & Co
00-00-52	Optical Data Systems
00-00-58	Racore Computer Products Inc
00-00-5A	S & Koch
00-00-5E	USC Information Science Inst (IANA)
00-00-5F	Sumitomo Electric Ind., Ltd
00-00-61	Gateway Communications
00-00-64	Yokogawa Digital Computer Corp
00-00-65	Network General Corp
00-00-68	Rosemount Controls
00-00-6B	MIPS
00-00-6D	Cray Communications, Ltd
00-00-6E	Artisoft, Inc
00-00-6F	Madge Networks Ltd
00-00-74	Ricoh Company Ltd
00-00-77	MIPS
00-00-79	Networth Inc
00-00-7A	Ardent
00-00-7D	Cray Research Superservers, Inc
00-00-7F	Linotype-Hell AG
00-00-80	Cray Communications A/S
00-00-89	Cayman System Gatorbox
00-00-8A	Datahouse Information Systems
00-00-93	Proteon
00-00-94	Asante Technologies
00-00-98	Crosscomm Corp
00-00-99	Memorex Telex Corp
00-00-9F	Ameristar Technology
00-00-A2	Wellfleet
00-00-A3	Network Application Technology
00-00-A4	Acorn Computers Ltd
00-00-A5	Compatible Systems Corp.
00-00-A6	Network General (utilisation interne)
00-00-A7	NCD (Network Computing Devices)
00-00-A8	Stratus Computer Inc.
00-00-A9	Network Systems Corp.
00-00-AA	Xerox Corp.
00-00-AE	Dassault Automatismes et telecom.
00-00-B1	Alpha Microsystems Inc.
00-00-B3	CIMlinc
00-00-B6	Micro-Matic Research
00-00-B7	Dove Computer Corp Fastnet
00-00-BC	Allen-Bradley Co. Inc
00-00-C0	Western Digital
00-00-C1	Olicom A/S
00-00-C5	Farallon phone net card
00-00-C6	HP Intelligent Net. Oper. (ex Eon S.)
00-00-C8	Altos
00-00-C9	Emulex, Terminal Servers
00-00-CC	Dersan Co., Ltd
00-00-CD	Industrial Research Ltd
00-00-D0	Develcon Electronics Ltd
00-00-D2	SBE, Inc
00-00-D7	Dartmouth College (NED Router)
00-00-D8	3Com ? Novell ? PS/2 ?
00-00-DD	Gould
00-00-DE	Unigraph
00-00-E2	Acer Counterpoint
00-00-E3	Integrated Micro Products Ltd
00-00-E6	Aptor Produits De Comm Indust
00-00-E7	Star Gate Technologies
00-00-E8	Accton Technologies Corp.
00-00-E9	Isicad, Inc
00-00-ED	April
00-00-EF	Alantec
00-00-F2	Spider Communications
00-00-F4	Allied Telesis, Inc.
00-00-F8	Digital Equipment Corporation
00-00-FB	Rechner Zur Kommunikation
00-00-FD	High Level Hardware (Orion, UK)
00-01-02	BBN (internal usage, not registered)
00-02-67	Node Runner, Inc
00-07-01	Racal-Datacom
00-17-00	Kabel
00-20-00	Lexmark International, Inc.
00-20-02	Seritech Entreprise Co., Ltd.
00-20-03	Pixel Power Ltd
00-20-04	Yamatake-Honeywell Co., Ltd
00-20-05	Simple Technology
00-20-06	Garett Communications, Inc
00-20-07	SFA, Inc
00-20-08	Cable & Computer Technology
00-20-09	Packard Bell Elec., Inc
00-20-0A	Source-Comm Corp.
00-20-0B	Octagonsystems Corp.
00-20-0C	Adastra Systems Corp.
00-20-0D	Carl Zeiss
00-20-0E	Satellite Technology Mgmt, Inc
00-20-0F	Tanbac Co., Ltd
00-20-10	Jeol System Technology Co. Ltd
00-20-11	Canopus Co., Ltd
00-20-12	Camtronics Medical Systems
00-20-13	Diversified Technology, Inc
00-20-14	Global View Co., Ltd
00-20-15	Actis Computer SA
00-20-16	Showa Electric Wire & cable Co
00-20-17	Orbotech
00-20-18	CIS Technology Inc
00-20-19	Ohler Gmbh
00-20-1C	Excel, Inc
00-20-1E	Netquest Corporation
00-20-1F	Best Power Technology, Inc
00-20-20	N-Base Switch Communications
00-20-21	Algorithms Software Pvt. Ltd
00-20-22	Teknique, Inc
00-20-23	T.C. Technologies Pty. Ltd
00-20-24	Pacific Communication Sciences
00-20-25	Control Technology, Inc
00-20-26	Amkly Systems Inc
00-20-27	Ming Fortune Industry Co., Ltd
00-20-28	West Egg Systems, Inc
00-20-29	Teleprocessing Products, Inc
00-20-2B	Advanced Telecommunications
00-20-2C	Welltronix Co., Ltd
00-20-2D	Taiyo Corporation
00-20-2E	Daystar Digital
00-20-2F	Zeta Communications Ltd
00-20-30	Analog & Digital Systems
00-20-31	Ertec Gmbh
00-20-32	Alcatel Taisel
00-20-33	Synapse Technologies, Inc
00-20-34	Rotec IndustrieAutomation Gmbh
00-20-35	CPN Architectures/IBM Corp
00-20-36	BMC Software
00-20-37	Seagate Technology
00-20-38	VME Microsystems International
00-20-39	Scinets
00-20-3A	Digitall Biometrics Inc
00-20-3B	WISDM Ltd
00-20-3C	Eurotime AB
00-20-3D	Novar Electronics Corp
00-20-3E	Logican Technologies Inc
00-20-3F	Juki Corp
00-20-42	Datametrics Corp
00-20-43	Neuron Company Ltd
00-20-44	Genitech PTY Ltd
00-20-45	Solcom Systems, Ltd
00-20-46	Ciprico, Inc
00-20-48	Fore Systems, Inc
00-20-49	Comtron, Inc
00-20-4A	Pronet Gmbh
00-20-4B	Autocomputer Co., Ltd
00-20-4C	Mitron Computer PTE Ltd
00-20-4D	Inovis Gmbh
00-20-4E	Network Security Systems, Inc
00-20-4F	Deutsche Aerospace AG
00-20-50	Korea Computer Inc
00-20-51	Phoenix Data Communications
00-20-52	Ragula Systems
00-20-53	Huntsville Microsystems, Inc
00-20-54	Eastern Research, Inc
00-20-55	Altech Co. Ltd
00-20-56	Neoproduct
00-20-57	Titze Datentechnik Gmbh
00-20-58	Allied Signal Inc
00-20-59	Microcomputer Products AG
00-20-5A	Computer Identics
00-20-5B	Skyline Technology
00-20-5C	Internet Systems/Florida Inc
00-20-5D	Nanomatic OY
00-20-5E	Castle Rock Inc
00-20-5F	Gammadata Computer Gmbh
00-20-60	Alcatel Italia S.P.A.
00-20-61	Dynatech Communications, Inc
00-20-62	Scorpion Logic, Ltd
00-20-63	Wipro Infotech Ltd
00-20-64	Protec Microsystems, Inc
00-20-65	Supernet Networking Inc
00-20-66	General Magic, Inc
00-20-68	Isdyne
00-20-69	ISDN Systems Corp
00-20-6A	Osaka Computer Corp
00-20-6B	Minolta Co. Ltd
00-20-6C	Evergreen Technology Corp
00-20-6D	Data Race Inc
00-20-6E	Xact, Inc
00-20-6F	Flowpoint Corp
00-20-70	Hynet, Ltd
00-20-71	IBR Gmbh
00-20-72	Working Innovation
00-20-73	Fusion Systems Corp
00-20-74	Sungwoon Systems
00-20-75	Motorola Communication Israel
00-20-76	Reudo Corp
00-20-77	Kardios Systems Corp
00-20-78	Runtop, Inc
00-20-79	Mikron Gmbh
00-20-7A	Wise Communications, Inc
00-20-7B	Level One Communications
00-20-7C	Autec Gmbh
00-20-7D	Advanced Computer Applications
00-20-7E	Finecom Co. Ltd
00-20-7F	Kyoei Sangyo Co. Ltd
00-20-80	Synergy (UK) Ltd
00-20-81	Titan Electronics
00-20-82	Oneac Corp
00-20-83	Presticom Inc
00-20-84	OCE Graphics USA, Inc
00-20-85	Exide Electronics
00-20-86	Microtech Electronics Ltd
00-20-87	Memotec Communications Corp
00-20-88	Global Village Communication
00-20-89	T3Plus Networking, Inc
00-20-8A	Sonix Communications, Ltd
00-20-8B	Lapis Technologies, Inc
00-20-8C	Galaxy Netorks, Inc
00-20-8D	CMD Technology
00-20-8E	Chevin Software Eng. Ltd
00-20-8F	ECI Telecom Ltd
00-20-90	Advanced Compression
00-20-91	J125n National Security Agency
00-20-92	Chess Engineering B.V.
00-20-94	Cubix Corp
00-20-95	Riva Electronics
00-20-96	Siebe Environmental Controls
00-20-98	Hectronix AB
00-20-99	BON Electric Co. Ltd
00-20-9A	The 3DO Company
00-20-9B	Ersat Electronic Gmbh
00-20-9C	Primary Access Corp
00-20-9D	Lippert Automationstechnik
00-20-9E	Brown's Operating System
00-20-9F	Mercury Computer Systems, Inc
00-20-A0	OA Laboratory Co. Ltd
00-20-A1	Dovatron
00-20-A2	Galcom Networking Ltd
00-20-A3	Divicom Inc
00-20-A4	Multipoint Networks
00-20-A5	API Engineering
00-20-A6	Proxim, Inc
00-20-A7	Pairgain Technologies Inc
00-20-A9	White Horse Industrial
00-20-AA	NTL
00-20-AB	Micro Industries Corp
00-20-AC	Interflex Datensysteme Gmbh
00-20-AD	Linq Systems
00-20-AE	Ornet Data Communication tech.
00-20-AF	3Com Corp
00-20-B0	Gateway Devices Inc

Table 9.1 (cont'd)

00-20-B1	Comtech Research Inc	00-40-26	Melco, Inc	00-40-F0	Micro Systems, Inc
00-20-B2	GKD Gesellschaft Fur Kommunikat.	00-40-27	SMC Massachusetts, Inc	00-40-F1	Chuo Electronics Co. Ltd
00-20-B3	SCLTEC Communications Systems	00-40-2A	Canoga-Perkins	00-40-F4	Cameo Communications Inc
00-20-B4	Terma Elektronik AS	00-40-2F	XLNT Designs Inc	00-40-F5	OEM Engines
00-20-B5	Yaskawa Electric Corp	00-40-30	GK Computer	00-40-F6	Katron Computers Inc
00-20-B6	Agile Networks Inc	00-40-32	Digital Communications	00-40-F9	Combinet
00-20-B7	Namaqua Computerware	00-40-33	Addtron Technology Co. Ltd	00-40-FA	Microboards, Inc
00-20-B8	Prime Option, Inc	00-40-39	Optec Daiichi Denko Co. Ltd	00-40-FD	LXE
00-20-B9	Metricom, Inc	00-40-3C	Forks, Inc	00-40-FF	Telebit Corp
00-20-BA	Center for High Perf Computing WPI	00-40-3F	Ssangyong Computer Systems	00-60-F3	NetCom Systems
00-20-BB	ZAX Corp	00-40-41	Fujikura Ltd	00-60-8C	3Com Corp
00-20-BC	JTEC PTY Ltd	00-40-43	Nokia Data Communications	00-80-00	Multitech Systems Inc
00-20-BD	Niobrara R & D Corp	00-40-48	SMD Informatica S.A.	00-80-04	Antlow Computers Ltd
00-20-BE	LAN Access Corp	00-40-4C	Hypertec Pty Ltd	00-80-05	Cacctus Computer Inc
00-20-BF	AEHR Test Systems	00-40-4D	Telecommunications Techniques	00-80-06	Compuadd Corporation Engineering
00-20-C0	Pulse Electronics	00-40-4F	Space & Naval Warfare Systems	00-80-07	Dlog NC-Ssysteme
00-20-C1	Taiko Electric Works, Ltd	00-40-50	Ironics, Inc	00-80-09	Jupiter Systems
00-20-C2	Texas Memory Systems, Inc	00-40-52	Star Technologies Inc	00-80-0D	Vosswwinkel F.U.
00-20-C3	Counter Solutions Ltd	00-40-54	Thinking Machines Corporation	00-80-15	Seiko Systems Inc
00-20-C5	Eagle Technology	00-40-57	Lockeed – Sanders	00-80-16	Wandel and Goltermann
00-20-C6	Nectec	00-40-59	Yoshida Kogvo K. K.	00-80-18	Kobe Steel Ltd
00-20-C7	Akai Electric Co. Ltd	00-40-5B	Funasset Ltd	00-80-19	Davna Communications Inc
00-20-C8	Larscom Inc	00-40-5D	Star-Tek Inc	00-80-1A	Bell Atlantic
00-20-C9	Victron By	00-40-66	Hitachi Cable Ltd	00-80-21	Newbridge Research Corp
00-20-CA	Digital Ocean	00-40-67	Omnibyte Corp	00-80-23	Integrated Business Networks
00-20-CB	Pretec Electronics Corp	00-40-68	Extended Systems	00-80-24	Kalpana Inc
00-20-CC	Digital Services, Ltd	00-40-69	Lemcom Systems Inc	00-80-26	Network Products Corp
00-20-CD	Hybrid Networks, Inc	00-40-6A	Kentek Information Systems, Inc	00-80-2A	Test Systems & Simulation Inc
00-20-CE	Logical Design Group, Inc	00-40-6E	Corollary, Inc	00-80-2B	Imac
00-20-CF	Test & Measurement Systems Inc	00-40-6F	Sync Research Inc	00-80-2C	The Sage Group PLC
00-20-D0	Versalynx Corporation	00-40-74	Cable and Wireless	00-80-2D	Xylogics INC Annex terminal servers
00-20-D1	Microcomputer Systems (M) Sdn	00-40-76	AMP Inc	00-80-37	Telefon AB LM Ericsson Corp
00-20-D2	RAD Data Communications, Ltd	00-40-78	Wearnes Automation PTE Ltd	00-80-38	Data Research & Applications
00-20-D3	OST (Ouest Standard Telematique)	00-40-7F	Agema Infrared Systems AB	00-80-3B	APT Commmunications Inc
00-20-D4	Zeitnet Inc	00-40-82	Laboratory Equipment Corp	00-80-3D	Surigiken Co. Ltd
00-20-D5	Vipa Gmbh	00-40-85	Saab Instruments AB	00-80-3E	Synernetics
00-20-D6	Lannair, Ltd	00-40-86	Michels & Kleberoff Computer	00-80-42	Force Computers
00-20-D7	Japan Minicomputer Systems Co.	00-40-87	Ubitrex Corp	00-80-43	Networld Inc
00-20-D9	Panasonic Technologies, Inc	00-40-8A	TPS Teleprocessing Sys. Gmbh	00-80-44	Systech Computer Corp
00-20-DA	Xylan Corp	00-40-8C	Axis Communications AB	00-80-45	Matsushita Electric Ind. Co.
00-20-DB	XNET Technology, Inc	00-40-8E	CXR/DIgilog	00-80-46	University of Toronto
00-20-DC	Densitron Taiwan Ltd	00-40-8F	WM-Data Minfo AB	00-80-49	Nissin Electric Co. Ltd
00-20-DD	Awa Ltd	00-40-91	Procom Industria Eletronica	00-80-4C	Contec Co. Ltd
00-20-DE	Japan Digital Laboratory Co. Ltd	00-40-92	ASP Computer Products Inc	00-80-4D	Cyclone Microsystems Inc
00-20-DF	Kyosan Electric MFG. Co. Ltd	00-40-94	Shographics Inc	00-80-51	Fibermux
00-20-E0	Premax Electronics, Inc	00-40-95	R.P.T. Intergroups Int'l Ltd	00-80-57	Adsoft Ltd
00-20-E1	Alamar Electronics	00-40-96	Telesystems SLW Inc	00-80-5A	Tulip Computers Internat'l B.V.
00-20-E2	Information Resource	00-40-98	Dressler Gmbh & Co	00-80-5B	Condor Systems Inc
00-20-E3	MCD Kencom Corp	00-40-9A	Network Express Inc	00-80-62	Interface Co.
00-20-E6	Lidkoping Machine Tools AB	00-40-9C	Transware	00-80-63	Richard Hirschmann Gmbh & Co.
00-20-E7	B&W Nuclear Service Company	00-40-9D	Digiboard Inc	00-80-64	Wyse Technology / Link Technolog.
00-20-E8	Datatrek Corp	00-40-9E	Concurrent Technologies Ltd	00-80-67	quare D Company
00-20-E9	Dantel	00-40-9F	Lancast/Casat Technology, Inc	00-80-69	Computone Systems
00-20-EA	Efficient Networks, Inc	00-40-A4	Rose Electronics	00-80-6A	ERI (Empac Research Inc)
00-20-EB	Cincinati Microwave, Inc	00-40-A6	Cray Research Inc	00-80-6B	Schmid Telecommunication
00-20-EC	Techware Systems Corp	00-40-AA	Valmet Automation Inc	00-80-6C	Cegelec Projetcs Ltd
00-20-ED	Giga-Byte Technology Co., Ltd	00-40-AD	SMA Regelsysteme Gmbh	00-80-6D	Century Systems Corp
00-20-EE	Gtech Corp	00-40-AE	Delta Controls, Inc	00-80-6E	Nippon Steel Corp
00-20-EF	U S C Corp	00-40-B4	3Com K.K.	00-80-6F	Onelan Ltd
00-20-F1	Altos India Ltd	00-40-B5	Video Technology Computers Ltd	00-80-71	SAI Technology
00-20-F2	Maximum Strategy Inc	00-40-B6	Computerm Corp	00-80-72	Microplex Systems Ltd
00-20-F3	Raynet Corp	00-40-B9	Macq Electronique SA	00-80-74	Fisher Controls
00-20-F4	Spectrix Corp	00-40-BD	Starlight Networks, Inc	00-80-79	Microbus Designs Ltd
00-20-F5	Pan Dacom Telecom'cations Gmbh	00-40-C0	Vista Controls Corp	00-80-7B	Artel Communications Corp
00-20-F6	Nettek and Karlnet, Inc	00-40-C1	Bizerba-Werke Wilheim Kraut	00-80-7E	Southern Pacific Ltd
00-20-F7	Cyberdata	00-40-C2	Applied Computing Devices	00-80-82	PEP Modular Computers Gmbh
00-20-F8	Carrera Computers, Inc	00-40-C3	Fischer and Porter Co.	00-80-86	Computer Generation Inc
00-20-F9	Paralink Networks, Inc	00-40-C6	Fibernet Research Inc	00-80-88	Victor Company of Japan Ltd
00-20-FA	GDE Systems, Inc	00-40-C8	Milan Technology Corp	00-80-89	Tecnetics (PTY) Ltd
00-20-FB	Octel Communications Corp	00-40-CC	Silcom Manuf'g Technology Inc	00-80-8A	Summit Microsystems Corp
00-20-FC	Matrox	00-40-CF	Strawberry Tree Inc	00-80-8B	Dacoll Ltd
00-20-FD	ITV Technologies, Inc	00-40-D2	Pagine Corp	00-80-8C	Frontier Software Development
00-20-FE	Topware Inc / Grand Computer	00-40-D4	Gage Talker Corp	00-80-8D	Westcoast Technology B.V.
00-20-FF	Symmetrical technologies	00-40-D7	Studio Gen Inc	00-80-8E	Radstone Technology
00-40-01	Zero One Technology Co. Ltd	00-40-D8	Ocean Office Automation Ltd	00-80-90	Microtek International Inc
00-40-09	Tachibana tectron Co. Ltd	00-40-DC	Tritec Electronic Gmbh	00-80-92	Japan Computer Industry, Inc
00-40-0C	General Micro Systems, Inc	00-40-DF	Digalog Systems, Inc	00-80-93	Xyron Corp
00-40-0D	Lannet Data Communications, Ltd	00-40-E1	Marner International, Inc	00-80-94	Sattcontrol AB
00-40-10	Sonic Systems	00-40-E2	Mesa Ridge Technologies, Inc	00-80-96	Human Designed Systems, Inc
00-40-13	NTT Data Comm. Systems Corp	00-40-E3	Quin Systems Ltd	00-80-98	TDK Corp
00-40-14	Comsoft Gmbh	00-40-E4	E-M Technology Inc	00-80-9A	Novus Networks Ltd
00-40-15	Ascom Infrasys AG	00-40-E5	Sybus Corp	00-80-9B	Justsystem Corp
00-40-1F	Colorgraph	00-40-E7	Arnos Instruments & Comp. Syst Co.	00-80-9D	Datacraft Manufactur'G PTY Ltd
00-40-20	Pinacl Communication	00-40-E9	Accord Systems Inc	00-80-9F	Alcatel Business Systems
00-40-23	Logic Corp	00-40-EA	Plain Tree Systems Inc	00-80-A1	Microtest, Inc
00-40-25	Molecular Dynamics	00-40-ED	Network Controls Int'natl Inc	00-80-A3	Lantronix

Table 9.1 (cont'd)

00-80-A6	Republic Technology Inc	00-A0-55	Linktech, Inc	00-A0-E0	Tennyson Technologies PTY Ltd
00-80-A7	Measurex Corp	00-A0-5B	Marquip, Inc	00-A0-E3	XKL Systems Corp
00-80-AC	Imlogix Division of Genesys	00-A0-5C	Inventory Conversion, Inc	00-A0-E4	Optiquest
00-80-AD	Cughes Technololgy Inc	00-A0-62	AES Prodata	00-A0-E5	NHC Communications
00-80-AE	Hughes Network Systems	00-A0-64	KVB/Analect	00-A0-E6	Dialogic Corp
00-80-AF	Allumer Co. Ltd	00-A0-65	Nexland, Inc	00-A0-E7	Central Data Corp
00-80-B1	Softcom A/S	00-A0-66	Isa Co. Ltd	00-A0-E8	Reuters Holding PLC
00-80-B8	Bug, Inc	00-A0-67	Network Services Group	00-A0-E9	Electronic Retailing Systems
00-80-BA	Specialix (Asia) PTE Ltd	00-A0-6A	Verilink Corp	00-A0-EB	Fastcom Communications Corp
00-80-BB	Hughes LAN Systems	00-A0-6B	DMS Dorsch Mikrosystem Gmbh	00-A0-EC	Transmitton Ltd
00-80-C2	IEEE 802 Committee (802.1)	00-A0-6E	Austron, Inc	00-A0-EE	Nashoba Networks
00-80-C9	Alberta Microelectronic Centre	00-A0-6F	The Appcon Group, Inc	00-A0-F1	MTI
00-80-CD	Micronics Computer, Inc	00-A0-70	Coastcom	00-A0-F3	Staubli
00-80-CE	Broadcast Television Systems	00-A0-72	Ovation Systems Ltd	00-A0-F4	GE Medical Systems
00-80-D3	Shiva	00-A0-73	Com21, Inc	00-A0-F5	Radguard Ltd
00-80-D7	Fantum Engineering Inc	00-A0-74	Perception Technology	00-A0-F8	Symbol Technologies, Inc
00-80-DA	Bruel & Kjaer	00-A0-75	Zeos International, Ltd	00-A0-F9	Bintec Computor Systeme Gmbh
00-80-DD	GMX Inc/GIMIX	00-A0-76	Cardware Lab, Inc	00-A0-FA	Ant Nachrichtentechnik Gmbh
00-80-E0	XTP Systems Inc	00-A0-79	Alps Electric (USA) Inc	00-A0-FB	Toray Engineering Co. Ltd
00-80-E7	Lynwood Scientific Dev Ltd	00-A0-7B	Dawn Computer Inc	00-A0-FD	Scitex Digital Printing, Inc
00-80-EA	The Fiber Company	00-A0-7C	Tonyang Nylon Co. Ltd	00-A0-FE	Boston Technology, Inc
00-80-F0	Kyushu Matsushita Electric Co	00-A0-7D	Seeq Technology, Inc	00-A0-FF	Tellabs Operations, Inc
00-80-F3	Sun Electronics Corp	00-A0-7E	Avid Technology, Inc	00-AA-00	Intel
00-80-F4	Telemecanique Electrique	00-A0-7F	GSM-Syntel, Ltd	00-C0-00	Lanoptics Ltd
00-80-F5	Quantel Ltd	00-A0-80	Antares Microsystems	00-C0-01	Diatek Patient Managment Systems
00-80-F9	Heurikon Corp	00-A0-81	Alcatel Data Networks	00-C0-02	Sercomm Corporation
00-80-FB	BVM Ltd	00-A0-82	NKT Elektronik A/S	00-C0-03	Globalnet Communications
00-80-FE	Azure Technologies Inc	00-A0-84	Dataplex PTY. LTD	00-C0-04	Japan Business Computer Co. Ltd
00-A0-00	Centillion	00-A0-87	GEC Plessey Semiconductors	00-C0-05	Livingston Enterprises Inc
00-A0-01	Watkins-Johnson Company	00-A0-88	Essential Communications	00-C0-06	Nippon Avionics Co. Ltd
00-A0-02	Leeds & Northrup Australia	00-A0-89	Xpoint Technologies, Inc	00-C0-07	Pinnacle Data Systems, Inc
00-A0-03	Staefa Control System	00-A0-8A	Brooktrout Technology, Inc	00-C0-08	Seco SRL
00-A0-04	Netpower, Inc	00-A0-8C	Multimedia LANs, Inc	00-C0-09	KT Technology (S) PTE Ltd
00-A0-07	Apexx Technology, Inc	00-A0-8D	Jacomo Corp	00-C0-0A	Micro Craft
00-A0-08	Netcorp	00-A0-8E	Ipsilon Networks, Inc	00-C0-0B	Norcontrol A.S.
00-A0-09	Whitetree Network	00-A0-91	Applicom International	00-C0-0D	Advanced Logic Research, Inc
00-A0-0A	R.D.C. Communication	00-A0-92	H. Bollmann Manufacturers, Ltd	00-C0-0E	Psitech Inc
00-A0-0C	Kingmax Technology, Inc	00-A0-97	JC Information Systems	00-C0-0F	Quantum Software Systems Ltd
00-A0-0D	The Panda Project	00-A0-98	Network Appliance Corp	00-C0-11	Interactive Computing Devices
00-A0-0E	Visual Networks, Inc	00-A0-99	K-Net Ltd	00-C0-12	Netspan Corp
00-A0-0F	Broadband Technologies	00-A0-9B	QPSX Communications, Ltd	00-C0-13	Netrix
00-A0-11	Mtoh Industries Ltd	00-A0-9D	Johnathon Freeman Technologies	00-C0-14	Telematics Calabasas Int'l Inc
00-A0-14	CSIR	00-A0-9E	ICTV	00-C0-15	New Media Corp
00-A0-15	Wyle	00-A0-9F	Commvision Corp	00-C0-16	Electronic Theatre Controls
00-A0-17	J B M Corp	00-A0-A0	Compact Data, Ltd	00-C0-18	Lanart Corp
00-A0-18	Creative Controllers, Inc	00-A0-A1	Epic Data Inc	00-C0-19	Leap Technology Inc
00-A0-1A	Binar Elektronik AB	00-A0-A2	Digicom S.P.A.	00-C0-1A	Corometrics Medical Systems
00-A0-1B	Premisys Communications, Inc	00-A0-A3	Reliable Power Meters	00-C0-1B	Socket Communications Inc
00-A0-1E	Est Corp	00-A0-A4	Micros Systems, Inc	00-C0-1C	Interlink Communications Ltd
00-A0-1F	Tricord Systems, Inc	00-A0-A5	Teknor Microsysteme, Inc	00-C0-1D	Grand Junction Networks, Inc
00-A0-21	GTE Government Systems Corp	00-A0-A7	Vorax Corp	00-C0-1F	S.E.R.C.E.L.
00-A0-22	Centre for Development of Adv. Comp.	00-A0-A8	Renex Corp	00-C0-20	Arco Electronic, Control Ltd
00-A0-23	Applied Creative Technology, Inc	00-A0-AA	Spacelabs Medical	00-C0-21	Netexpress
00-A0-24	3Com Corp	00-A0-AB	Netcs Informationstechnik Gmbh	00-C0-23	Tutankhamon Electronics
00-A0-25	Redcom Labs Inc	00-A0-AE	Nucom Systems, Inc	00-C0-24	Eden Sistemas de Computacao SA
00-A0-26	Teldat, S.A.	00-A0-B1	First Virtual Corp	00-C0-25	Dataproducts Corp
00-A0-27	Firepower Systems, Inc	00-A0-B2	Shima Seiki	00-C0-27	Cipher Systems Inc
00-A0-28	Conner Peripherals	00-A0-B3	Zykronix	00-C0-28	Jasco Corp
00-A0-29	Coulter Corp	00-A0-B4	Texas Microsystems, Inc	00-C0-29	Kabel Rheydt AG
00-A0-2B	Transition Research Corp	00-A0-B5	3H Technology	00-C0-2A	Ohkura Electric Co., Ltd
00-A0-2D	1394 Trade Association % Skipstone	00-A0-B6	Sanritz Automation Co. Ltd	00-C0-2B	Gerloff Gesellschaft fur Elek System.
00-A0-30	Captor NV/SA	00-A0-BA	Patton Electronics Co.	00-C0-2C	Centrum Communications, Inc
00-A0-32	GES Singapore PTE. Ltd	00-A0-BC	Viasat, Inc	00-C0-2D	Fuji Photo Film Co. Ltd
00-A0-34	Axel	00-A0-BE	Integrated Circuit Systems, Inc	00-C0-2E	Netwiz
00-A0-35	Cylink Corp	00-A0-C0	Digital Link Corp	00-C0-2F	Okuma Corp
00-A0-36	Applied Network Technology	00-A0-C1	Ortivus Medical AB	00-C0-30	Integrated Engineering B. V.
00-A0-37	Datascope Corp	00-A0-C2	R.A. Systems Co. Ltd	00-C0-31	Design ESIGN Research Systems
00-A0-3A	Kubotek Corp	00-A0-C3	Unicomputer Gmbh	00-C0-32	I-Cubed Ltd
00-A0-3B	Toshin Electric Co. Ltd	00-A0-C6	Qualcomm Inc	00-C0-33	Telebit Communication APS
00-A0-3D	Opto – 22	00-A0-C7	Tadiran Telecommunications	00-C0-34	Dale Computer Corp
00-A0-3E	ATM Forum	00-A0-C8	Adtran Inc	00-C0-35	Quintar Company
00-A0-3F	Computer Society Micropr. & Stds Com	00-A0-CA	Fujitsu Denso Ltd	00-C0-36	Raytech Electronic Corp
00-A0-40	Apple Computer	00-A0-CB	Ark Telecommunications, Inc	00-C0-39	Silicon Systems
00-A0-41	Leybold-Inficon	00-A0-CF	SWL, Inc	00-C0-3B	Multiaccess Computing Corp
00-A0-42	Spur Products Corp	00-A0-D0	Ten X Technology, Inc	00-C0-3C	Tower Tech S.R.L.
00-A0-43	American Technology Labs, Inc	00-A0-D1	Inventec Corp	00-C0-3D	Wiesemann & Theis Gmbh
00-A0-45	Phoenix Contact Gmbh & Co.	00-A0-D2	Allied Telesis, Inc	00-C0-3E	FA. Gebr. Heller Gmbh
00-A0-46	Scitex Corp. Ltd	00-A0-D3	Instem Computer Systems, Ltd	00-C0-3F	Stores Automated Systems,
00-A0-47	Integrated Fitness Corp	00-A0-D4	Radiolan, Inc	00-C0-40	ECCI
00-A0-49	Digitech Industries, Inc	00-A0-D5	Sierra Wireless Inc	00-C0-41	Digital Transmission Systelms
00-A0-4A	Nisshin Electric Co. Ltd	00-A0-D7	Kasten Chase Applied Research	00-C0-42	Datalux Corp
00-A0-4B	TFL LAN Inc	00-A0-D8	Spectra – Tek	00-C0-43	Stratacom
00-A0-4C	Innovative Systems & Tech. Inc	00-A0-D9	Convex Computer Corp	00-C0-44	Emcom Corp
00-A0-4D	EDA Instruments, Inc	00-A0-DB	Fisher & Paykel Production	00-C0-45	Isolation Systems Ltd
00-A0-4F	Ameritec Corp	00-A0-DD	Azonix Corp	00-C0-46	Kemitron Ltd
00-A0-50	Cypress Semiconductor	00-A0-DE	Yamaha Corp	00-C0-47	Unimicro Systems Inc

Table 9.1 (cont'd)

00-C0-48	Bay Technical Associates	00-C0-A8	GVC Corp	00-C0-FD	Prosum
00-C0-4B	Creative Microsystems	00-C0-A9	Barron Mccann Ltd	00-C0-FF	Box Hill Systems Corp
00-C0-4D	Mitec Inc	00-C0-AA	Silicon Valley Computer	00-DD-00	Ungermann-Bass
00-C0-4E	Comtrol Corp	00-C0-AB	Jupiter Technology Inc	00-DD-01	Ungermann-Bass
00-C0-50	Toyo Denki Seizo K.K.	00-C0-AC	Gambit Computer Communications	02-04-06	BBN (internal usage, not registered)
00-C0-51	Advanced Integration Research	00-C0-AD	Marben Communication Systems	02-07-01	Racal-Datacom (InterLan)
00-C0-55	Modular Computing Technologies	00-C0-AE	Towercom Co. Inc DBA PC House	02-60-86	Satelcom MegaPac (UK)
00-C0-56	Somelec	00-C0-AF	Teklogix Inc	02-60-8C	3Com
00-C0-57	Mvco Electronics	00-C0-B0	GCC Technologies Inc	02-CF-1F	CMC
00-C0-58	Dataexpert Corp	00-C0-B2	Norand Corp	08-00-02	3Com (formerly Bridge)
00-C0-59	Nippondenso Co. Ltd	00-C0-B3	Comstat Datacomm Corp	08-00-03	ACC (Advanced Computer Comm)
00-C0-5B	Networks Northwest Inc	00-C0-B4	Myson Technology Inc	08-00-05	Symbolics LISP machines
00-C0-5C	Elonex PLC	00-C0-B5	Corporate Network Systems Inc	08-00-07	Apple Computer Inc
00-C0-5D	L&N Technologies	00-C0-B6	Meridian Data Inc	08-00-08	BBN
00-C0-5E	Vari-Lite Inc	00-C0-B7	American Power Conversion Corp	08-00-09	Hewlett-Packard
00-C0-60	ID Scandinavia AS	00-C0-B8	Fraser Hill Ltd	08-00-0A	Nestar Systems
00-C0-61	Solectek Corp	00-C0-B9	Funk Software Inc	08-00-0B	Unisys Corp
00-C0-63	Morning Star Technologies, Inc	00-C0-BA	Netvantage	08-00-0D	International Computers LTD.
00-C0-64	General Datacomm Ind. Inc	00-C0-BB	Forval Creative Inc	08-00-11	Tektronix Inc.
00-C0-65	Scope Communications Inc	00-C0-BD	Inex Technologies Inc	08-00-14	Excelan
00-C0-66	Docupoint Inc	00-C0-BE	Alcatel – SEL	08-00-17	NSC
00-C0-67	United Barcode Industries	00-C0-BF	Technology Concepts Ltd	08-00-1A	Data General
00-C0-68	Philip Drake Electonics Ltd	00-C0-C0	Shore Microsystems Inc	08-00-1B	Data General
00-C0-69	California Microwave Inc	00-C0-C1	Quad/Graphics Inc	08-00-1E	Apollo
00-C0-6A	Zahner-Elektrik Gmbh & Co. KG	00-C0-C2	Infinite Networks Ltd	08-00-1F	Sharp Corp
00-C0-6B	OSI Plus Corp	00-C0-C3	Acuson Computed Sonography	08-00-20	Sun
00-C0-6C	Syec Computer Corp	00-C0-C4	Computer Operat. Requir Analysts	08-00-22	NBI
00-C0-6D	Boca Rsearch Inc	00-C0-C5	SID Informatica	08-00-25	CDC
00-C0-6F	Komatsu Ltd	00-C0-C6	Personal Media Corp	08-00-26	Norsk Data (Nord)
00-C0-70	Sectra Secure-Transmission AB	00-C0-C8	Micro Byte PTY Ltd	08-00-27	PCS Computer Systems GmbH
00-C0-71	Areanex Communications, Inc	00-C0-C9	Bailey Controls Co.	08-00-28	Texas Instruments
00-C0-72	KNX td	00-C0-CA	Alfa, Inc	08-00-2B	DEC (Digital Equipment Corporation)
00-C0-73	Xedia Corp	00-C0-CB	Control Tevhnology Corporation	08-00-2E	Metaphor
00-C0-74	Toyoda Automatic Loom Works, Ltd	00-C0-CD	Comelta, S.A.	08-00-2F	Prime Computer
00-C0-75	Xante Corp	00-C0-D0	Ratoc System Inc	08-00-30	CERN
00-C0-76	I-Data Internation A-S	00-C0-D1	Comtree Technology Corporation	08-00-36	Intergraph
00-C0-77	Daewoo Telecom Ltd	00-C0-D2	Syntellect Inc	08-00-37	Fujitsu-Xerox
00-C0-78	Computer Sytems Engineering	00-C0-D4	Axon Networks Inc	08-00-38	Bull
00-C0-79	Fonsys Co. Ltd	00-C0-D5	Quancom Electronic Gmbh	08-00-39	Spider Systems Ltd
00-C0-7A	Priva B.Y.	00-C0-D6	J1 Systems, Inc	08-00-41	DCA (Digital Comm. Assoc.)
00-C0-7D	Risc Developments Ltd	00-C0-D9	Quinte Network Confidentiality Equip	08-00-45	Xylogic ?
00-C0-7F	Nupon Computing Corp	00-C0-DB	IPC Corp (PTE) Ltd	08-00-46	Sony
00-C0-80	Netstart Inc	00-C0-DC	EOS Technologies Inc	08-00-47	Sequent
00-C0-81	Metrodata Ltd	00-C0-DE	Zcomm, Inc	08-00-48	Eurotherm Gauging Systems
00-C0-82	Moore Products Co.	00-C0-DF	KYE Systems Corp	08-00-49	Univation
00-C0-84	Data Link Corp. Ltd	00-C0-E1	Sonic Solutions	08-00-4C	Encore
00-C0-86	The Lynk Corp	00-C0-E2	Calcomp Inc	08-00-4E	BICC
00-C0-87	Uunet Technologies, Inc	00-C0-E3	Ositech Communications Inc	08-00-51	Experdata
00-C0-89	Telindus Distribution	00-C0-E4	Landis & Gyr Powers Inc	08-00-56	Stanford University
00-C0-8A	Lauterbach Datentechnik Gmbh	00-C0-E5	Gespac, S.A.	08-00-5A	IBM : Int'l Business Machines Corp
00-C0-8B	Risq Modular Systems Inc	00-C0-E6	TXPort	08-00-67	Comdesign
00-C0-8C	Performance Technologies Inc	00-C0-E7	Fiberdata AB	08-00-68	Ridge (Bull)
00-C0-8D	Tronix Procduct Development	00-C0-E8	Plexcom Inc	08-00-69	Silicon Graphics Inc
00-C0-8E	Network Information Technology	00-C0-E9	OAK Solutions Ltd	08-00-6E	Concurrent
00-C0-8F	Matsushita Electric Works, Ltd	00-C0-EA	Array Technology Ltd	08-00-74	Casio Computer Co. Ltd
00-C0-90	Praim S.R.L.	00-C0-EB	SEH Computer Technik Gmbh	08-00-75	DDE (Danish Data Elektronik A/S)
00-C0-91	Jabil Circuit Inc	00-C0-EC	Dauphin Technology	08-00-7C	Vitalink
00-C0-92	Mennen Medical Inc	00-C0-ED	US Army Electronic	08-00-80	XIOS
00-C0-93	Alta Research Corp	00-C0-EE	Kyocera Corp	08-00-86	Imagen/QMS
00-C0-96	Tamura Corp	00-C0-EF	Abit Corp	08-00-87	Xyplex
00-C0-97	Archipel SA	00-C0-F0	Kingston Technology Corp	08-00-89	Kinetics
00-C0-98	Chuntex Electronic Co. Ltd	00-C0-F1	Shinko Electric Co. Ltd	08-00-8B	Pyramid
00-C0-99	Yoshiki Industrial Co. Ltd	00-C0-F2	Transition Engineering Inc	08-00-8D	XyVision
00-C0-9B	Reliance Comm/Tec, R-Tec Syst. Inc	00-C0-F3	Network Communications Corp.	08-00-8F	Chipcom Corp
00-C0-9C	TOA Electronic Ltd	00-C0-F4	Interlink System Co. Ltd	08-00-90	Retix Inc
00-C0-9D	Distributed Systems Int'l Inc	00-C0-F5	Metacomp Inc	10-00-5A	IBM Corp
00-C0-9F	Quanta Computer Inc	00-C0-F6	Celan Technology Inc	48-44-53	HDS ?
00-C0-A0	Advance Micro Research Inc	00-C0-F7	Engage Communication Inc	80-00-19	AT&T
00-C0-A1	Tokyo Denshi Sekei Co	00-C0-F8	About Computing Inc	AA-00-00	DEC (Digital Equip. Corp) obsolete
00-C0-A2	Intermedium A/S	00-C0-F9	Harris and Jeffries Inc	AA-00-01	DEC obsolete
00-C0-A3	Dual Enterprises Corp	00-C0-FA	Canary Communications Inc	AA-00-02	DEC obsolete
00-C0-A4	Unigrapf OV	00-C0-FB	Advanced Technology Labs	AA-00-03	DEC Globl Phy addr some DEC host
00-C0-A7	Seel Ltd	00-C0-FC	ASDG, Inc	AA-00-04	DEC Local logical addr DECNET syst

Table 9.2 contains the list of prefixes used by certain multicast (group destination) traffic, the first byte of which is necessarily odd. Note, however, that the type field can provide complementary information.

In the IEEE 802 structure, the first bit of an address (long or short) is termed the Individual/Group (I/G) bit (Figure 9.3). However, for long addresses, the second

Table 9.2 List of prefixes for diffusion.

Address	Type	Use
01-00-5E-00-00-00- 01-00-5E-7F-FF-FF	0800	Internet Multicast [RFC1112]
01-00-5E-80-00-00- 01-00-5E-FF-FF-FF	????	Internet reserved by IANA
01-80-C2-00-00-00	-802-	Spanning tree (for bridges)
01-80-C2-00-00-2X	-802-	GARP
09-00-02-04-00-01	8080	Vitalink printer
09-00-02-04-00-02	8080	Vitalink management
09-00-09-00-00-01	8005	HP Probe
09-00-09-00-00-01	-802-	HP Probe
09-00-09-00-00-04	8005	HP DTC
09-00-1E-00-00-00	8019	Apollo DOMAIN
09-00-2B-00-00-00	6009	DEC MUMPS
09-00-2B-00-00-01	8039	DEC DSM/DTP
09-00-2B-00-00-02	803B	DEC VAXELN
09-00-2B-00-00-03	8038	DEC Lanbridge Traffic Monitor (LTM)
09-00-2B-00-00-04	????	DEC MAP End System Hello
09-00-2B-00-00-05	????	DEC MAP Intermediate System Hello
09-00-2B-00-00-06	803D?	DEC CSMA/CD Encryption
09-00-2B-00-00-07	8040?	DEC NetBios Emulator
09-00-2B-00-00-0F	6004	DEC Local Area Transport (LAT)
09-00-2B-00-00-1x	????	DEC Experimental
09-00-2B-01-00-00	8038	DEC LanBridge Copy packets (All bridges)
09-00-2B-01-00-01	8038	DEC LanBridge Hello packets (All local bridges) 1 packet per second sent by the designated LanBridge
09-00-2B-02-00-00	????	DEC DNA Lev. 2 Routing Layer routers
09-00-2B-02-01-00	803C	DEC DNA Naming Service Advertisement
09-00-2B-02-01-01	803C	DEC DNA Naming Service Solicitation
09-00-2B-02-01-02	803E	DEC DNA Time Service
09-00-2B-03-xx-xx	????	DEC default filtering by bridges
09-00-2B-04-00-00	8041	DEC Local Area Sys. Transport (LAST)
09-00-2B-23-00-00	803A	DEC Argonaut Console
09-00-4E-00-00-02	8137	Novell IPX
09-00-56-00-00-00- 09-00-56-FE-FF-FF	????	Stanford reserved
09-00-56-FF-00-00- 09-00-56-FF-FF-FF	805C	Stanford V Kernel, version 6.0
09-00-77-00-00-01	????	Retix spanning tree bridges
09-00-7C-02-00-05	8080	Vitalink diagnostics
09-00-7C-05-00-01	8080	Vitalink gateway
0D-1E-15-BA-DD-06	????	HP
AB-00-00-01-00-00	6001	DEC Maintenance Operation Protocol (MOP) Dump/Load Assistance

Table 9.2   (cont'd)

Adresse Ethernet	Type	Utilisation
AB-00-00-02-00-00	6002	DEC Maintenance Operation Protocol (MOP) Remote Console 1 System ID, 1 packet every 8–10 minutes, by every DEC LanBridge and DEC DEUNA DEC DELUA, DEC DEQNA (in certain mode)
AB-00-00-03-00-00	6003	DECNET Phase IV end node Hello packets 1 packet every 15 seconds, sent by the DECNET router
AB-00-00-04-00-00	6003	DECNET Phase IV Router Hello packets: 1 packet every 15 seconds, DECNET router
AB-00-00-05-00-00- AB-00-03-FF-FF-FF		Reserved for DEC
AB-00-03-00-00-00	6004	DEC Local Area Transport (LAT) – old
AB-00-04-00-xx-xx	????	Reserved DEC customer private use
AB-00-04-01-xx-yy	6007	DEC Local Area VAX Cluster groups Sys. Communication Architecture (SCA)
CF-00-00-00-00-00	9000	Ethernet Configuration Test protocol (Loopback)

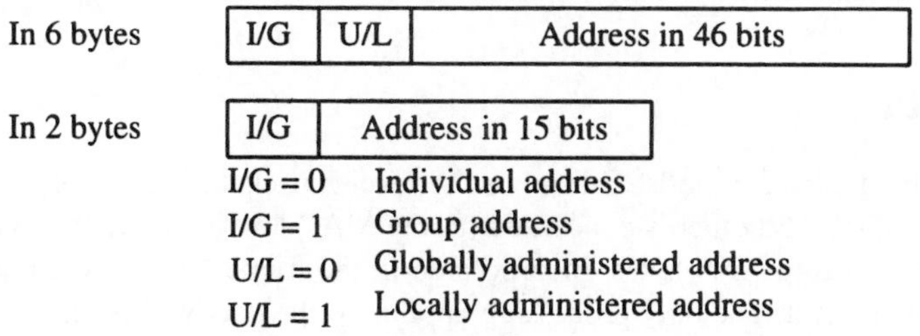

In 6 bytes | I/G | U/L | Address in 46 bits |

In 2 bytes | I/G | Address in 15 bits |

I/G = 0   Individual address
I/G = 1   Group address
U/L = 0   Globally administered address
U/L = 1   Locally administered address

Figure 9.3   IEEE 802 address format.

bit transmitted also has a special meaning and indicates whether the address is of a universal type (as described above) or whether it is administered locally. In the latter case, the following 46 bits are chosen by the user and are not necessarily the manufacturer and interface Card IDs. This second bit is called the Universally/ Locally (U/L) administered bit. These address formats are also found in other IEEE standards such as Token Ring and in ANSI's FDDI.

The type/length field

This two-byte field was defined in the Ethernet standard to indicate the type of level 3 protocol used to transport the message. This information could thus be used to switch the frame towards the software (driver) adapted for its decoding.

However, the meaning of this field changed with standardization (IEEE 802.3, then IS 8802-3), and it now carries length information about the data field (the following field), according to the standard. This length is not indispensable to the operation of the receiver, since the start and end of the frame can be deduced from the end of the preamble (two consecutive bits set to 1) and the fall in the carrier in the last bit; moreover, the lengths of other fixed fields (addresses, type, FCS) are known. This information is of interest both when the data field is not entirely full (a case in which it is desired to transmit only a few bytes using a short frame) and to verify the consistency between the total length of the frame received and the number of bytes as given by this field.

In all cases, the important question is to know how Ethernet frames can be distinguished from IEEE 802.3 frames on the network. The two may coexist perfectly well, which is often the case in reality. We know that the data field has a length of between 46 bytes (with insertion of a PAD, if necessary) and 1500 bytes, which makes 2E (or less, if there is a PAD) or 5DC in hexadecimal. Thus, if the content of the field following the two addresses is greater than 5DC, it is determined to be a type field and hence an Ethernet frame; otherwise, it must be a length field and an IEEE 802.3 frame.

Table 2.3 lists the most common protocol types, which may help readers to identify the traffic to which the frames circulating on their network belong.

We note that certain protocol types with numbers less than 5DC (prior to the IEEE 802.3 standard) have been reproduced further in the list.

The data

The data field contains the LLC-level or the level-3 packet, thus it has no intrinsic meaning as far as Ethernet is concerned (at the MAC level). The field is viewed as a sequence of 46 to 1500 bytes, incorporated in the frame, and no attempt will be made to interpret it. The only processing applied to the data will be the calculation of the CRC.

Within an ISO architecture, the IEEE 802.3 frame will encapsulate an IEEE 802.2 LLC packet.

Finally, if less than 46 bytes are provided by the layer above, the data field is filled out by the PAD.

The PAD

The PAD or stuffing sequence is only used to fill the data field to obtain at least 46 bytes. It is therefore indispensable in completing the generation of a short frame from a message consisting of only a few bytes. It consists of a sequence of meaningless bits placed after the data itself.

In the case of Ethernet V 2.0, the MAC level of the frame did not transport any information about the number of data bytes. The differentiation between the useful bytes and the stuffing therefore had to be provided by the upper layers. In IEEE 802.3, the length field indicates whether the data field contains a PAD and gives its length (obtained by subtraction).

The FCS

Frame Check Sequence (FCS) is a four-byte field placed at the end of frames which is used to check the validity of the frame after receipt, up to a one bit. It uses a Cyclic Redundancy Check (CRC) calculated using a generator polynomial of degree 32. It covers the two address fields, the type/length field and the data (including PAD), and is thus used by the receiving station to decide whether the frame is perfectly correct and can be forwarded to the layer above (LLC or level 3).

On the subject of FCS transmission, we note that it is the only field of the frame to be transmitted beginning with the most significant bit (coefficient of X^{31} first, coefficient of X^0 last).

The interframe gap

We saw with the description of the method that all machines can take their turn on a single network in which regular exchanges between other equipment take place, with a relatively small delay. This is due in part to the fact that a machine cannot transmit all the frames it has to transmit one after the other. There is an obligatory 9.6 μs interval (at 10 Mbps) between the fall of the signal occupying the medium and the start of the frame emitted; this is known as the interframe gap (IFG), or spacing. This silence allows the electronic circuits to recover the rest state of the medium (absence of signal), and it may enable other stations wishing to transmit to take over at that time.

We note that this delay would correspond to the time taken to emit 96 bits, or 8 bytes, which is quite substantial. We shall see later that after the crossing of the repeaters this interframe gap may be reduced to less than 9.6 μs.

Summary To review the important elements of the composition of a frame, Figure 9.4 gives a representation of the typical frame with its various fields together with the order of emission of the bits of each byte. The frame thus consists of bytes which are emitted on the cable in serial mode. Therefore, an order of transmission for the bits of each byte must be chosen. For Ethernet networks, the first bit emitted is the least-significant bit and the last is the most-significant (eighth) bit (MSB). This

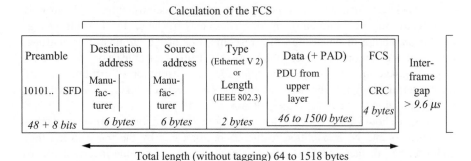

Calculation of the FCS

Preamble	Destination address	Source address	Type (Ethernet V 2) or Length (IEEE 802.3)	Data (+ PAD) PDU from upper layer	FCS CRC	Inter-frame gap > 9.6 μs
10101..	SFD	Manu-fac-turer	Manu-fac-turer			4 bytes	
48 + 8 bits	6 bytes	6 bytes	2 bytes	46 to 1500 bytes		

Total length (without tagging) 64 to 1518 bytes

Figure 9.4 Schematic view of the structure of a complete frame.

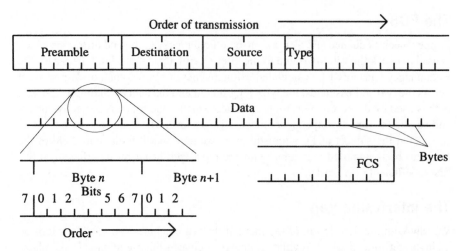

Figure 9.5 Details of a short frame and order of transmission of the bits and bytes.

order, also referred to as little endian, is respected for all the fields of the frame, with the exception, as we have seen, of the FCS (see Figure 9.5). Readers should be aware that not all IEEE local area networks necessarily use this order.

To conclude, we note that sometimes a special (and partially inexact) terminology is used in the literature, whereby the term 'packet' is used to denote the succession of the eight fields discussed here (preamble, SFD, destination address, source address, type/length, data, PAD, FCS) and the term 'frame' refers to a packet without a preamble or SFD (this corresponds to the significant data).

9.2 Defective frames

The frame as described above is the entity intended for emission to exchange data between the stations of the network. However, problems may hinder its emission or propagation.

Packets which do not respect a consistent frame structure, or do so only imperfectly, may be found on the media. These may be the result of events such as a collision, abrupt disconnection of a machine, loss of the terminator or malfunctioning of one or more machines in the network. In all cases, at least one of the fields of the message infringes one of the rules for the constitution of a frame. Thus, a precise terminology may be used to denote each defective packet. As you will see, this vocabulary is, of course, largely of American origin.

One should also be aware that, although all these dubious frames may cross the repeaters and be transmitted to the connector cards by the transceivers, they go no further. In fact, the MAC layer of each station deletes the incorrect frames immediately and retains no trace of any field of the defective packet type (except for certain internal software for monitoring and statistical purposes).

The runt

This term is used to denote a frame which is too short, that is, less than 64 bytes. In most cases, this is a frame which has been truncated for some reason (often because of a collision), and what remains of the original frame no longer has any meaning. In fact, the receiver does not necessarily know whether it has received the complete data field and whether the last four bytes are those of the CRC. Since this frame might actually be the result of a collision, its presence on a healthy network is perfectly acceptable. However, in this case the runt frame will usually be misaligned (non-integral number of bytes) with a bad FCS.

The jabber

The jabber is a frame which is too long, that is, with a length greater than 1518 bytes. Theoretically, this type of fault should never occur in a healthy network. However, the original causes of instances in which the frame contains between 1500 and 3000 bytes or several tens of thousands of bytes vary.

In the first case, we shall suppose that it is a superposition of two long frames involved in an undetected collision. The fact that a collision has not been detected reveals an important problem. In fact, we have seen that the Ethernet technology is based on a CSMA/CD method; now, if the CD (collision detection) is no longer guaranteed, the Ethernet layers 1 and 2 can no longer offer the same level of performance. Of course, a frame may be lost entirely, when it enters the MAC layer (if its emission is subject to 16 successive collisions), but that should not happen too regularly, otherwise this lack of Ethernet reliability will result in numerous retransmissions which, in turn, will disturb all the traffic and degrade the global performance.

In the second case, the packet probably does not have a frame structure and must be produced by a defective component which has remained in emission mode for far too long. *A priori*, there will be a tendency to accuse low-level elements (transceivers, repeaters, interface cards) rather than the software driver or the application used. This is because the problem appears rudimentary and directly linked to the production of the physical signals, and because, as we shall see later, there exist watchdogs upstream of the driver.

This fault should be located and repaired quickly since it may be very injurious for the network. It is clear that an element which takes over to emit for several milliseconds blocks the network totally and unnecessarily for this period.

The misaligned frame

A misaligned frame is one in which the number of bits is not divisible by eight and which, therefore, cannot be reconstituted in the format of a sequence of complete bytes. This is one proof that the frame is unusable, for the receiver has no way of knowing whether it has counted too many or too few bits at the start of the frame, in the middle or at the end. Thus, all the bytes are potentially incorrect.

In practice, the misaligned frame may have an arbitrary length (from 64 to 1518 bytes, plus or minus several bits), but it almost always has a bad CRC. In fact, it is clear that a reading of the bytes of the frame which is shifted by several bits cannot produce a CRC value consistent with the last four bytes.

The bad FCS

The frame with a bad FCS is a frame for which the CRC calculated by the receiving (or reading) machine does not correspond to the last four bytes of the frame received. This may occur when one or more bits of the frame is incorrect (because of poor transmission, interference, and so on), in which case the calculation of the redundancy checksum finds its justification. However, it is also possible to obtain a frame with a bad FCS when the frame is truncated and thus the last four bytes which are compared with the calculated CRC are not those of the CRC for the whole frame (in this case, the frame is often misaligned and runt, since, first, there is little chance of the truncation occurring at the end of a byte and, second, the collisions must have occurred before 64 bytes). We recall that in this instance a truncated frame normally results from a collision.

In conclusion, the frame with a bad FCS is either a complete frame, in which at least one bit was not received as it was emitted, or the residue of a collision.

Table 9.3 Different types of error.

	< 64 bytes	64 to 1518 bytes	> 1518 bytes
Packet correctly constituted	Undersized	Packet correct	Oversized
Bad FCS	Fragment	CRC error or misaligned	Jabber

9.3 Collision

The collision is the phenomenon resulting from the superposition of two signals (*a priori* two frames) on the medium. Of course, the collision occurs if the two emitters started up simultaneously (or at a sufficiently short interval apart) (Figure 9.6).

This event is normally linked to and resolved by the access method. However, its occurrence should not exceed certain thresholds (for example, one collision per 1000 frames) otherwise the traffic flow will be harmed. We shall now discuss the conditions under which the collision occurs.

Let us suppose that two machines wish to transmit a frame at the same time. They will sense the medium and, assuming that it is free at that time, will both decide that they can act and move simultaneously to transmit mode. What happens? Their signals are superimposed and the two frames become invisible, even for the two addressees.

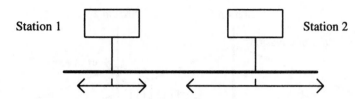

Figure 9.6 Two quasi-simultaneous emissions on a segment.

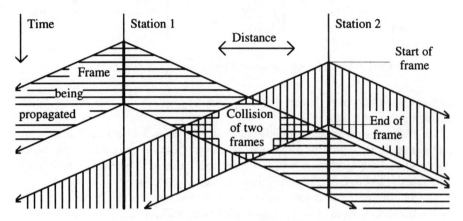

Figure 9.7 Illustration of an undetected collision.

In fact, it is not necessary for the machines to set off the process at exactly the same time; it is sufficient for the time separating the two decisions to be less than the transmission time between their two points of attachment to the network. If this is the case, it was quite possible for the two machines to find the medium empty at the time they sensed the carrier before emission. However, a conflict will arise after a delay of less than the transit time separating them.

This event is acceptable if the emitters are informed of it. Thus, they should be able to detect this event which prevents correct reading of the signal at any point on the medium. For this, it is decided to extend the collision sufficiently. In fact, the aim is to ensure that the collision does not go undetected, when the network would be incapable of detecting the problem which has arisen and would fail to recover the frame or pass the information on to the layer above.

Figure 9.7 illustrates the occurrence of an undetected collision. Note that the collision is not visible at any point on the medium and that the emitters see the two packets pass one after the other.

There is a way of avoiding this type of event, which is difficult to manage. For this, one must ensure that the time taken to transmit a frame is always greater than twice the transit time between the two points of emission. Since the size of an Ethernet network is bounded (the number of segments, transceivers and repeaters is limited, as is the maximum length of each segment), the round-trip delay for an Ethernet network should not exceed a fixed value (499 bit times), and the

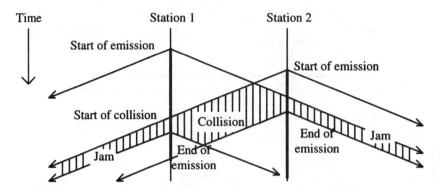

Figure 9.8 Collision correctly detected and followed by the jam.

corresponding minimum frame should consist of at least 512 bits (or 64 bytes, excluding preamble and SFD).

With this constraint, all collisions last long enough to ensure that they are propagated to the emitters concerned, wherever these are located, which, when informed that the last frame was lost, may then attempt to retransmit from their buffer, according to an algorithm which we shall describe later.

In practice, when a collision occurs, the MAC layer of the station is alerted by the transceiver which emits on the Signal Quality Error (SQE) pair of the drop cable. This indicates that the transceiver considers that the quality of the signal being emitted is unacceptable (Figure 9.8). The coaxial transceiver (10Base5 or 10Base2) detects the collision either because it cannot read the bits it is emitting correctly or because the continuous component of the signal on the cable is greater than that for a signal emission (–1 V). Other types of transceiver operate on point-to-point links (10BaseT, FOIRL, 10BaseFB and 10BaseFL) with a channel in each direction; there can be no superposition and the collision simply involves the detection of a reception during a transmission. The collision on a 10BaseFP network is a special case, which is handled in Section 12.6.

We shall see later that, although 100BaseT operates on point-to-point links, collision detection is implemented differently for UTP cables of category 3 and 4.

Up to now, we have seen that the collision was an inevitable, but not grave, event. However, if one or more elements of the network are operating incorrectly all of the traffic may be affected. We stress that the collision rates per frame and per second are generally good indicators of the health of a network. If these increase abnormally, users may experience a loss of quality in their exchanges. Thus, it is useful to be able to judge a collision rate in order to quantify the state of a network.

The probability of a collision is difficult to calculate rigorously, but it is known to be linked to (and increase with) the following parameters:

- The total traffic on the network at a given time (measured in frames per second).
- The number of active stations on the network (sharing the global load).
- The separation of the machines (in terms of distance and number of repeaters).

There exist simulation programs which provide indicative results based on these parameters as input. Unfortunately, it is generally difficult to know the parameters to be provided with accuracy, since that corresponds to modeling a real network with all its intrinsic irregularity.

Remark An elementary way of provoking collisions involves removing the imped-ance adaptation plug or terminator at the coax cable end. Then any frame emitted in the circuit is reflected on the open circuit and collides with itself.

This exemplifies the attention which must be paid to the cabling and to its protection, since an untimely disconnection of this 50 Ohm plug may block a net-work completely.

The backoff algorithm

The access method used for Ethernet is of the persistent CSMA/CD type. Moreover, it is capable of returning to its transmission process after collisions have occurred. As we shall see, the Ethernet access method manages transmission attempts after the incident using a random distribution on an increasing time interval.

More precisely, Ethernet uses the backoff algorithm (Figure 9.9) to handle collision during attempts to transmit a frame. When the emission of a frame is

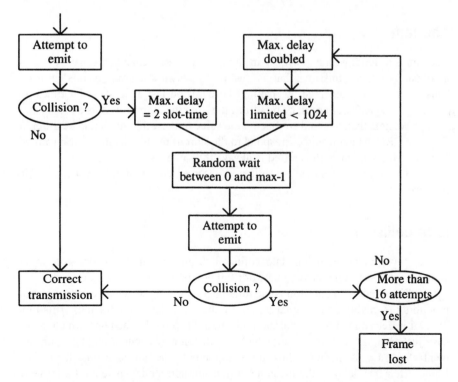

Figure 9.9 Block diagram summarizing the backoff algorithm.

perturbed by a collision, the machine produces a jam, then ceases all emission until the medium becomes free again. After an interval, randomly determined so as not to restart simultaneously with its 'rival', it again tries to send its message and loops on the same emission procedure as before. If a serious problem prevents all transmission, the Ethernet MAC level ensures that the station stops its series of attempts to emit by simply deleting the frame to be emitted from its buffers after 16 unsuccessful attempts.

It is here that one notes the unreliability of the network, since, in certain cases, it authorizes the loss of a packet without informing the layers above.

Moreover, if the collisions are due to the network load, the more the stations try to re-emit their data rapidly, the more they load the network, resulting in an avalanche effect which tends towards a complete network blockage. To counter this eventuality, Ethernet uses a waiting time randomly chosen in an increasing window of possible delays. Thus, after the first collision, there are two possible choices for the window (0 or 1 slot times), which increases by a factor of two with every new attempt. Finally, after the tenth attempt, this window is bounded by 1023 slot times, which is already a relatively high value ($1024 \times 512 \times 0.1$ μs = 52.4 ms). The attempts then continue, if necessary, up to the sixteenth time, with this same delay window. The backoff algorithm is also referred to as the BEB (Binary Exponential Backoff), as the interval length increases per every two iterations.

The jam

The jam is a signal with no intrinsic meaning; it assures elements that have detected a collision on their emissions that the rest of the network is aware of this collision. This is simply implemented by making the collision last at least 32 bit times, by emitting a sequence of arbitrary bits from the time the emitter detects a collision.

We note that, to avoid confusion, the value of these 32 bits should be different from the CRC, which would correspond to the start of the frame already transmitted. In reality, the sequence transmitted is always the same.

This signal is also called 'collision enforcement', which is evocative of its purpose.

Late collision

Unlike 'in-window' collision, late collision is an abnormal phenomenon which should never occur on a healthy network (all equipment functioning correctly).

The window in question is the time interval during which an emitting station monitors the quality of its signal (and may therefore detect a collision). This time interval is determined by the duration of a round trip on the medium, which, as we have just seen, is the delay during which a collision may occur without an infringement of the access method. Thus, it corresponds to the emission time for a short frame. After this delay, if the machine in transmission mode has to emit a frame of a length greater than 64 bytes, it continues its emission and ceases to observe the signals on the medium. After the round-trip delay all the attached stations should have seen the emission and, having determined that the medium is busy, will have moved to the wait state. Thus, a collision which occurs after 512 bit times have elapsed (equivalent to the length of a minimum frame) can only be the consequence of an infringement of the basic rule of the CSMA/CD access method, namely the carrier sensing.

In addition to its known intrinsic limitations and its lack of robustness under heavy load, CSMA/CD, as defined in Ethernet, proved not to be as fair as expected. A phenomenon called Capture Effect tends to prove that in case of collision the station that has already just transmitted a frame is more privileged, as it will use the same random process as the station that has not transmitted recently. This appears as though the first station has somehow captured the medium. A proposal, sometimes referred to as the CABEB (Capture Avoidance BEB), has been made to eliminate this unfairness by changing the two first intervals for a station that has just transmitted a frame and encountered a collision on the following attempt. The other stations do not have to change their behavior.

Instead of waiting for a random number chosen in (0,1) and (0,1,2,3) times the slot-time, the 'privileged' station that has just transmitted the last frame seen on the segment will have to wait exactly 2 slot-times after the first collision before the attempt to transmit, and if ever it encounters a second collision, it will have to wait 0 slot-times. If collisions keep happening the process resumes like the normal back-off with interval (0 . . . 7) and so on. We can see that the average delay for the first 2 consecutive collisions is maintained: $0.5 + 1.5 = 2$, meaning that the CABEB just tries to reduce the probability after a successful transmission followed by a collision, and that the same station 'keeps' the medium.

9.4 The idle signal

The idle signal is a waiting signal which may occupy the medium, voluntarily and regularly, during periods of inactivity. This signal is only used on point-to-point links (twisted pair and optical fiber) and provides information about the presence of an active element at the other end. It is a safeguard, designed to protect the network against a breakdown on a link. For example, a machine which is unaware that its transceiver's reception pair is defective might emit without respecting the CSMA and cause numerous collisions.

In the case of 10 Mbps Ethernet on twisted pair, the transceiver (external or built into the hub), whenever it is switched on and there is no traffic, emits a peak with a frequency of approximately 5 MHz every 16 milliseconds. The hub or receiver opposite is thus informed that the transceiver connected to this port is active and that the pair in its direction (reception) is in good condition. The idle signal is known as the Link Test Pulse (in the 10BaseT Addendum) or NLP (Normal Link Pulse). We note that this description applies in one direction only and that the quality of the hub's emission pair to the transceiver has to be determined from an exchange.

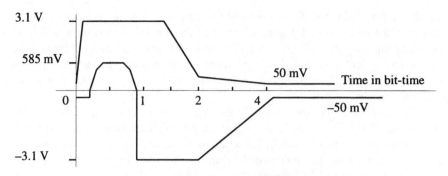

Figure 9.10 Template of an idle signal pulse in 10BaseT.

The hub, knowing the state of the transceiver for each port, may adapt its behavior to isolate the port completely (transmission and reception) after an excessively long period of silence.

More precisely, the 10 Mbps idle signal consists of a unique oscillation, whose first part is positive and has a duration of between 250 and 600 ns. In the absence of useful traffic, the emission of these peaks is periodic, with silences of 16 ± 8 ms separating the pulses. If the 10BaseT port does not receive a valid signal or pulse from its correspondent during a maximum delay interval (from 50 to 150 ms), it decides that it has lost communication with the port which has become silent, and partitions it. After receiving 2 to 10 pulses, the port should recover its normal operational state. Two pulses are deemed to be consecutive if they are not too far apart (between 25 and 150 ms).

In reality, the sequence of pulses in a period of inactivity begins with a TP_IDL (Twisted Pair Idle) signal whose template is similar to that of the Link Test Pulse (see Figure 9.10), where the homothety depends upon the time axis. The TP_IDL emitted after the last frame has a global duration twice that of a Link Test Pulse, whence half the corresponding frequency (approximately 2 MHz). When a transceiver decides it has lost communication with its peer it begins to emit a sequence of pulses, beginning with a TP_IDL to the silent transceiver.

Finally, we note that the idle signal provides an indication in one direction only (unidirectional). If only one of these two directions of communication of a link is cut or perturbed, one end will detect the absence of correct pulses, but will still generate its idle signal in return, since it cannot inform the other end that it thinks the link is inoperable. Some manufacturers have improved the idle signal by varying the level and/or frequency within the standard template, to transport information similar to the 'remote fault' of 10BaseFB. The idle then becomes a more complete, bidirectional means of communication.

Chapter 10

Higher speed

- 100BaseT

- 100BaseT2

- Auto-negotiation

- 1000BaseX

- 1000BaseT

- Ethernet 10 Gbps

10.1 100BaseT

The simplest solution, in terms of continuous evolution, that offers Ethernet access at 100 Mbps is the one proposed under the label of 100BaseT or Fast Ethernet (FE), which preserves the CSMA/CD access method and can use existing cabling consisting of two non-shielded twisted pairs of category 5 (they may also be shielded), or of four non-shielded twisted pairs of category 3 or 4. It is also possible to use multimode optical fiber. The fact that 100BaseT proposes a tenfold increase in throughput without major modifications implicitly means an equivalent reduction in terms of distance (the round-trip time being proportional to the emission delay of a short frame, a value that remains unchanged). After having envisaged creating a specific IEEE 802.14 working group, 100BaseT has been reintegrated into IEEE 802.3 as supplement u. This is an obvious sign of respect towards the functionality of Ethernet and has also contributed to the success of this technology by presenting it as an extension of Ethernet, and not as a competitor or as a simple revival.

Standard 100BaseT is divided into three major categories: 100BaseX which takes two PMDs coming from FDDI and 100BaseT4, specifically designed for support of UTP 3 and 4 and 100BaseT2, more recent supplement for UTP 3 and 4.

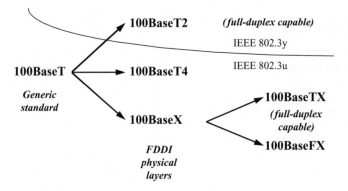

Figure 10.1 Decomposition of 100BaseT.

100BaseX proceeds with a particularly pragmatic and economically interesting approach, taking advantage of an already existing, perfectly standardized and stable 100 Mbps technology, and electronic emitter and receiver components that implement its specifications in twisted pair and optical fiber cabling currently available on the market. Thus, 100BaseX has two implementations: 100BaseFX which corresponds to FDDI's MMF-PMD and 100BaseTX which corresponds to FDDI's TP-PMD.

Fast Ethernet technology is nearly inevitably associated with dynamic packet switching. Indeed, transparent bridging is indispensable to pass from 100 Mbps ports to 10 Mbps Ethernet standard ports. This conversion is directly connected to the coexistence of the two throughputs during the phase of progressive migration.

100BaseTX

100BaseTX uses the cable type of FDDI's TP-PMD: UTP category 5 (IEC 11801), also called Data Grade TP (DTP) and Shielded Twisted Pair (STP) such as IBM's type 1, using two pairs of a length limited to 100 meters: one pair for emission and one for receipt.

100BaseTX uses 4B/5B conversion (which includes an intrinsic consistency check, and raises the bit rate to 125 Mbps), followed by stream cipher scrambling and MLT-3 encoding (multiline transmission) (Figure 10.2).

4B/5B ensures that all symbols corresponding to numerical data include at least two changes of state (bit set to 1), and never more than three bits with the same value are emitted successively (which would correspond to two bits set to 0, see Figure 10.2). The scrambler is responsible for distributing the signal energy across the whole spectrum. MLT-3 uses three physical levels to reduce the main signal frequency to 31.25 MHz (over a four-bit period).

Data symbols

11110	0	0000
01001	1	0001
10100	2	0010
10101	3	0011
01010	4	0100
01011	5	0101
01110	6	0110
01111	7	0111
10010	8	1000
10011	9	1001
10110	A	1010
10111	B	1011
11010	C	1100
11011	D	1101
11100	E	1110
11101	F	1111

Line status symbols

00000	Q	Quiet
11111	I	Idle
00100	H	Halt

Starting delimiters

11000	J
10001	K

Ending delimiter

01101	T	Terminator

Control indicators

00111	R	Reset
11001	S	Set

Figure 10.2 Table of legal values for the 4B/5B encoding.

The pairs used are still 1–2 and 3–6, for perfect compatibility with existing Ethernet cabling certified at 100 Mbps, rather than the pairs 1–2 and 7–8 used in

Table 10.1 RJ45 pinout assignment for 100BaseTX port.

Pins	Signal on station or repeater port side without crossover	Signal on repeater side with internal crossover
1 and 2	Tx+ and –	Rx+ and –
3 and 6	Rx+ and –	Tx+ and –

FDDI's TP-PMD. UTP category 5 cables and STP cables must have an attenuation less than 10 dB for UTP5 and 5.2 dB for STP at 16 MHz, a propagation speed of 0.6 c, and a maximum round-trip delay of 1112 ns per segment.

100BaseTX is most frequently implemented on UTP5, with a shielded RJ45 connector. In an inter-switch configuration, full duplex is always preferable because it is more powerful, but it is also beginning to become generally used between switch and station. Finally, let us not forget that if 100BaseTX appears as an attractive solution, it requires category 5 cables to be able to connect the machines at 100 Mbps. Since in the majority of cases these machines are servers, often centralized in one computer room, cabling is no problem because in practice it is simply a question of tying together network equipment and neighboring servers within one wiring closet.

Note that the currently marketed Ethernet 10/100 cards are generally capable of supporting both 10BaseT and 100BaseTX modes by means of auto-negotiation.

100BaseT4

To respect the investments made in UTP3 or 4 cabling for Ethernet networks, 100BaseT wanted to define an adapted mode of functioning which, however, needed 4 pairs instead of 2 (the reason for the 4 in 100BaseT4). Now we are facing a dilemma, because if 10BaseT needed 2 pairs of UTP 3/4/5, 100BaseTX too needs only 2 pairs, but of category 5, whereas 100BaseT4 uses any category of UTP (3/4/ 5) but on 4 pairs. Finally those users who as a money-saving measure have only cabled 2 pairs of UTP 3 on their RJ45s had no simple means of upgrading to 100 Mbps (we will see how the 100BaseT2 specifications proposes to help them).

100BaseT4 (standard specification derived from 4T+ which appeared in the first proposals) employs an 8B/6T coding where each byte is converted into a sequence of six ternary levels, transmitted in parallel on 3 pairs simultaneously. Among the 4 pairs, 2 are used indifferently for transmission in both senses (bidirectional), and 2 are reserved to a single direction. The pair, exclusively Rx, easily guarantees collision detection (that is, transmission and reception at the same time). Because of the fact that the two pairs are used indistinguishably in both senses, 100BaseT4 cannot function in full duplex, and is thus the only point-to-point Ethernet technology presenting this limitation.

Note that 8B/6T coding and multiplexing on 3 physical channels is relatively complex, but allows the throughput per pair to be limited to 25 Mbaud. The cabling

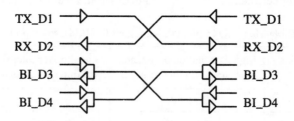

Figure 10.3 Transmission on three pairs, two of which are bidirectional.

Table 10.2 RJ45 pinout assignment for 100BaseT4 port.

Pins	Signal on station or repeater port side (without crossover)	Signal on repeater side with internal crossover
1 and 2	Tx_D1+ and –	Rx_D2+ and –
3 and 6	Rx_D2+ and –	Tx_D1+ and –
4 and 5	BI_D3+ and –	BI_D4+ and –
7 and 8	BI_D4+ and –	BI_D3+ and –

must show less than 12 dB of attenuation between 2 and 12.5 MHz. Each ternary sextet is transmitted with an interval of one third of a sextet. The preamble is a sequence of specific sextets (non-data symbols) which allow these phase differences to initiate. It also triggers the reading of the data symbols in the SFD manner to be triggered.

The three SOSB symbols constitute the Start of Stream Delimiter (SSD). Note that the complete preamble still consists of the equivalent of eight bytes.

Since the number of bytes in the original frame is arbitrary (between permitted limits of 64 to 1518 bytes), the last byte of the frame, DATA_N, may be on any one of the three pairs, at random: TX_D1, BI_D3 or BI_D4 (see Figure 10.4).

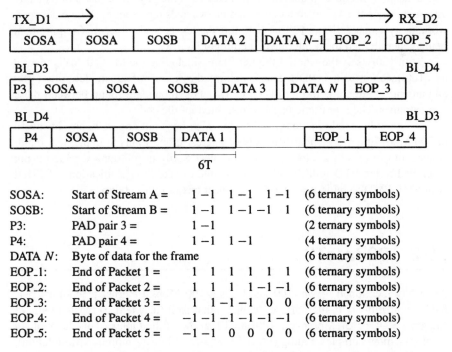

SOSA:	Start of Stream A =	1 –1 1 –1 1 –1	(6 ternary symbols)
SOSB:	Start of Stream B =	1 –1 1 –1 –1 1	(6 ternary symbols)
P3:	PAD pair 3 =	1 –1	(2 ternary symbols)
P4:	PAD pair 4 =	1 –1 1 –1	(4 ternary symbols)
DATA N:	Byte of data for the frame		(6 ternary symbols)
EOP_1:	End of Packet 1 =	1 1 1 1 1 1	(6 ternary symbols)
EOP_2:	End of Packet 2 =	1 1 1 1 –1 –1	(6 ternary symbols)
EOP_3:	End of Packet 3 =	1 1 –1 –1 0 0	(6 ternary symbols)
EOP_4:	End of Packet 4 =	–1 –1 –1 –1 –1 –1	(6 ternary symbols)
EOP_5:	End of Packet 5 =	–1 –1 0 0 0 0	(6 ternary symbols)

Figure 10.4 Decomposition of the transmission of a frame on the three pairs.

This 100BaseT4 technology is important in that it means that 100BaseT is not restricted to UTP category 5 installations. Cables of category 3 or 4 have a propagation speed of 0.5852 c, a maximum round-trip delay of 1140 ns per segment and an attenuation less than or equal to 12.5 dB from 2 to 12.5 MHz (where the latter is the highest fundamental sequence). Note that a ternary symbol effectively lasts 40 ns so that, on a pair, a period comprises 80 ns or more.

In practice, in spite of the larger number of supported media, 100BaseT4 has no wide diffusion and risks never having much of it.

100BaseFX

As we have seen, 100BaseFX takes over the principal characteristics of FDDI MMF-PMD and of PHY (equivalent to the transceiver): optical signal wavelength of 1300 nm and 4B/5B & NRZI coding. Thus, emitter and receiver components can be re-employed. The maximum attenuation is 11 dB for 62.5/125 μm multimode fiber.

The only difference from FDDI at the physical level lies in the choice of the SC connector instead of MIC (key M) or ST duplex, which are also described. It should, however, be noted that the round-trip time, as mentioned above, limits the lengths of a half-duplex fiber connection to 412 m (408 bit times = 4080 ns: one tenth of the diameter of a 10 Mbps Ethernet network). The traditional 2 km can only be reached in full-duplex mode, this time because of the physical constraints (mainly attenuation). As the 412 m connection and its two ends represent the whole network, working systematically in 100BaseFX full duplex is preferable, this requirement being generally tied to an inter-switch configuration.

In 100BaseX the whole Ethernet frame (including the MAC field) is viewed as a 100BaseX stream or PDU. This is delimited by a start of stream delimiter (J-K) and an end of stream delimiter (T-R). Only data symbols are found between these two extremes. The interframe gap is transmitted in idle code.

Note: the single mode optical fiber which does not appear in any of the 10 or 100 Mbps Ethernet standards is only of interest if one wants to implement major connections of tens of kilometers, therefore necessarily in full duplex, which is not submitted to the RTD limit. Here, it is possible to take the specifications of FDDI with SMF-PMD to build non-standard connections of up to 60 km.

10.2 100BaseT2

As briefly mentioned above, 100BaseT2 is a 100 Mbps Ethernet technology perfectly compatible with the 10BaseT cabling, that is, 2 (unshielded) twisted pairs of category 3, 4 or 5. Moreover, 100BaseT2 allows full duplex. This technology employs a more complex coding (PAM 5 × 5: 5-level Pulse Amplitude Modulation), and should serve as a base for the development of 1000BaseT. The specifications are elaborated as a complement to 100BaseT by the 802.3y subcommittee. They allow throughout of 25 MBd on each pair, with a signal frequency of 25 MHz, compatible with autonegotiation.

Given that 100BaseTX is already relatively common, at the expense of 100BaseT4, it is difficult to foresee a development of 100BaseT2, whose technology appears as a supplementary choice that can only disturb the market.

10.3 Auto-negotiation

At 100 Mbps

Auto-negotiation refers to the capability of network elements to handle their mode of communication automatically as a function of their common capacities. This optional capacity has been introduced with Fast Ethernet on twisted pair, but can be applied to all Ethernet throughputs (from 10 Mbps to 1 Gbps), to related technologies, such as IsoEthernet, and thus theoretically to other LAN, Token Ring or WLAN (Wireless LAN) technologies.

This capacity is employed on twisted pair in the transceiver/PHY, hub, or switch, and allows provision for so-called 10/100 or 100/1000 equipment, capable of switching to the highest throughput accepted by the two edge devices. Equally, auto-negotiation should allow automatic exploitation of full duplex if it is supported by both edge devices of a dedicated connection. It should be noted, however, that the dual speed capability is not envisaged for optical fiber at 10 and 100 Mbps.

Auto-negotiation builds on the exchange, between PHYs, of words (Link Code Word) that describe the capacities supported at each side, followed by the choice of the greatest common denominator. The emission of these messages is

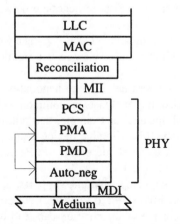

Figure 10.5   Position of the auto-negotiation functions in the model.

carried out in the form of quick pulses that represent the different bits, but remain perfectly compatible with the existing standard, that is, the Link Pulses (or NLPs: Normal Link Pulses) defined in 10BaseT to inform about the active state of the opposite endpoint. The FLPs (Fast Link Pulses) code the 1 bits of the 16-bit words to be exchanged. More precisely, the FLP sequence is sent every 16 ± 8 ms (frequency of the NLP). This is composed of 17 clock pulses every 125 μs, between which the bits of the transmitted register are transmitted: a 1 is represented by a pulse, a 0 by the absence of a pulse. Each burst lasts 2.125 ms and consists of peaks separated by at least 62.5 ± 7 μs.

A 10BaseT device or transceiver will see the FLP sequence as a simple Link Test and will reply with a Normal Link Pulse (periodic peaks every 16 ± 8 ms, in the absence of traffic). In turn, receipt of the NLP by the 100BaseT PHY will force the activation of 10BaseT operation.

The coding of the 16 bits (and pulses) of the base page is shown in Figure 10.6.

This information can thus be emitted at both edges during the initialization phase, and can also be acknowledged to prove understanding by the addressee, which does not necessarily mean approval of the proposed technology.

If the two edge devices support other pages (NP = 1), they transmit them in the same way. Message page (MP = 1) potentially allows transmission of 2048 messages.

Ack2 means that it is possible to conform to the message, whereas Ack simply means that the message has been read.

The Unformatted page (MP = 0) has the following format:

U0 U1 U2 U3 U4 U5 U6 U7 U8 U9 U10 T Ack2 MP Ack NP

The information contained in these words also circulates on the MII between PHY and the reconciliation layer in form of management registers.

With 100BaseT, a classification was initiated to allow the choice of the 'best' available technology, (see Table 10.3, and note that the most powerful one is shown at the bottom. It has been extended with 1000BaseT, but concerns only those connections where the possibility exists to negotiate between the different speeds (i.e. UTP).

Note that with fixed throughput, a technology is always preferable when it is less demanding from a cabling point of view or if it employs fewer pairs with the same type of cable.

If one of the edge devices has no auto-negotiation capacity, the other one must adapt its working mode. If there exists no common technology, the connection must be interrupted, which means, for example, that auto-negation FLPs must no longer be sent to a uniquely 10BaseT edge device if this mode is not supported, because the 10BaseT interface would interpret the FLPs as a simple Idle, indicating that the counterpart is ready to receive.

The capability of announcing what one supports, but without the capability to auto-adapt itself, is sometimes referred to as auto-detection, as opposed to auto-negotiation, where the exchange of information can lead to a modification on the transmission mode (speed, half/full-duplex, Flow Control support).

In practice, auto-negotiation does not always proceed in an ideal way and sometimes ends up with the smallest common denominator (10 Mbps). Problems

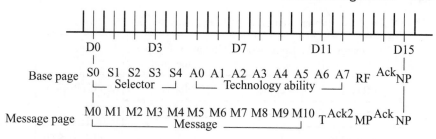

Selector, of 32 possible message types, the following are already defined:

    0 = reserved for future developments

    1 = IEEE 802.3

    2 = IEEE 802.9a

    31 = reserved for future developments

Technology ability (technologies supported), 5 independent bits are defined:

    A0 = 10BaseT

    A1 = 10BaseT full duplex

    A2 = 100BaseTX

    A3 = 100BaseTX full duplex

    A4 = 100BaseT4

    A5 = Pause Operation for full duplex links

RF: Remote Fault

    0 = no remote fault

    1 = indication of remote fault

Ack: Acknowledge

    0 = acknowledgment of receipt not yet received

    1 = acknowledgment of receipt of message after 3 successive consistent receipts

NP: Next Page

    0 = last page

    1 = another page follows

Message, 2048 possible messages, of which the first codes are:

    0 = reserved for a future auto-negotiation use

    1 = zero message (during an exchange with Next Page)

    2 = UP message with Technology Ability extension follows

    3 = Two UP messages with TA extension follow

    4 = UP message followed by the code for remote fault

    5 = message followed by 4 others encoding the OUI

    6 = message followed by 4 others encoding the PHY ID

    7 = 100BaseT2 Ability Page Follow

    2047 = reserved for a future auto-negotiation use

T: Toggle, inverse of the value of the toggle for the previous message

Ack2: Acknowledge 2

    0 = inability to conform with the previous message

    1 = will conform with the previous message

MP: Message Page

    0 = Unformatted Page (UP)

    1 = Message page

Figure 10.6   Encoding or pages in FLP.

Table 10.3   Preferential order of Ethernet technologies on twisted pair.

Technology	Working mode	Global throughput/ connection	Media
10BaseT	half duplex	10 Mbps	2 p UTP 3/4/5
10BaseT	full duplex	2 × 10 Mbps	
100BaseTX			2 p UTP5/STP
100BaseT4	half duplex	100 Mbps	4 p UTP 3/4/5
100BaseT2			2 p UTP 3/4/5
100BaseTX	full duplex	2 × 100 Mbps	2 p UTP5/STP
100BaseT2			2 p UTP 3/4/5
1000BaseT	half duplex	1 Gbps	4 p UTP 5
1000BaseT	full duplex	2 × 1 Gbps	

encountered with the selection of the throughput or of half- or full-duplex mode. The solution usually consists of using management procedures to force one of the edge devices to the highest throughput mode.

Note: In the case of a hub, the auto-negotiation function can be approached in different ways. Either the hub imposes 100 Mbps speed via its messages, and does not change its working mode, or it handles connections dynamically, knowing that it is a 10/100 multi-port repeater, and the first mono-speed connection established will force its throughput for the following ones. To be democratic, the hub could select the speed supported by the majority. One can also imagine a 10 and 100 Mbps double repeater, which must also be equipped with an internal bridge to be complete. Caution: the case of a switch is completely different because each of its interfaces possesses an independent MAC layer, potentially 10/100.

At 1 Gbps

While it was only optional at 10 or 100 Mbps, auto-negotiation becomes indispensable in 1000BaseT (there is no more parallel automatic detection). Besides the definition of a new page (Next Page) which indicates whether the working mode is 1000BaseX or 1000BaseT, half or full duplex, DTE port or repeater, the supplement includes support of the Asymmetric Pause mode (from IEEE 802.3x). Moreover, the auto-negotiation incorporates specific information on transmission coding at 3 or 6 dB in 1000BaseT. Obviously, this information also circulates on the GMII by means of new registers (two of which are shared with 100BaseT2). At 1 Gbps, the 8B/10B coding is used to transport ordered set (/C/ and /I/), which vehicle messages as the FLP do in autonegotiation. Please note that the ordered set do not provide a cable test capability. The Code Group /C1/ and /C2/ followed by /K28.5/D*.*/ are used for configuration, whereas /I1/ and /I2/ are used for Idle. As this code applies to 1000BaseSX,

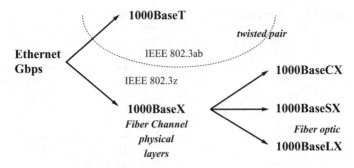

Figure 10.7   Gbps Ethernet technologies.

FX and CX, autonegotiation is therefore available on twisted pair and fiber (for full-duplex and Flow Control support, but without any speed negotiation capacity.

10.4 1000BaseX

After having succeeded in bringing Ethernet up to 100 Mbps (10 times its original throughput), the next step was to multiply the bandwidth once again by 10. This is the heart of 1000BaseX, more commonly called GigaEthernet (GE), dealt with by the IEEE 802.3z subcommittee which has specified the working mode of shared or switched Ethernet with a throughput of 1 Gbps.

In the same way as for 100BaseT, the IEEE has adopted a pragmatic attitude which allowed, as much as possible, the CSMA/CD access method and the MAC frame format to be maintained, recovering an existing Physical level working approximately at this throughput. While supplement u was based on the FDDI specifications for the lower layers, supplement z took up the work done by the ANSI X3.230-1994 committee on Fiber Channel (Physical and Signaling Interface) functioning at up to 800 Mbps.

We should remember, however, that the ever-present requirement to be able to function in shared mode (and thus in half duplex) and to be able to build networks incorporating at least one level of repeaters (to remain inside the Ethernet continuity) imposes very strong constraints on 1 Gbps, such as the lengthening of short frames or the development of the repeater function. In fact, by multiplying the throughput once again by 10 and consequentially dividing the emission time of a frame by 10 (0.51 μs for a frame of 64 bytes), the propagation time (round trip delay) becomes unacceptably restrictive (of the order of 40 m). In half duplex, the solution therefore consists in modifying the minimum slot-time size, changing it from 512 bits (64 bytes) to 512 bytes (8 times more). Therefore, when the emitting coupler has the task of transmitting less than 512 bytes, it has the choice between emitting a frame padded up to 512 bytes by non-data symbols of carrier extension or, to be more efficient, concatenating 2 or more consecutive frames, possibly separated by extension symbols, but without IFG, to constitute a sequence of at least 512 bytes. The result is that a shared network consisting of a unique point-to-point connection can reach 320 m (in optical fiber), with a possible reach of up to somewhere near 412 m in Fast Ethernet.

Table 10.4 Principal characteristics of GigaEthernet technologies.

	1000BaseSX (850 nm)	1000BaseLX (1300 nm)	1000BaseCX	1000BaseT
Max length of connection	220–275 m in 62.5 µm 500–550 m in 50/125 µm	550 m in MMF 5 km in SMF	25 m in STP	100 m in UTP5
Connectors	SC	SC	DB9/ shielded RJ45	RJ45
Attenuation	3.75 dB/km in 62.5 µm 3.5 dB/km in 50/125 µm	1.5 dB/km in MMF 0.5 dB/km in SMF	35.2 dB/100 m @ 625 MHz	24 dB/100 m
Modal bandwidth MHz.km	160–200 in 62.5 µm 400–500 in 50/125 µm	500 in 62.5/125 µm 400–500 in 50/125 µm	–	–

The 1000BaseX technology is subdivided into 3 technologies, CX, SX, and LX, one on twisted pair and two on optical fiber. C stands for Copper for the STP, S means Short Wave Length (in this case, 850 nm) and L means Long Wave Length (that is, 1300 nm). In the first drafts, 1000BaseCX was an implementation on Twinax cable; this was subsequently replaced by shielded twisted pair. The 1000BaseSX technology shows an obvious desire to offer products at affordable cost (thanks to the prices of 850 nm components) and should theoretically meet a vast majority of requirements in terms of distance. In fact, the GEA has inquired about the number and length of multimode fibers already in place to determine the necessity of and interest in each technology. Furthermore, 1000BaseX has been confronted with the problem of DMD, which significantly limits the accessible lengths in 62.5/125 µm.

The code employed in 1000BaseX is of type 8B/10B, which is responsible for the difference between payload and binary line throughput (only four fifths of the bandwidth is used for data transfer). This code is composed of a 5B/6B function applied to the 5 first bits of each byte and a 3B/4B function which globally provide an efficient error detection capacity.

Moreover, the code is balanced and presents a transition density that allows simplified clock recovery.

10.5 1000BaseT

The support of UTP media could have been described in supplement z. But the specific difficulties of defining the adequate coding have postponed its specification, and a dedicated supplement, number ab, has been created. The aim was to define a GigaEthernet working mode on 4 pairs of UTP 5 (thus, 250 Mbps per pair, and 125 Mbaud in practice per pair), on connections of at most 100 m, and capable of working in full duplex with the aid of echo canceling devices.

The inevitably complex coding partly re-utilizes work carried out for 100BaseT2, that is E-Tx/T2, building on PAM5. Coding of 250 Mbps in 125 Mbaud with 5 levels allows integration of a code redundancy higher than 100%, which guarantees good immunity against noise. Moreover, the frequency of 125 MHz allows simplification of cross-compatibility for 100/1000 cards autonegotiation as 100BaseTX also works at this frequency.

The attenuation of a connection must be less than $2.1 \times f^{0.529} + 0.4 / f$; where f is the frequency, going from 1 to 100 MHz. Thus, at 100 MHz, the attenuation must be limited to less than 24 dB/100 m. This formula is an approximation of the figures given by the ANSI/TIA/EIA-568-A standard (see Table 4.5).

10.6 Ethernet 10 Gbps

Although work on the 1 Gbps Ethernet has not yet been completed, and therefore the real impact of this technology on the market is not yet known, those who firmly believe in the long-term durability of Ethernet are already investing into study and research of solutions at 10 Gbps. This could eventually be achieved easily through WDM (Wavelength Division Multiplexing), i.e. using multiple frequency laser emission to transport 10 different Gigabit Ethernet 'channels' on a single fiber.

Chapter 11

Other technical developments

- Full-duplex

- WLAN

- 100VG-AnyLAN

- IsoEthernet

- Daisy chain

11.1 Full-duplex

The IEEE 802.3x subcommittee has begun (belatedly) to deal with the already widespread capacity of functioning in full duplex (simultaneous transmission in both directions). Originally, this was a relatively simple development for Ethernet which, however, allows a non negligible improvement of performance (up to a factor of 2). It consists in exploiting the point-to-point connection of any 10BaseT, 10BaseFL, 100BaseTX, or 100BaseFX type of link, using each connection in full duplex mode: simultaneous transmission and reception are authorized and mean that there is no longer a collision. This solution has the advantage that it needs only minimal modifications on the interface cards (the notion of collision disappears) and sometimes removes the RTD (Round Trip Delay) constraints on certain connections (optical fiber at 100 Mbps and higher). This full-duplex working mode should allow 2×10 Mbps per 10BaseT/F connection to be achieved, which is only possible if the concentrator is a packet switching device (capable of handling at least 2 packets per port concurrently). Obviously, the bus media (10Base5, 10Base2, 10BaseFP, 10Base36) cannot be used in full duplex because the transmission medium is unique (symmetrical pair of coaxial cables, heart of the passive star) whatever the direction of the signal.

Full-duplex technology can also be applied to the 100 Mbps Ethernet, always with switching concentrator devices, but not with an arbitrary Physical layer; thus, 100BaseT4 is intrinsically unable to support full-duplex mode.

Note that in Ethernet, full-duplex mode is substantially simpler to implement than in Token Ring (because at 10 Mbps there was no frame exchange corresponding to a negotiation), but consequently, it could only be used with an explicit declaration at both edge devices. In fact, if one of the two transceivers works in full duplex and its counterpart does not, one will authorize itself to receive and transmit simultaneously, whereas the other will treat this event as a collision. The result is a noticeable dysfunction.

Today, the IEEE specifications on full duplex obviously envisage the use of auto-negotiation to handle its usage dynamically. Moreover, IEEE 802.3x also describes a flow control whose support is also conveyed by the auto-negotiation on twisted pair. It is a simple protocol, independent of the throughput (10/100/1000 Mbps), using Pause messages to silence the counterpart temporarily in case of congestion. This command for the remote partner is represented by a MAC frame demanding a stop of N slot-times (from 0 to 65535 times 512 bit-time).

The flow control meets the requirement of switching devices in case one of them is congested, and is in this case implemented symmetrically, but possibly also

6 bytes	6 bytes	2 bytes	2 bytes	2 bytes	42 bytes	4 bytes
DA = 0180C2 000001	SA	Type = 0x8808	OpCode = 0001	Pause Time	PAD = 0...0	FCS

Figure 11.1 Structure of the MAC Control Pause frame.

between switch and station (or better, server). It could then be implemented asymmetrically, with the switch having the right to impose silence but the server having no possibility of slowing down the flow coming from the switch. The reason for this is simply that the global capacity of the buffers of all stations is considered largely superior to that of the switch or switches. The auto-negotiation allows specification of whether the capacity of the supporting flow control includes the asymmetric mode.

In a 'modern' switched environment, flow control could be improved by being capable of considering the priority of the waiting frames (with the institution of several queues), or their VLAN, or the MAC destination address (to identify the frames affected by the congestion: no-HOL blocking capacity).

Finally, and theoretically, one should know that IEEE 802.3x inserts a MAC control sublayer (responsible for handling Pause messages) between the traditional layer MAC and the MAC client: LLC or other. This new sublayer is proof that flow control is the only function that creates a purely MAC Ethernet frame (except for the old Loopback test frames).

Moreover, IEEE 802.3x recognizes (for the first time) the two MAC frame formats in CSMA/CD, that is, Ethernet V 2.0 (with a type field) as a complement of IEEE 802.3 (with a length field).

11.2 WLAN

Even though the new technologies of wireless local networks are noticeably different from Ethernet, they usually propose simple means of interconnection with Ethernet networks (bearing in mind that currently WLANs only propose throughputs of 1 or 2 Mbps).

WLANs are dealt with by the IEEE committee 802.11, but studies are also carried out at the ETSI (HIPERLAN). The IEEE standard we describe here proposes functioning in the ISM range (Industrial, Scientific & Medical, electromagnetic waves around 2.4 GHz) using a spectrum spreading method (of type FHSS: Frequency Hopping Spread Spectrum, or DSSS: Direct Sequence Spread Spectrum) or in the infrared range.

RTS/CTS:	Request To Send/Clear To Send
PPM:	Pulse Position Modulation
NPMA:	NonPreemptive Multiple Access

The frequency band around 2.4 GHz has the unique advantage of being available in the USA, in Europe, and in Japan, but with different maximum power.

The codings used are robust and require only weak transmission power. The main problem lies in the wish to be able to have several systems function near to each other without having to declare them to each other, and also in disturbed

Table 11.1 Characteristics of the two principal WLAN technologies.

Technology	Frequency band	Type of modulation	Throughput Mbps	Access method	MAC service
IEEE 802.11	2.4–2.4835 GHz (FHSS & DSSS) 850–950 nm infrared	2/4GFSK (FHSS) DB/QPSK (DSSS) 4/16 PPM (ir)	1 or 2	Basic CSMA/CA, RTS/CTS	Authentication, Encryption, energy saving, service time restricted
HIPERLAN	5.15–5.3 GHz	FSK or GMSK	1.47 or 23.53	NPMA	Encryption, energy saving, routing and retransmission, service time restricted

environments. Thus, the product must receive a unique approval by country and not by installation.

Since wireless technologies have a natural affinity with mobile workstations, the problem of power consumption has been studied in detail. In fact, it is important that the WLAN network interface uses as little power as possible, but, above all, that it is able to switch into a 'sleeping' state when inactive. This optimizes the duration of battery operation of portable computers.

Introduction

First of all, we must consider the difficulty represented by wireless communication inside a building, given that it must work with a medium quality that varies in time and space and with interference due to reflections of the signal and electromagnetic disturbances (by similar or other systems). Thus, two stations belonging to the same system (effectively being part of the same cell) are not always guaranteed to see each other (hidden node phenomenon). Obstacles can hide them from each other although both can see the access point of the cell.

Moreover, WLANs must be able to function with movable stations, possibly even with mobile stations. Two services have been defined: an asynchronous delivery of MSDUs (MAC Service Data Units) which must always be supported, and a temporarily limited (plesiochronous) carriage. Mobility also introduces a complexity at level 3 (the station can move from one side of an IP router to the other) which will not be treated in this book.

The IEEE 802.11 model distinguishes two sublayers for level 1: PLCP (Physical Layer Convergence Protocol) and PMD (Physical Medium Dependent). In addition, several blocks are defined concerning management and administration of a system.

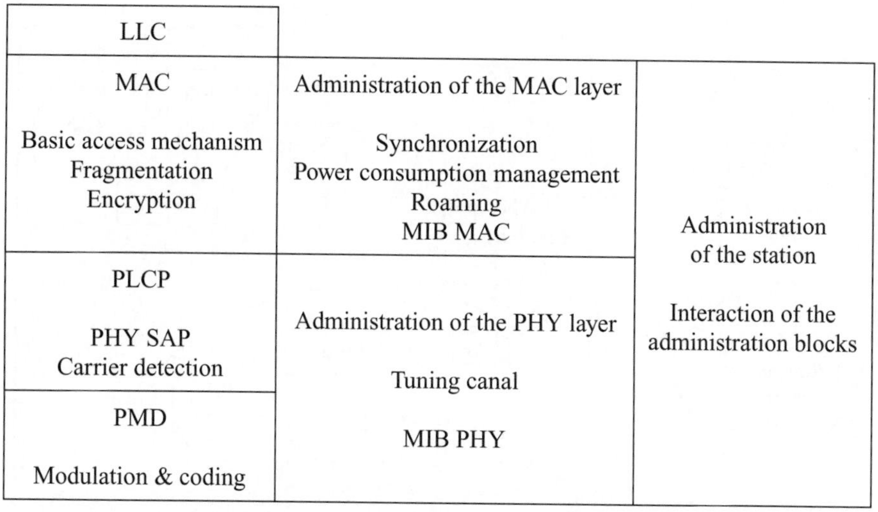

LLC		
MAC Basic access mechanism Fragmentation Encryption	Administration of the MAC layer Synchronization Power consumption management Roaming MIB MAC	Administration of the station Interaction of the administration blocks
PLCP PHY SAP Carrier detection	Administration of the PHY layer Tuning canal	
PMD Modulation & coding	MIB PHY	

Figure 11.2   Layers and sublayers of IEEE 802.11.

Two working modes are described. The first consists of a BSA or BSS (Basic Service Area or Set) network inside which the stations can communicate directly with each other or via an AP (Access Point). The second mode (ESA or ESS: Extended Service Area or Set) relates several BSS cells by means of Access Points. This allows mobile stations to maintain their access to fixed resources (see Figure 11.3).

The use of an Access Point is generally preferred. Thus, the stations begin by searching for the nearest AP (in terms of signal quality) and connect to it. The traffic is then carried from one station to the other by the AP.

MAC functioning

The MAC layer builds on a CSMA/CA method. It includes an acknowledgment at MAC level for unicast frames. It must be able to handle hidden nodes, limited delay services, and the requirements of confidentiality and security (access control).

The CSMA/CA attempts to minimize the probability of collision and to guarantee a good efficiency under heavy load. For this, it imposes verification of a minimum duration of a DIFS before sending if the medium is found to be free. In addition, it includes a complementary random delay (Backoff) in the DIFS before sending if the medium was found to be engaged. DIFS is the DCF Inter Frame Space, where DCF represents the Distributed Coordination Function between all stations of the BSS. Note that the backoff has an exponential growth factor in case of retransmission. In the case of correct reception of the frame (CRC correct), the addressee immediately returns an acknowledgment.

The MAC service provides an interface towards LLC, authorizing frames of at most 2304 bytes. It also includes the capacity of fragmentation to adapt itself to the real characteristics of the different PHYs.

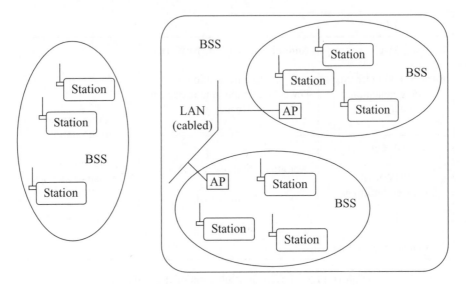

Figure 11.3 BSS and ESS cells.

2 bytes	2 bytes	6 bytes	6 bytes	6 bytes	2 bytes	6 bytes	0–2312	4 bytes
Frame control	Duration ID	Address 1	Address 2	Address 3	Sequence control	Address 4	Data	CRC

Figure 11.4 MAC frame in IEEE 802.11.

2 bits	2 bits	4 bits	1 bit	1 bit	1 bit	1 bit	1 bit	1 bit	1 bit	1 bit
Protocol version	Type	Sub-type	To DS	From DS	More Frag	Retry	Power Mgt	More Data	WEP	Rsvd

Figure 11.5 Frame Control field.

The optional PCF (Point Coordination Function) allows a faster delivery system to be provided (limited in time) in conjunction with the asynchronous service. The PCF resides in the Access Point. This function can carry voice and data, as opposed to the distributed coordination function (DCF) capabilities. DCF and PCF successively distribute the occupation among themselves, with alternate phases with and without contention.

There are three types of frame, control frames, administration frames, and data frames. They differ by their headers.

The sequence control field is used to filter out the duplicates generated by the acknowledgment mechanism.

In Figure 11.5, DS is the Distribution System, used to interconnect a set of BSSs and LANs to create an ESS, and WEP stands for Wired Equivalent Privacy, which allows a confidentiality function to be provided from station to station. It allows encryption of data encapsulated in the frame, using an algorithm based on a secret key of 40 bits and an initialization vector (IV) of 24 bits sent together with the data. This IV can be used for several consecutive frames, or can be different for each frame.

The PHY interfaces

The PHY layer must be able to function at different speeds. It must be capable of determining whether the medium is free (for CSMA/CA). This is called CCA (Clear Channel Assessment), also known as Virtual Carrier Sense. Finally, with the aid of PHY administration, it realizes channel tuning.

Three types of PHY are defined, two with spectrum spreading around 2.4 GHz with frequency hopping (FHSS) or direct sequence (DSSS), plus one infrared base band technology. They must all be capable of functioning at 1 or 2 Mbps.

FHSS

FHSS uses 79 channels of disjoint frequencies (23 in Japan) with a spacing of 1 MHz. The authorized power of 100 mW in Europe and 1W in the USA allows realization of cells of nearly 200 m in size within a building, and of 1 to 5 km outside (using external antennas). The channel hopping sequence follows a pseudo-random order, the kth sequence being of type: $2402 + (b[i] + k)$ mod 79, where b[i] is the basic sequence from 0 to 78. This technique theoretically allows cohabitation of 26 similar networks, which also represents an even more important global throughput.

The throughput is 1 or 2 Mbps, using a 2- or 4-level GFSK code. Support of 2 Mbps is optional. The broadcast traffic (at MAC level) is usually transported at 1 Mbps.

PLCP (Figure 11.6)

10 bytes	2 bytes	12 bits	4 bits	2 bytes	N bytes
Sync	SFD = 0x0CBD	Length	Signaling field	CRC (PLCP header)	PPDU (PLCP_PDU)
PLCP preamble		PLCP header			PPDU

Figure 11.6   The PLCP field in FHSS.

The preamble and header are always sent at 1 Mbps and in 2-level GFSK; the change of speed in transmission and reception takes place after the CRC.

Only one of the 4 bits of the Signaling field is used to indicate the speed of 1 Mbps (in 2GFSK) or 2 Mbps (in 4GFSK), the remaining 3 bits are reserved for future use.

DSSS

DSSS tries to transmit in an intentionally large spectrum with a more feeble power density to protect itself against perturbations localized in a frequency band. The Barker emission sequence corresponding to one bit is composed of multiple levels possessing good auto-correlation properties. Thus, the coding brings a gain of 10.4 dB with respect to noise, and an interesting robustness against echo superposition.

The power for transmission differs according to country (as with FHSS): 1 W in the USA, 100 mW in Europe, and 10 mW/MHz in Japan.

PLCP (Figure 11.7)

16 bytes	2 bytes	1 byte	1 byte	2 bytes	2 bytes	N bytes
Sync	SFD = 0xF3A0	Signal = N.100 kbps	Service = 00 (802.11)	Length	CRC (PLCP header)	MPDU
PLCP preamble		PLCP header				MPDU
PPDU (PLCP_PDU)						

Figure 11.7 The PLCP field in DSSS.

Preamble and header are always sent at 1 Mbps and in DBPSK; the change of speed also takes place after the CRC.

The Signal field specifies the speed in steps of 100 kbps; thus 0x0A indicates 1 Mbps in DBPSK, and 0x14 indicates 2 Mbps in DQPSK.

For stations which can save energy by changing automatically into a sleeping state in phases of inactivity, the AP has the task of temporarily storing the frames addressed to them. The AP informs the sleeping stations that they have frames waiting for them by means of the TIM (Traffic Indication Map) sent together with each Beacon frame.

Given the simplicity offered by the complete absence of a physical connection for a portable PC, it seems reasonable to foresee an important development for wireless LAN technologies. The period of full expansion is obviously more difficult to estimate, but should be reached at most five years from now, when the technology will allow higher throughputs and even more Plug & Play.

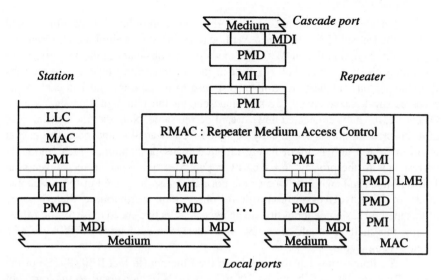

PMI: Physical Medium Independent
MII: Medium Independent Interface
PMD: Physical Medium Dependent
MDI: Medium Dependent Interface
LME: Layer Management Entity

Figure 11.8   Decomposition of the 100VG-AnyLAN elements: station and repeater. The four connections shown between the PMI and the MII correspond to the four channels of the physical architecture.

11.3 100VG-AnyLAN

The 100VG-AnyLAN technology, which denotes 100 Mbps on voice-grade twisted pair cables that support all LAN technologies (in fact, Ethernet and Token Ring), was introduced by Hewlett-Packard (Figure 11.8). It represents an ambitious proposal for an evolution of Ethernet, since, apart from the physical layer, it will involve a change in the access method to eliminate the probabilistic aspect and a merging of the two most common types of LANs. However, it retains a shared access method, sharing the bandwidth over all the accesses by time-division multiplexing.

Nevertheless, it should be stressed that the compatibility with Ethernet and Token Ring applications does not imply that 100VG-AnyLAN will be able to act as a gateway between these local area networks. In fact, interconnection elements, of the bridge or router type, will be needed systematically to access the traditional networks.

The first consequence of these differences has been the assignment to a new IEEE committee, 802.12. This is despite the fact that originally (in 1992) the project, then called 100BaseVG, only concerned Ethernet.

A new deterministic access method has been introduced: the polling round robin or the Demand Priority Access Method (DPAM), which eliminates the penalizing phenomenon of collision. With this method, the hubs manage the network. After a learning phase, the root hub (highest in the tree structure) records the requests from the stations (requests to emit in response to its polling) and lets each of its accesses speak successively (by stopping sending the idle signal on their links). Of course, the hubs connected downstream do the same. Note that the UpLink port of a downstream hub is specifically designed for cascaded connection. The packet received by the hub is immediately directed to its destination, which implicitly corresponds to the privacy and security capabilities developed in recent years on 10BaseT hubs and switches. One of the ports may also be placed in 'promiscuous' mode, so that it receives all the traffic for observation. Furthermore, the efficiency of this method has made it possible to achieve an effective speed close to 100 Mbps. Finally, this method should also have short delays in comparison with those of a token passing method.

The frames may equally well be in the Ethernet (in fact IEEE 802.3) or the Token Ring format, which makes 100VG-AnyLAN a 'universal' technology, but also shows the distance separating these conventional LANs, just like FDDI several years ago.

Two different priority levels may be associated with the traffic (normal and high), which makes it possible to incorporate synchronous traffic in the data communications and at the same time guarantee a given bandwidth for this type of communication. The Target Transmission Time (TTT) means that an upper bound can be placed on the access delay and a constant average speed can be guaranteed. However, traffic with normal priority is automatically assigned a high priority after a waiting time of 200 to 300 ms.

The 'intelligence' of the 100VG-AnyLAN hub includes the ability to modify its behavior on request, to monitor the traffic as a function of the packets and transmission requests and assemble more detailed management information than in the case of a simple 10BaseT hub.

In terms of cabling, 100VG-AnyLAN can operate on twisted pair or optical fiber. Fiber allows lengths of 1 km for Ethernet and 2 km for Token Ring. On UTP category 3, 4 or 5 cables, four pairs are needed to reach 100 m, against two pairs for STP. Note that, for UTP5 and STP, a length of 200 meters per segment would be possible. The draft also describes the use of UTP cable with 25 pairs.

100VG-AnyLAN uses a 5-bit conversion of type 5B/6B, which requires three mapping tables to ensure that the signal is balanced in terms of 0s and 1s, and an upstream scrambler. There exist 6-bit codes with two 1s and four 0s, which are said to be of weight two (and unbalanced), codes with three 0s and three 1s, which are said to be balanced, and codes with two 0s and 4s, which are said to be of weight four (also unbalanced). These processes run on each pair as shown in Figure 11.9 and give the pattern structure of Figure 11.10.

The bits are transmitted on the four pairs in full multiplexing mode, with an offset of half a sextet between pairs 1 and 2 and pairs 3 and 4. Thus, each pair operates at 30 Mbps, with a main frequency at 15 MHz, similar to that of 10BaseT (10 MHz).

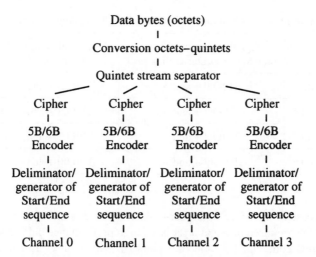

Figure 11.9 Partitioning of the data transmission. The scrambler uses the generator polynomial $x^{11} + x^9 + 1$.

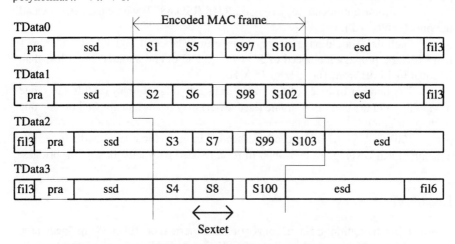

pra: preamble, succession of 24 times the two bits 01 for each channel of the MII
ssd: Start of Frame Delimiter Normal priority (SFDN) = 111100 000011
or   Start of Frame Delimiter High priority (SFDH)   = 100000 111110
Fil3: FillPr = 101 padding before the preamble on channels 2 and 3
or   Fill3L = 100 padding associated with EFD2 when necessary
or   Fill3H = 011 padding associated with EFD4 or IPM when necessary
esd: EFD2 (End of Frame Delimiter for following code of weight two) = 111111 000011 000001
or   EDF4 (End of Frame Delimiter for following code of weight four) = 000000 111100 111110
or   Invalid Packet Marker (IPM) = 110000 011111 110000
fil6: Fill6L = 100011 padding associated with EFD2 when necessary
or   Fill6H = 011100 padding associated with EFD4 or IPM when necessary

Figure 11.10 Decomposition of a 64-byte frame across the four pairs.

Table 11.2   RJ45 pinout assignment for 100VG-AnyLAN port.

Pins	Signal on station side or on that of repeater Uplink port	Signal side of repeater Downlink port
1 and 2	TPIO:0 + and −	TPIO:3 + and −
3 and 6	TPIO:1 + and −	TPIO:2 + and −
4 and 5	TPIO:2 + and −	TPIO:1 + and −
7 and 8	TPIO:3 + and −	TPIO:0 + and −

A future increase in the speed on higher-quality cables can therefore be envisaged. We note that the proposed physical layer has a high performance but is complicated; it uses a 5B/6B code and NRZ on four pairs (in half duplex) instead of two (in simplex) to multiply the bandwidth of 10BaseT by 10. However, VG cables with two pairs should make it possible to achieve speeds of 50 Mbps.

The connector technology is again RJ45 (ISO 8877) where the MDI uses all the pins (Table 11.2).

Each link should have a characteristic impedance of 100 ± 15 Ohm from 1 to 15 MHz, a propagation speed of 5.7 ns/m (0.585 c) and an attenuation less than or equal to 14 dB from 100 kHz to 15 MHz.

The number of bytes of the frame transmitted is arbitrary (within the range of validity) and the end of the frame (last sextet) may occur equally well on any one of the four pairs.

100VG-AnyLAN hubs can be cascaded in up to three levels, which permits a geographical coverage of up to 600 m for a twisted pair network with no bridges.

Evolution

A priori the transition from a conventional Ethernet or Token Ring local area network based on structured cabling to 100VG-AnyLAN does not present a problem. Four pairs per port are vital for operation at 100 Mbps (except on STP), otherwise only half the bandwidth will be available (50 Mbps if there are only two UTP pairs).

Once the problem of the medium has been settled, the existing topology (tree or ring structure) and the existing structured cabling (UTP, STP and optical fiber) can be retained, and it only remains to swap the active elements (interface cards and hubs, not forgetting interconnection devices).

This migration, which may be progressive, will enable the attached stations to access a very comfortable bandwidth, while retaining the associated network software. In addition, 100VG-AnyLAN provides plesiochronous transport of traffic for future multimedia applications.

Conclusion

For managers confronted with the requirement for higher speeds on their Ethernet networks who wish to improve the architecture, the choice has been difficult up to now. Until now, they might have envisaged eliminating the bottlenecks by inserting a technology with a higher performance in the infrastructure, such as FDDI; but this amounted to a wager on the future of a new network.

Then, 100BaseT and 100VG-AnyLAN provided access to 100 Mbps, either by a simple evolution of the speed of Ethernet or by correcting the main shortcomings of the access method. These two concurrent offerings provide for re-use of the existing cabling in the case of twisted pairs and optical fibers and the transport of frames in the standard format.

But 100BaseT has the appearance of a natural evolution which retains the characteristics of Ethernet, while 100VG-AnyLAN is much more ambitious in that it incorporates the Token Ring technology and defines the transport of plesiochronous traffic, therefore appears more revolutionary, as it imposes drastic changes to the network equipment.

11.4 IsoEthernet

Another evolution of Ethernet involves the incorporation of support for synchronous channels, that is, the transport in parallel with the standard traffic of asynchronous data of one or more channels in which the transit time and the bandwidth are fixed and bounded. This type of local area network, called ISLAN (IsoLAN for isochronous) falls under the IEEE 802.9 committee with Supplements a, b, c and d. IEEE 802.9 describes data rates of 4 and 20 Mbps (3.584 and 19.968 Mbps, to be precise).

Supplement a deals with the IsoEthernet PHY at 16 Mbps, while Supplement b deals with AU to AU internetworking (AU: access unit, that is, an IsoEthernet hub). Supplements c and d deal with the Managed Object Conformance Statement (MOCS) and Protocol Implementation Conformance Statement (PICS). We note that the end station becomes the Integrated Services Terminal Equipment (ISTE).

More precisely, IsoEthernet offers two services: a primary service (Multiservice) retaining the usual 10 Mbps but with an extra 6 Mbps full duplex channel (like the WBC offered by FDDI-II) and a secondary, all isochronous service with a 16 Mbps full duplex channel, which can be used, for example, for video. In all cases, IsoEthernet, like FDDI, uses a 4B/5B encoding which is more efficient than the Manchester code. To achieve synchronous operation, IsoEthernet is based on a periodic emission of cells or cycles every 125 μs. These cycles, which consist of 512 symbols (5B) corresponding to 256 bytes, are the result of a multiplexing of the various channels transported.

Table 11.3 Comparative table for the main 100 Mbps technologies.

Technology	**Ethernet**	**100baseT**	**100VG-AnyLAN**	**FDDI**
Standard/draft	IEEE 802.3	IEEE 802.3u	IEEE 802.12	ANSI X3T9.5
Bit rate	10 Mbps	100 Mbps	100 Mbps	100 Mbps
Access method	CSMA/CD	CSMA/CD	Demand priority	Token passing
Characteristics	Probabilistic	Probabilistic	Deterministic	Deterministic
Frames transported	Ethernet	Ethernet	Ethernet Token Ring plesiochronous	FDDI: asynchronous and plesiochronous
Types of medium	Coaxial cable Twisted pair Optical fiber	Twisted pair Optical fiber	Twisted pair Optical fiber	Optical fiber Multi/single mode twisted pair
Twisted pair segment length	100 m 250 m realizable	100 m	100 m (200 m possible)	100 m
Multimode optical segment	2 km	400 km	1 km 2 km (Token Ring)	2 km
Repeaters/series	4	2	5	[500]
Network diameter	4 km (+ AUI)	400 m	1 km (Ethernet)	100 km
TP network	500 m (+ AUI)	200 m (+ 5 m)	600 m	200 m
2 twisted pairs	UTP 3/4/5	STP and UTP5	STP	STP and UTP5
Supplement	10baseT	100baseTX	–	TP-PMD
Transmission mode	1 Tx and 1 Rx	1 Tx and 1 Rx	2 p. full duplex	1 Tx and 1 Rx
Coding used	Manchester	4B/5B + MLT-3	5B/6B	4B/5B + MLT-3
Main frequency	10 MHz/pair	31.25 MHz/p.	30 MHz/pair	31.25 MHz/p.
4 twisted pairs		UTP 3/4/5	UTP 3/4/5	
Supplement		100baseT4	–	
Transmission mode	N.A.	3 pairs data + 1 pair collision	4 pairs full duplex	N.A.
Coding used		8B/6T	5B/6B	
Main frequency		25 MHz/pair	15 MHz/pair	

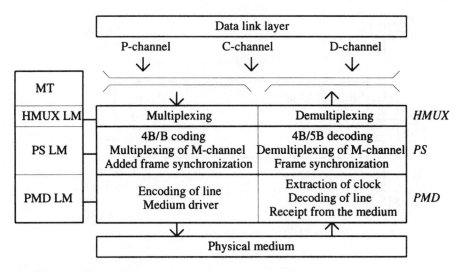

HMUX: Hybrid Multiplexer
PS: Physical Signaling
PMD: Physical Medium Dependent
MT: Management

Figure 11.11 Decomposition of the physical layer (HMUX, PS, PMD).

Thus, the multi-service mode of operation incorporates (see Figure 11.11):

- A half-duplex Ethernet packet channel (P-channel) at 10.016 Mbps
- An isochronous full duplex channel (C-channel or 96 dedicated B channels) at 6.144 Mbps
- A full duplex channel (D-channel) at 64 kbps
- A full-duplex maintenance channel (M-channel) at 96 kbps
- A full-duplex frame-synchronization channel at 64 kbps.

This amounts to a total of 16.384 Mbps. All these channels are multiplexed in each cycle, representing, 313, 192, 2, 3 and 2 symbols per cycle, respectively.

As far as the all-isochronous service is concerned, it comprises:

- A full-duplex isochronous channel (C-channel or 248 dedicated B-channels) at 15.872 Mbps
- A full-duplex channel (D-channel) at 64 kbps
- A full-duplex maintenance channel (M-channel) at 96 kbps
- A full-duplex frame synchronization channel at 64 kbps
- An empty (idle) channel at 288 kbps.

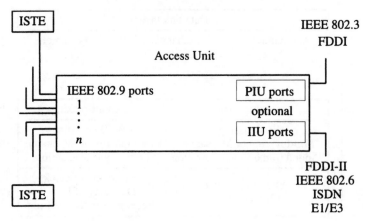

Figure 11.12 Example of an Access Unit.

In both cases, with a 4B/5B and NRZI encoding, the total speed of 16.384 Mbps becomes an effective speed of 20.48 Mbps on the medium. This also gives a main frequency of 10.24 MHz, which is almost the same as in standard Ethernet with a Manchester encoding. This means that it is possible to retain the same implementation rules as for 10BaseT, namely 11.5 dB maximum attenuation from 5 to 10 MHz on a twisted pair link and a maximum delay of 1000 ns. However, the isochronous constraints impose additional limits on a complete path, as indicated in the table in the section on repeaters in Chapter 10.

The M-channel is managed at the Physical Signaling level between the Layer Management and the corresponding PHY blocks.

IEEE 802.9a describes all the LAN functionality, but also that of the PABX type, which makes IsoEthernet the only LAN service with such an isochronous capability. In fact, the Access Unit (or repeater) may have isochronous IEEE 802.9 ports and also, optionally, Ethernet packet or FDDI ports (PIU: Packet Interface Unit) and isochronous ISDN, DQDB, FDDI-II, ATM, E1/T1 or E3/T3 ports (IIU: Isochronous Interface Unit) (see Figure 11.12).

It is apparent that such a device must incorporate a switching capability, embodied in the Packet Switching/Multiplexing Unit (PSMU) and the Isochronous Switching/Multiplexing Unit (ISMU).

The IEEE 802.9 standardization is effective, but it does not appear to have been followed by product announcements. IEEE 802.9a and b, scheduled for issue in 1995, were more encouraging, since they permitted a flexible integration into the Ethernet architectures. In fact, the multi-service mode includes a standard 10 Mbps channel and functions on the same type of cabling. However, as we have seen, terminal equipment is notably different from and much more complex than the usual hubs.

Nevertheless, this is a very complete technology which provides a perfect answer to the requirement to integrate synchronous traffic in data communication infrastructures.

11.5 Daisy chain

Finally, another solution derived from Ethernet on twisted pairs has been proposed by a number of manufacturers which involves chaining the elements, rather than arranging them in a star around the hub as in the standard topology. We note that certain implementations of StarLAN (1Base5) already had this capability at 1 Mbps. This non-standardized method allows one to install a minimum length of physical medium (if the user does not envisage structured prewiring) or to re-use the cables of a LocalTalk network. Approximately ten accesses can be chained in this way.

Chapter 12

Elements of the network

- The medium

- Transceivers

- The AUI cable

- The MII and GMII interfaces

- The interface card

- 10 Mbps repeaters

- 100 Mbps and 1 Gbps repeaters

- Test equipment

The network consists of the passive medium and the active components (Figure 12.1). The medium is the base to which the devices that will use it for their communications are attached. The transceiver (sometimes abbreviated to Xver) is the medium attachment unit, which is attached to the connector card by the drop cable. The connector card is the interface which interprets the packets from the network for the station or, conversely, which adapts the data from the applications to send them on the cable.

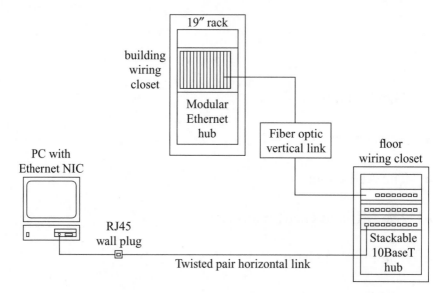

Figure 12.1   Schematic view of the main components of the network.

12.1 The medium

The physical carrier for Ethernet consists of segments of coaxial cable, possibly interconnected by fiber optic links. Other media were subsequently added to these possibilities, such as the twisted pair or, more recently, the air.

50 Ohm coaxial cables

Originally, Ethernet was defined for operation with a coaxial cable (relatively bulky) as the bus. Later, a much more practical solution, with a lower performance, on a cable with similar characteristics was developed.

The standard coaxial cable

The basic medium is the yellow coaxial cable with a characteristic impedance of 50 Ohm. This was the first medium defined, being initially associated with transceiver connection points with a tap connection, then, more generally, with a type N connector technology. As opposed to thin cable, which we shall discuss later, this cable is sometimes called thick cable. The most important mechanical characteristics of the cable are the following:

- The central conductor is made of solid copper and has a diameter of 2.17 ± 0.013 mm.

- The dielectric which insulates the two conductors is such that the desired propagation rate can be achieved and the attenuation is limited to the required value.

- The cylindrical conductor consisting of an aluminum shield (braid and foil elements) has an internal diameter of 6.15 mm and an external diameter of 8.28 ± 0.18 mm. This braid, which also acts as a screen, must be grounded at just one of its two ends (to avoid the passage of current in the cable due to masses with different potentials). The intermediate connectors should thus be insulated from the metal components on the cable path.

- The external sheath is either of colored PVC (polyvinyl chloride – yellow is recommended) with an external diameter of 10.29 ± 0.18 mm, or of fluoropolymer (for example, FEP or E-CTFE) with an external diameter of 9.53 ± 0.25 mm. It should have a black ring drawn on it every 2.5 m as a unit of measurement for the taps.

- A length of at most 500 m per segment.

- A distance of at least 2.5 m between each attachment point.

- At most 100 connections per segment.

- A minimum bend radius of 25 cm (10 inches). Note that, while it is not advisable to split the coaxial cable segment, the cable sections should have a length of 23.4, 70.2 or 117 m. These three lengths, which are multiples of 23.4 m (one, three or fives times the dimension of a bit on the cable) are such that the reflections which occur on the lines are superimposed out of phase.

The physical characteristics of the cable are as follows:

- A characteristic impedance of 50 Ohm (reminder: $Z = 138/\sqrt{\varepsilon}.\log(D/d)$).

- An attenuation less than 17 dB/km at 10 MHz and less than 12 dB/km at 5 MHz.

- A resistance for the two wires (round trip) of less than 10 Ohm/km.

- A signal propagation speed greater than or equal to $0.77c = 2.3 \times 10^8$ m/s, corresponding to a maximum period of 21.65 bit times to cross a segment.

- A cable attachment point should not give rise to a signal reflection greater than 4%.

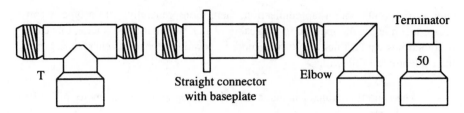

Figure 12.2 Elements of the basic BNC connector technology.

The standard coaxial cable costs around 4 US dollars per meter, which makes it a relatively expensive medium. This price, like the prices given elsewhere in the book, is only given for information, as an order of magnitude.

The associated connector technology is of type N (Figure 12.2). Each cable segment ends with a male connector. The segments may be interlinked by straight female–female connectors, with or without a baseplate (the baseplate is used to fix the connector to a patch-cabinet plate) or by Ts, which allow the connection of a transceiver. At each end of the complete segment a terminator (50 ± 1% Ohm from 0 to 20 MHz and a phase shift of < 5°) should be screwed on for the purposes of load adaptation. There are other type N connector modules such as the straight–straight male connector, the male–female elbow (with a right angle), the male terminator, the female terminator, and the N–BNC adapter.

In most cases, the cable sheath consists of PVC for use within buildings, polyethylene being reserved for passage to the outside. PVC burns less easily than polyethylene and thus tends to limit the spread of fires. However, PVC releases toxic and corrosive gases when it is burnt, together with opaque smoke. The toxic gases include halides and may also degrade to hydrochloric acid. Its drawbacks may have non-trivial consequences for the occupants of buildings in case of fire.

Thin coaxial cable

Another type of coaxial cable was introduced in an IEEE supplement and was even incorporated in the ISO standard, namely thin coaxial cable of the RG58 type. Like the yellow cable, it has a characteristic impedance of 50 Ohm, but is much thinner, so less resistant and considerably cheaper. Its main characteristics are:

- A central conductor of electroplated copper with a diameter of 0.89 ± 0.05 mm.
- A dielectric of a quality such that the cable has the required electrical characteristics.
- A cylindrical conductor consisting of aluminum tape and electroplated copper braid, with an external diameter of 2.95 ± 0.15 mm.
- An external sheath of either PVC (often black) with a diameter of 4.9 ± 0.3 mm or FEP with external diameter 4.8 ± 0.3 mm.

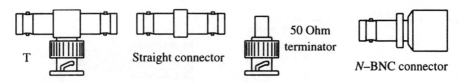

Figure 12.3   Basic BNC connectors.

- A maximum length of 185 m per segment.
- A minimum distance of 50 cm between two attachment points.
- At most 30 connections per segment.
- A minimum bend radius of 5 cm.
- A signal propagation speed greater than or equal to 0.65 c.

The other electrical specifications are the same as those above.

Thin coaxial cable is associated with a BNC connector technology (Figure 12.3), which is also less expensive than the type N connector technology. When using thin cable, it is general practise to run the cable right up to the machine, where the connection is then made using a T (BNC), the transceiver being built into the interface card. In this case, care should be taken to ensure that the T does not separate the cable of the BNC connector from the card by more than 4 cm, otherwise there is a risk of impedance disturbance.

In the above, we saw that there exists a straight N–BNC connector which can be used to connect a standard coaxial cable segment to a thin coaxial cable segment. This type of connection is not described in the standard, but works provided the distances are proportionately respected. A segment consisting of cables of the two types (x meters of standard cable and y meters of thin cable) should satisfy $x/500 + y/185 < 1$.

Thin coaxial cable costs less than 1 US dollar per meter, which is much more affordable than the standard coaxial cable, making this a preferable physical medium for small installations where economy is desirable.

Optical fibers

Ethernet V 2.0 defined point-to-point optical links over 1 km, without specifying the media from which they should be constructed. This could only be fiber optic cable.

Since the IEEE standardization has taken a great deal of time, various types of fiber and connector have been used by manufacturers. However, the optical fiber retained for Ethernet in FOIRL, then 10BaseF, is the graded-index multimode silica fiber with a core of diameter 62.5 μm. The ST connector technology is recommended from 10BaseF, to replace SMA. Exceeding the one kilometer limit for FOIRL, links may extend to two kilometers with 10BaseF; however, in fact, manufacturers have for some years offered (non-standardized) hardware capable of supporting much longer optical lines (4 km).

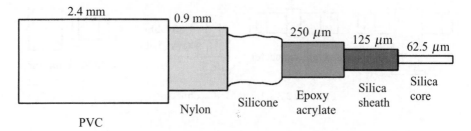

Figure 12.4   Overall structure of an optical fiber.

In practice, fiber remains an expensive physical carrier; for example, a ten-fiber cable costs less than 15 US dollars per meter. Finally, we note that, in practice, fibers in the form in which they can be handled have a diameter of 250 μm rather than 62.5 μm. This is explained by Figure 12.4.

The main characteristics of optical fiber suitable for all Ethernet installations, bearing in mind preparations for 10BaseF and 100BaseT, are listed below.

Multimode graded-index silica optical fiber has a core diameter of 62.5 $\pm$ 3 μm, a sheath diameter of 125 $\pm$ 2 μm, a numerical aperture of 0.275 $\pm$ 0.015, and attenuation at 850 nm of less than 3.5 dB/km, a bandwidth greater than 160 MHz.km at 850 nm (IEC 793-2 type A1b requires more: 200 MHz.km) and a propagation speed of 0.67 c (5 μs/km).

With a view to future use of FDDI or 100BaseFX, one might ensure that the fiber proposed also has the following characteristics: an attenuation at 1300 nm of less than 1.5 dB/km and a bandwidth greater than 500 MHz.km at 1300 nm. Links of a length of at most 2 km should also be used, in conformance with 10BaseF (except for the passive case) and FDDI MMF-PMD.

10BaseF mentions a relatively self-evident practical detail, in that it recommends that all unused optical connectors should be covered with a cap. This provides a protection against dust and also ensures that operation of the active devices is not disturbed by parasitic optical signals. Finally, this limits the risk of someone involuntarily looking directly at the light ray from an emitter.

Twisted pairs

StarLAN already used the unshielded twisted pair, but its rate was only one tenth that of 10Base5. Thus, the development of 10BaseT had to be accompanied by a deployment of hardware.

In fact, the twisted pair is an inexpensive medium, which is easy to install and may possibly be used for other types of network, which is not the case for the thick 50 Ohm cable. Within a few years users became so infatuated with it that it became a preferred medium for Ethernet installations, and today shares with optical fiber the privilege of being viewed as a physical carrier for the future.

10BaseT repeated the specifications for the twisted pair given in 1Base5, namely, two UTPs with a characteristic impedance of 100 Ohm, an attenuation less than 11.5 dB (from 5 to 10 MHz) per segment, a propagation speed of 0.585 c (or 5.7 ns/m), and a maximum recommended length of 100 m per segment. However, the choice of the unshielded twisted pair is governed by the desire to take over the existing telephone cable in buildings for data communication purposes. Unfortunately, this praiseworthy intention is rarely implemented in practice, since telephone signals may have a high voltage (48 V for the bell circuits) and may perturb the data transfer if all the cables are contiguous.

In spite of everything, the quasi-universality of the UTP, on which signals for Token Ring (with maximum lengths less than for STP), LocalTalk, ISDN, ARCnet, 100BaseT and FDDI and ATM make it the favored physical carrier for prewired installations. In brief, prewiring involves providing services to all the offices when the cables are laid and the wall sockets installed, independently of the immediate needs, but with a view to medium- or long-term gain. The physical topology is still a star around the plant room, even though it can be adapted by relooping the segments at the level of the patch cabinet. Provided the lengths are suitable (generally limited to 100 m per segment), the twisted pair is a preferred medium, since it can accommodate both Ethernet and rival local area networks. However, when long lines are involved (to be specific, longer than 100 m), one should then think in terms of optical fiber, which has far superior qualities (low attenuation, wide bandwidth). Fiber optic cables have their place in prewiring since they often represent the most practical medium for interlinking the plant rooms in one or more buildings.

Although STPs are not well adapted in terms of characteristic impedance (150 Ohm rather than 100 Ohm), given their better characteristics they will be suitable for and will permit (using products from certain manufacturers) lengths greater than 200 m, still in 10BaseT technology. We note that STP should be used to advantage, since the quality of the adaptation on twisted pair is far less important than on coaxial cable. This is because a mismatch on coaxial cable generates a reflected signal whose power is proportional to the difference in impedance. This undesirable signal circulates backwards and may be superposed on the valid signals (with the frame moving in both directions on the cable, from the point of emission). However, on twisted pair, the reflected signal circulates in the opposite direction to the valid signals, and can only be superimposed after a second reflection, when its power is even weaker (function of the square of the coefficient of reflection).

By way of indication, a cable of four twisted pairs costs less than 1 US dollar per meter.

Other possibilities

Some companies have developed transmission facilities outside the specifications of the standard and its supplements. There have been two approaches in the domain of local area networks, first in response to a need for point-to-point, face-to-face links, and second, in order to provide accesses in the offices in a building, based on the capillary cabling.

As far as the first requirement is concerned, solutions have existed for several years which permit links, for example, between two buildings, without the need to install any cable (which may be a crucial advantage in certain cases, such as when a road is crossed). Thus, it is possible to implement a duplex frequency-modulated microwave link at 23 GHz between two points which may be several kilometers apart, or a link using centimeter waves with the spread-spectrum technology (DS-SS, direct sequence spread spectrum; and FH-SS, frequency-hopped spread spectrum) generally with a rate of several hundred kbps. The accessible coverage is a direct function of the authorized emitted power.

In the same area, we find a laser link extending up to 1 km, with a rate of 10 Mbps or above. This type of equipment is mounted on the roof of a building or on a window sill, and must be aligned in a precise direction. It is designed to be perturbed relatively little by climatic variations, fog, rain or snow. The last technique is the only one which is not subject to authorization by public authorities or by the authority responsible for the assignment and use of frequency ranges.

Conclusion   The original medium, the yellow coaxial cable, is being progressively abandoned in favor of unshielded twisted pair and optical fiber.

In fact, the most commonly drawn structure is constructed as a star on a fiber optic backbone with terminating cables in twisted pair serving the offices. The standard coaxial cable no longer has a great attraction, since its capabilities have been exceeded by those of fiber and its cost is too high in comparison with cabling based on twisted pair. Only qualities of the thin coaxial cable are still of interest for the particular case of small installations with a high numerical connection density, for which the bus topology is still the most advantageous.

In Part III, we shall see why the recent choices of cabling are almost all oriented towards twisted-pair and fiber optic cables.

12.2 Transceivers

The transceiver (its name comes from the fusion of the two words *transmitter* and *receiver*), called the MAU in the IEEE 802.3 document, is the active element that is connected to the cable on which it emits or receives the electrical signals. It then communicates these to the connector card via the AUI cable.

The monoport transceiver

The most common transceiver has two connections, one to the medium (coaxial cable, twisted pair, optical fiber) and the other to the drop cable, via a male socket.

We have described the types of connector technology associated with each medium; however, a special type of connector technology exists on the standard coaxial cable. This is the tap connector. As its name suggests, this technique involves perforating the cable using 'needles' capable of reaching the two conductors without causing a short circuit. This method was the first to appear and is very consistent with the spirit in which Ethernet has been developed, that is, the wish to produce a network which is simple to install (the cable laying) and easy to modify (by

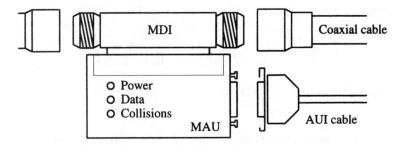

Figure 12.5 Sketch of insertion transceiver (type N).

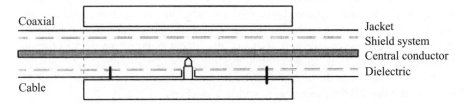

Figure 12.6 Schematic cross section of a tap on yellow coaxial cable.

moving the taps almost anywhere without cutting the network). The cable was then seen as offering a self-service facility for communication. In Part III, we shall see that rigorous rules for installation and modification are vital to the maintenance of reasonably consistent networks. The tap technique is no longer recommended since former tapping points may age, leading to a considerable variation in impedance due to this connection mode.

The method of connection by insertion is more expensive, since it requires a severing of the cable at each site of a future transceiver, together with the incorporation of two male connectors of type N. Thus, it is more troublesome since one has to open the cable and thus interrupt the traffic during operation. However, the overall quality is better and the contact more reliable.

As shown in Figure 12.5, the MDI part of the transceiver is fitted onto the MAU and thus can be changed conveniently. The MDI is a simple connection element and can be used to adapt the transceiver to N connectors, BNC connectors or a tapping module (Figure 12.6).

The electrical characteristics

A 10Base5 transceiver should have the following main electrical characteristics.

Toward the medium To minimize the variation in impedance due to the transceiver, the latter must have a resistance greater than 100 kOhm and a capacitance less then 2 pF (which covers the influence of the circuits and also that of the connectors).

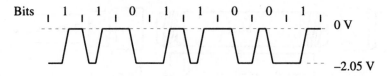

Figure 12.7 Electrical signal and rise time (~25 ns) on the coaxial cable.

We have seen that the 10 Mbps code was of the Manchester type, where 1 is encoded by a rising edge and 0 by a descending edge. The signal emitted should have a continuous component (or offset) of -41 ± 4 mA (or between -37 and -45 mA). The alternating component should be between the offset ± 28 mA. Thus, the resulting signal should range between 0 and -90 ± 4 mA. The corresponding voltages are 0 and -2.05 V. Since the coaxial cable has a characteristic impedance of 50 Ohm the transceiver sees two sections from its attachment point, or twice 50 Ohm in parallel $= 25$ Ohm. Thus, for example, Ohm's law $U = Z \times I$ implies -2.05 V $= 25$ Ohm $\times -82$ mA. The rise time should be between 20 and 30 ns (for the 10–90% portion) and the fall time identical to within 1 ns (Figure 12.7).

The continuous component of the signal (its average) is thus -1 V on emission, which is already an indication of activity since the free state of the medium (complete absence of signals) is at 0 V. Since the collision corresponds to the superposition of two signals, the resulting continuous component of the signal is therefore greater than that of a valid signal. Thus, the transceiver's collision detection threshold should be -1.56 ± 0.07 V (which reduces to a threshold of between -1.49 and -1.63 V). For 10Base2, the threshold should be between -1.4 and -1.58 V.

Toward the AUI cable   The power supply should be between 12 and 15 V, and the transceiver's electrical consumption should be less than 0.5 A. The impedance of the pairs of the 15 point socket should be less than 15 Ohm from 3 to 30 MHz. The signals emitted on the drop cable are encoded using the Manchester code with continuous component zero and voltage references of the order of ± 1 V (the gap should effectively be located between 0.45 and 1.315 V).

Crossing delay

The limits on the transceiver crossing delay are defined so that a network can be constructed based on simple rules (such as the maximum number of repeaters, coaxial segments, inter-repeater links, transceivers) without the need to recalculate the time taken to cross the network by the longest path every time (Figure 12.8).

They are thus assigned the following fixed values: a delay time for transmission of the data valid in a state of continuous flow of less than 1/2 bit time (50 ns) with a loss of at most the five first bits in the direction from the coaxial cable to the drop cable and at most the two first bits in the direction from the drop cable to the coaxial cable. In fact, the transceiver is authorized to lose several of the leading bits of the preamble of the frame to be transmitted. The transmission time for a collision

Continuous component on the coaxial cable

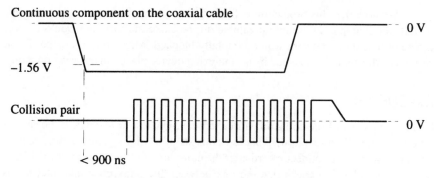

Figure 12.8 Delays in detecting a collision.

(naturally, in the direction from the coaxial cable to the AUI cable) should be less than or equal to 9 bit times. After this delay, of less than 900 ns, the transceiver emits a 10 MHz signal on the collision pair (Control In) to the connector interface.

Jabber protection

The transceiver has a method for protecting the network against malfunctioning of the interface card to which it is attached. Thus, if the interface card requests an excessively long or uninterrupted emission, the transceiver is able to truncate this and notify the connector via the drop cable collision pair (or signal quality).

This security is called jabber protection and should be triggered after 20 to 150 ms of continuous transmission (Figure 12.9). The truncation of the emission is accompanied by a signal indicating the presence of a collision (10 MHz on the Control In pair). The truncated state should be inhibited 0.5 ± 0.25 s after the end of the emission from the interface card.

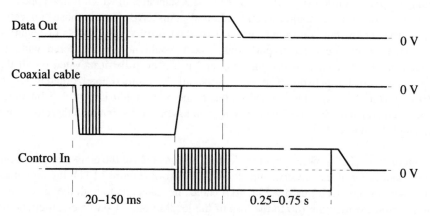

Figure 12.9 Illustration of the triggering of jabber protection.

We note that this protection is fundamental since, if a defective device were to emit, for example, an infinite preamble on the cable, no machine would be able to take over and the network would be totally blocked. Moreover, in this particular case, no traffic could be detected by an analyzing device placed in observation mode.

The SQE test

There exists a test of the collision pair called the SQE test or *heart beat* (because it is very regular) (Figure 12.10). This test consists of a brief signal which is sent by the transceiver to the connector card after the emission of each frame on the collision pair (or Control In) to check that the link between the transceiver and interface is operating properly. The arrival of this signal at the card means that if the card has not received a collision indication during transmission, it is because emission has passed off well and not because the collision pair is cut.

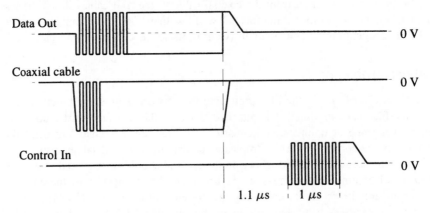

Figure 12.10 Heart beat after an emission of a correct frame.

This test may be activated, if necessary, on each transceiver (usually using a jumper wire or a microswitch). The IEEE 802.3 standard, in which it first appeared, recommended that it should be activated on all transceivers except those connected to a repeater (or the equivalent: hub, active star), so that the process of counting collisions when the repeater partitions a port would not be interfered with. In practice, very few stations use this test, and it can even be deactivated on all the transceivers of the network. The SQE test should be emitted approximately 1.1 μs (from 0.6 to 1.6 μs) after the end of the frame and should last 10 ± 5 bit times (between 500 and 1500 ns). The receiving window for this signal will therefore have a length from 4 to 8 μs.

Conclusion The transceiver is the element responsible for the emission, reception, and monitoring of the physical signals on the network (Figure 12.11). It communicates with the connector card via the AUI cable and transmits to it all the data it sees passing on the medium (up to the loss of the leading bits). Conversely, it emits the data sent to it by the interface card on the physical medium, essentially as it is

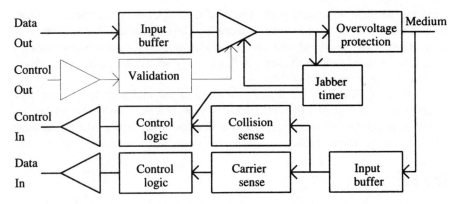

Figure 12.11   Schematic illustration of the circuits of a transceiver.

Table 12.1   Delays of different types of transceivers (in bit time).

	10Base5	10Base2	FOIRL	10BaseT	10BaseFP	10BaseFB	10BaseFL
Tx	3.5	3.5	3.5	5	4	2	5
Rx	6.5	6.5	3.5	8	3	2	5
Coll	9	9	3.5	9	11.5	3.5	3.5

received. Its only intelligence comprises its capability to interrupt an excessively long emission and to test the validity of the collision pair after the emission of each frame.

In practice, transceivers often have LEDs. These are quite useful, as they may be used to carry out elementary diagnostics when problems arise. They can indicate the state of emission, reception and collision detection, the triggering of the jabber protection or the position of the switch validating the SQE test.

Figure 12.11 illustrates the main functional blocks of a transceiver and their inter-relationship. Finally, the accompanying table gives the crossing delays for the different types of transceiver, for valid signals and for collision detection; these times may be used to calculate the round-trip delay on the network.

All the times in Table 12.1 are given in bit time (0.1 μs). Note that on the coaxial cable, this time does not include the rise time of the collision, if not a value of 17 bit times should be used. In the section on repeaters we shall see that transceivers built into repeaters often have slightly lower times.

The multiport transceiver

The multiport transceiver is a transceiver with several male AUI connectors, generally two or four. Its internal structure simply amounts to a set of several transceivers accessing the cable at the same point. Thus, its advantage lies in its compactness and the fact that it can be used to connect more than one machine to the network at a single point, since the perturbation due to the local impedance perturbation remains unitary. Its crossing delay is the same as that of a transceiver and, like a transceiver, it is fed by one or more drop cables.

If two terminators are directly attached to the multiport transceiver, this becomes a small virtual Ethernet, which is very practical when one wishes to establish intercommunication between two devices with female AUI connectors (repeater, bridge, router, probe).

The FanOut

The FanOut is a concentrator for male AUI ports, which also has a female AUI port. This element is capable of collecting together several (generally eight) drop cables attached to stations and connecting the whole to the network using a single trans-ceiver (monoport) (Figure 12.12).

This is a very useful device, which makes it easy to simulate a small Ethernet network that is not attached to a true transceiver. It is even possible to cascade several FanOuts if there is a requirement for a large number of AUI connectors, thereby creating a large virtual Ethernet. The FanOut used to be quite common and afford-able. Note, however, that it generally requires a power supply and that it has a non-zero crossing delay (less than 1 μs, but of the order of several hundred ns). This means that this time must be included in the calculation of the length of the maximum path for the network. One also needs to know the length of the AUI cable connecting the transceiver, and then to add this to that of the cable leading to the station (the sum of the two should be less than ~45 m).

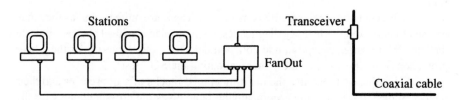

Figure 12.12 Four stations attached to the network via a FanOut.

12.3 The AUI cable

The cable linking the transceiver to the interface card (PLS) is often called the drop cable (for attachment unit interface) in the standard, and is also referred to as the drop cable (since it often descends from a transceiver placed in a suspended ceiling to a wall socket) or the blue cable (as it is usually blue).

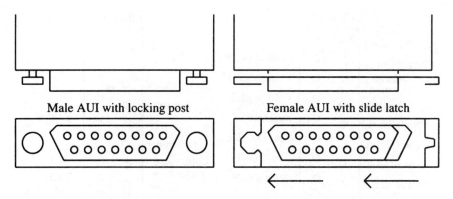

Figure 12.13 Representation of two types of end connector.

This cable serves no purpose if the station interface has a 10Base2 port (in BNC connector technology) or a 10BaseT port (in RJ45 connector technology), since then the coaxial cable or the twisted-pair line leads right to the machine. Otherwise (10Base5, FOIRL and 10BaseF) the AUI cable is indispensable. Its maximum length authorized by the standard is 50 meters; however, caution is advisable, as some manufacturers only certify the connection of their hardware for 30 or 15 meters.

The cable has a male DB15 jack at one end and a female DB15 plug at the other (Figure 12.13). One special feature of this cable is the locking of its 15-point connectors. These are not of the screw type, as is usual in computer technology, but use a slide latch and locking post. This form of locking (standardized by MIL-C-24308), which belongs to the philosophy of the initial development under which Ethernet was to be easy to manipulate, has proved to be a source of problems. It is unreliable because when the slide latch is eventually slid around the two ports it becomes twisted, and cannot provide sufficient rigidity. In answer to this problem, manufacturers have provided their interfaces with screw connectors, thereby creating an undesirable heterogeneity. We could dwell on the quality of production of the slide latch, since there are various models, some of which are relatively reliable.

The main characteristics of the drop cable (according to IEEE 802.3) are:

- Five individually shielded twisted pairs.
- A characteristic impedance of 78 ± 3 Ohm between 5 and 10 MHz.
- A total length less than 50 meters.
- A propagation speed greater than or equal to 0.65 c.
- A maximum transit time of 257 ns (2.57 bit times).
- An attenuation of less than 3 dB at 10 MHz (per pair).
- A total resistance for a conductor of less than 1.75 Ohm.
- Finally, the cable costs usually less than 4 US dollars per meter.

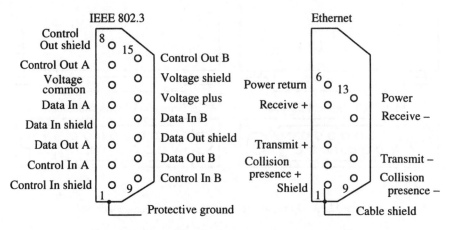

Figure 12.14 Different pin layouts for the AUI cable.

The definition of the AUI cable belongs to those chapters which the IEEE has supplemented with new material. Thus, the cable has changed from four to five pairs, the shielding on each pair has become accessible by the connector and the cladding ground (in contact with the global shielding) is no longer linked to pin 1 (Figure 12.14). Some connector cards designed to operate in the IEEE 802.3 world will require appropriate drop cables.

We recall that the 'Control In' pair (or collision presence) is used by the transceiver to notify the connector card of the presence of a collision or the triggering of the jabber protection and to transmit the SQE test. In all cases, the signal emitted on this pair (2–9) has a fixed frequency of 10 MHz. A smaller AUI, called AAUI has been developed for small computers and laptops (as Apple Macintosh), but has not been standardized. It benefits from a reduced size and a better locking system.

12.4 The MII and GMII interfaces

Media Independent Interface (MII) is defined by the 100BaseT specifications of the IEEE 802.3u supplement, section 22 (Figure 12.15). Simplifying somewhat, it can be said to correspond to the AUI interface in the 100BaseT environment, but only on the MAC (or station) side. The transceiver or PHY is directly attached to the MII cable. This is the transition point between the so-called reconciliation sublayer (in fact, MII can support speeds of 10 and 100 Mbps, but not 1 Mbps) and the PLS. The reconciliation layer itself lies between the MAC and the PLS.

The AUI is optional and is only specified at 10 Mbps. The MII is also optional, but is specified at 10 and 100 Mbps.

Note that the PMD layer is not defined by 100BaseT4, but only by 100BaseX (100BaseTX and 100BaseFX). The PCS layer implements the 8B/6T encoding for 100BaseT4 and the 4B/5B encoding for 100BaseX.

On the MII link the data is transmitted in each direction by 4 bits (nibble) in parallel. Note that this is not directly related to the retransmission mode that is used on the medium.

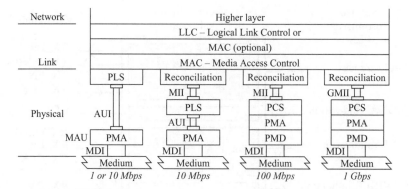

LLC: Logical Link Control
MAC: Medium Access Control
PLS: Physical Layer Signaling
PCS: Physical Coding Sublayer
AUI: Attachment Unit Interface
MII: Media Independent Interface
MAU: Medium Attachment Unit
PMA: Physical Medium Attachment
PMD: Physical Medium Dependent
PHY: Physical Layer Device
MDI: Medium Dependent Interface
GMII: Gigabit MII

Figure 12.15   Three different types of Ethernet interface.

The signals transported are MAC level transmission and reception, collision detection, carrier detection, and transmit enable. In fact, the clock signal used for the emission is also transmitted by the transceiver, as is the clock signal for reception derived from the received signal (Figure 12.16).

This represents a total of 19 different signals (8 for the data itself).

The MII cable should not be longer than 50 cm, which gives a total of 1 m for the two extremities of a link. The maximum delay corresponding to this total is 10 ns per segment, but also 2.5 ns for the MII–PHY connector. Moreover, the lengths of the MII cables have to be reduced to the lengths permitted by 100BaseT on the segments.

The connector of the IEC/SC 48B type has 40 pins on two lines and has a jack-type locking mechanism. It is female on the MAC side and male on the side of the cable attached to the PHY. The connector template should be less than 1.5 cm high and 5 cm wide.

The conductors of the MII cable should have a diameter of 0.32 mm (28 AWG) with a characteristic impedance of 68 ± 10% Ohm, and they are used at TTL electrical levels 0 and 3.3 at 5 V.

The management signals (MDIO) are used to communicate information registers which indicate, for example, the state or type of the PHY, which may result from an auto-negotiation phase, as follows:

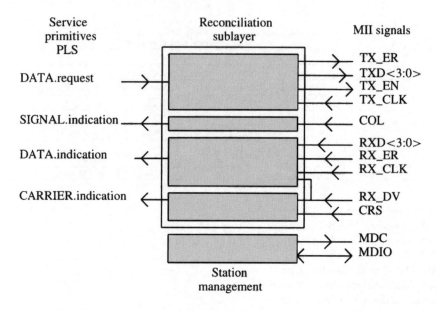

Signal	Meaning	Pin
TX_ER	Transmit Error	11
TX_CLK	Transmit Clock	12
TXD n ($n = 0, \ldots, 3$)	Transmit Data	14–17
TX_EN	Transmit Enable	13
COL	Collision	18
CRS	Carrier Sense	19
RX_CLK	Receive Clock	9
RXD n ($n = 0, 1, \ldots, 3$)	Receive Data	4–7
RX_DV	Receive Data Valid	8
RX_ER	Receive Error	10
MDC	Management Data Clock	3
MDIO	Management Data Input/Output	2
Power	+5 V	1, 20, 21, 40

Figure 12.16   Logical and physical signals.

- 100BaseT4
- 100BaseTX full duplex
- 100BaseTX half duplex
- 10 Mbps full duplex
- 10 Mbps half duplex

In fact, the MII interface permits the exchange (read and write) of management data between the PHY and the station management entity. This information consists of 32 registers, of which only the first eleven are defined explicitly by 100BaseT, 100BaseT2 and 100BaseX. The following five registers are reserved and the last 16 are dedicated to the manufacturers. All the registers have 16 bits. The first eleven registers have the meaning shown in Table 12.2.

Table 12.2 Meaning of auto-negotiation registers.

Register address	Register name
0	MII Control
1	MII Status
2 and 3	PHY identifier
4	Auto-Negotiation advertisement
5	Auto-Negotiation Link Partner Ability
6	Auto-Negotiation Expansion
7	Auto-Negotiation Next Page Transmit
8	Auto-Negotiation Link Partner Next Page
9	100BaseT2 Control Register
10	100BaseT2 Status Register

Table 12.3 Control register (0).

Bit	Name	Meaning of 0	Meaning of 1
15	Reset	Normal operation	PHY reset (< 0.5 s)
14	Loopback	Disable loop back mode and isolate the medium	Isolate the medium and enable loop back mode Tx→Rx
13	Speed selection	10 Mbps	100 Mbps
12	Auto-Negotiation Enable	Disable Auto-Negotiation Process	Enable Auto-Negotiation Process
11	Power Down	Normal operation	Power down
10	Isolate	Normal operation	Electrically isolate PHY from MII
9	Restart Auto-Negotiation	Normal operation	Restart Auto-Negotiation Process
8	Duplex mode	Half duplex	Full duplex
7	Collision test	Disable COL signal test	Enable COL signal test

Only the first two registers (control and state) are base registers which are necessarily implemented by all PHYs. The contents of the control register (register 0) and the status register (register 1) are shown in Tables 12.3 and 12.4, respectively.

Table 12.4 Status register (1).

Bit	Name	Meaning of 0	Meaning of 1
15	100BaseT4	PHY not able to perform 100BaseT4	PHY able to perform 100BaseT4
14	100BaseX full duplex	PHY not able to perform full duplex 100BaseX	PHY able to perform full duplex 100BaseX
13	100BaseX half duplex	PHY not able to perform half duplex 100BaseX	PHY able to perform half duplex 100BaseX
12	10 Mbps full duplex	PHY not able to operate at 10 Mbps in full duplex mode	PHY able to operate at 10 Mbps in full duplex mode
11	10 Mbps half duplex	PHY not able to operate at 10 Mbps in half duplex mode	PHY able to operate at 10 Mbps in half duplex mode
5	Auto-negotiation terminated	Auto-negotiation process not completed	Auto-negotiation process completed Registers 4, 5, 6, 7 valid
4	Remote fault	No remote fault detected	Remote fault condition detected
3	Auto-negotiation ability	PHY not able to perform auto-negotiation	PHY able to perform auto-negotiation
2	Link status	Link is down	Link is up
1	Jabber detect	No jabber condition detected	Jabber condition detected
0	Extended capability	Base register set capabilities only	Extended register capabilities

Bits 0 to 7 of register 0 are reserved, all the other bits of register 0 can be read or written. All the bits of register 1 are read only.

Remote faults may arise under four conditions:

- Test of remote fault operation.
- Loss of the link.
- Jabber.
- Failure to detect a valid link by more than one PMA in parallel (10BaseT, 100BaseTX, 100BaseT4).

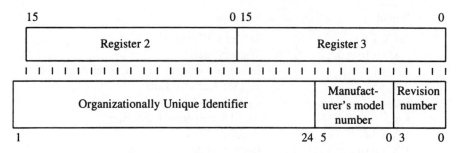

Figure 12.17   Decomposition of registers 2 and 3.

The next two registers (2 and 3) are used to communicate numbers identifying the PHY precisely: the OUI, the manufacturer's model number and the number of the revision. Only 22 bits of the OUI are taken into account; the first two bits need not necessarily be transmitted as 0 (since they have special meanings: unicast/multicast address and local/universal address) (Figure 12.17).

All the management registers are communicated by the MII MDIO signal, where the frames have the form shown in Figure 12.18. In this figure, Z indicates a high-impedance state. The physical address (PHYAD) corresponds to the number of the PHY with which the management entity wishes to correspond. An entity may have up to 32 PHY. The register address corresponds to its number (as before), and is also limited to 32. The Turnaround is a 2 bit time spacing used to avoid the risk of signal conflicts (on return) for operations to read a register.

Preamble 32 bits at 1	Start of frame ST = 01	Operation code : OP Read = 10, Write = 01	Physical address PHYAD

Register address REGAD	Turnaround : TA Read = Z0, Write = 10	Register contents 16 bits of data	Idle Z

Figure 12.18   Management frame.

The GMII interface

The GMII interface is a superset of MII, and can support throughputs of 10 Mbps, 100 Mbps, and 1 Gbps. A GMII mode is defined as a complement of previously possible functions. The carried signals are more or less the same, except that data is transmitted 8 bits at a time instead of 4, and that a GTX_CLK transmission clock is added. This clock runs at 1/8 of the throughput, that is 125 MHz at 1 Gbps.

Signal	Meaning
GTX_CLK	Transmit Clock
TXD n ($n = 0, \ldots, 7$)	Transmit data
TX_ER	Indicates Transmit Error/Carrier Extension
TX_EN	Frames Transmit Data
COL	Collision Indication
CRS	Non-Idle Medium Indication
RX_CLK	Receive Clock
RXD n ($n = 0, \ldots, 7$)	Receive Data
RX_DV	Frames Receive SFD and DATA
RX_ER	Receive Error Indication/Carrier Extension
MDC	Management Data Clock
MDIO	Management Data

12.5 The interface card

Straddling levels 1 and 2, the connector card covers the functions of an interface with the transceiver (the PLS in the IEEE 802.3 model) and the MAC functions. The card is called the Network Interface Card (NIC).

The NIC consists of electronic circuits and carries out a fixed processing defined by the physical implantation of the components. It can be said to form part of the hardware, apart from the communication work carried out by the machine (processing according to the higher protocols) which corresponds to the execution of software code.

One of the circuits on the card is dedicated to the local area network and is specific to a particular technology. For example, chips for Ethernet have been available for a long time and can be found in interface cards and in all bridges and routers. Known circuits include, for example, AMD's LANCE Am 7990 and 79C960, Intel's 82586, 82593 and 82596, and National Semiconductor's DP83902 and 83910. Comparable dedicated circuits also exist for Token Ring, LocalTalk, and ARCnet.

As far as the physical layer is concerned, the card originally had a single AUI female port. With the arrival of 10Base2, some manufacturers preferred to give their hardware a unique BNC port, while others chose to add the BNC port (which, in fact, incorporates a transceiver) next to the AUI jack. Finally, interface cards adapted to FOIRL and 10BaseT are also available, and we note that it is even possible to obtain three sockets (AUI, BNC and RJ45) on a single PC card, leaving the user free to choose between these types of attachment, with a minimum number of complementary attachment elements.

As far as the higher layers are concerned, since the card is a commonplace computer interface, it can exchange data with the computer via the machine bus. The packet formatting follows from the Ethernet technology at the MAC level and the indications are managed by the card driver.

In the case of PCs, the card exchanges data with the software driver provided by the card manufacturer, which has standardized accesses to cooperate with the various software of the microcomputer world (NOS: servers and clients, emulation of passive terminals, network applications: file transfer, electronic mail, network management).

With the rapid evolution of workstations and microcomputers, the frequency of central microprocessors is increasing as are the speeds of internal buses. This is accompanied by an increasingly greater consumption of bandwidth by each machine (up to several Mbps).

Smart cards

It is important to be aware that, in most cases, the interface card is an element which imposes constraints on the use of an Ethernet network. In fact, all the elements defined in the standard, together with certain recent bridges and routers are capable of processing the network traffic, whatever the load. However, interface cards were generally incapable of emitting at 10 Mbps, even on an empty network. The maximum speed for current cards often lies between 100 kbps and 8 Mbps. The receive capacity is also limited, among other things, by the buffer capacity and the speed of transfer to the CPU card processing the protocol decoding. This brings to light the close relationship that exists between the processing capacity of the mother board's microprocessor and the amount of information the computer is able to communicate per unit of time. This dependence is due to the fact that the processing for the protocols of level 3 and above is carried out entirely by software using appropriate decoding programs.

To counter this limitation, some of the decoding functions may be implemented in hardware. This is what is done in so-called smart cards. These have circuits and microprograms which are useful in the processing of protocols from the LLC or (DoD) IP level to the transport layer and thus relieve the central system of these additional tasks. However, the performance of these cards, which are clearly more expensive than conventional equipment since they are more complex, while greater, may still be constrained by the capacity for communication between the smart interface card and the mother board for data exchange at level 5 and above. Moreover, these cards cannot evolve as easily as a program module, following the modification of the contents of a field or of a procedure in a protocol, and for this reason they are less flexible in their use. The smart cards available for PCs generally handle the DoD protocols (IP, TCP) using their own microprocessor and their local memory.

12.6 10 Mbps repeaters

It was mentioned earlier that the repeater is an interconnection device which is an integral part of the Ethernet network (Figure 12.19). It is defined in brief in the ISO standard (section 9) and more fully and in more detail in the supplements IEEE 802.3c and d. However, the 10BaseF standard redefines this section 9 again, enlarging the application domains.

We note that the repeater is located at the level of the physical layer and thus has no knowledge of the fields of the frame which belong to the MAC level. It reproduces the frame exactly, without deciphering it and without being able to check whether or not it is valid. The segments it links together form a single Ethernet. Finally, since it is located at level 1, it cannot interconnect two segments with different speeds, such as 10Base5, 1Base5 (StarLAN) or 100BaseT.

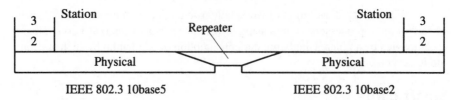

Figure 12.19 Representation of a biport repeater between standard Ethernet and thin Ethernet.

The simple repeater

The function of the repeater is to interconnect the medium segments in order to extend the network by linking several segments. It may have two or more ports and may or may not incorporate transceivers. Note that when it has many ports the repeater becomes the center of a star topology.

Its work thus involves transporting the Ethernet packets from the medium segment which provides them to the others. In so doing, it reshapes the electrical signals; it is also responsible for extending the fragments, completing the preambles, detecting and propagating collisions, interrupting excessively long emissions, and partitioning defective ports.

The regeneration of the electrical signals eliminates jitter and reduces noise problems by compensating for the attenuation of the signal. One reason why a segment of coaxial cable cannot be as long as the round-trip delay on the network would allow is that there is always a need to detect collisions (as required by CSMA/CD), in other words, to distinguish a valid signal from the superposition of two signals, which may have been attenuated. The repeater allows signals to recover their original level.

The crossing delay for a simple repeater (with female AUI ports) is 8 bit times. This becomes 4 bit times for the repeater part of a box incorporating the transceivers (the delays due to the built-in transceivers are given below).

The repeater also has to extend very short bit sequences (less than 96 bits) circulating on the network (called fragments). It is prudent to ensure that all the stations have seen these signals (carrier sense present), which is done by extending them to at least 96 bits. When these fragments are the result of collisions, their presence is not abnormal and does not signify malfunctioning.

The repeater is also responsible for completing short preambles by extending them to 56 bits and making them followed by the SFD. In the case where the repeater transmits an excessively long preamble, this should be no more than six bits longer than the received preamble.

If a collision occurs on one side of a repeater, as a result of its action, or between two other stations, the repeater is responsible for detecting this collision and propagating it on the other segment. In this way, any station concerned about the result of its emission will be informed that a collision has occurred and the others will detect that the whole of the network is busy for the duration of the collision.

When a collision is detected on a port, the repeater then emits a jam-type signal on the other segment(s). The jam is a sequence of at least 62 bits, consisting of alternate 1 and 0, beginning with a 1. The propagation of the jam should stop less than 5 bit times after the end of the collision. The crossing delay for a collision should be less than 6.5 bit times for a repeater with external transceivers and 19 bit times (9 extra on input and 3.5 on output) for a repeater with built-in coaxial transceivers.

Like the transceiver, the repeater has a function to monitor emissions judged to be excessively long and will interrupt its own retransmission after more than 5 + 50% − 20% ms or 40 000 to 75 000 bit times. The repeater reactivates its retransmission after 10.6 ± 1 μs. We note that the repeater's jabber protection is triggered well before the jabber protection for the transceivers, which enables the repeater to avoid cutting off its transceivers, which would block it.

Finally, the repeater may (optionally) implement a partition function, which involves deactivating a port that is judged to be a source of repeated collisions. Two conditions may trigger this protection: the passing of a threshold corresponding to a number of successive collisions; and a collision deemed to be abnormally long. The threshold for the maximum permissible number of consecutive collisions should be greater than 30 (generally chosen to be 32, or twice 16, or the equivalent of two successive *excessive collisions*). An abnormally long collision causes auto-partitioning after 1000 to 30 000 bit times (from 100 μs to 3 ms). The repeater reactivates the port after having detected an activity corresponding to approximately 500 collision free bits (between 450 and 560 bits, to be precise). In practice, all repeaters have an auto-partition function.

The term 'auto-partition' relates to the capability of some repeaters to let the user choose the state of the interfaces (activated, deactivated) using simple access software. Transition to a silent state corresponds to a manual partitioning; the inverse corresponds to a departitioning.

Remark   On reflection, it is apparent that as the repeater is responsible for extending short fragments and preambles, it cannot always respect the interframe delay.

In fact, if several frames with short preambles reach it in succession, it will have to add the complementary bits to each before retransmitting it. Forced to transport each frame in less than 8 bit times, it will not always be able to respect the interframe minimum and will therefore violate the 9.6 μs rule. A modification of the standard is envisaged (as indicated in specification of 10BaseF) to stipulate in section 4.4.2.1 that the interpacket gap (IPG) may be reduced to 47 bit times after the crossing of a network, because of variable network crossing delays, possible bits added to preambles and misalignment of clocks.

A new parameter which also appears in the 10BaseF standard is the Path Delay Value (PDV). This time is useful in evaluation and validation of the longest Round-Trip Delay (RTD) of a network. The PDV is divided into Segment Delay Values (SDV). One difference arises at the level of the SDV, depending on whether the segment concerned is the first segment on the path, the last segment or a segment between the two. For the calculation of each SDV, times associated with the minimum and the maximum admissible values for each segment are given in Table 12.5. The

Table 12.5   Table of bases and coefficients for computing the maximum RTD on a given path of the shared network.

Segment type	Base for for first segment	Base for for intermediate segment	Base for for last segment	Coefficient (bit times)	Maximum length (m)
10Base5	11.75	46.5	169.5	0.0866	500
10Base2	11.75	46.5	169.5	0.1026	185
FOIRL	7.75	29	152	0.1	1000
10BaseT	15.25	42	165	0.113	100
10BaseFP	11.25	61	183.5	0.1	1000
10BaseFB	–	24	–	0.1	2000
10BaseFL	12.25	33.5	156.5	0.1	2000
ISLAN	72	86.5	209.5	0.113	100
AUI (–2 m)	0	0	0	0.1026	48

SDV is calculated as follows: basic number + coefficient $\times$ segment length (in meters). The drop cables on the path are assumed, by default, to have a length of 2 meters, and the extra meters have to be added into the calculation.

The total PDV, the sum of the SDV, should never exceed 575 bit times. The base numbers are given in bit time.

Note that 10BaseFB has not been defined to constitute terminal connections (to stations or DTEs), even though some manufacturers offer this with synchronous transceivers.

The rule is given by the following inequality (lengths of AUI cables greater than 2 m should be included in the calculation):

$$PDV = \sum SDV = \sum(\text{base} + \text{coefficient} \times \text{length}) \leq 527 \text{ bit times.}$$

Respect for the PDV, which corresponds to the delay in crossing, should be ensured in parallel with the evaluation of the interpacket gap (IPG) shrinkage (see Table 12.6), which is measured by the Path Variability Value (PVV). No path through the network should exceed these two limits.

$$PVV = \sum SVV \leq 49.$$

Note that the receiving segment is not included in the calculation, so the calculation is not necessarily symmetrical.

Table 12.6   Table of values for computing the maximum IPG shrinkage on a given path of the network.

Segment type	Emitter segment	Intermediate segment
Coaxial cable	16	11
All links, except 10BaseFP	10.5	8
10BaseFB	–	2
10BaseFP	11	8

In conclusion, this provides a convenient method for evaluating the validity of a configuration or a topology including different types of medium.

The multimedia active star

The star should primarily be viewed as a multiport repeater, the term star being derived logically from the topology created by this repeater attached to several segments.

Based on technical progress, manufacturers have done their utmost to incorporate the maximum number of facilities in a single apparatus, which is often modular and takes the form of a rack in which each card represents a type of attachment to a chosen medium. Originally, the backplane of these devices consisted of a passive bus equivalent to an Ethernet segment. Things have changed since then and several independent buses are now implemented, giving a choice of the network to which the card to be inserted is to be connected.

The following types of card are available:

- Female AUI connectors to link coaxial transceivers of type N (as on a standard repeater).
- Male AUI connectors to link stations directly (in this case, the star functions as a FanOut).
- Type N coaxial connectors to interlink 10Base5 segments (relatively rare option due to the connector size).
- BNC coaxial connectors to link 10Base2 segments to a T or directly at the cable end (high impedance or 50 Ohm internal terminator).
- RJ45 connectors to interlink 10BaseT segments.
- 50-point Telco connectors to interlink 12 10BaseT segments.
- ST or SMA optical connectors to interlink FOIRL links or synchronous optical links.

Normally, each card has several ports of the same kind, where the number of ports is generally a function of the size of the card.

Furthermore, recent developments have led to the production of cards with capabilities going beyond the simple function of access to a repeater stage. For example, there are cards which act as:

- A bridge between two ports (female AUI connectors) or between two backplane buses, or a combination of the two,

- A remote bridge between an AUI port (or backplane) and one or two sockets for remote connection (for example, RS232 or V.35),

- A router (dealing with protocols such as TCP/IP, NetWare, DECnet, XNS, AppleTalk, ISO) between two ports, two backplane buses or a combination of the two,

- A remote router, identical to a remote bridge with the routing function,

- A management card or SNMP probe, with an *out of band* port, generally of type DB25 or DB9 for RS232 connection.

The management card is now discussed in more detail, since its incorporation in the range of multimedia stars was associated with the qualification of smart hubs. Its main function is to permit remote monitoring of equipment with, initially, reporting of the light indicators from the front panels of these modules (self test, transmit, receive, jabber, collision, partitioning). It then proved possible to obtain statistics about the whole star (global traffic, per card, per port, error rate, load curve) and to observe and learn Ethernet addresses. This was followed by the configuration of certain parameters and the activation or deactivation of a card or port. All the supplementary functions which do not form part of the basic work of the star multiport repeater provide information about the traffic flow in various parts of the star. If the star is constructed from a number of manageable stars, the overall traffic can be monitored by the load on each card and the state of each port. In this case, it is even possible to locate a machine and even to follow the movements of stations. Used properly, the management card may prove to be a very useful tool for validating the current architecture of the network or causing it to evolve, and foreseeing the overloading of certain nodes or segments. Furthermore, these cards generally communicate their information to a PC or a Unix station on the network, but also have a serial external port (out of band) for a direct access via a modem, which is indispensable in the case of complete blockage of the network.

Finally, these stars now accommodate several technologies in addition to their Ethernet capabilities, and even the following cards can be available for them:

- MAU Token Ring card in DB9, RJ11, RJ45 or hermaphrodite (rarer) connector technology

- Token Ring repeaters on fiber optic links in ST or biconic connector technology

- LocalTalk in RJ11 connector technology

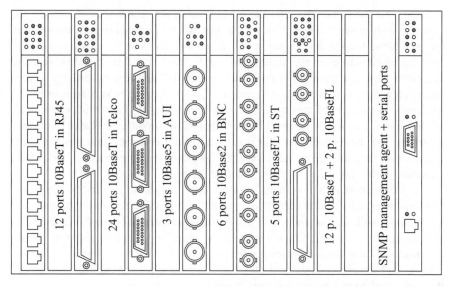

Figure 12.20 Symbolic representation of a multimedia star.

- FDDI in single or multimode fiber with ST duplex or MIC connector technology, or twisted pair with DB9 or RJ45 connectors.

Connection between these networks and with Ethernet is made possible using module or card bridges and/or router modules which are able to access different backplane buses.

One final type of common card for use with multimedia stars is (Figure 12.20):

- The terminal server in RJ45 or 50-point Telco connector technology, whose functionality is described in a later section.

To be perfectly multimedia, stars should support synchronous (10BaseFB) and asynchronous transmission modes. Some manufacturers offer hardware which functions synchronously, with some standard accesses (AUI, BNC, 10BaseT, FOIRL). These ranges also include solutions on twisted pair (which do not conform to IEEE 802.3) but which are able to extend point-to-point links over longer distances.

In addition to the diverse types of connection provided by multimedia stars, these stars also implement richer capabilities than a simple repeater. Independently of the functions of a bridge and a router and of monitoring possibilities, the functions provided by multimedia stars include the management of point-to-point redundant links and, recently, the implementation of elementary filtering.

The point-to-point links such as the twisted-pair segments for 10BaseT and fiber optic segments (FOIRL, 10BaseF) may be duplicated. One of these two links is active and used operationally; the other is used for redundancy. To secure the connections between two stars it is sufficient to use two ports on each. If transceivers are used, these must then have two ports. When a problem arises on the active link, or in the active end elements, the second link replaces it and the network manager is notified via his or her monitoring system. In certain cases, the switch may be very rapid (a few bit times), since fault detection is so much easier in synchronous mode. Moreover, protection of this type can also be envisaged on coaxial cable, with duplication of the access points. This corresponds to linking the star to two transceivers on the same cable. The star is responsible for detecting faults in the transceivers, the drop cable or one of the AUI cards and for executing the switch. However, in this case, the medium cannot be duplicated.

To ensure that their systems are available for even longer periods, the manufacturers offer racks with a redundant power supply and the possibility of changing the modules while leaving the whole powered up (hot swap). Thus, one may envisage building totally secure multimedia stars for the crucial nodes of the network. Breakdown does not involve any stoppage time, as once the defective element is deactivated, it can be replaced and reactivated and return to take over the link provided by the back-up elements during the breakdown.

In addition to management functions, which can be used to validate/invalidate a port or monitor it in a particular way, 10BaseT cards also offer an address filtering (source or destination). In fact, it is recognized that, in the majority of cases, a 10BaseT link from a hub ends at a transceiver feeding a unique machine. Thus, an RJ45 port of the star can be associated with the address of the station attached at this point which adds security to the network by allowing only that machine to talk on that link. With the potential for filtering currently available, it is sufficient to define the type of link for each port to a unique machine or a set of machines and, in the first case, to enter the only authorized Ethernet address. The 10BaseT will not only filter this port as requested, but may also indicate the illegal address which has attempted to use this port recently. Conversely, a machine attached to a port can be allowed to see only the traffic which concerns it. This is a way of limiting eavesdropping which provides surplus privacy. This new filtering functionality, which is quite simple, when available at each port individually, provides additional security, but also requires a stricter management of the network. In fact, to make it easy for users to use the network, one has to be able to modify the filtering addresses in parallel with the movements of machines on relocation or at the time of new installations, that is, quickly and without error.

When the multi LAN technology repeaters have several networks of each type on the backplane, it is of course possible to assign each module freely to one of the buses (or rings) of the backplane, but it is also sometimes possible to link each port of a given module to one of its internal networks. This is static per port switching. This parametrization can be carried out directly on the module or, preferably, from the management console.

Finally, the most advanced modular designs are able to support concentration modules implementing a dynamic packet switching technology. In this case, each card inserted in the device corresponds to added dedicated bandwidth (see Chapter 13.3).

Stackable hubs

A new generation of hub or multiport repeater has emerged recently, which could eliminate so-called stand-alone equipment once and for all and threatens to be an advantageous replacement for modular hubs. These are stackable hubs, sometimes referred to as cascadable hubs (Figure 12.21).

These hubs may consist of a limited number of elements interconnected in a chain or star by short proprietary links (generally a few centimeters long). This means that the overall stack formed in this way can only be presented as a single repeater level as far as Ethernet is concerned. The manufacturers offer a minimum modularity, perfectly oriented towards the most common requirements: numerous 10BaseT ports (for example, 16 or 24 per module) with RJ45 or Telco connectors, a few AUI or optical ports for backbone links, and an optional SNMP management agent. The main aim is to preserve the main functionality and advantages of a modular chassis in a more affordable range.

Some manufacturers allow one to mix modules for different LAN technologies, where only the management is common to all. Moreover, there exist interconnection modules, such as local or remote bridges, multi-protocol brouters, and SNA gateways. Finally, we note that these devices in general correspond in a particular way to the capillary service from secondary plant rooms for a hundred attachment points.

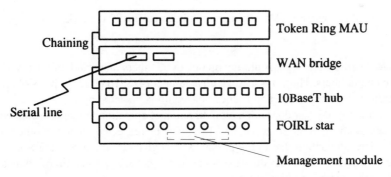

Figure 12.21 Example of a stackable hybrid Ethernet/Token Ring stack.

The passive optical star

The passive optical star (Figure 12.22) is a special instance of a star, as it has no active elements and can only process optical signals from transceivers. Its internal structure is particularly simple, since it comprises optical fibers fused together with one another

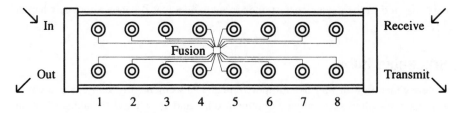

Figure 12.22 Symbolic diagram of a passive star with eight ports.

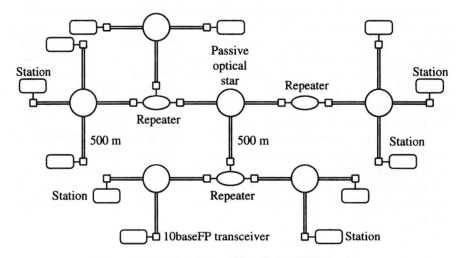

Figure 12.23 Example of a large 10BaseFP network.

so as to distribute any signal entering on one of the fibers fairly and uniformly across all the output fibers. Thus, it is a box with a number (4, 8, 16 or 32) of pairs of optical connectors (input–output), and it does not require a power supply.

Initially, the star does not have a direction of operation, but once a connection has been established the same Tx/Rx order must be respected on all the other ports.

The attenuation due to the passive star is given by the formula $2 \times C + E + 10\log N$, where C is the loss due to a connector, E is the star's margin of attenuation and N is the number of optical ports.

The fact that it has no electronic circuits makes it very valuable for sites where the electromagnetic disturbance is large and where the safety restrictions (for example, overheating, risk of fire) are important. One example might be a tentative application as an interconnection box for a computer network in a car.

This type of technology has been in existence for some time but has only been standardized lately, since it has been included in the 10BaseFP standard (Figure 12.23). However, it also has non-trivial shortcomings, since it is not easy to guarantee the detection of all collisions under all circumstances, for example in the presence of optical noise (which is inevitable). The internal structure of the star is as simple as the method of managing the signals by the transceivers is elaborate.

We have seen that, to ensure that the data it transmits is emitted without difficulty, the transceiver has to continually check the validity of its emission, which corresponds to an elementary function on coaxial cable (reception = emission), twisted-pair or point-to-point optical fibers (reception = none during the emission) but not in the case of passive optics. In fact, when the transceiver emits, it does not know either the segment length (and the associated transit delay) or the number of ports of the star (and the resulting attenuation) and, despite everything, it has to be able to interpret the signals received to judge whether a frame is its own frame and whether it is intact or superposed on another.

With a view to improving this technology, IEEE 802.3 10BaseFP defined a more elaborate technique than simple transposition of the Ethernet frames on optical fiber. Here, the first 56 bits of a frame preamble are replaced by two fields of four bits (a synchronization structure, a packet header) and a unique 32-bit word, followed by at least 12 bits (always an even number) of a normal preamble (Figure 12.24). Next come the standard SFD and the frame itself. The synchronization structure is 1010 (in that order), and the packet header is a violation of the Manchester code (code rule violation: CRV) which can be used to identify it. The unique word consists of the manufacturer identifier on 12 bits and 20 bits giving the transceiver number. The least significant bit is transmitted first. Thus, the preambles transmitted by all transceivers are different.

4 bits	4 bits	12 bits	20 bits	≥12 bits	8 bits
Sync	PHCRV	Unique word		Rest of preamble	SFD
1 0 1 0	1 MV 0 1	Manufacturer	MAU ID	101010...101010	

Figure 12.24 Preamble for a frame in 10BaseFP.

A collision is detected in the following two cases: if the transceiver receives on its AUI cable a frame to be emitted while it is receiving (except if it is receiving the return of a previous signal sent back by the passive star), and if it receives a CRV without having detected a silence of at least 125 ns. To detect the superposition of two (or more) simultaneous frames, use is made of the fact that each contains a Manchester code violation. After correct receipt of a start of frame the signal is sampled at 20 MHz and a check is made to ensure that the average signal is zero. Since the phasing at this frequency is not necessarily known, two sums are calculated, one between two consecutive samples and the other between two samples with one sample in between. If neither of these sums is zero a collision has occurred. This method is designed to detect 100% of collisions between two or more stations; it is proposed but not obligatory, since manufacturers achieve the same results in a different way.

Summary We now summarize the crossing delays for all transceiver types. Tables of the total crossing delays for a repeater with built-in transceivers (such as a hub), for a valid signal (Table 12.7) and then for a collision (Table 12.8) are given below.

Table 12.7 Delays of different repeaters for a valid signal (frame).

Transceiver type	Delays due to the transceiver Input + Output	Total time in bit times
10Base5	6.5 + 3.5	14
10Base2	6.5 + 3.5	14
FOIRL	3.5 + 3.5	11
10BaseT	8 + 5	17
10BaseFP	3 + 4	11*
10BaseFB	2 + 2	4
10BaseFL	5 + 5	11

*: for 10BaseFP the calculation involves a repeater incorporating two transceivers and not a passive star.

Table 12.8 Delays of different repeaters for a collision.

Transceiver type	Delays due to the transceiver Input + Output	Total time in bit times
10Base5	9 + 3.5	19
10Base2	9 + 3.5	19
FOIRL	3.5 + 3.5	13.5
10BaseT	9 + 5	20.5
10BaseFP	11.5 + 1	19*
10BaseFB	3.5 + 2	12
10BaseFL	3.5 + 5	15

*: for 10BaseFP the calculation involves a repeater incorporating two transceivers and not a passive star.

The switching hub

The most efficient solution to the new bandwidth requirements is to increase the global speed of the network without jeopardizing the architectures previously chosen. The idea is, in fact, to improve the existing MAC technology by moving from an access mode in which all the connections share the global bandwidth to one in which the total bandwidth is dedicated to each pair of items of equipment for the duration of the transmission of each packet.

Taking advantage of the star topology linked to all installations with structured cabling (twisted pair and optical fiber), it is effectively possible to guarantee that the maximum throughput is available to each port for each of its communications. The hub is then called a switching hub, since it is responsible for the dynamic switching of the packets between the ports, simulating the operation of a switching matrix.

The main practical advantage of switching lies in the fact that it can make use of the majority of existing network hardware, whether cabling, connectors, all the network interface cards (and, of course, their drivers) and, in certain cases, even the multi LAN technology modular chassis. In addition, the concept of packet switching is applicable to all shared LAN technology, whether Ethernet (recently including 100BaseT), Token Ring, LocalTalk or FDDI. However, the popularity and vulnerability of the CSMA/CD access method has made this requirement very beneficial to Ethernet, in order to help users who are already in a difficult situation with overloaded networks.

No LAN standard deals precisely with packet switching yet, although this is not a completely separate new technology with its own qualities and characteristics. We note in passing that the switch is an intermediate hardware element between the hub and the multiport bridge. Like a hub it has a large number of ports, but operates like a bridge in that it works on the MAC addresses. Given that it operates at the MAC level, we shall describe it in further detail in Chapter 13, as an interconnection hardware.

12.7 100 Mbps and 1 Gbps repeaters

Regarding 100 and 1000 Mbps shared networks, as there can not be more than 2 repeaters in a 100 Mbps network and only one in a 1 Gbps network, calculation is much simpler, knowing that:

$$LSDV = 2 \times \text{segment length} \times \text{media delay in bit-time/meter}$$

where LSVD : Link Segment Delay Value, is a segment delay (different from SDV)

$$PDV = \sum LSDV + \sum \text{repeaters} + DTE \text{ delay} + \text{security margin}$$

where PDV has to be lower than 512 bit-time at 100 Mbps, and lower than 4096 bit-time at 1 Gbps, with a recommended security margin of 4 bit-time at 100 Mbps, and 32 bit-time at 1 Gbps:

PVD < 508 bit-time at 100 Mbps, and
PVD < 4064 bit-time at 1 Gbps

Naturally, those numbers for RTD calculation correspond to a shared environments, not switched. Fibre optic links for instance have different constraints in full-duplex mode (as shown in Table 8.1).

Besides, a network consisting of one repeater (with integrated PHY) and different types of link will have to respect the following rules:

1000BaseT + 1000BaseSX/LX ≤ 210 m (100 + 110 m)
1000BaseCX + 1000BaseSX/LX ≤ 220 m (195 + 25 m)

Table 12.9 Round-Trip Delay calculation at 100 and 1000 Mbps.

Component	RTD in bit-time/m	RTD max	max length
2 DTE 100B-TX or FX		100 bit-time	
2 DTE 100BaseT4		138 bit-time	
2 DTE 100BaseT2		96 bit-time	
1 DTE 100B-T2 or T4 & 1 DTE 100B-TX/FX		127 bit-time	
UTP 3/4 link in 100BaseT	1.14	114 bit-time	100 m
UTP 5 link in 100BaseT	1.112	111.2 bit-time	100 m
STP link in 100BaseTX	1.112	111.2 bit-time	100 m
100BaseFX link	1	412 bit-time	412 m
100 Mbps Class I repeater		140 bit-time	
100 Mbps Class II repeater (TX and FX)		92 bit-time	
100 Mbps Class II repeater (with T4 port)		67 bit-time	
100 Mbps Class II repeater (with T2 port)		90 bit-time	

Component	RTD in bit-time/m	RTD max	max length
2 DTE at 1 Gbps		864 bit-time	
UTP 5 link in 1000BaseT	11.12	1112 bit-time	100 m
1000BaseCX link	10.10	253 bit-time	25 m
1000BaseSX/LX link DTE-DTE	10.10	3232 bit-time	≤ 320 m
1000BaseSX/FX repeated link (exter. PHY)	10.10	1111 bit-time	110 m
1 Gbps repeater		976 bit-time	

Table 12.10 Main characteristics of twisted pair supplements.

Technology	Throughput	Link length	No. of hubs	Number and type of twisted pair	Pair usage	Full-duplex
1Base5	1 Mbps	250 m	7	2 UTP 3/4/5 ou STP		NA
10BaseT	10 Mbps	100 m (177 m)	3 (4)		1 Tx/1 Rx	possible
100BaseTX				2 UTP 5 ou STP		
100BaseT4	100 Mbps	100 m	2	4 UTP 3/4/5	3 Tx/3 Rx	impossible
100BaseT2				2 UTP 3/4/5	2 Tx-Rx	
1000BaseCX	1 Gbps	25 m	1	2 STP	1 Tx/1 Rx	possible
1000BaseT		100 m		4 UTP 5	4 Tx-Rx	

100BaseT repeater

Since 100BaseT wants to define a technology that complies fully with the Ethernet functioning mode, it defines repeaters as (the only) means to build a shared 100 Mbps network. Because a network is constrained by the round-trip time of 5.12 μs, there can be at most two repeaters on the way between two stations (and thus at most two repeaters within a 100BaseT network).

The wish of the 802.3u committee to define the repeater at 100 Mbps is not entirely consistent with the needs of the market, where it is much more common to use 100BaseT technology in close conjunction with switching, and therefore often with a very limited use of 100BaseT hubs.

However, to find a compromise between the performance of the repeater (in terms of delay) and its flexibility (in terms of different coding of interfaces), the IEEE has defined two types of hub: a single Class I repeater may be placed in a network, whereas up to two Class II repeaters may compose a network. The Class II hub is faster than the Class I hub, and thus also allows networks to be built with one slightly bigger hub.

RTD (propagation delay of a frame + propagation of a collision)
Class I   = 140 bit-time
Class II   = 46 + 46 bit-time   all 100BaseTX and/or 100BaseFX ports
Class II   = 67 bit-time   at least one 100BaseT4 port

We notice that the Class I repeater is particularly ill-suited for the change of coding 4B/5B $\leftrightarrow$ 8B/6T (about thirty meters less).

Table 12.11   Diameter of a shared 100 Mbps Ethernet network.

Model	UTP	100BaseFX	100BaseFX & T4 or T2	100BaseFX & TX
DTE-DTE	100 m	412 m	NA	
1 Class I hub	200 m	272 m	231 m	260.8 m
1 Class II hub		320 m	304 m	308.8 m
2 Class II hubs	205 m	228 m	236.3 m	216.2 m

The full-duplex Giga repeater

The full-duplex buffer repeater (or Buffer Distributor) realizes a network architecture centered around a 1 Gigabps repeater, but without the limitations of half duplex in terms of global dimensions. For this purpose, the repeater, which still processes only one frame at a time, is equipped with one MAC layer per port and one more receiving buffer than the traditional PHY layer. In addition, the repeater must handle Flow Control to be able to react to its buffers filling up too quickly.

The use of a full-duplex repeater at 1 Gigabps is reasonably justified if the network requires this throughput both centrally and towards the first level of switches, but does not necessarily need a multiple of a Gigabps, as would be offered by a switching device.

Virtual collision

Among the proposals for modifying the functioning of the 1 Gbps repeater, a suggestion was made to handle Virtual Collisions (at that time in CSMA/VCD). This means that, when a collision occurs, the first frame received by the hub is not 'killed', only the subsequent ones. Thus, a collision no longer causes time loss because one of the frames is effectively transmitted. However, this solution would have by default introduced an imbalance in the equity of access.

12.8 Test equipment

Various types of hardware may be useful for testing a network, during receipt or when dealing with a breakdown. Some hardware has been specially developed for local area networks, other hardware is general purpose.

The oscilloscope

This traditional device is used to visualize the signals directly in the coaxial cable or on the twisted pairs of the drop cables. When it has a resolution significantly greater than 10 MHz, it can be used to check the shape of the signals, the rise and fall times and the interframe gap. Its main advantages are that it can be used to visualize packets passing through an active hardware element of the network (transceiver, repeater, bridge, star) and can measure precisely the crossing delay for the device (Figure 12.25).

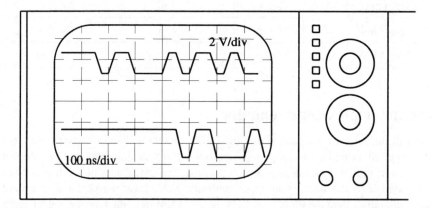

Figure 12.25   Ethernet signals on an oscilloscope screen.

It is easy to find tap points for the electrical signals, whether on the coaxial cable, the twisted pairs of the AUI cable or the 10BaseT lines, which can be used to establish the observation directly on the medium or between the MAU and the PLS without disturbing the communications. Measurements on the optical transceivers are usually made through the intermediary of the drop cable. Finally, one particular application is the qualification of the retransmission of intensive traffic by an interconnection device, where one seeks to detect irregularities such as bursty emissions which are detrimental for the other hardware.

Since it is a laboratory tool, one always needs to have available a minimum quantity of minor measurement hardware associated with the oscilloscope: a probe, crocodile clip, drop cable splitter and BNC and type N connectors.

The coaxial reflectometer

The reflectometer for coaxial cable measures the variation of the impedance along a medium segment (it does not cross the repeaters) (Figure 12.26). Its operation is based on the periodic emission of calibrated peaks at one end and the observation of the amplitude of the reflection of this signal in time. This measurement is known as Time-Domain Reflectometry (TDR). Note that the reflectometer screen is graduated in mρ/DIV rather than in Ohm and only measures differences in impedance.

These reflected peaks are processed in order to determine the impedance graph for the cable over its whole length. Thus it is possible to detect any abnormal variation which could lead to malfunctioning, to check that the maximum reflection rate of 7% at an arbitrary point (connection of a transceiver) or 4% at the straight connector points studied is not exceeded. The graph can also be used to locate the positions of cuts, junctions, and transceivers relatively exactly. If the opposite end is not fitted with a 50 Ohm terminator, the important reflection at this point can be used to obtain a reliable estimate of the length of the segment measured.

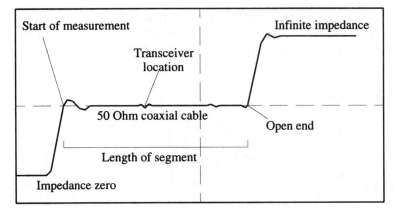

Figure 12.26 Example of a screen of a coaxial reflectometer.

A regular measurement campaign, for example every two years, may be used to monitor the aging of the medium, its hardware and its attachment points.

For increased freedom in measurement activities and operations one should choose a battery-operated device. Since the reflectometer generates electrical signals and quantizes their reflection on return, all the transceivers connected to the segment studied must be disconnected during the measurement so as not to disturb either the reflectometer or the attached stations. The greatest risk is that the emissions from the transceivers will lead to a deterioration of the reflectometer, if the latter does not have appropriate protection.

The optical dBmeter

The optical dBmeter has the simple function of measuring the power of a light signal reaching it. Thus, it can be used to evaluate the attenuation of a fiber optic link, with a view to checking that the maximum attenuation between the two ends authorized by the standard (12.5dB for 10BaseFL) is not exceeded (Figure 12.27).

Good quality work requires the choice as light emitter of a stable calibrated source (not an active transceiver for example) operating in the same frequency range as the network hardware to be installed (850 nm for Ethernet, 1300 nm for FDDI and 100BaseFX). The measurement is relative, that is, the attenuation due to the fiber is evaluated by taking the difference between the power received directly behind the source and the power of this same signal after it has crossed the link in question. Current hardware can usually store the first value as a reference, so that the display then gives the difference directly.

Since the connector technology for the optical source and the receiver cannot be universal (given the heterogeneity of this area) adapter cables are usually needed. Thus, it is important to carry out the reference measurement with the attachment cables which will be used subsequently.

The receiver indicates the power in dB (hence the name dBmeter) or in mW. The signal frequency used should also be indicated (820, 850, 1300 or 1550 nm) for greater accuracy.

Some emitters can accommodate different sources, each operating at a specific wavelength and being either an LED or a laser. The laser, which delivers a considerably greater power than the LED, is used for the measurement of very long

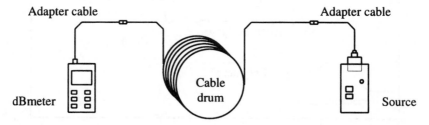

Figure 12.27   Configuration for measurement of the attenuation of an optical fiber.

lengths. In a practical way, the source and the dBmeter are both small battery-operated devices (which can be held in the hand) which are robust enough that they can be moved without difficulty.

We stress that this is an elementary measurement which cannot be used to locate a fault when the link is defective, but only gives a global figure. We shall see below that there exist instruments capable of analyzing the quality of the optical fiber in a much finer manner.

The optical reflectometer

The optical reflectometer operates on the same principle as the coaxial reflectometer but, of course, using light signals (Figure 12.28). It produces Optical Time-Domain Reflectometry (OTDR), measuring the reflection rate (or variation of index) along the fiber by emitting periodic peaks from one end. The result is a graph showing the attenuation due to the fiber at all points, which gives, among other things, the total length of the link.

Unlike measurement using the dBmeter, reflectometry gives information about the quality of the fiber over the whole path, except at the output end, where the reflection rate on the open connector is generally sufficiently large to mask any defect at this point. This device can be used to evaluate the attenuation per kilometer, visualize the quality of the attachments (pair of connectors) and the splices and locate these precisely. Like measurement using the dBmeter, it is preferable to carry out the reflectometry at the same frequency as that of the active elements which are to be used (850 nm for 10 Mbps Ethernet).

Specifically, the gradient of each section easily gives the attenuation as a function of the length (for example, 3.5 dB/km with the 62.5/125 μm at 850 nm); the difference between the two sides of a pair of connectors gives the attenuation due to this attachment (strictly, the stable tangents to each side should be used). One effect that is rapidly encountered is the dazzle in each large perturbation, such as that

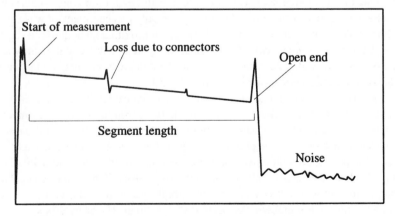

Figure 12.28   Example of the screen of an optical reflectometer.

produced by a connector. Since the reflectometer's receiver is saturated by the returning signal (comparatively much larger than the simple reflection due to the fiber itself), measurement near a connector is not reliable. To obtain a better resolution, one should choose a shorter peak (long peaks being reserved for measurements over long distances, which require more power). However, the measurement will still be partially masked around a strong source of reflection. This implies that the first and last connectors cannot be qualified, since a stabilized part of one of their sides is missing. To counter this disadvantage a trailer (extra length of fiber) can be inserted in front of the link to be studied, and possibly after it. This makes it possible to measure the end connectors since one then has a stable line segment, obtained before and after the fiber, on the screen. It is then possible to evaluate the total attenuation, although less accurately than using a dBmeter. Note that, since the majority of optical links are bi-fiber links, the two fibers may be looped together for measurement at the far end using a jumper wire; thus, it is possible to check the two distant connectors even if one does not have a trailer. However, measurement from the other end is still useful for checking the two other connectors.

In practice, the reflectometer is a top-of-the-range device, whose sources are often in the form of interchangeable slide valves, each with a unique fixed operating frequency.

In conclusion, we note that there exist elementary optical reflectometers called fault finders which give a graph very similar to that of a reflectometer, without being able to provide a reliable measurement of the attenuation. Since only the distance from the source of the observed reflection can be retained, they have to be reserved for use in an emergency (intervention in the case of breakdown), and cannot be used to qualify the optical fiber.

The tester for twisted pairs

The tester for twisted pairs is a small, easily transportable device (it fits into the hand). This is a more recent tool than the previous ones, being directly linked to the development of local area networks. It is a tool in full evolution which incorporates an increasing number of functions. Originally, the only measurements it was capable of taking related to twisted pairs. It could give the approximate length of the segment (using TDR) and indicate whether the segment was open or short-circuited or whether the pairs were crossed. The result is displayed in English (in text mode, without graphics) on a liquid crystal display (Figure 12.29).

Today, it is adapted to standard and thin coaxial cables (type N and BNC), to the shielded and the unshielded twisted pair (hermaphrodite and RJ45 connectors) and, indeed, to the palettes of patching modules. It is able to test several pairs at a time, check their order and detect crossings, measure the in-loop resistance and store the reflectometry curves obtained and print them or transmit them to a PC. It can generate Link Test Pulses to validate the ports of a 10BaseT hub, and is capable of measuring the network activity using a bar graph, generating alarms when events occur and dialing via a modem. Associated with a small RF receiver box, it can be used to track the path of the cabling in walls and suspended ceilings.

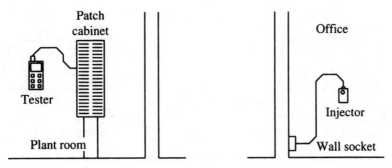

Figure 12.29   Test of a cabling link using a tester and an injector.

The Ethernet test set

The Ethernet test set is a simple, portable tool which implements part of the MAC layer. Thus, it can be used to carry out tests involving the emission and receipt of frames in the Ethernet format, in order to validate a network infrastructure including all types of medium, transceivers, repeaters, bridges and AUI cables.

The main desirable capability is the possibility of creating an automatic echo mode between two connection points. The two sets of the pair are generally assigned in a master–slave relationship. The master regularly generates frames (possibly numbered), which the slave receives and replies to with identical frames. The master set is responsible for checking that no frames are lost. This test is used to check a chain of devices on the route of the packets. Since no protocols above the MAC level are involved, this qualification is purely Ethernet. We note that for the traffic to pass through the bridges, the source and destination of the frames must be distinct (use of emission in multicast is possible, but not always desirable). Passage through routers is rarely possible because the contents of the MAC frames generated are meaningless in most cases. Since the presence of traffic on the medium does not always facilitate implementation of this echo mode (partly because of collisions), the use of test sets may be restricted to operations on empty networks.

In addition to their ability to carry out an exchange in echo mode (Figure 12.30), these test sets can provide other functions such as the test of the drop cable (continuity and insulation of each pair, determination of the type: Ethernet V 2.0 or IEEE 802.3) or the test of the transceiver with qualification of the electrical levels of emission, reception and detection, the delay in triggering the jabber, and the presence or absence of the SQE test. This collection of tests may be very useful when dealing with a network one of whose elements is conjectured to be defective. The Ethernet test set can be used to carry out a series of tests of the units. Some test sets offer the possibility of evaluating the round-trip delay for a network, either from a point, by the emission of a frame which is reflected against one end in an open circuit, or between two test sets with the voluntary generation of a collision. These measurements are generally less precise than those of a reflectometer, but quickly

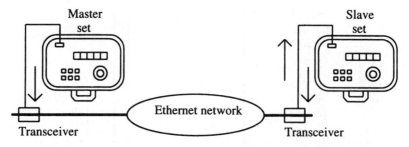

Figure 12.30   Pair of Ethernet test sets in echo mode.

give an order of magnitude measurement. Finally, the test set can also generate a given rate of traffic (from a few percent to the maximum) with frames of a parametrizable length, emit defective packets (too long, too short, with a bad CRC) or create collisions.

Some manufacturers offer Ethernet test sets with three AUI sockets (two of which are used to test the AUI cable from end to end), a BNC connection (for testing the transceiver outside the network when it can be attached by the AUI socket and the coaxial cable at the same time) and, sometimes, tap points on the drop cable pairs (this last option is essentially adapted to qualification operations in the laboratory using an oscilloscope).

The test set should be able to count all the frames received, the collisions and the faults. Since the device is relatively rudimentary, it is expected to be precise, reliable and easy to use and install. As we shall see in Part III, it used to be a very useful piece of hardware in repair work, when it can be used to validate one or more network access points. Note that the test set operates with frames whose fields are only important at the MAC level, and that the data field is generally just a sequence of bytes, independent of any protocol. Conversely, the test set is able to count the frames circulating in the network and recognize whether or not they are intended for it, although it cannot provide more information.

The analyzer

The Ethernet analyzer is the most complete MAC-level test equipment, which is still portable for use in repair work. It should be able to operate on the Ethernet fields for both reception and emission.

Moreover, over successive evolutions, the analyzer has acquired an understanding and a knowledge of the most common higher protocols, and can deal with all the fields of the frame (from the preamble up to level 7). It has also become programmable, which opens up a wealth of possibilities for implementation.

The analyzer should be able to measure the network traffic precisely and display the total number of frames, errors and collisions received, their rates per second in the form of an instantaneous value, and an average, together with the maximum rate recorded (associated with the time this occurred). It should also be

```
frame 3111    9 Sept 92      16h27'34"42536            length 60    no error
Ethernet : Dest :   Sun-07-51-17  Source   : HP-23-45-81  Type : DoD_IP
  IP Version : 4  Header length bytes : 20  Type of service : routine
            Total length : 41  Ident : 37562  Flags : May Frag Last Frag
            Frag offset: 0    Time to live : 30     Next protocol : TCP
            Chksum : OK 00-19 Source : 154.27.2.154  Dest : 154.27.35.48
  TCP Source : 1023    Dest : RWHO_RLOGIN      Sequence no : 142578296
            Acknowledge : 765774905    Data Offset : 20  Flags : ACK_PSH
            Window : 4096        Chksum : OK      Urgent point : not used 0
```

Figure 12.31 Example of a screen showing a decoded header.

able to capture complete frames, construct the list of addresses of machines using the network and decode the frames as finely as possible while automatically managing the standard protocols (TCP/IP, DECnet, XNS, IPX, ISO, and so on) (Figure 12.31). It will also be required to emit frames whose format and various higher-level fields will be defined by the user or recovered by capture on the network. All these tasks should be executable within as broad a range of speeds as possible, both during reception and counting and during emission, so that the use of the analyzer is independent of the measurement conditions. For example, the analyzer will be required not to lose traffic in reception, even when the load is very high, whether valid frames, very short frames (a few bytes), excessively long frames or collisions. In all cases, the counters should be exact so that the measurement is truly reliable and can be used with confidence. Similarly, in emission, the analyzer should be able to generate a maximum level of traffic, even with short frames (64 bytes). Even more demands will be placed on it if this device is used in assemblies for qualifying network hardware.

On this subject, we note that there are several ways of counting the traffic as a percentage (Figure 12.32). If one considers the frame with all its fields (preamble, addresses, type, data and CRC), the maximal traffic (100% theoretically) in short

View of the network							
Observed since 17h49'35" 5 July 92				9h25'20"	13 July 92		
Throughput				Frame info			
Instantaneous	Ave.	Peak	Unit	Average size	827 bytes		
3.25	2.86	42.17	%	Maximum size	2142 bytes		
323	2.74	4.087	kbps	Minimum size	7 bytes		
48	36	459	frm/s	Total frames	45 321 784		
Ave.: 1 min		Peak at 8h07'42"		Total bytes	3.729 E-10		

Collision and errors					
	Bad FCS	Runt	Jabber	Collision	
Instan.	2	1	0	0	
Total	1457	986	27	536	
Rate	3.2E-5	2.2E-5	6E-7	1.2E-5	
Ave.	5.4E-5	3.7E-5	0	2.3E-3	
Peak	4.2E-2	2.7E-2	1E-2	1.1E-2	

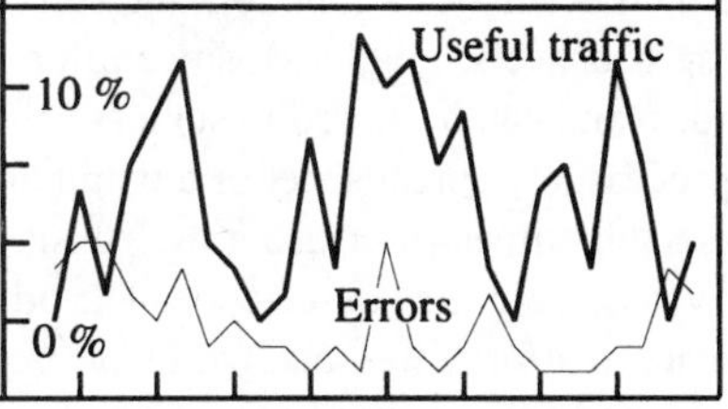

Figure 12.32 Examples screen of analyzer statistics (unit for errors: occurrences/frame).

frames (64 bytes + 64 bits = 576 bits) could be 85.7% (= $14880 \times 576/10^7$), while, if one ignores the preamble, the short frame comprises 64 bytes and the maximal traffic represents a usage of 76.2% (= $14880 \times 64 \times 8/10^7$). This explains why, excluding device faults and limitations, not all analyzers count in exactly the same way. Still on this subject, some analyzers include in their evaluation of the traffic (as a percentage or in kbps) all the bits read, whether they are part of a frame structure or isolated. The resulting information is sometimes very useful, as in the case of an infinitely long preamble which would occupy the medium without representing traffic in terms of frames per second.

The possibility of programming these devices with a few lines of code or a sequence of test conditions means that they can be used in an automated and diverse way. For example, it is possible to trigger an arbitrary action (alarm, storage, capture, emission) when different events occur, such as the receipt of certain special packets, the passing of a threshold or the elapsing of a timer. Applications can therefore be developed by users focusing on their own needs.

Finally, the industry has recently begun to produce analyzers with analytical capabilities and a certain autonomous reasoning power. Expert systems have been coupled to the functionality of the devices so as to relieve the novice user of level 2 or 3 analysis and repair tasks. Thus, these new analyzers claim to be able to detect defective frames at the MAC level or in the network and transport layer together with certain anomalies such as the duplication of logical addresses. Although this new facet is a noteworthy introduction, one should not expect too much from a PC with an analyzer card and an inference motor, which, in any case, cannot determine the topology of your network or the characteristics of the traffic of the stations.

In practice, there are two main categories of Ethernet analyzer, one based on slot-in cards for PCs (possibly portable), the other based on proprietary hardware, which is therefore closed. In the first case, either the card is 'smart' with its own microprocessor and RAM (a few Mbytes are needed) and capable of carrying out certain processing directly on certain packets received and stored in its memory, or it is a simple Ethernet interface card and all the processing is the responsibility of the microcomputer host. Up to now, this second type of card has not been able to offer the visibility capabilities of dedicated cards at high speed, which are sometimes expensive but have a high performance. The advantages of the analyzer in the form of a PC card lie first in its apparently few restrictions, in that it interfaces with any portable micro with extension slots that are not necessarily reserved solely for the Ethernet analyzer function and, second, in its openness to MS-Windows software (spreadsheets, graphics), since after processing the data is returned to the PC platform and can be stored in standard files. These files can then be recovered by a word processor, a spreadsheet or a commercial graphics program. Moreover, manufacturers sometimes offer users the possibility of enriching certain decoding themselves by accessing the source code. The advantage of the analyzer developed on a proprietary platform lies mainly in its performance, since its hardware architecture is oriented towards the processing of frames. Finally, we note that there are analyzers which combine the advantages of both categories, being constructed based on a PC but with a proprietary extensions adapted to fast message processing functions.

Moreover, for some time, analyzers have been available which are capable of holding connector cards for various local area networks (such as Ethernet, Token Ring and FDDI), but which have only one user interface with unique higher-level decoding capabilities for the two or three types of attachment.

The probe

The probe is a remote monitoring tool which, some years ago, was a small analyzer with a limited capability, fixed on the network to observe the traffic there and return its statistics to a master station (Figure 12.33). The probe generally comprises a small box with a network interface and sometimes a socket for serial connection; thus, it does not have a screen or any form of display. This implies that a non-trivial part of the processing is carried out at the level of the management station (calculation, averaging, storage, display).

The main data concerns network load statistics and graphs, covering valid frames, errors, and collisions over periods of various lengths. This includes the storage of maximal values and the evaluation of mean rates and peaks for each category of frame, together with a listing of the Ethernet addresses of active stations with their corresponding traffic and error rate. These figures are communicated regularly to the monitoring station, either by the network, if this is not defective or out of service, or by the intermediary of a serial link between the probe and the station.

Probes have evolved with the development of management protocols such as SNMP of the TCP/IP family. They still collect statistics on the network traffic, as an analyzer might, but they no longer simply present them in the manufacturer's format and now follow the SNMP standard and certain groups of the RMON (remote monitoring) MIB specifically defined for this purpose. The groups of RFC 1757 are statistics, history, alarms, hosts, host_top_N, traffic_matrix, filters, packet_capture, and events. These groups correspond to relatively rich analytical and observational capabilities, which also consume processing power, hence the need for a dedicated CPU. These standards also classify the errors in detailed categories.

In addition, SNMP defines the values to be monitored in the form of variables in a tree structure, the whole being defined in libraries called Management Information Bases (MIB). The manufacturers have naturally added to the amount of data that their probes can capture by adding proprietary MIBs to those already defined (MIB-I, MIB-II, and RMON). See Chapter 15.7 for more details.

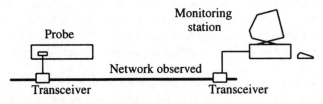

Figure 12.33 Monitoring system comprising a probe and the master station.

Finally, we note that if the network implements the dynamic packet switching technology at certain nodes, the probe becomes somewhat less interesting, since each port of the switch only allows traffic to pass which is either explicitly destined for interfaces connected behind this port or is in diffusion. Thus, as a probe alone on a switch port will only see the traffic in diffusion, switching requires a probe for each port, or better, a "virtual" global probe. This remark also applies to any network which is micro-segmented by numerous local bridges.

The multiport tester

A new type of testing equipment has come recently to the market. It typically consists of a rack able to receive multiple interface modules, the whole being controlled by a single station. The goal is then to be able to generate a high number of flows at level 2 (MAC frames), 3 (IP datagrams) or higher (TCP sessions, up to HTTP connection) in order to measure the performance of equipment or eventually of an entire network under a very precisely mastered situation. The simplest test consists of evaluating the global throughput of a switch or a router, and the behaviour of the retransmission while changing certain parameters (bursty aspect, type of frame, number of simulated end-station). But this equipment could also provide a generic means to operate very complete descriptions of a network item under common conditions, and automatically show its main drawback or limitations. In a second phase we can expect that the multiport tester could be able to monitor an active network (LAN or WAN) with a minimal impact on operational traffic by having multiple points of measurement spread over the infrastructure, each point still providing a coordinated reliable generator and measuring tool. Eventually it could then be able to simulate default or hacker attack, or help to simulate anticipated growth by multiplying artificially (but as realistically as possible) the existing traffic. In this way the network manager could know exactly how the network would react to a coming extension.

Management hardware

Here, we distinguish between the agent which accumulates the measurement data (such as the probe) and that which processes and analyzes the data and presents them to the person responsible for monitoring the network. This last element actually constitutes the management tool with which people communicate.

Several classes of device are capable of transmitting the data relating to the traffic they observe to a management center. This includes hardware dedicated to the monitoring function (probe, analyzer) or hardware involved in the network architecture (repeater, hub, star, bridge, router, terminal server, file server, peripheral server) which is equipped with sufficient intelligence to send statistical reports to a master station.

All these elements accumulate information about the parts of the network in which they are located and send their data stream to one or more concentration points whose job it is to synthesize all the data. The management station receiving the data streams first has to be able to understand them, which is not a self-evident matter. In fact, the proprietary formats of the messages exchanged for management of the hardware devices have given way to certain standard protocols. However, each manufacturer is able to record special information which it then includes in its database, in an extension of the standardized framework. For example, if the management station is meant to cover a large number of makes of hardware, it should be able to decode the packets of each and associate a meaning with each counter (knowledge of a private MIB).

If possible, the management station will present results of the analysis of the contents of all the messages in graphical form, associating graphs of various loads, changes in colors when certain thresholds are passed and requests for acknowledgment when warnings are issued. One possible method of navigating through the various layers of description avoids submerging a whole screen, in the case of a heavily populated network, and represents the network in a hierarchical fashion.

In addition to simply listening in to the packets of management information circulating on the network, monitoring systems should also be able to interrogate (poll) the machines managed to retrieve the desired counters at the appropriate time. They should also be able to parametrize certain acquisitions by defining the measurement periods, the addresses observed, the protocols concerned, the levels of alarms or notification on the traffic, the percentage of frames in diffusion, the errors, the collision rate, and so on.

In addition, a hierarchy of management stations may be developed with several successive levels of information retrieval. In this light, one can envisage that a single console may receive the synthesized overview from several machines, which themselves receive the information from smaller management systems. At each stage, the concentration of reports on the state of part of the network should be handled in such a way that only relevant new details are retained and only important or significant warnings are passed on. The objective remains the same, that is, to be able to monitor the network, whatever its size, from a single screen, while ensuring that no notable events are missed and without being submerged by a chain of alarms triggered by a single event.

When choosing a device of this type, care should therefore be taken to ensure that the tool is easy to use (or as undaunting as possible) to eliminate the risk of being faced by a sequence of indications with an impenetrable meaning. One should also look for a system with a rich knowledge of hardware from different manufacturers (possibly developed in collaboration), and which can be updated by adding modules describing recent or additional databases. The underlying standardized protocol should be SNMP today and possibly CMIP or SNMP v3 in the near future.

In fact, SNMP was not originally designed for such generalized and complex uses as those for which it is effectively employed today. It was to be a rudimentary and temporary solution. Consequently, its simplicity and intrinsic shortcomings (lack of security, low performance on important data, limited error management, no report for hierarchical or distributed configuration) have begun to become truly restrictive and must be overcome. SNMP v3 represents a recasting of this management protocol, which is applicable to network and application-related devices and to computer systems, and which supports other protocols in addition to those of the TCP/IP world. It covers the functionality developed for Secure SNMP and, of course, the description of objects by the MIB. We will come back to this topic in Chapter 15.7.

Chapter 13

Interconnection and switching

- MAC bridges

- Hybrid bridging

- Switching

- Routers

- Terminal servers

Up to now we have described the components which may constitute an Ethernet network, together with those which can be used to test it. Given the inherent limitations of the technology, in terms of the area covered and the number of machines, interconnection requirements appeared at a very early stage.

The first requirement was to extend an existing network or to interlink several more-or-less adjacent networks. Various types of hardware meet this requirement, including bridges, routers, and gateways. Repeaters and stars, which cannot extend the coverage of a single network, do not fall in this category, even when they can be used to exceed the standardized distances.

Bridge processing is at level 2 (more precisely, at the MAC level), and thus achieves a more than satisfactory performance (its functionality may be encoded entirely in hardware). The bridge has the advantage of being totally transparent as far as the use of the network is concerned. Its disadvantage is inherent in its function, namely that it cannot be used for logical segmentation of interconnected networks and therefore propagates the problems on all the networks attached to it.

The router provides connection at level 3, where the routing information is normally found. Its processing depends upon the encapsulated protocols and thus may be less extensive, in terms of its knowledge of protocol classes (mono- or multiprotocol). Since its work is much more elaborate, it is partially handled by software, which, several years ago, was an indicator of modest performance. Its advantages lie in its independence of the lower layers, since it may have all types of network interface (Token Ring, FDDI, serial lines). It is not transparent and has to be configured as a step toward the destination.

The gateway is concerned with links at the level of the higher layers and remains a specific hardware device. When it acts on application data (level 7), it may be developed on any protocol stack on each side of its interfaces.

Readers will have understood that the devices do not all meet exactly the same requirement, even if they all involve interconnection. Their respective advantages inevitably mean that they are each preferred in different situations.

These three types of hardware are relatively old and only their performance has evolved at different times. Bridges were the first to provide suitable capabilities, followed by routers. Gateways, being specific devices, are somewhat separate.

13.1 MAC bridges

Introduction

Bridges are devices that allow two or more networks to connect with each other. Thus, they are not really part of the elements that constitute a network, and they are not defined by the LAN or MAN technology standard employed, but by a complementary document.

Requirements

The principal role of a bridge lies in the interconnection of several networks at MAC level. This means that it allows stations connected to different networks to communicate with each other, thus authorizing the construction of more extended and more populated architectures than that of a single network.

The fact that it works at MAC level means that it has no knowledge of the higher protocols (of Network level and higher) used by the traffic it lets through. Consequently, its operation is independent of the contents of the data (or Info) field of the MAC frame, and applies to all protocols in exactly the same way.

History

Standardization of bridging was carried out, as with the majority of LAN technologies, by the IEEE. The 802.1D committee dealt with the subject and in 1990 produced a document which was taken on by the ISO in 1993, adding the different modes of bridging. Moreover, the resulting IS 10038 standard equally concerns Ethernet, Token Bus, Token Ring, and FDDI networks. More recently, the 802.1p draft proposes including handling of multicast and priority queues, and the 802.1Q draft describes VLANs setting up and operation.

By default, a bridge connects two networks of the same technology, but with possibly different speeds. Thus, the various implementations of Ethernet corresponding to the existing supplements (1, 10, 100 Mbps, and 1 Gbps) can communicate via a MAC bridge, whereas a repeater cannot provide this service. However, there are also so-called hybrid bridges which connect heterogeneous networks with each other (Ethernet $\leftrightarrow$ Token-Ring). We will look at them in more detail in the section on conversion bridging (see Chapter 13.2).

It is important to remember that, at MAC level, the bridge must be considered as a station. It can have one or more MAC-level addresses, and surrounds all its basic operations with a MAC interface, that is, validity check of the frame (minimum and maximum length, whole number of bytes, FCS recalculation, and, more specifically, reading of the Signal Quality Error: collision detection).

General principles

The only type of bridging used in Ethernet is Transparent Bridging (TB). Transparent Bridging requires that the bridge deals with the set of operations needed for bridging, freeing the end-stations of all extra computing load specific to the position of their counterparts. In this case, the interface card has no knowledge of the bridge and creates the same MAC headers, whether the addressee is in the same network or behind one (or more) bridge(s). This bridging is called transparent (to the stations at the extremes). The bridge must be powerful to guarantee the processing of all frames (be they retransmitted or not) with a reasonable pps rate (packets per second) and delay.

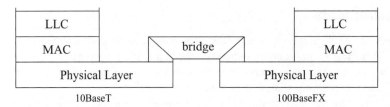

Figure 13.1   Example of a bridge between Ethernet and Fast Ethernet.

Note that the transparent type bridge perceives all frames whatever their destination may be, and not only those addressed to itself (packets explicitly addressed to the transparent bridge consist of multicast messages exchanged by the Spanning Tree Protocol, and management information, such as SNMP requests). If a received frame is valid, the bridge learns its source address, which amounts to storing the pair (source address, number of port at which received). Thus, it knows from then on that the station which emitted that frame lies behind the port through which the frame reached it. This information is stored in its learning table, which the bridge will use for any forwarding decision. Simultaneously with the learning, the bridge processes the frames reaching it. If the destination address of the frame received on the port N is not in its table it retransmits (forwards) the frame on all the ports other than N. If the address of the frame is in its table and associated with port N, it discards the frame from its processing procedure, since, in the meantime, the frame will necessarily have reached the destination station, which is on the same network or at least on the same side of the bridge. Finally, if it finds the address in its table, but associated with a port other than N, it forwards the message on this port only. This whole process is called natural filtering or filtering by learning (Figure 13.2). It is standardized by the IEEE under the name of transparent bridging. All Ethernet bridges must implement this filtering function, as a minimum.

Depending on the hardware, the learning of an address may take place immediately, or after one or more frames have passed (this last case is rare and undesirable). In the best of circumstances, the frame that is used to update the learning table is subject to filtering with the new table, which amounts to saying that a frame with identical source and destination addresses will never cross a bridge. Some bridges, the device will let the first frame through, but not subsequent frames.

The learning function associated with natural filtering is not simply additive, that is, it does not accumulate the addresses observed indefinitely in its tables. In fact, such behavior would be a handicap in the case of evolving networks in which machines may change sides after a move or even disappear for good from the network. There is then no point in retaining a memory of the address, by taking the risk of progressively building gigantic and partially obsolete tables. Bridges employing natural filtering therefore carry out a regular refreshment of their table, by simply eliminating from their memory any entries corresponding to addresses which have not emitted for a certain time (for example, several minutes). This implies that if a station has not emitted for a long time (more than the delay after which it is forgotten), the frames destined for it will be forwarded by the bridges on all their ports, like packets with an unknown destination. Another condition which results in

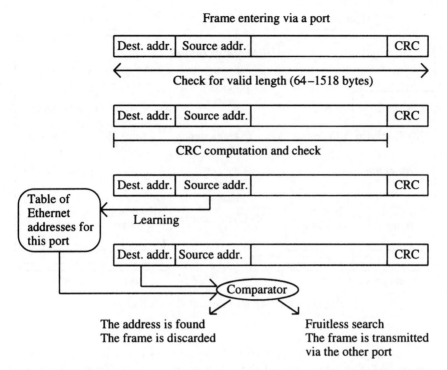

Figure 13.2   Stages in the natural filtering operation on one side of a biport bridge.

the modification of the learning table is the change of side of an address (a physical address previously seen on a port of the bridge is later detected on another port). In this case, too, the bridge updates its table as a function of the recent information. However, if the address changes sides regularly and relatively quickly, some bridges then refuse to register the address, considering this to be an abnormal situation.

We note that, in the case of several networks interlinked by several bridges, it is not crucial for a bridge to be able to differentiate between every existing network. It is sufficient for it to have a local view and, without risk of upsetting the operation of the network, it may confuse all the networks which are finally linked to it through the same port.

IEEE 802.1D represents the bridge as shown in Figure 13.3. This figure picks out the vital functional blocks for the bridging function (the two MAC entities and the MAC relay entity) and the supplementary blocks (the LLC entities and the higher layers). The MAC level is implemented for observation of the traffic and to forward frames, while the level above is used for communication between bridges.

The spanning tree

The vulnerability of the transparent bridge to loops is a crucial problem which was settled by the implementation of an interaction between bridges and a capability to detect and eliminate looped paths. In fact, the loop, if it is not detected, causes the

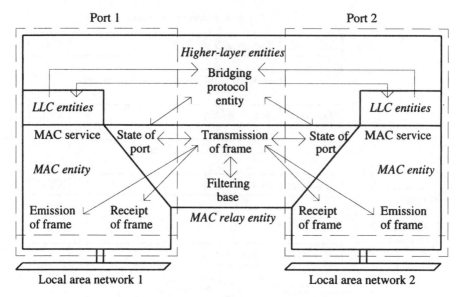

Figure 13.3 Architecture of a biport bridge.

bridge learning tables to lose all their validity and gives rise to a continuous circulation of the frames which then fill all the linked networks. We note that the solution chosen to resolve the loop problem by deactivating ports on certain bridges is simple, but not optimal. In fact, it would be more effective to distribute the traffic on the different possible routes, thereby increasing the global bandwidth of the interconnections, but it would be much more complex.

Nevertheless, the manufacturers of transparent bridges soon implemented a version of the spanning tree algorithm (the term 'spanning tree' refers to a loop-free topology extending over all the interconnected networks). However, as soon as the IEEE 802.1D committee had finalized the Spanning Tree Protocol/Algorithm (STP/A) all the manufacturers rallied to it, with the concomitant advantage that bridges of different makes take part in the same exchanges to establish the desired tree. DEC's implementation, which was very common, is also supported by certain interconnection equipment.

In summary, the STA's function is to define one of the bridges of the architecture as the root bridge and to establish a ramified topology based on this, without loops, of course. The loops are suppressed by deactivating certain bridges port and all the networks are thus attached to the root bridge by a unique path (see changes from Figure 13.4 to 13.5). On each network, one of the bridges is chosen as a designated bridge, this being the bridge that leads to the root bridge. Similarly, each designated bridge has a root port which leads to the root bridge, while the other ports which provide this access to more distant networks are called designated ports. Ports involved in the creation of loops are placed in a completely passive state (blocking), except as far as listening to BPDU packets is concerned. Note that, before the

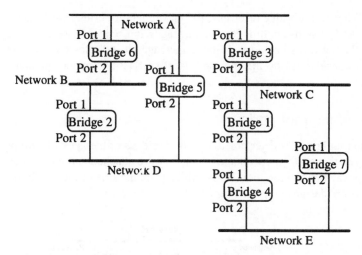

Figure 13.4 Example of networks bridged before the spanning tree is established.

configuration stabilizes, the bridges exchange information but do not forward the frames of real traffic which they receive and do not yet learn the MAC addresses.

For this, the bridges communicate using frames specific to the STP, called Bridge Protocol Data Units (BPDU). These frames have a format of type IEEE 802.3 or IEEE 802.2 (LLC type 1, connectionless, unacknowledged). They use a group destination address 01-80-C2-00-00-00 and an SAP $= 0 \times 42$ (which has a symmetrical binary value). On Token Ring, the function address 03-00-00-00-80-00 is used (due to the difficulty of managing multicasts with the NIC). The bridge has MAC addresses (one per port), which it uses naturally as source in its frames.

In addition, a management group address is defined for all the networks: 01-80-C2-00-00-10.

Finally, for future evolutions, 15 other group addresses have been reserved (01-80-C2-00-00-01 to -0F), which can be used to define different bridging areas that may be superposed on the same network interconnection architecture.

The procedure for establishing the spanning tree is described below in more detail.

Choice of the root bridge

When it is powered up, or when it is isolated (in the absence of any external information), any bridge thinks that it is itself the root bridge. It therefore periodically (every 2 seconds) broadcasts frames on the networks to which it is attached, indicating that it is the root and giving its 8-byte identifier. This identifier consists of the priority and the MAC address of the bridge (it is recommended that this should be the address of the port with the smallest number). The frames are sent to all the bridges, but do not cross them. The bridge chosen is that with the highest priority, that is, whose identifier has the smallest value. This root bridge is therefore a designated bridge for the LANs to which it is connected.

Whenever a bridge receives a BPDU from a root bridge which is effectively superior to it, it stops emitting its own messages and echoes those coming from the root on the networks behind it. In these messages it indicates the identifier of the bridge it considers to be the root and uses the STP parameters implemented by the latter.

Choice of the root ports

Once the root bridge is determined, the other bridges of the network will propagate this information on the networks to which they are attached and position their ports in such a way that the root port is that which is on the side of the root bridge, while the others are designated ports (Figure 13.5).

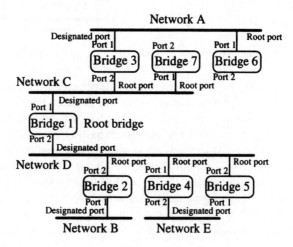

Figure 13.5 Example of a tree-like topology emanating from the root port.

Choice of the designated bridges and ports

On each distant network (on which the root is not directly connected) the bridges will inform each other of the bridge identifier for the bridge that they have chosen as the root and of the cost of the path they propose to this root bridge. After a joint survey of the root, the bridge proposing the least expensive path will win. This cost is normally proportional to the sum of the inverses of the speeds of the networks crossed, or the sum of the delays in emission. The other bridges will place their port in a passive (or blocked) state so as to eliminate loops (Figure 13.6). The ports are chosen using a system of preferential selection based on the priority, then the number.

For this calculation, it is recommended that the cost of each network should be 1000/(speed in Mbps of the connected network), which gives: ≈ 4000 for a serial link at 256 kbps, 250 for Token Ring at 4 Mbps, 100 for Ethernet at 10 Mbps, 62 for Token Ring at 16 Mbps and 10 for FDDI or 100BaseT.

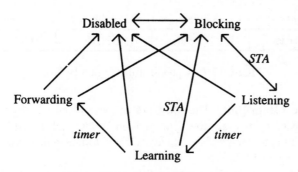

Figure 13.6 Diagram of port states.

Table 13.1 Recommended value of path cost.

Throughput of the link	Recommended value	Recommended range
4 Mbps	250	100–1000
10 Mbps	100	50–600
16 Mbps	62	40–400
100 Mbps	19	10–60
1 Gbps	4	3–10
10 Gbps	2	1–5

Traditionally, the recommended global value was $\Sigma1000$/throughputs of the traversed networks in Mbps, but since this was no longer applicable for the Gbps and higher range, a slightly more logarithmic table of recommended values is provided by IEEE 802.1p (Table 13.1). The global value remains the sum of the costs of each link.

In the case of a dispute, when the bridges propose the same path cost, the decision is based on the priority level of the bridges (that is, on the identifier) and, in the case where a bridge has several ports connected to the network, the port with the smallest identifier is chosen. Note that all the ports of a bridge should have an identifier consisting of a priority and their number.

In the simplified example shown in Figure 13.4 and 13.5, we used the number of the bridge as the identifier and we supposed that the costs of all the networks (and the costs of the associated ports) were identical.

All in all, the ports move between four different states, plus a deactivated state. The listening and learning states are transitory phases.

Once the port is declared to be part of the spanning tree topology, the transition from the listening phase to the learning phase and then to the forwarding phase takes 15 seconds in each case, or a total of 30 seconds.

The transition to the deactivated state is not part of the STP, but may be imposed by the management system.

n bytes	3 bytes	35 or 4 bytes	p bytes
MAC header	LLC1 header	BPDU	MAC postfix

Figure 13.7 General structure of a BPDU.

Bridge Protocol Data Unit The two types of message emitted by the bridges to manage the spanning tree are the configuration BPDU and the BPDU indicating modification of the topology. They all have a frame format conforming to the structure shown in Figure 13.7.

The MAC source address is that of the emitting port of the bridge. The LLC header includes the DSAP and SSAP = 0×42 indicating the STP.

The configuration BPDUs are emitted periodically by the root bridge on its networks. The bridges receiving them in turn forward them on all the networks they feed, and thus propagate the identifier of the root bridge, while incrementing the path cost as a function of the last network crossed (path cost of the receiving port). Thus, these BPDUs leave the root and are echoed on each branch of the tree, up to the extremities. Note that they transport the parameters imposed by the root, including the maximum age of a message, the interval between hellos and the delay in forwarding.

The messages emitted by the root have an age of 0 and are forwarded with this same age along the branches of the network. However, if a bridge of the network temporarily receives no further BPDUs, it will continue to emit the same packet periodically (every two seconds), increasing the age of the message relative to that from which it is derived. Thus, it indicates that its original information is not perfectly up to date, but is beginning to age. After the delay of *max age* (20 seconds recommended) the information coming from the root where these BPDUs were constructed is suppressed and the bridge redefines the path to the root (path cost and root port) based on other indications which it receives.

Figure 13.8 shows the format of a configuration BPDU; the individual fields are constructed as follows.

- **Flags**
- **TCA (most significant bit): Topology Change Acknowledgment** Bit positioned by the root bridge to acknowledge receipt of a message notifying a topology modification and indicating that the emitter should stop sending other messages of this type.
- **TC (least significant bit): Topology Change** Bit positioned by the root to inform the bridges that a change has occurred and that the forward delay should be used for the timer of fast aging for the learning table (15 seconds instead of 5 minutes).
- **Bridge identifier**
  - Priority of the bridge (two most significant bytes): 32768 by default, from 0 (high) to 65535 (low).
  - MAC address of the bridge (six least significant bytes).

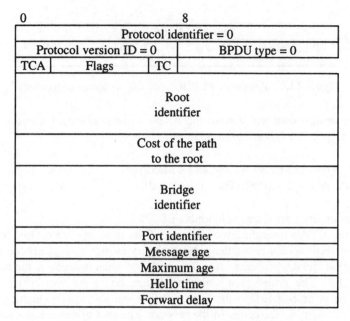

Figure 13.8 Format of a configuration BPDU.

- **Port identifier**
  - Priority of the port (most significant byte) to force the selection of the port in the case of a double connection: 128 by default, from 0 (high) to 255 (low)
  - Port number (least significant byte).
- **Root path cost** Cost of the path to the root: from 1 to 65535. Recommended value used to be = Σ1000 Mbps/speed of networks crossed (see Table 13.1).
- **Message age** Delay which has arisen between the receipt of the last source BPDU carrying information from the root and the emission of the present BPDU which is derived from that. This delay may be overestimated by 1 second at most (4 seconds is an absolute maximum) but should never be underestimated.
- **Max age** Maximum age that a message may have, once stored, without being updated, after which it should be discarded: 20 seconds recommended, value of from 6 to 40 seconds imposed by the root bridge.
- **Hello time** Minimum interval for periodic transmission of information from the root: 2 seconds recommended, from 1 to 10 seconds.
- **Forward delay** Delay serving as timer between the stages of listening and learning and then of forwarding and also as the age of aging during the changeover phase, value imposed by the root bridge: 15 seconds recommended, from 4 to 30 seconds.

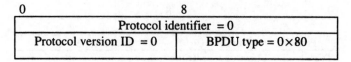

0	8
Protocol identifier = 0	
Protocol version ID = 0	BPDU type = 0×80

Figure 13.9 Format of a BPDU notifying a change of topology.

When the bridge does not choose the default values indicated above it should, however, respect the following inequalities:

2 × (Forward Delay − 1 second) ≥ Max Age
Max Age ≥ 2 × (Hello Time + 1 second).

Note: the durations are encoded in units of 1/256 s.

The BPDUs indicating modification of the topology are emitted by a port when it detects a change in the network, such as the non-receipt of periodic configuration BPDUs on one of its active ports, or when it becomes the root itself (Figure 13.9). The bridge then emits this indication to the root bridge and the information is propagated, in the opposite direction to the configuration BPDU, from the periphery to the center of the network. The root bridge acknowledges this message with a configuration BPDU (with the Topology Change bit activated), and all ports receiving it reduce the age of the dynamic entries in their learning table. Normal operation is resumed as soon as the topology change bit of the flag field of the following BPDU is reset to zero.

Other parameters, such as the crossing delay for the bridge, are defined by the standard:

- **Maximum bridge transit delay** Maximum acceptable delay in forwarding a frame, after which it should be discarded: 1 second recommended, 4 seconds absolute maximum.

- **Maximum BPDU transmission delay** Maximum delay in transmission of a BPDU by the bridge: 1 second recommended, 4 seconds absolute maximum.

- **Hold time** Minimum interval between the emission of successive BPDUs on a port: 1 second.

Finally, the standard specifies that the maximum recommended diameter for the architecture is seven bridges. This means that at most seven bridges can be crossed when passing between two different networks; this is equivalent to a maximum diameter of eight networks.

The filters

In addition to the natural filtering function, some so-called programmable bridges offer client-defined parametrization of filters. The number of these filters is generally a multiple of eight, and they can be applied at one or more ports, on input or output.

There are several categories of filter, such as those which involve the modification of the natural filtering by the forcing of static addresses in the learning table or the prevention of the insertion of a given address. It is thus possible to give a partial definition of a permanent address to be fixed in the learning table, which may, for example, only involve the manufacturer part (first three bytes). These static filters always correspond to a test on the destination field of the frame in transit. However, another category of filters can also be used to define tests on the source address of frames, on the type/length field or on any other byte sequence. In fact, serious programmable bridges can be used to read and test any field, defined by its offset (from the first byte of the frame), its length, a binary mask (used to ensure that only the desired bits are taken into account) and a reference value. In the case of equality with the reference value, the action may be to forward the frame and not the others or, conversely, to discard the frame and not the others, to associate it with a priority level within the bridge, or simply to count the frame and leave the behavior of the bridge unchanged.

These different categories of filtering are applied in serial and in a well-determined order (Figure 13.10). Natural filtering (possibly modified by the addition of static addresses) is generally the first test performed. It is followed by the test of the source address, that of the type field, and finally, the establishment of the correspondence with a given bit sequence.

We note, in passing, that this filtering capability enables the bridges to work on fields of the network layer or higher. It is easy to see that the bridges are then capable of eliminating frames in general IP broadcast (it is sufficient to take the IP destination address and compare it with 255.255.255.255). However, since the filter is always fixed, it cannot, for example, take into account a variable-length header, and thus its domain of application remains limited.

Here is one last point on the subject of the intelligent filtering of certain devices which are able to discard frames according to the consistency of their fields. Thus, bridges may reject frames whose type field does not have a meaningful value (such as 0000), frames with an unauthorized source or destination address (for example, manufacturer field set to 00-00-00) or frames using a MAC level protocol which they do not support (such as the Loopback). This is a plus, because the bridge does not forward these frames, however minor their illegality, but one should bear this in mind when carrying out tests with an analyzer, which generates valid frames (MAC level) that are not necessarily perfectly rational (at the LLC or network level).

Unlike simple bridges which do not implement additional filtering, programmable bridges can modify their operation according to the parametrized filters. Thus, they must provide access enabling the user to input the necessary commands and a back-up mode to save this configuration. In general, programmable ports have a serial RS-232 port of the DB25 type for connection of a VT100 terminal or equivalent. This direct access mode is often associated with a possibility of communication via the network between the bridge and a management station, where both devices come from the same manufacturer. Since this station has a copy of the configuration of each port of the machines it monitors, it can load the configuration

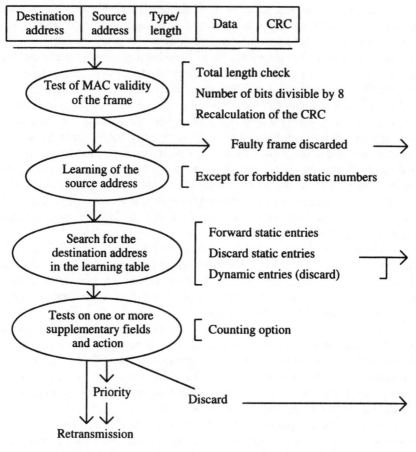

Figure 13.10 Stages of filtering in a programmable bridge.

remotely at any time, if necessary (for example, new hardware installed after repair, modification of filters). Direct access via a terminal is generally less convenient, since all the commands are passed in line mode. As far as the preservation of the parameters is concerned, there are various possible ways of saving the filters. The simplest such way is to store the configuration of the bridge in RAM (volatile memory) only. In this case, after each reset, the bridge returns to a basic mode of operation (natural filtering) and calls the master station so that the latter carries out a remote load of its configuration defined by the manager. We note that if the master station does not reply (being inaccessible for one reason or another) or does not reply immediately (busy communicating with other bridges), the bridge will have lost all its parameters and, while awaiting the station's reply, may let through traffic which would normally be forbidden by the filters. Thus, this is a simple solution which involves a risk. Another classical solution is to provide the bridge with a diskette reader on which the desired configuration is stored. The image of the parameters thus remains local and will always be available. The only disadvantage is that the bridge has to be equipped with an element containing mechanical components which are necessarily less reliable than the electronics. The advantage is that it is easy to manipulate the diskettes on which the configuration is held (for example, to duplicate them or modify them in advance). The third solution involves the implementation of memory of the NVRAM or better, of Flash PCMCIA card, which can be used to save the data even when the device is powered down. In the last two cases the device may associate an internal back-up capability with the possibility of receiving its configuration by remote loading.

As we noted earlier, bridges are relatively old elements, but their capabilities have evolved considerably. The first devices had quite modest filtering and forwarding rates, but their use could not be considered to be truly transparent since they could easily lose part of the signal sent to them. The interconnection of segments by bridges was essentially imposed by an inescapable requirement (to extend a network, to enable two networks to intercommunicate). Conversely, today, the choice of a bridge may result from a desire to reduce the traffic of a large network by segmentation (using the natural filtering function), in the implicit hope that the set of all the networks interconnected by bridges will function better than the original heavily loaded network, which of course implies a reliance on the device capabilities.

The multiport bridge

In the case of multiport bridges, the mode of operation is more or less identical to that of a biport bridge. The main difference is that the learning table has to contain two fields per entry, namely the Ethernet address and the port on which it was seen. In fact, with the multiport bridge, three different behaviors exist: discard the frame, retransmit to relevant output port, or forward to all ports (except input port). Instead, the correspondence should be sought and broadcast should only take place after a fruitless search of all the addresses stored by the bridge.

The multiport bridge is nevertheless subject to a constraint on its processing capability which is a direct function of the number of bridges. In fact, although a biport bridge should theoretically be able to filter twice 14 880 frames per second and be able to transport up to 14 880 frames per second (in the worst case, a network will be saturated by short frames with a non-local destination), the N port bridge should be able to filter $N \times 14\,880$ frames per second and transport $(N/2) \times 14\,880$ frames per second.

Although some local bridges now manage to process the maximum Ethernet traffic, that has not always been the case; in fact, it requires a well-adapted hardware architecture. Thus, bridges should not only increase the number of interfaces, but should also, as far as possible, be capable of not losing frames because of overflow (which would imply a lack of reliability).

The MAC bridge based on the PC

At the bottom of the range in terms of performance are local bridges, developed based on PC hardware, which have been supplemented by two Ethernet cards. These devices have the advantage of being affordable and easy to modify (hardware and software). However, their capabilities are often too limited to permit the intercommunication of two networks with a medium-to-high load. Thus, they are reserved for relatively undemanding applications.

However, these devices have recently undergone an evolution with the support for serial links offering low-cost WAN connections and the routing of various common protocol stacks.

13.2 Hybrid bridging

Translation

Bridging by translation stands for the ability to carry out bridging between networks of different technologies in a transparent way. Thus, bridging between Ethernet and Token Ring or FDDI with frame format conversion in transparent bridging (in such a way that the frames are meaningful on any medium) is called translation bridging. By means of this type of bridging, it is possible to make devices connected to heterogeneous networks communicate with each other without any knowledge of the technology of their interlocutors. The networks interconnected by translation bridges constitute only one single logical network (at the level of the Network layer) because no routing takes place between them. This means that all stations are visible from all other stations, with the associated advantages (and disadvantages).

It is important to understand that this process is merely a question of re-ordering the bits in certain fields, inserting or extracting type, length, LLC and/or SNAP headers, and recalculating the CRC. It does not involve the creation or extraction of an RIF field (Source Routing bridging information). The packets must be handled by translation bridging in the same way as they would be handled by transparent bridging. Note that in general, the Ethernet – Token Ring bridge has two separate tasks to perform: a conversion of the TB – SR bridging mode and a translation of the frame including the reconstruction of its MAC and/or LLC header and the ordering of the bits in the bytes.

Since the methods of data conversion from a parallel to a serial mode format are different in the cases of Ethernet and Token Ring or FDDI (big/little-endian), and this conversion does not apply to MAC addresses, not all fields can be processed in the same way.

In addition, the addresses managed locally under Token Ring must be converted and the functional addresses retranscribed (in multicast), since they generally do not have an Ethernet equivalent.

Finally, the requirement of changing the encapsulation of Ethernet V2.0 frames into frames with LLC and SNAP and vice versa complicates the function of translation bridges. In fact, if several formats coexist on Ethernet, then all the frames should theoretically incorporate an LLC level on Token Ring and FDDI.

The problem is exactly the same in the case of bridging between a network that is entirely Ethernet V2.0 and a network that is totally IEEE 802.3. In spite of the homogeneity of the Physical layer, this bridging is not transparent but translation bridging.

Let us also not forget that the minimum or maximum frame length depends on the characteristics of the traversed networks. With regard to this specific difficulty, the manufacturers of translation bridges have preferred not to deal at all with packets which are 'too long' for the technology of the destination network. Only some devices have the capacity of fragmenting at Network level, for the most diffused protocols (one of which is usually IP). In fact, this fragmentation requires the capacity to reconstruct the Network header of each fragment in a consistent way, as a router would do. Obviously, the reassembly is left to the terminal station. If the bridge does not implement this function at all (or not for some of the used protocols), users who will not be able to make their packets cross the bridge will inevitably be led to modify the MTU of the stations to take it down to the smallest MTU of the LAN technologies concerned. Note that there is no MAC protocol capable of automatically determining this value, but that this is, however, possible at Network level. Thus, in IP, a station can determine by itself which is the MTU towards which addressee. For this purpose, it emits ping (ICMP Echo request) frames of different lengths, with the Do Not Fragment bit set, prohibiting the cutting up of the frame on the way towards its destination. Proceeding by simple dichotomy, and on the basis of the answers (Echo Reply), the station is thus capable of dynamically discovering the MTU for IP packets.

Also note that short Token Ring or FDDI frames pose a problem when they must be carried towards Ethernet. In this case, the translation bridge has the task of adding a PAD and adapting the MAC header accordingly if required (as for IEEE 802.3 frames with their length field, which must be consistent with the size of the data field). Vice versa, the IEEE 802.3 frames that include a PAD will see their info field reduced to only data during its passage towards Token Ring or FDDI (the notion of padding has no equivalent in Token Ring or FDDI).

The fact that the number of bytes of the data (or info) field can be odd is also one of the differences between Ethernet (where certain protocol families construct only frames with an info field of even length) and FDDI. If necessary, a PAD byte will be added to the Ethernet info field.

Conversion and/or propagation of priority is an additional difficulty, because Ethernet possesses no means to code it *a priori*. Thus, a frame emitted by a Token Ring bridge has a priority of 4, the same as an LLC frame in FDDI. It was therefore decided that if an FDDI frame passes through an Ethernet network on the way to its destination, its priority is set back to 0 by the Ethernet ↔ FDDI bridge.

Finally, it should be noted that all protocols cannot simply pass through a translation bridge, although this may appear contradictory. In fact, the protocols that use the MAC address as a subfield of their network address reproduce this outside the MAC field, but sometimes with a consistency check at reception. If such a frame is converted, the MAC addresses do not follow the same treatment as the addresses that are part of the Info field.

This is a common problem, because a large number of protocols use the MAC address to compose the Network address (such as IPX and XNS) or simply reproduce the MAC address in the contents of the frame (such as ARP). For certain combinations of Ethernet, Token Ring, and FDDI, and depending on the MAC

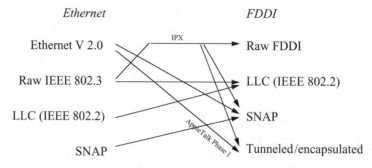

Figure 13.11 Detailed scheme of Ethernet → FDDI conversion modes.

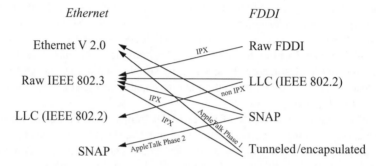

Figure 13.12 Detailed scheme of Ethernet ← FDDI conversion modes.

encapsulations and the capabilities of the bridge, the translation can make the frame lose its global consistency in reception.

Note that IPX and AppleTalk require specific treatments.

Standards

The majority of existing standards deal with different encapsulations of a given protocol stack in some type of LAN technology. Only the standards IEEE 802.1D, H, and Q deal, in a theoretical manner, with the means of encapsulation and translation.

Thus, in IP, RFC 1042 describes the operation of the TCP/IP protocol family on IEEE 802.X LANs, RFCs 894 and 826 describes it on Ethernet, and RFCs 1188 and 1390 on FDDI.

The practical conversion modes are thus deduced from the study of the encapsulation specifications on each side of the bridge, taking into consideration the fact that the peculiarities of the different protocols are not always clearly specified.

The case of the AppleTalk protocol is slightly different because the particulars of its translation are given in several standards. Thus, when the bridge detects an Ethernet (V2.0) frame encapsulating AppleTalk Phase 1 (MAC Type field = 0x80F3), it is converted on an FDDI network into a SNAP format where the OUI is 00-00-F8 (which indicates bridging by tunneling). When, on the other hand, the bridge detects an AppleTalk Phase 2 frame (SNAP field = 0x80F3, OUI = 00-00-00), it is retransmitted without special modification. In addition, tunneling is sometimes used to transport on FDDI an IPX Raw encapsulation (directly in IEEE 802.3, without LLC).

Conversion

Conversion between bridging modes (SR and TB) differs from the bridgings seen up to now, because (in addition to the functions of a translation bridge) it allows insertion or extraction of the RIF field in a frame during its passage across the bridge. The interconnection devices must also handle the storage of information contained in the removed fields, together with its coherent reconstruction.

The design of a crossover functionality between two different modes of bridging does not present any conceptual problems because one knows the functioning modes of different types of bridging very well. The task is to provide the element that links a network in TB and a network in SR, handling the exchange of packets between the two without the terminal stations having to modify their behavior (software drivers defining encapsulation and table management of SR).

The case where one passes from a network supporting one type of bridging to another is relatively simple. On the SR side, the bridge must handle a real network number and must have a bridge number as any traditional SR bridge. But it is the last bridge of the sequence of couples (ring bridge) and must thus represent the TB domain by means of a virtual ring number.

The case where one traverses a network that does not function with the same type of bridging as the surrounding networks is more particular.

SR – TB – SR

In the case where a TB network separates two SR environments, loss of knowledge of the ring numbers occurs during the passage. In fact, to each SR domain, the rest ($-$ TB $-$ SR) appears as one and the same ring. The consequence is that the two SR parts ignore each other and can thus be put under different administrations, but above all, an economy in numbers of rings has been achieved. In fact, if the SR domains handle N and P rings respectively, each machine only sees $N + 1$ or $P + 1$ rings, not $N + P + 1$. This can even be envisaged without an intermediate TB stage, and it consists in artificially hiding the sequence of rings placed behind a bridge, presenting just one single number.

Note: The case TB $-$ SR $-$TB can simply be understood as two distinct TB– SR operations.

SR + TB

Finally, to conclude, it should be noted that theoretically nothing will prevent the bridge from concurrently supporting conversion and SRTB, or translation bridging. The bridge must be capable of handling an SRTB port and a TB port. If it receives frames in TB on the SRTB port, it can retransmit them as they are, except for a translation operation. If it receives frames in SR on the SRTB port, it must convert them before retransmitting them on the TB port, not forgetting to preserve the significant RIF information in its tables. Vice versa, if it receives frames on its TB port, it must be able to decide whether they need conversion or not, which it can only do on the basis of its tables filled in during previous receptions. In the case where the bridge does not know the destination (it does not know whether the addressee functions in SR or in TB, nor where it is located), and if the first frame to be sent μ is not in diffusion, the bridge will have a higher chance of reaching its goal by reproducing the frame in SR and in exploration in a first phase (as a NIC would behave).

Thus, different bridging methods can coexist in the same multimedia bridge and confer it a great flexibility of use. They inevitably entail more complex handling, but do have their important functions.

Encapsulation

Bridging by encapsulation (sometimes referred to as tunneling) is a simple and efficient solution which allows heterogeneous networks to be connected, avoiding dealing with their differences at MAC level. This technique consists in encapsulating the frames coming from a network of type X upon their passage through a network of type Y, and then de-encapsulating them upon their arrival at the destination network of type X.

This is still proper bridging because the processing remains at MAC level (with generation of a complementary header and postfix), and never lets the higher protocol(s) used come into play.

The first solution to connecting Ethernet and FDDI networks used for this method employed the traversed FDDI network(s) as simple unifying backbone.

The principal drawback of this technique was that the bridged frames were proprietary on FDDI (non-compliant with the structure of standard frames), because they had two consecutive MAC headers, among other things, and could therefore not be interpreted by possible stations placed on the intermediate network.

On the other hand, this solution had the advantage of being simple to set up, because the bridges had a fairly reduced operation to carry out, and it could be applied to any interconnection requirement of heterogeneous networks, given that all that was involved was to traverse the intermediate connecting technology. Simplicity of functioning generally has a very positive impact on equipment performance.

More recently, the IEEE 802.1Q has undertaken standardization of transporting different frame formats (Ethernet V2.0, Token Ring and FDDI) on all networks. For this purpose, the 802.1Q tagging allows the specification of which format (canonical or not) of MAC frames appears in the data field. The format of addresses in the header and data bytes other than MAC addresses obviously respects the LAN specification.

Moreover, as seen above, the IEEE 802.1H has realized tunneling on a network by setting the OUI to 00-00-F8 to indicate that it is not sensible to read the frame on the transition network, because it needs a service specific to its originating network.

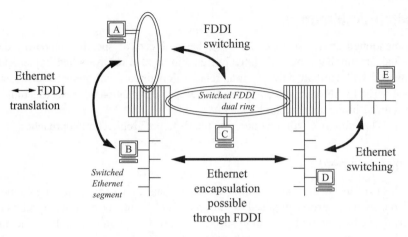

Figure 13.13 Switched FDDI and Ethernet.

Developments

Several complements and corrections concerning the standards of bridging are currently being elaborated. We will look at them in more detail in the chapter on switching. Thus, IEEE 802.1Q and IEEE 802.1p introduce the notion of virtual LAN, flow priorities, multicast filtering and multiple queues inside a bridge. These specifications will appear in new and more complete versions in the years to come (with support for multiple Spanning Trees in parallel, for example). To provide a certain homogeneity vis-à-vis these novelties, the IEEE 802.1D (ISO 10038) is currently under revision too.

13.3 Switching

Presentation

Switching, an indisputable revival of LANs, ensures that in the years to come we will not have to face complex new choices. It allows a nearly unlimited plurality of bandwidths, implicit access to high speeds, and above all the almost complete elimination of the flaws of the MAC layers, which have with time become more and more critical. Thus, sharing the total bandwidth is no longer as penalizing because the machines have become less numerous in each segment, and the degradation of CSMA/CD under heavy loads is pushed back outside the functioning ranges.

Originally based on the proliferation of two-port bridges (micro-segmentation), switched solutions build on the intrinsic qualities of the switches and the functional richness they offer, where the majority of these technologies are non-standard.

Switch architecture

As mentioned above, switches have not been objects of specific standards; their internal functioning mode is relatively free and has led to diversified implementations. We will see that only the four related domains of full-duplex transmission mode, virtual LAN management, priority queues and limitation of broadcasts must be normalized in the near future.

Therefore, we will now describe the different architecture approaches.

Central element

The heart of the switch can be of several types, based on a true switching element, called a switch matrix, composed of multiple subelements, or on a bus which is the equivalent of an internal, very high speed, LAN, or finally on a centralized memory capable of supporting several simultaneous accesses.

Matrix The matrix, in the form of multiple, more or less complex architectures, is relatively rare in the domain of LAN switches because its qualities are not essential there. In fact, sophisticated Banyan-type matrices have the property of allowing the construction of switches with N ports, using $NlogN$ elementary components instead of N^2 in the case of a simple matrix, the elementary component being a 2-port mini-switch. This is particularly important when the issue is to have switches with a large number of ports, or which reach a total bandwidth that exceeds the current capacities of bus or central memory technologies (which is still fairly rare in LANs). Moreover, matrix technologies have the disadvantage of possessing a non-zero probability of blocking. Blocking means that certain combinations of incoming data and information flow can provoke a supplementary transport delay due to an internal access conflict with an elementary component. This probability can be greatly reduced by sorting algorithms placed upstream (Batcher Banyan), but it is never zero.

Bus The bus architecture corresponds to the construction of a high-throughput simil-LAN in a (generally modular) chassis. The interface modules connect to this bus on the backplane and share the bandwidth with the other modules. Different methods of bandwidth sharing can be envisaged: principally, temporary multiplexing, synchronous or asynchronous, in the second case managed by a deterministic access method. The bus is indeed a 'collapsed backbone' because it is a high-throughput LAN accessible inside a device. This solution has the advantage of simplicity, and of possessing a good natural suitability for scalability. To be non-blocking, it is sufficient that the sum of bandwidths that the forward facing ports can require does not exceed the capacity of the bus. Once again, be careful: if the switch has N 10 Mbps half-duplex ports, it is sufficient that the backplane bus works at $N/2 \times 10$ Mbps (that is, $5 \times N$). Because of its similarity to a LAN, this solution allows natural processing of the frames in diffusion, which is not the case with the matrix solution, and is particularly suited to the construction of modular switches of different sizes, all using exactly the same components.

There is, however, a limitation in a particular case. Let us imagine that an output port is saturated: it does not manage to get rid of all the traffic flow that it receives from the backplane (either because the flow is higher than its bandwidth or because the segment attached to it is already heavily loaded itself). Now, let us consider another port of the switch which is charged with transmitting two types of incoming traffic, one flow towards the already saturated port, closely linked to a flow directed to another port which is in a fluid state. Very quickly, this port will receive an indication that the traffic it is trying to forward is blocked, and it will start to accumulate the incoming traffic in a local reception buffer. Alas, if this buffer cannot differentiate between the different incoming flows and allocate different memory areas to each of them, it will affect all incoming flows by blocking all traffic it receives in exactly the same way. This blocking phenomenon is called HOL type (Head Of Line) blocking, and it is difficult to deal with in the case of a bus architecture because it requires this capacity of distinguishing the flows of traffic (by MAC destination address or by output module *a priori*) on each port or group of ports. Note that a partial solution consists in placing relatively large buffers in the output, thus reducing the probability of blocking the input, without, however, really solving the problem.

Shared memory   Finally, the last current architecture is that of shared memory, which consists of providing the heart of the switch with a memory across which all switched frames will transit. In order not to be blocking, this memory must have an access capacity that corresponds to the global bandwidth of the switch. This is usually realized by means of a memory with multiple simultaneous access, managed by several specific reading and writing components. This architecture also allows the HOL blocking problems to be dealt with at minimum cost, because this substantial central memory obviously allows all flows to be differentiated according to their destination, with the retransmission components charged with disposing of all flows that can effectively leave the switch. Note that for good HOL management it is preferable to be able to dynamically vary the memory zones assigned to each incoming port or group of ports, if there are any.

Hardware/software

Another fundamental distinction lies in the type of components employed to realize the switch. Very schematically, we differentiate between architectures which employ one or more traditional CPUs which run code corresponding to the switching function (for which reason they are called software architectures), and architectures which use specific VLSIs (usually ASICs), specifically developed for switching operations (called hardware architectures).

The first option has two big advantages, which are, on the one hand, its ease of development, because for years all bridges and routers were produced that way and only a simple adaptation was needed to transform them into switches, and on the other hand, its functional progressivity, because an update of the code allows the functions of the switch to be modified or enriched. Evidently, this flexibility is only possible at the expense of performance. In fact, a standard CPU only processes some ten thousands of frames per second, and with a relatively variable delay as a function of its load.

The second option requires the development and production of dedicated integrated circuits, restricted in their function, but substantially more powerful than a normal CPU (capable of processing several hundred thousand headers per second). Evidently, the progressive nature of these electronic components is relatively limited, but this limitation is usually compensated by the development of other circuits dedicated to complementary functions (filtering, level 3 switching, translation, and so on). This is an approach that takes on the development principles of concentrators, for which the repetition functions and the complementary functions (statistics, static switching) were produced in the form of dedicated circuits.

Pragmatically speaking, we can observe that the switches market tends towards hardware architectures which allow switches to be constructed with a larger number of ports, more powerful and more rigorous in their behavior. To a certain extent, this corresponds to optimizing the architecture of the products according to their function and use. The same question arises now for layer 3 or 4 switches.

Centralized/distributed

The distinction between centralized architecture (where there is only one single processing element at the heart of the switch) and distributed architecture (where several elements share the global task of switching equally) is closely related to the two previous choices. In fact, a software architecture will generally be centralized, since the task of synchronization and distribution of work between several CPUs appears hard. A distributed architecture, on the other hand, is easier to set up on the basis of hardware constructed around a bus.

Evidently, each of these architectures has its advantages and disadvantages. Nevertheless, the market visibly tends towards hardware solutions whose development is made even easier because a certain number of elementary components is available on the market. In this context, distributed architectures can be interesting with regard to redundancy aspects, but a centralized solution with a redundant central element can provide the same quality of service with less complexity.

Table 13.2 Preferential combinations.

	Bus	Matrix	Central memory
Hardware	Distributed or centralized	Distributed	Centralized
Software	Centralized	N/A	Centralized

Cut-Through/Store & Forward

Since the principal function of the switch is to bridge frames between its ports, it is quite natural to try to do this as quickly as possible, in throughput by achieving the maximum bandwidth (wire speed), but also in delay. As the information needed for switching is located at the beginning of the frame: MAC destination address for TB, (and RIF field for SR), with the aim of retransmitting a frame as quickly as possible, one could thus begin to do it before the frame has been entirely received (which is contrary to the functioning of a true bridge, which must be able to validate the received frame before processing it). Thus, two major categories can be distinguished:

- Store & Forward mode which requires receipt of the entire frame before deciding to retransmit it; this is the traditional mode for all interconnection equipment: bridge, router, gateway, and so on.
- Cut-Through or On-the-Fly mode where the switch tries to start the transmission as soon as it has the necessary elements.

Table 13.3 Simplified comparison of retransmission modes.

	Store & Forward	On the Fly
Minimum retransmission delay of a frame	$\geq$ Reading time	Some $10\,\mu s$
Variation of this delay	Proportional to frame length	Independent of frame length
Error detection	All (potentially)	Jabber (misaligned)
Different throughputs in input and output	Yes	Not if Tx >> Rx
Heterogeneous LAN: Ethernet, Token Ring, FDDI, ATM	Indispensable	Impossible

Note that a bridge as defined by IEEE 802.1D can only be Store & Forward because it has to implement a complete MAC layer per port.

Finally, it is important to note that the wish to retransmit as quickly as possible is quite consistent with the notion of switching. This is probably the reason why the On the Fly method, which positions the switch as an intermediate product between hub and bridge but which has significant intrinsic flaws, has been substantially improved in practice. In fact, the principal disadvantage of this method lies in the possibility of retransmitting erroneous frames from one network to the other(s) (runt, misaligned, bad FCS). In the worst, but not unrealistic case, where one of the segments connected to the switch is faulty and/or saturated, this will create a retransmission of the vast majority of errors on all the other ports, and eventually provoke the collapse of all networks linked to the switch (note that many errors effectively appear to the switch as multicasts, which explains why they can be reproduced on all ports).

The first improvement consists in eliminating the risk of retransmitting the most common erroneous frames: the runts (frame too short, usually the result of a collision). For this purpose, the switch sets itself a minimum reading delay corresponding to a correct short frame (64 bytes = 51.2 μs at 10 Mbps, which is quite short) before starting retransmission. We thus obtain a retransmission whose delay is constant (more precisely, independent of the frame length) and only passes along the beginning of the most infrequent errors: bad FCS and misaligned frames of length more than 64 bytes, and jabber (abnormal error as we have seen earlier).

The second type of improvement consists in monitoring the quality of the traffic (its error rate) in parallel with the retransmission, without influencing the speed. If the error rate exceeds a certain threshold, it is possible to switch the port *a posteriori* into a (passive) observation state, waiting to revalidate it or, more intelligently, to change its functioning mode dynamically into Store & Forward (which evidently filters out all the errors) until the traffic has again reached an acceptable error rate. It is the adaptive Cut-through that benefits from the qualities of both environments, minimum delay, and cleanness of the generated flows. Evidently, this duality of functioning must not affect the other capacities of the switch (global performance and, above all, complementary functionalities).

Note that, in half duplex, the switch always activates the access method on its retransmission port and must therefore wait for its turn to transmit (medium free in CSMA/CD). This means that the minimum delays are obtained in the case of virgin destination networks. For example, if the switch must systematically wait and store temporarily frames into its buffers because the output network is loaded, Cut-through does not present any particular advantage.

Specific issues of switching

Full duplex

As opposed to the internal functioning mode of the switch, transmission in full duplex (simultaneous transmission and reception) applicable to point-to-point links (on twisted pair or optical fiber) has been standardized by the IEEE. In fact, in Ethernet the 802.3x subcommittee after several manufacturers' implementations have emerged, defines an operational and cross-operative reference mode (incorporating capacities of automation).

With regard to Ethernet, full-duplex operation on a point-to-point link requires only two things, namely that each edge device deactivates its collision detection mechanism (on simultaneous transmission and reception) and that it can handle at least two frames simultaneously (which is obviously the case with a switch that, due to its very nature, can deal with several frames concurrently). In addition, the standard provides two functionalities: the capacity for auto-negotiation of the functioning mode derived from the exchange of pages and the capacity to notify the other side that there is a situation of congestion, that is, the capacity of flow control (see Section 11.1). Naturally, the Flow Control support can be announced by AutoNegotiation.

Handling of congestion

We have seen earlier with HOL blocking that congestion phenomena could occur. These can have two causes, the first one being that the sum of traffic flows is directed towards a port and these flows represent more than the bandwidth of that port, and the second that the bandwidth directed (inside the switch) towards the output port is higher than the availability left by the other accesses present on the segment. In all cases, the switch cannot handle the traffic it receives as fast as it would like. This is independent of its own performance. The first reaction is to use the memory buffers available in output, then those in input. Once the input buffer(s) is (are) full, we find ourselves again in a critical phase, where there are two possible alternatives:

- to lose part of the incoming traffic because it can neither be dealt with nor temporarily stored: so-called passive congestion management;
- to act on the incoming flows to limit their throughput at the source (NIC or other switch placed upstream): so-called active congestion management.

These problems are identical for all interconnection devices equipped with a MAC layer per port. In fact, these equipments are supposed to be able to read the frames in arrival, but they have no *a priori* means of signaling back that they are congested. Certain protocols include this kind of message, such as ICMP for IP, or better TCP with Source Quench, but they only apply to a few protocol families and in any case do not belong to the MAC level.

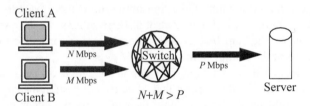

Figure 13.14   Congestion on two ports of a switch.

Passive congestion management usually needs relatively consistent buffers so that switching into frame losing mode only occurs in the case of long-term congestion. It has the disadvantage that it shows an eminently variable forwarding delay because the retransmission delay for the last frame filling the buffer will be considerably longer than the normal delay. However, this disadvantage also has an associated benefit: in the case of congestion, the loss of frames will probably produce a resumption of the sessions by the connection-oriented Transport protocols (if there is one), and thus a reset to zero of all flows, which can be healthy. Note that the Transport protocols usually demand retransmission of the sequence of all frames starting with the first non-received one, which can also prolong the congestion in a transitory way. Moreover, flows that do not employ connection-oriented layers will be lost without any indication.

Naturally, a means of optimizing passive congestion management consists in handling multiple waiting queues in input. Thus, if a flow provokes the congestion of the switch and a loss of frames arriving at a port, being able to isolate it without affecting all flows arriving at that port represents a clear improvement. The underlying question lies in the determination of the optimum number of buffers per port and in the choice of the criterion of switching the incoming flows towards these different buffers. Evidently, the ideal solution would be switching according to the output port, which on the one hand represents a large number (possibly of the order of a hundred in a big switch) and on the other hand is not easily realizable because each input buffer would need knowledge of the whole of the switch.

Active congestion management can build on an existing signaling protocol, such as the one proposed by IEEE 802.3x for flow control, or can be designed in other ways.

A clever means of setting up this active congestion management in a shared way lies in an optimized use of the access method to guarantee that the switch will not be submerged by the traffic received. The switch will thus make use of the access method, but will not necessarily conform to it entirely. Thus, in CSMA/CD (and in half duplex), a simple means to guarantee that the switch does not receive more frames than it can handle at an instant t on each port consists in sending a busy signal on the saturated lines in reception. This signal, preferably non-significant, must have the duration of the congestion and can be subdivided into pseudo-frames to prevent it from being interpreted as jabber. Evidently, in the case of collision during emission of this signal, the switch maintains its transmission, forcing the other couplers to wait for release of the medium. Thus, this active mechanism is safe because it takes the need to keep the information to be transmitted in memory back to the original devices. With the asymmetrical flow control of IEEE 802.3x, we have seen that it is normal to consider the sum of the workstations' storage capacities to be largely superior to those of the central elements.

The principal flaw of this system lies in its action on the entirety of the workstations located behind a port. In fact, if active congestion management poses no acceptance problem in port switching, then in segment switching it is reasonable to study the global consequences of a bandwidth limitation. Monopolizing the medium for a certain proportion of time not only penalizes the stations that transmitted the flows that provoked the congestion, but also the stations that communicate between each other or with non-saturated destinations. Once again, the ideal transposition of this technology is a little complicated. Thus, the switch should be capable of limiting only the machines that take part in the congestion, for example, by verifying on the fly the MAC source address of the frames it receives, before entering deliberately in collision with the undesirable frames. On the one hand, this would provoke collisions and no longer a simple occupation of the medium, which entails the risk of provoking a partitioning on an upstream hub and the loss of undesirable frames after 16 collisions. On the other hand, if the concerned stations also have non-disturbing frames to exchange, these are penalized as well.

Moreover, active congestion management that uses whichever access method can also be seen as a transposition of the conflict management mechanisms integrated in the MAC layers. In fact, if the CSMA/CD allow the best possible distribution of the right to transmit on a concentrator when several components want to transmit at the same time, active management does not leave the switch unprovided. In the same way as a simple hub has the capacity to 'refuse' access to the network, a switch can act on the apparent availability of each segment so that it does not receive more than it is able to handle and forward.

We conclude by reminding the reader that the problem with active congestion management is that it sometimes acts on the entire segment and not only on the sending machine(s) responsible for the congestion, thus penalizing both 'neighbors' and 'disturbers'.

Priorities

Priority of flows   As with all interconnection devices provided with MAC layers, we have seen above that the switch must be able to handle congestion phenomena. Independently of the choice of congestion management technique, the switch (as the bridge or the router) can attempt to privilege certain traffic flows at the expense of others. This is the outcome of the need to differentiate between multimedia and pure data flows or, more simply, between traffic flows associated with applications considered as critical and secondary traffic. In all cases, since the reaction capacities of the switch are given, different priority levels will allow modification of the subdivision of the remaining bandwidth. The priority levels can serve as weighting factors in the distribution of the accessible throughput, or sequentially, of retransmissions. Thus, it is possible either to distribute the bandwidth between incoming flows affected by congestion in proportion to their priority, or to let higher priority traffic always pass first. In the first case (known as WFQ: Weight Fair Queuing), during congestion, the forwarding delay affects all traffic flows, but is inversely proportional to their priority; in the second case, the higher-priority traffic will not see a degradation (provided that it occupies less than the available bandwidth). This distinction of functioning modes may have a relevant impact on synchronous type traffic flows.

Later we will see that IEEE 802.1p and Q have undertaken standardization of the management of several levels of priority, implementation of several queues in switching bridges, and an associated tagging to indicate this frame priority.

Priority of switches   There is a second approach to priority which lies in the positioning of the switches with respect to other network devices, and this time when there is a conflict in accessing the medium.

In fact, in a switched network, it is often useful to privilege the switch compared with other user devices.

By default, if a single machine is connected to each port of the switch, it has virtually the maximum bandwidth with its interlocutors. If, on the other hand, loaded networks are connected, the probability of collision on each Ethernet port impacts on the benefit users may obtain from their switching bridge.

It may therefore be desirable to make the behavior of the switch more 'aggressive' than that of a normal coupler.

In the absence of the priority mechanism in Ethernet, the manufacturers who found it wise to privilege their switch with respect to other accesses in the network do this in two ways, generally by implementing a 'strong' back-off algorithm for which the random waiting delay in the case of collision is always (or often) 0 (the switch will always win in case of contention), but also by going below the 9.6 μs of interframe gap (at 10 Mbps) and thus noticeably exceeding a 100% load in emission. Note that both cases break the standards and risk ending up in blocking situations if the switch is not exclusively connected to Ethernet-conformant interfaces. Thus, two switches that implement a 'strong' back-off attached to the same Ethernet network will quickly end up with the complete immobilization of the network: collisions without end. And an illegally short inter-frame gap can provoke the loss (or non-visibility) of frames by devices exactly conforming to the standard.

Note that luckily enough these priority modes are often only employed during congestion phenomena and have the aim of helping the switch to process much traffic as quickly as possible. We always consider that the buffers of the switch are substantially smaller than the sum of the buffers of all interfaces of the network.

Virtual LANs

The notion of Virtual LANs (VLANs) is currently widely diffused in switched environments, and we shall therefore explain it in some detail.

Introduction

Schematically, machines belonging to the same virtual LAN can normally communicate with each other, but two machines that do not belong to the same VLAN cannot communicate.

When switching is introduced into a network architecture, it allows this to be provided with high throughputs. Sharing the bandwidth between several groups of users thus becomes a natural thing to want to do. Therefore, for example, the same switch can provide access to different networks 'simulated as distinct', and carry all these accesses concurrently on each (high-speed) connecting link, with the virtual LAN corresponding to the capacity for artificially separating the traffic flows. It responds to two major requirement categories:

- Security (in the sense of confidentiality: eavesdropping) for enterprises wishing to maintain a totally secure gap, with no possible leakage, between different groups of users whose access rights and resources are kept distinct (by the network administrator) as a function of their group membership. Thus, the user is not considered to be trustworthy.

- Limitation of 'pollution' by adjacent traffic flows, which is the case with frames in broadcast between different protocol families or even between different IP networks (for example). A VLAN is the equivalent of a broadcast domain (not to be confused with a collision domain). We will insist later on the fact that frames in diffusion are not (and are never) switched, but are treated by the switch as they would be treated by a simple hub, and that consequently broadcasts do not benefit from the combined bandwidth represented by the switch, but only from one channel equivalent to the unitary bandwidth (*a priori* 10 Mbps in traditional Ethernet).

Note that this separation of traffic flows obviously reinforces the shunting of frames carried out by the switch: in port switching, the frame passing from A to B is in any case only visible by stations A and B. With VLANs, the aim is to prevent A and B from communicating with each other if the network administrator so wishes, or to avoid A and B receiving exchange broadcasts that do not concern them.

Shared networks   Also note that in shared networks, the notion of a virtual LAN already existed implicitly when, for example, several IP networks coexisted on the same segment, without 'mixing up' and almost without disturbing each other, or when more than one IPX MAC encapsulation method (among Ethernet V 2.0, raw 802.3, 802.2, SNAP) coexisted on the same Ethernet network, or even more simply when an Ethernet network supported traffic flows of several Network or higher protocols: IP, IPX, CLNP, AppleTalk, DECnet, NetBIOS, LAT, and so on, which do not interact and ignore each other (SIN: Ships In the Night).

Finally, a notion of veritable shared virtual Ethernet network has also (briefly) existed with the capacity of handling subgroups inside the same shared network, and this independently of a potential distinction by the higher layers. For this purpose, a product generally called 'Frame Killer' had the task of preventing communication between subgroups, which it did simply by systematic collision with the undesirable frames. This means that the said product had to listen to everything which goes through the network, and verify on the fly whether the couple MAC destination–source address was authorized or not. If it was not authorized, it had to 'kill' the frame by means of an almost immediate collision.

By preventing it from communicating with the rest of the network one seeks to limit the disturbance it causes (for example, broadcast avalanche). Note that, since the test is carried out at the MAC level, the frame killer must be located in the same network as the machines in question and not beyond a router or a gateway.

Need   One must also remember that before switching became widespread, the majority of hubs on the market had the capacity to handle distinct 'networks' by segmenting the hub into different independent repeaters. This allowed N Ethernet networks ($N \ll 10$ in practice) to be made available in each node of the network (but carried by N inter-hub connecting links). VLANs can also be seen as an extension of this multi-LAN hub principle, then realized by several backplane buses.

After several years of existence of manufacturers solutions, which have the major fault of not being able to exchange VLAN information in heterogeneous environments on connecting links (the notion of a virtual LAN getting lost in the passage from a product X to a switch Y), the IEEE has integrated this need and charged the 802.1Q committee with the task of specifying a standard solution.

But before we come to this belated standard, we will summarize the various existing methods of meeting this need.

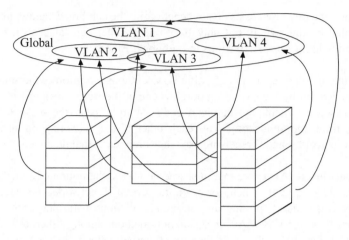

Figure 13.15 Representation of how to split a site into VLANs.

Functioning

Constitution modes   Generally, 3 or 4 types of VLAN can be identified: VLANs by port (or level 1), by MAC address (level 2), by Network address: IP, IPX, and so on (thus, level 3) or conditioned by a higher level (4: Transport Protocol to 7: Application). This distinction is based on the association mode frame – VLAN.

In fact, when the product handles VLANs by port, all frames coming from a port located in VLAN X are associated with this VLAN. If a multi-station LAN segment (Ethernet hub) is connected to this port, all stations are automatically placed in this VLAN X. This is natural, because in any case, the switch cannot prevent them from communicating with each other through the intermediary of the hub.

When the switch handles VLANs by MAC address, each coupler card, and thus each station, is treated as a unit, whether it is directly connected to the switch, or by the intermediary of a segment, a hub, or another switch. The granularity of administration is thus all the finer, and one can in this case differentiate between devices arriving at the switch by the same port, but one cannot, however, prevent them from communicating with each other downstream of the switch.

If VLANs are level 3, the switch handles the membership in a VLAN according to the network protocol used, or better according to the network address of each station. This is a particularly consistent mode of functioning because it allows the task of assignment to be automated and always provides a certain level of security. In addition, whether the task is to separate the stations according to the communication protocol family employed (TCP/IP, NetWare, OSI, AppleTalk, and so on) or to segment networks already disjointed from the point of view of the network protocol (such as IP subnets) into distinct VLANs, this functionality responds to an obvious and frequent need of network administrators. As can easily be imagined, this capacity is not easy to implement in environments where the network addresses are dynamically allocated, as in DHCP.

Finally, when VLANs are constituted as a function of a higher-level parameter, this allows us to regroup the stations of the network by Transport protocol or even by application. This is undeniably a complementary tool, but the question lies more in the *raison d'être* of this type of VLAN. VLAN type can even integrate an authentication process, requiring a login to the switch before being assigned to a VLAN. Clearly the switch is then partly playing the role of the server, managing a high-level entry check point.

These different processing modes all have individual advantages and disadvantages, which fall into two groups, depending on one's point of view: either as issues of management and dissemination of information concerning these VLANs, at switch level, or as issues of help concerning VLAN development and implementation.

Table 13.4   Characteristics of VLAN constitution modes.

Type of VLAN	Creation	Scalability	Granularity	Automation	Mobility	Security
By port	Easy	Average	Limited	Little natural	Difficult	Strong
By MAC address	Heavy	Weak	Fine	Little natural	Possible	Medium
By Network Protocol	Easy	Good	Limited	Logical	Natural	Weak
By IP, IPX, addr	Simple	Good	Implicit	Logical	Natural	Weak
By application	Simple	Good	Implicit	Implicit	Natural	Weak

Proper consideration must be given to the currently important need represented by VLAN automation. Clearly, segmentation into virtual LANs is a useful tool and beneficial for both administrators and users. But setting up, development, and administration should really be carried out with careful reference to the need for ease of access by human beings. Since ports of switches and MAC addresses are not very meaningful, it is certainly preferable to deal with network protocols and addresses, above all if the addressing plan is clearly defined and follows a structure representing the organization of the site and its users.

Thus computer-aided constitution of VLANs can be carried out without too much concern for the consistency of the result.

Intersection   Leaving aside the mode of VLAN constitution, there is an important requirement regarding the intersection of VLANs. More or less as we will see with the question of interconnection of VLANs, which arises as soon as a segmentation has been carried out, splitting into independent VLANs often appears to be too radical a solution. In a large number of cases, it is desirable that certain devices belong to two or more VLANs (but always starting from a single coupler).

There are two ways to respond to this requirement of inter-VLAN intersection, either by allowing one interface to belong effectively to N VLANs, or by defining a hierarchy between VLANs.

Note that the first solution can be applied to all types of VLAN described above.

In the second option, a tree structure with several levels can be built. In this functioning mode, the superior of a set of VLANs is able to communicate with any of these, still maintaining a segmentation between the subordinate VLANs. The superior VLAN is located at the common intersection of all VLANs it encompasses. Thus, to illustrate a system with 2 levels, VLAN X.0 is the superior of all VLANs X.Y where Y ≠ 0, whereas VLAN 0 in turn is the superior of all VLANs X, and thus by definition of all VLANs X.Y.

Uniqueness of addresses   A specific question generated by segmentation into VLANs concerns the support of the existence (and visibility) of the same MAC address (in the Source field) on several VLANs. Although the standard, as we will see shortly, authorizes the two possible modes, it must be understood that this is not natural for a switch. In fact, all switches or transparent bridges learn to localize the machines by their MAC source address and to associate these addresses with the reception ports so as to carry out what has been called natural filtering.

Now, putting two VLANs in selective communication via a stage of bridging with various filtering (for example, for security reasons) implies that a frame can re-enter the switch by a port other than the one which received its first transmission. The learning process is therefore unnecessarily duplicated. All the same, one can imagine that an interface able to tag its frames could emit frames in different VLANs with the same MAC address.

This ubiquity of an address can only be supported if the switches are equipped with a learning table distinguishing the VLANs, which is not yet very common. To justify this limitation of the products on the market, we note that this is not a frequent requirement.

VLAN transport   Ideally, knowledge of the virtual LANs should be extended to all elements of the network, but with a high priority for the switches. In fact, if all the switches have the same level of information on the splitting of the network into VLANs, they can work in a perfectly consistent way. Two means can be envisaged:

- manually providing exhaustive and global knowledge of the network to each switch, or
- parametrizing them with only a partial and local view and letting them dynamically communicate the notion of belonging to the VLANs.

The second option is clearly preferable, because it is more automatic and more evolutionary, as well as charging the network administrator only with a unitary (and not multiple) workload. This inter-switch communication (*a priori* on high-speed links of 100 Mbps and more) can take on different aspects:

- transmission of synthetic information regarding the correspondence (station – VLAN) through a subsidiary distribution protocol circulating in parallel with the data frames
- transmission of information regarding each frame exchanged via explicit tagging.

The first solution has the advantage of not burdening the readability of the frames for devices that do not handle VLANs. Inversely, it provides little protection vis-à-vis unwanted eavesdropping, since the frames pass in the clear on the trunk connections (such as an FDDI ring).

The second solution, more common and also retained by IEEE 802.1Q, imposes adding complementary fields that change the MAC structure of the frame (including its length). This means that if the frames are tagged, all MAC devices having to retransmit them must be able to interpret them. Consequently, the first switches to implement tagging will obviously be capable of de-tagging the frames towards all ports where there are one or more pieces of equipment that do not understand these new fields.

Leaking In transparent bridging, the notion of 'leaking' or open virtual LANs is applied to unicast frames. The idea is that the open VLANs effectively segment only traffic flows in diffusion. If two workstations wish to communicate with each other (and know their MAC addresses) the exchange can take place directly. This type of VLAN has the main advantage of limiting pollution by broadcasts and multicasts, but allows only limited security. It is therefore fairly well suited for level 3 switching of short-cut type in LANs (which we will see below).

IEEE 802.1Q standard

The IEEE has an interesting theoretical approach to virtual LANs. Thus, the first part of the standard defines an adapted terminology which we will describe below. However, it should not be forgotten that the IEEE is a latecomer, relatively speaking, with respect to the developments of the manufacturers on the market.

A maximum of 4095 VLANs are envisaged, bearing in mind that a frame can only belong to one of them.

In addition to the notion of a VLAN, the IEEE 802.1Q also defines a communication mode of priority levels by means of tagging.

The IEEE 802.1Q divides edge devices and bridges into two categories: VLAN-aware devices which know that there are virtual LANs and are able to handle them, and VLAN-unaware devices which work without this knowledge. With regard to bridges, this means functioning according to the current IEEE 802.1D specifications. Compatibility between the two environments is desired, and the devices of all categories can thus coexist on the same network. Thus, there is one VLAN by default.

IEEE 802.1Q also defines three types of links for a bridge. The segments leading to links with VLAN-unaware stations (without tagging) are called access links. The inter-switch segments that carry only tagged frames are called trunk links. These segments can be point-to-point connections or true, potentially shared, networks. Finally, the segments that can see tagged and non-tagged frames transit are called hybrid links. On these segments one will therefore find VLAN-aware and VLAN-unaware devices. Note that on a hybrid link, all frames circulating in a given VLAN must comply with the same format (tagged or not). The requirement

6 bytes	6 bytes	2 bytes	2 bytes	2 bytes	N bytes	4 bytes
DA	SA	TPID = 8100	TCI	Long/Type	Data	FCS

Figure 13.16 Structure of the tagged Ethernet frame.

3 bits	1 bit	12 bits
User priority	CFI	VID

Figure 13.17 Structure of the TCI.

for compatibility with existing implementations means that most of the links are hybrid.

Tagging Membership in a virtual LAN can be denoted by explicit or implicit tagging. Explicit tagging consists of a 4 bytes header inserted in the frame, whereas implicit tagging consists of being able to determine the VLAN number in function of the frame contents (MAC or network addresses, protocol, and so on) or its reception port on the switch.

If the format of the frame is of Ethernet or IEEE 802.3 type (meaning without LLC), tagging consisting of TPID (Tag Protocol Identifier = 8100) and TCI (Tag Control Information) is placed as shown in Figure 13.16.

Note that since the tagging inserted in the frame adds 4 bytes, the length of the data field could accordingly be reduced by 4 bytes (46–1496). The minimum size could also go from 64 to 68 bytes. In fact, the IEEE 802.3ac supplement describes a maximum frame length depending on the value of the field following the MAC source address. If this field contains the value which indicates that it is a TPID, the maximum size passes from 1518 to 1522 bytes (all fields counted, except for the preamble), whereas the minimum length remains unchanged at 64 bytes. The aim is to avoid a tagged frame being erroneously eliminated as jabber error.

The TCI is composed as shown in Figure 13.17.

The level of priority as defined by IEEE 802.1p can thus be carried by the same header as the VLAN number (VID: VLAN Identifier).

CFI (Canonical Format Indicator) is a bit which can be used in the encapsulation of a frame format from one LAN towards another. It specifies whether the MAC addresses that can occur in the data field follow a canonical or a non-canonical format. For an Ethernet or IEEE 802.3 frame, CFI = 1 indicates that an RIF (Routing Information Field) is present after the tagging (which is not represented in the illustration). Thus, it is the NCFI bit of the RIF that specifies whether the format of the MAC addresses contained in the data field is canonical or not. If, on the contrary, the frame is Token Ring or FDDI (thus, with SNAP tagging), CFI = 1 indicates directly that the format of the MAC frames present in the data field is non-canonical, and CFI = 0 indicates the opposite.

VLAN (or VID) 0 is special because it corresponds to the absence of a VLAN number. This does not mean that the frame cannot be classified, but that the tagging does not specify a VLAN number. Thus, the association frame / VLAN will be carried out as for a non-tagged frame (*a priori* by port). This case can occur when the station uses tagging only to denote priority, or to exploit an encapsulation mode of IEEE 802.1Q. Note that a bridge must not generate tagged frames without VLAN and with priority. VLAN 1 is theoretically the default VLAN.

VLANs In the framework of the first version of the standard, the VLAN constitution mode for non-tagged frames is based on the VLAN of the reception port (VLAN by port), while tagged frames can use more elaborate notions to determine their VLAN. In fact, the classification by port is also presented (in a supplement) as a basic solution which, in the case of a switch capable of elaborating the VLANs on the basis of other parameters (MAC address, network, protocol, and so on), is the essential fallback solution if the received frame cannot be decoded by means of one of the higher-level criteria. On that occasion, a hierarchy is presented, starting from the lowest level: port number, MAC address, network protocol, range of network addresses, and so on.

Once again, the coexistence of the two tagging modes imposes non-negligible 'translation' capacities on the switching bridges which can be charged with insertion or suppression of tagging, according to the MAC format, and with recalculation of the CRC. Moreover, as IEEE 802.1Q comprises all LAN technologies and their bridging, the input and output MAC formats can be substantially different. We will see below that capabilities of encapsulation have been introduced as well.

The standard has chosen to allow only one occurrence of a spanning tree in the bridged topology, and not one spanning tree per VLAN. This choice implies that the topology of each VLAN is a subset of the tree topology determined by the STP, with blocked ports being blocked for all VLANs. The second solution was obviously possible, but seemed relatively complex and has been reserved for future extensions of the standard.

On the other hand, the choice is left to the switching bridge to implement a learning facility for MAC addresses by VLAN (MFD: Multiple Filtering Database) or a learning facility for global addresses (SFD: Single Filtering Database). This difference has a direct effect on the use of the same MAC address in different VLANs, or on inter-VLAN bridging. In MFD, the same interface, by means of explicit tagging, can belong to several VLANs simultaneously, whereas this is not always possible in SFD. Also, communication between VLANs by means of a dedicated filtering bridge will pose critical problems to SFD bridges which will see the same MAC address enter through different ports (without maintaining the association to different VLANs in their learning table).

GVRP Furthermore, IEEE 802.1Q exploits the GARP protocol of IEEE 802.1p to define a protocol for flagging the presence of a VLAN in a segment. GVRP (GARP VLAN Registration Protocol) allows VLAN-aware switches and stations to let the other switches know that they actively manage that particular VLAN on a LAN segment. The aim here is to allow the rediffusion of traffic that does not concern any device on a segment to be limited. This is made possible by proceeding the other way round, namely by registering potentially on each port of the necessary VLANs. Note that the protocol allows registration of the presence of elements belonging to a VLAN behind a port of the bridge, and thus activation of the extension of the VLAN on this port, but not unitary registration of the terminal devices. For this purpose, the registered value is the VLAN number (in 12 bits) but not the MAC address.

GVRP uses only one type of attribute in GARP corresponding to the VLAN, namely the VID Attribute Type (value of the type = 1). As it does not specify the MAC address of the interface, the registering is unitary for each VLAN.

Note that VLAN-unaware workstations can *a priori* not use GVRP and therefore are unable to automatically indicate the presence of the VLAN to which they belong.

While waiting for the diffusion of devices conforming to IEEE 802.1Q, a heterogeneity will persist, forcing VLAN-aware switches to include and extract the tags (with CRC recalculation) from one port towards the other every time that the frame comes from a VLAN-aware device and is directed towards a VLAN-unaware device and vice versa. Also note that this is not necessarily managed by port (hybrid link), but by destination.

Encapsulation   As mentioned earlier, IEEE 802.1Q takes advantage of the introduction of tagging, which on the one hand allows you to insert an RIF into an Ethernet frame, and on the other hand to specify the format of MAC frames which are not present in the MAC header, to redefine the bridging modes in a heterogeneous environment. Since frequently explicit tagging is introduced to allow coding of the conversion options, we can often consider this as a kind of encapsulation or tunneling.

To determine all necessary and possible formats, IEEE 802.1Q uses several criteria and looks at all combinations:

E/L: Ethernet V2.0 (E) or LLC (L) frame format
C/N: MAC addresses present in the data field in
       Canonical (C) or Non-canonical (N) format
R/T: Source Route (R) or Transparent (T) bridging
C/R: CSMA/CD (C) or Token Ring/FDDI (R) LAN technology
I/T: Implicit (I) or present (T) tagging

The CSMA/CD technologies are Ethernet and IEEE 802.3.

This represents 32 possible combinations, and 48 methods of bi-directional (symmetric) bridging. Each combination is represented as a sequence of the letters identifying each selection. Thus E-C-T/C-I is the most common Ethernet.

All these possibilities of conversion are then broken down into three categories, namely those which refer only to the IEEE 802.1H (or ISO 11802-5) standard and to RFC 1042, called H; those which refer only to IEEE 802.1Q, called Q; and those which imply all three specifications, called Q + H.

H: X-X-X/C-I   ↔   X-X-X/R-I   where X is arbitrary
Q: X-X-X/C-I   ↔   X-X-X/C-T
         X-X-X/R-I   ↔   X-X-X/R-T
Q + H: X-X-X/Y-T   ↔   X-X-X/Z-T   where Y ≠ Z
         X-X-X/U-W   ↔   X-X-X/V-Y   where U ≠ V and W ≠ Y

This classification appears heavy and complex, but it is an unambiguous method which allows media to be changed without having to bother about the notions one could lose (bridging) or the necessary conversions. In this sense, it proposes the use of tagging to specify the frame representation format without burdening the translation function.

With regard to recalculation of the CRC for a frame whose format has been modified or enriched, a study of the means of recalculation or modification of the CRC can be found in the supplement of IEEE 802.1p.

Broadcast control

Switching undeniably allows populated and powerful 'flat' networks of vast dimensions to be constructed. In fact, because it overcomes the limitations of the access methods, switching allows realization of networks, without having to worry about their size (as long as the total transporting delay remains reasonable), by connecting all the machines one wishes to connect, since each of them can be assigned a dedicated bandwidth (or at least a non-negligible part of it), and finally, by accumulating the required number of Mbps by means of introducing switches of suitable size. However, if all this appears to meet the requirements, it must still be noted that multicast and unicast traffic flows are processed differently. Direct switching of each frame according to its destination allows a growing quantity of unicast flows to be met, but the frames in diffusion are always reproduced on all ports belonging to a VLAN. It is indeed the role of the switch, as is that of a bridge, to diffuse broadcasts and multicasts in the same way that a hub would do. Thus, while unicast traffic is switched, traffic in diffusion is treated as in a shared technology.

To illustrate this notion, consider a hypothetical station which emits an average of 1 Mbps of traffic (and 200 pps), and generates 1 broadcast per second (top value); then 100 machines of this type generate 100 Mbps (20 000 pps) which are redirected by the switches, but also 100 broadcast/s (which is a lot). Thus, the accumulation of broadcast frames that always interrupt the NIC of all stations that receive them rapidly becomes penalizing.

Thus, a disproportion is created between the flows, because if each machine emits less than one frame out of 100 in diffusion, it receives one out of 3 in return.

In addition, it should be noted that on a switch with 100 ports at 10 Mbps, we have $(100 / 2) \times 10 = 500$ Mbps for flows to unique destinations, but still only 10 Mbps for all flows in diffusion.

The solution to this background pollution lies in the reduction of the broadcast domain, which can be achieved by two methods: splitting into VLANs (each

VLAN being a broadcast domain), or intelligent reduction of the frames in diffusion during their transit through the switch. The first solution is relatively simple and can be applied to all flows in diffusion, whereas the second solution can integrate different elaborated mechanisms which, however, concern only broadcasts.

For example, a switch can be asked to follow all ARP frames (requests and answers) it retransmits, so as to be able to limit diffusion of the subsequent requests, that is, to answer them directly. In fact, if the switch listens to all ARP frames, it will progressively learn the whole IP topology which surrounds it. This knowledge can be used to limit the pollution of the subsequent searches, either by switching them directly to the port on which the target machine is located, or by answering in place of the machine. The first solution is the least intrusive and most secure one, because the switch never takes the place of a device charged with answering the frame in diffusion. The second solution is the most economical one in terms of traffic, because it limits the distance that the request and answer have to travel.

This principle can be applied to all frames in diffusion or advertisement frames of current protocols which correspond to a search for a unique element or to an announcement of the presence of a service. Thus in IPX, RIP/SAP and Type 20 frames (used for NetBIOS in IPX) can be cleverly filtered. In NetBIOS, the Name Query can be switched following a previous learning process of the server locations, and Retries can be explicitly limited in their number of repetitions.

If the frame in diffusion has the function of informing a set of devices (which is different from a search), the principle is not exactly the same, but it is always possible to reduce the range of retransmissions. Thus, in a client–server environment, it is possible to divide all ports into two categories: those that only feed client stations, and those that feed servers (and maybe also clients). Considering that it is not sensible to have any traffic circulate between client stations, it is possible to limit the diffusion of frames generated on client ports to server ports only. Note that the opposite is not true; server broadcasts must always arrive at all ports.

As a complement to the previous solutions of limitation of broadcasts, we will now see how, with IEEE 802.1p, we can efficiently reduce diffusion of multicast frames.

IEEE 802.1p standard

The IEEE is currently drawing up a supplement to the IEEE 802.1D standard which deals with the management of distinct classes of traffic and the filtering of multicast frames by MAC bridges. This draft is consistent with the update of ISO 10038 (or IEEE 802.1D) and the specifications of supplement IEEE 802.1Q. Moreover, the GVRP protocol of IEEE 802.1Q builds on the functioning of the GARP protocol defined by IEEE 802.1p.

Traffic classes Management of several classes of service must allow traffic flows considered to be of high priority to be placed into 'faster' queues in the case of congestion or saturation of the bridge's performance. The notion underlying this functionality is the differentiation of the traffic flows, and their more or less privileged

Table 13.5 Traffic types and priorities.

Queues	Type of traffic
Low priority	Background
	Best effort
	Excellent effort
	Controlled load
	Video
	Voice
High priority	Network control

treatment according to their importance, criticality or urgency. It also appears evident that the wish to support multimedia flows has contributed to the elaboration of this principle.

Eight different levels of priority are defined, from 0 (low) to 7 (high), knowing that no number of queues (or buffers) per port is imposed. This can, indeed, vary between 1 and 7 queues.

Obviously, for LANs that incorporate a notion of explicit priority by frame in the MAC header, such as Token Ring and FDDI, establishing the correspondence is trivial. For others, such as Ethernet, the lowest priority is chosen by default.

Where voice data must undergo less than 10 ms of delay, video data less than 100 ms, and where controlled-load traffic is supposed to have been previously studied and dimensioned in function of the network capacities.

Retransmission follows a rather simple procedure, namely that the frames waiting in the output of a port in a queue of priority N can only be output if the queues $N + 1$ and higher are empty. The subdivision of flows is thus not proportional to the level of priority, but follows a selective and sequential treatment. Note that this also means that the ordering of frames is only maintained by queue, and not between the queues. Traffic flows of different priorities can be retransmitted in a different order from that of their reception.

Multicast filtering The GMRP protocol (GARP Multicast Registration Protocol) allows stations to tell bridges which groups of diffusion they wish to attach themselves to. The aim clearly is to manage the diffusion of multicast frames as cleverly as possible. Broadcast frames, instead, must be forwarded to all ports.

Two types of attribute are defined, allowing specification of the multicast MAC address concerned (in 6 bytes), and the type of generic action (registering of all groups, or of all undeclared groups), respectively.

This mechanism can potentially be put in parallel with the one proposed by IGMP and DVMRP in the IP world. As IGMP is already used, this means that (layer

3 but also layer 2) switches may need to be capable of managing IGMP exchanges, typically by IGMP spooling on each port, as a router would do.

Let us nevertheless not forget that if multicast frames needlessly take up global bandwidth, as do broadcasts, they do not penalize the NICs, as do the latter.

GARP The GARP protocol (Generic Attribute Registration Protocol) allows devices that implement it to register with bridges, passing them certain parameters. This is indeed a generic indication (or registration) protocol in the sense that it is perfectly neutral. Only applications developed under this protocol have a meaning. We have already seen two applications of GARP, namely GVRP in 802.1Q and GMRP in 802.1p.

GARP is designed to operate in an environment where a frame can be lost (the MAC still being connectionless). Thus, the registration of a machine with a certain number of parameters is not for ever, and the bridge periodically (every 10 s by default) informs that it will cancel all its registrations. Machines wishing to maintain the same attributes are thus forced to declare themselves again.

The GARP frame format (Figure 13.18) respects LLC encapsulation, obvious for an IEEE protocol.

The distinction between applications using GARP is made via the MAC address used. Each application shares the same first bytes of the multicast address, and is attributed the last half byte (GMRP: 0, GVRP:1) (Figure 13.19).

Protocol ID = 0x0001 identifying the GARP protocol
End Mark = 0

= 14 bytes	3 bytes	M bytes	= 4 bytes
MAC header where DA = group address of the application	LLC header	PDU GARP	MAC postfix

Figure 13.18   GARP frame.

2 bytes	N bytes	. . .	P bytes	1 byte
Protocol ID	Message A	. . .	Message Z	End mark

Figure 13.19   GARP PDU.

1 byte	1 byte	1 byte	X bytes	. . .	1 byte	1 byte	Y bytes	1 byte
Attribute Type	Attribute Length 1	Attribute Event 1	Attribute Value 1	. . .	Attribute Length M	Attribute Event M	Attribute Value M	End mark

Figure 13.20   Structure of a message.

The structure of a message is shown in Figure 13.20 and described below:

Attribute Type:	defined by the application using GARP (1 to 255 included)
Attribute Length:	length of the 3 fields Length + Event + Value (2 to 255)
Attribute Event	operator
0: LeaveAll	all registrations will be canceled
1: JoinEmpty	declaration of the attribute value, without registration of the station
2: JoinIn	declaration of the value, after previous registration
3: LeaveEmpty	de-registration of the value, without registration
4: LeaveIn	de-registration of the value, after registration
5: Empty	neither declaration nor registration of the value
Attribute Value:	according to the application using GARP.

Each time, the Attribute Type code defines which type of information can be found in the Attribute Value field.

The stations can adopt an active or passive behavior; they are thus silent and monitor the GARP messages in transit.

If the bridge that receives a GARP frame does not implement the protocol, it obviously retransmits the frame, because it is a frame in diffusion, towards the bridges possibly located behind it.

GMRP   The first GARP application defined thus concerns the inscription of multicast addresses that must be diffused on each port of the switch.

It defines two types of attribute:

- the Group Attribute Type, which is 1 and indicates that the Group Attribute Value is the MAC multicast address (in 48 bits) representing the multicast group to which one wishes to attach;
- the Service Requirement Attribute Type, which is 2 and indicates that the required service is either the diffusion of all multicast groups (coded by a value of 0) or only of the unregistered groups (value of 1).

Thus, either the station explicitly asks the bridge to be served by the diffusions of the MAC addresses expressly communicated, or – in a more global way – to be integrated into all multicast groups (without specifying multicast addresses), or into the multicast groups not expressly registered with this bridge.

GMRP proposes an interesting solution to multicast traffic limitation, but it will only be of real practical benefit if it is effectively implemented everywhere.

Layer 3 switching

In all switched environments, the problem of performance of routing occurs. In fact, switches (whether LAN or ATM) easily present some Gigabps of global bandwidth, possibly associated with guaranteed retransmission delays. The router, instead, even though it has substantially evolved, cannot hope to compete with these capacities, because its treatment is usually much more complex (multi-protocol, multi-technology LAN/WAN routers). This is due to the bandwidth of each network having increased with the aid of switching, adding the throughputs of several links, while the router, which at one time had equivalent access to the bandwidth of an entire network (10 Mbps, for example, for a shared Ethernet network), is today linked to this network by a single link which is inevitably a potential bottleneck (even at 100 Mbps). We may say that the router as we know it has been conceived to suit shared architectures, but is not quite suited to switched LAN infrastructures.

Obviously, this problem only manifests itself when transverse flows (those which go from one logical network to another) are required to present the same level of performance as though they occurred within one network. Unfortunately, it appears that the evolution of the IT world, with tendencies such as centralization of servers and Intranet, demands that vertical and transverse flows are conveyed in similar conditions.

This requirement for routing also results from the inevitable segmentation, during these past years, at the level of network addresses, with IP subnetting, for example, but also with splitting into VLANs. In effect, this segmentation, which had become necessary because of the overpopulation of address classes, because of the requirement to refine the granularity of administration, or because of security rules, has ended up creating distinct subsets, whose need for inter-group communication, however, has been growing ever since.

With regard to administration, we must state that even though a switched flat network can technically accommodate several hundred machines, it will not be easily manageable because it lacks any substructure capable of identifying, distinguishing or localizing access. Moreover, as we have seen, pollution by frames in diffusion is all the more penalizing the more the network is populated.

Two major approaches can be identified to satisfy this need for powerful routing:

- to route very quickly, preferably inside the very heart of the LAN switch (called hop-by-hop);

- to route without passing through a router, by short-cutting it (also called cut-through).

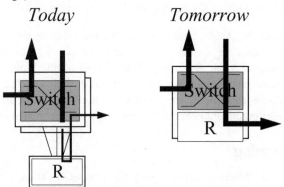

Figure 13.21 Use of switched routing.

The two approaches are part of what is commonly called switching at level 3 (Network layer) or Layer 3 Switching.

In both cases, we fundamentally differentiate between retransmitting functions (with modification of MAC and network headers) and route calculation functions. The first function (Frame Forwarding) is demanding in speed, but extremely repetitive. It systematically exploits the knowledge the router has of the network topologies to determine the routing to be followed by the packet. The second function is considerably more intelligent. It exploits the routing protocols such as RIP or OSPF, but requires computing power only at specific times, when the network topology is modified. The route calculation function fills in a table of knowledge which is used for forwarding, and can potentially be distributed if the element is a route server.

Super routers

The first approach, also sometimes called Giga-Router, has the big advantage of not needing any modification at protocol level. It shifts the problem on to the manufacturers, who must develop retransmission devices which process (and modify) network headers as fast as MAC headers. However, at this point we should remind ourselves that if the current LAN switches show attractive performance, this is simply because manufacturers have implemented the technical improvements needed to make the old bridges powerful enough to hide the (relative) complexity of bridging. Similarly, we can expect that manufacturers will succeed in implementing ever faster routing technologies, and this, as with LAN switches, probably at the expense of the functional richness of the current routers. We can thus imagine that these switches/routers will concentrate on the principal protocol families: IP, IPX and their routing protocols (RIP, OSPF and RIP, NLSP, respectively). These routers, even if integrated, always find their main *raison d'être* in selectively putting several sub-groups in communication with each other. For this purpose, they must be able to use filtering of the same kind as that of traditional routers (on network address, transport protocol and application port), preferably without any noticeable impact on their performance.

Moreover, as mentioned before, this super router (mainly hardware) must be integrated into the switch so as not to be dependent on the bandwidth of its links with the switch. The ideal situation would be that these routers could process several hundreds of Mbps of traffic, and thus have direct access to the heart of the switch (bus, shared memory or other). Furthermore, this direct access dynamically subdivides the global routed bandwidth between all the flows. Once again, the performance of such super routers is generally evaluated in network headers processed per second (pps). To illustrate this, a routing element able to handle 100 k pps, for example, can only output 67 Mbps in short frames (64 bytes) but up to 1.23 Gbps in long frames (1500 bytes). The significance of being connected to the very core of the switch is thus evident.

The much more traditional alternative (to be avoided) is to connect a big external router by N high-speed ports to the switch, each of the N ports being linked to one of the VLANs to interconnect. The worst case in terms of performance is to share a single access of the router to the switch, this link being shared by all logical networks which are to be linked with each other.

The coexistence of several IP networks on the same port does not pose problems, and this can also be realized in IPX by means of the different MAC encapsulations (four on Ethernet). This last solution is only acceptable for not very demanding routed traffic (towards the WAN, for example), but is obviously the most affordable one.

Short-cut

The second approach is interesting because it does not require the development of a 'super router', and theoretically allows data to be transmitted with the same speed inside a network or between two networks, because it only influences the functioning mode of the cards at the endpoints. However, it requires a modification of traditional routing methods that theoretically cannot do without a router. Unless one wants to modify the functioning of all NICs together, it is not systematically applicable in LANs. It is, however, the basis of very promising technologies, such as NHRP and MPOA in ATM.

There are, however, two approaches that allow 'on-the-fly' routing in IP by cheating a little.

The first solution requires each station to be told that it is its own default gateway and thus force it to output an ARP frame, even for stations that are not located in its IP network. If the machine is directly accessible, it responds to the ARP request, and if it is located in another VLAN, it is the task of the layer 3 switch to propagate the request or to answer it instead of the true addressee. If the two interlocutors are located in distinct networks, it is the task of the switch to reproduce the frames of one VLAN towards the other systematically for the new flow. This change of VLAN is fairly simple and uses only few resources, and can even be completely avoided in the case of leaky VLANs, as discussed earlier. Since layer 3 switching employs the same path as MAC switching, it enjoys exactly the same performance in terms of pps and delay.

Moreover, interaction with traditional WAN routers is not trivial, because the station always considers itself to be the default gateway. It is therefore necessary either to declare the WAN router explicitly in the routing tables of the workstations, provided that the station accepts a routing table of several entries, or to employ the Proxy-ARP protocol on the WAN routers, which is not an ideal solution.

A short-cut solution that respects the standards more than the previous one consists in obtaining the change of router by sending ICMP redirection frames. The Redirect packet asks the station requesting the MAC address of an addressee to apply to the specified router, that is to the station itself. This derivative has the advantage over the initial solution of not requiring any manual modification of the IP stacks of the client stations (a potentially heavy undertaking), because a dynamic protocol (ICMP) is used to manage the router change.

The second solution consists in employing a specific free class A or B address (10.X.X.X or 172.16.X.X–172.31.X.X), and carrying out a subnetting not declared inside this class where each subnet corresponds to a VLAN. This solution does not require any modification of the functioning of the workstations, and the layer 3 switch has, as before, the function of propagating the ARP request to the destination VLAN. If the VLANs are open to unicast frames, the switch only intervenes in the search for the addressee. If, on the contrary, the VLANs are closed (or secure), the switch must reproduce each unicast frame following the phase of discovery of the interlocutor.

In this solution, the interconnection with the WAN obviously requires caching the addresses used locally by a stage of the Network Address Translation (NAT, RFC 1918), and converting them into official IP addresses.

Note that these short-cut solutions have the major disadvantage of providing a low level of security, because once the stations are in direct communication, no control over the protocol or the application can be exercised by the switch. Thus, even if the switch controls the protocols during the connection phase (more precisely, during the search for MAC addresses via ARP), it is afterwards no longer in the circuit and has no means of verification. Its only possible action is to cut the inter-VLAN retransmission.

Since these solutions do not provide all the advantages of a router, they are sometimes described as layer 2.5 switching solutions.

Finally, as we have seen, both short-cut solutions concern IP traffic only, and will not function on all current IP derivatives.

Development

If we try to understand layer 3 switching from a practical and summary point of view, we must accept that MAC switching requires development of routers aiming for integrated high-performance solutions. It is therefore reasonable to believe that layer 3 switching will probably become very common by the year 2000.

Presently, if we try to imagine its near future, we must say that layer 3 switching is an evolution of the MAC switch which places LAN technologies within the same aspirational framework as ATM. In fact, ATM is natively switched at the levels of cells and frames (via LAN_E), but also integrates multi-protocol layer 3 switching with MPOA and NHRP. However, as an answer to the multimedia

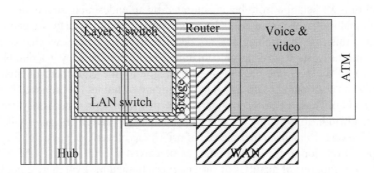

Figure 13.22   Domains covered by switching.

Table 13.6 Fields used for switching.

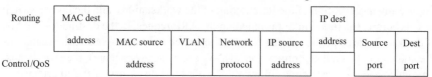

	MAC dest address					IP dest address		
Routing								
		MAC source address	VLAN	Network protocol	IP source address		Source port	Dest port
Control/QoS								

capacities of ATM, the switched LAN could also integrate priorities (consistent with TOS bits RSVP) for supporting service qualities.

After switching at layer 2, then 3, it is currently layer 4 which is at the forefront (while waiting for AnyLayer switching). This, indeed, is no longer generic 'routing', but classification. The complementary requirement that the two preceding levels of switching did not meet is to assign priorities to flows as a function of the application which is identified by IP addresses or the port number specified in the Transport layer. Thus, a network administrator can demand, independently of the machines at the endpoints, that a better service be guaranteed to certain communications considered more critical. This is undeniably a significant complementary service, but it intervenes only in the case of congestion or passage to a lower throughput (LAN–WAN for example). Otherwise, transport is fluid for all exchanges. These products are commonly referred to as Bandwidth Manager or Bandwidth Controller. On the other hand, Layer 4 switches would focus on TCP connection redirection for redundancy, security and load sharing purpose.

Finally, we insist on the fact that the term of layer 4 switching is only justified if we consider that the only switching really carried out by the switch is situated between internal queues of different priorities.

QOS

The last major subject related to switching concerns quality of service and transport of multimedia traffic. With the advent of switching, many thought that finally, with their powerful switches, synchronous traffic could easily be transported via LANs. In fact, by dedicating the entire bandwidth, possibly in full duplex, to two stations, one is sure not to disturb their exchanges. Nothing, however, prevents the reception channel of a workstation from being saturated by an undesirable stream at the very moment that it is expecting a critical transmission in terms of delay. We can clearly see that in this case the problem has not been resolved inside the switch, and moreover, no means exists at MAC level to guarantee bandwidth or delay in a reliable way.

At MAC level, the only means of integrating the equivalent of quality of service is the positioning of priorities in the tagging of frames (as proposed by IEEE 802.1p and Q). Thus, the flows considered critical will benefit, if necessary, from the entire bandwidth, followed by the other communication categories sub-divided into at most 8 levels. To manage these levels of priority as cleverly as possible, they need to be put in relation to the critical point as perceived at level 3. Since the network level has descriptions of qualities of service (very limited in IPv4, more complete in IPv6 and RSVP), it would be interesting if routers and stations at the extremes could concurrently manage the reservation of resources (with RSVP, for example) and the setting of more or less high priorities for the transmitted frames.

In reality, we must be well aware that there is still no real guarantee of throughput or delay because there is no true resource reservation mechanism in LAN switches. However, this establishment of a correspondence would at least allow the user to benefit from the maximum efficiency of the MAC level in conditions of congestion.

Future refinements at the MAC level should allow optimization of the behavior of a switched network in the case of saturation, for example by managing the flow control (defined in full-duplex Ethernet) as a function of traffic priority.

13.4 Routers

The router is an interconnection device that uses the logical address information contained in the headers of levels above Ethernet to retransmit packets within a set of networks (Figure 13.23). In fact, most (but not all) protocols have ways of identifying the machines independently of their attachment, using a logical address. This description is placed in the network layer. In addition to the level 3 source and destination addresses, the protocol defines the so-called routing parameters, such as the default gateway, the maximum number of routers that can be crossed before reaching the destination, the choice of a route according to type of service (small delay, high speed, high reliability, low cost). It is these fields that the router will use to switch and re-emit the frame. It should be noted that in its work, the router is led to modify the physical-level frame. It will change the layer 1 addresses and replace them by its own address as source and the station address as destination, if the latter is on a network attached to it or by the address of the next router to be passed through. This is a fundamental concept, which means, for example, that the observation of MAC level frames leaving a router is of no interest, since they then all have the same source address and the frames entering have the same destination address.

The monitoring of the traffic on the networks between which routers have been installed requires observation tools to visualize the level-3 fields.

Finally, as routers have a knowledge of the different possible routes between the logical networks attached to them, it is advantageous for them to be able to

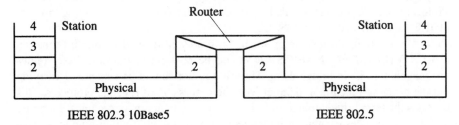

Figure 13.23   Example of an Ethernet and Token Ring router.

intercommunicate to exchange their tables or information on the availability of a route at a given time. This means that they are able to work in a concerted manner to choose the fastest channel, distribute the load over various serial lines, select another interconnection technology if loops are detected or switch to a back-up link if the main link fails. So-called routing protocols have been defined to encode these exchanges of data between routers; these incorporate an algorithm (sometimes relatively complicated) for modifying the tables and propagating recent information. In fact, on networks with a large number of interconnection devices, it is crucial to be able to ensure the evolution of routing when incidents occur without losing too much time and without creating an oscillatory phenomenon involving the circulation of contradictory information on the network. One should not forget that each element only has a knowledge of its own interface, and has to reconstitute the overall configuration of the global network from the information reaching it.

To ensure maximum security, all the routing tables may be predefined and fixed. In this case, the routing is no longer dynamic but static, and only evolves when routes which the manager wishes to incorporate in his or her network are added.

Since the router function lies at level 3, it processes the decapsulated packet and is not concerned with the type of interface. Thus, a router may have virtually any type of interface, provided this transports the packets whose format it knows. Thus, routers can easily be made multimedia devices with local area network interfaces for, for example, Ethernet, Token Ring and FDDI, and wide area network interfaces for, for example, E1 & E3 (T1 & T3 in the USA), X.25, HDLC, LAPB, PPP, Frame Relay and, more recently, ATM. The serial ports are of the RS-232, X.21, V.35, G.703, and, more recently, High Speed Serial Interface (HSSI) type.

This capability to function with various types of low-level technology implies an ability to divide excessively long packets, and reconstruct the header of each segment produced. In fact, the networks do not all support the same maximum packet size and the router may very well have to route frames exceeding the maximum length of the destination network. Since it understands information relating to level 3, it will be able to intervene actively in fields containing, for example, the total length of the datagram or the fragment offset.

The routers now available are almost all multi-protocol, with the ability to handle successive frames corresponding to the main protocols such as IP (DoD), CLNP (ISO), DECnet (Digital), IPX (Novell), AppleTalk (Apple), VINES (Banyan), and XNS (Xerox). They also support a number of routing protocols such as the Routing Information Protocol (RIP), Border Gateway Protocol (BGP), Exterior Gateway Protocol (EGP), Open Shortest Path First (OSPF), Interior Gateway Routing Protocol (IGRP), and ISO's ES–IS and IS–IS.

In addition, since some protocols have no well-defined routing information at level 3 (LAT, SNA, NetBIOS), it should be possible to transmit these frames unchanged, that is, to bridge them. Thus, the router should be capable of carrying out the bridging function in parallel with the processing of routable protocols. This explains the term bridge–router, or brouter, which is found in the technical literature and denotes devices capable of implementing bridging and routing functions. Like bridges, these devices can accept filters, taking advantage of their knowledge of the level above.

We note that the operation of a router depends entirely upon its use (prefixes to the logical network and sub-network addresses to be communicated, choice of the routing system, contents of the routing table if a static method is chosen, and so on). This means that it is vital to configure the router to adapt it to the desired function, and that the device should be able to save this configuration, otherwise it will be useless. Thus, routers have a port for connection of a VT100 console, so that the commands to implement the different types of routing can be typed in directly. But they can also be accessed via the network (for example, using the Telnet protocol) and generally in a more user-friendly manner. In addition, they store their configuration locally (diskette or flash memory) and can also receive their parametrization via the network. This remote loading via the network may be carried out using the FTP protocols (which provides some security since FTP relies on TCP and IP) or TFTP (unguaranteed, because the lower layers are UDP and IP) with a possible call to BOOTP. Finally, many have the facility for modification of their software by remote loading, in a similar manner to the acquisition of the configuration. Two cases must be distinguished. The first comprises devices whose code is stored in ROM, PROM or EPROM (and cannot therefore be altered) but which can execute procedures stored in RAM. The second comprises devices whose code is stored in non-volatile RAM or EEPROM, and which implement a complete upgrade by means of remote loading. The first case still requires a change of ROM if the router is not to restart with an old version after a reboot, while the second solution involves the risk that the hardware may become unusable if the transfer cannot proceed in a single integral action. In fact, if a power failure occurs, the code having been only partially loaded, no more attempts may be permitted and the circuits might need to be physically changed.

The IP router

Let us consider the specific case of an IP router, in order to give examples of the processing carried out for routing.

The IP router is undoubtedly the most common router, given the popularity of the DoD protocol stack. Its function is to enable (at least) two different logical networks to intercommunicate by translating the physical addresses of the frames it has to transport. Logical networks are distinguished by the first part of the logical level addresses (IP).

There are various classes of IP address defined by the apportionment between the number of bits giving the network number and the following bits which give the number of the host in that network (Figure 2.16). Each network number is assigned uniquely by a centralized official body, the Network Information Center (NIC). However, note that the use of addresses which have not been assigned is not dangerous as long as the traffic remains confined and there is no risk of giving rise to conflict or confusion with the machines of the network that officially holds the network number used.

An additional concept allows each group of users with an official address to divide their domain locally into sub-networks. This is based on the use of a sub-network mask (see Figure 13.24). This mask consists of a sequence of 32 bits, and

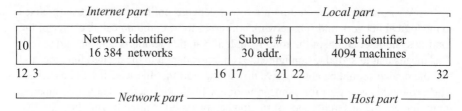

Example: Class B address with a 5-bit subnet
(30 subnetwork addresses)

Subnet mask: 255.255.248.0

Figure 13.24   Example of partitioning by the mask 255.255.248.0 (21 bits set to 1, then 11 bits set to 0).

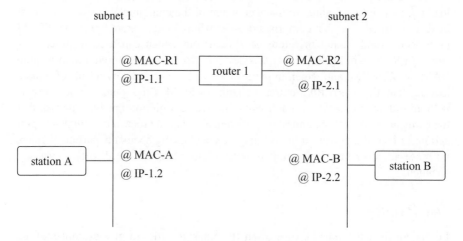

Figure 13.25   Routing example.

can be used to distinguish between the bits which form part of the sub-network address (corresponding to the bits of the mask set to 1) and those which identify the host (the bits of the mask set to 0). See RFC 950 for more details.

For a station or a router, the sub-network field is treated as though it were associated with the Internet part. Thus, the traffic between two stations in different sub-networks will necessarily have to be routed.

Note that, since IP addressing is user defined, it is not necessarily associated with the physical topology. Thus, machines on a single Ethernet cable may be divided into two logical subsets (each with a different network number). Stations belonging to different networks will then have to pass through a router to communicate, even if the stations and the router are all attached to the same Ethernet network. Conversely, a single IP network may consist of several Ethernet networks, some of which may be remote (provided only repeaters, bridges, and remote bridges are used).

The values corresponding to a sequence of 0s or 1s in the network part, the sub-network part and the station number have particular meanings and should be reserved for this application. The 0 (sequence of bits set to 0) is used to implicitly denote the entity (IP network or sub-network) in which one is located, the host in question. The sequence of 1s (for example, 255 for a byte) corresponds to broadcast and denotes all the networks, all the sub-networks, all the hosts or the whole system (in case of the address 255.255.255.255). Some implementations of IP give the sequence of 0s the meaning of broadcast, which could be a source of confusion and lead to major problems. Finally, the address 127.X.X.X corresponds to a looping internal to the station and does not affect the network.

The basic task of the router is to transmit the packet to be routed, modifying the physical addresses to ensure that it is routed to its destination (which is given by the IP address). Here is a simplified description of how it does this.

Station A wishes to emit a frame to station B. It only knows the IP-level logical address of the latter. Perhaps with the help of the sub-network mask, if it has one, station A determines whether station B is on the same network (or sub-network) as itself. If this is not the case, it refers to its routing table to find which router is the transit point for this network. If it does not find this explicitly it will send this frame to the default router. Thus, station A's interface card sends the frame, as illustrated in Figure 13.26, on the physical network. When it receives it the router will read it, interpret it and re-emit it on station B's network.

If the router is not directly connected to B's network, it too will have to pass through one or more intermediate routers, and the frame will bounce from router to router until it reaches its destination (Figure 13.27). On each occasion, the physical addresses change and certain parameters such as the number of jumps taken are modified. Thus, it is conceivable that on the path leading to the target machine, the frame is obliged to pass through a network of a different technology, which would force one of the routers to segment the packets and to reconstruct the header of each segment produced.

7	12	15	26	31	34

MAC destination address: Router 1	MAC source address: Station A	IP type	IP header	IP source address: Station A	IP destination address: Station B

1	6	13	14	27	30

Figure 13.26 IP frame encapsulated in Ethernet with the numbers of the bytes.

MAC destination address: Station B	MAC source address: Router 1	IP type	IP header	IP source address: Station A	IP destination address: Station B

Figure 13.27 Frame leaving the router for its destination.

Unlike bridges with a relatively limited overall view of the networks, the router has to know which direction to take to return to a particular logical network. Today, IP networks of nearly all countries are interconnected and permit international exchanges by the intermediary of a sequence of routers. The complexity arising from the ability to manage such configurations has forced the existing routing protocols to evolve with the size of the networks. Some complete high-performance products are now available and the constitution of large-scale compositions can be envisaged. Protocols such as OSPF try to ensure the reliability of the large enterprise network, and treat modification or evolution information cautiously to ensure stability. In addition, they are also able to evaluate the capabilities and cost of each network in a refined way, and to track the state of adjacent or nearby routers and thus provide dynamic management of a large number of devices.

Before ending, note that a multi-protocol router is capable of processing IP frames, as just mentioned, and also other protocols simultaneously. Moreover, it can bridge certain frames and, like bridges, see its natural behavior modified by the addition of specific filters relating to the fields of the network layers it supports. Unlike the bridge, the router, which knows how to interpret network protocol headers, is able to find a particular field independently of the encapsulation of the lower levels. Thus, if the frame is encapsulated directly in Ethernet or in IEEE 802.3 followed by IEEE 802.2, the IP header (Figure 13.28) does not begin at the same offset; but this will not affect filtering required of a router.

Finally, the router has sufficient knowledge to analyze the validity of a packet and reply to it autonomously if it can (for example, search for correspondence between logical and physical address) or even discard it and inform the sender (if the packet destination is unknown, if it has exceeded the maximum number of hops permitted for its journey).

Just as some bridges have sight of the layer above, some IP routers understand the TCP protocol and are capable of implementing filters similar to those of bridges (forwarding, discarding, priority transfer) on the value of transport-level fields.

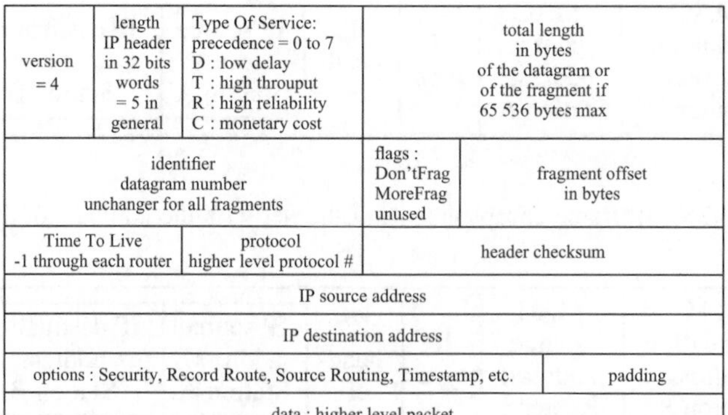

version = 4	length IP header in 32 bits words = 5 in general	Type Of Service: precedence = 0 to 7 D : low delay T : high throuput R : high reliability C : monetary cost	total length in bytes of the datagram or of the fragment if 65 536 bytes max	
identifier datagram number unchanger for all fragments			flags : Don'tFrag MoreFrag unused	fragment offset in bytes
Time To Live -1 through each router		protocol higher level protocol #	header checksum	
IP source address				
IP destination address				
options : Security, Record Route, Source Routing, Timestamp, etc.				padding
data : higher level packet				

Figure 13.28 Fields of the IP protocol header.

It should be stressed that, unlike the bridge with which it often competes, the router links two segments that remain disjoint at the logical level, although the bridge gathers them into a single network. Consequently, the possible problems of a network do not necessarily disturb the nearby networks, as they would in a configuration consisting of non-programmed bridges (natural filtering). Thus, it follows that the router carries out elaborate and complex processing, and that the dimensions of its hardware architecture should be determined as a function of this constraint if the interconnection point is not to put a strain on the overall performance.

IPng

The considerable success of the Internet network has stretched the IP protocol to its limits. In fact, IP is approaching exhaustion of its addressing potential. The 32 bits provided for this field for logical identification of terminal equipment and the associated partitioning structure did not anticipate such growth.

There are two possible solutions. For the medium term (five years or thereabouts) some of the address bands which have already been allocated but are clearly underused could be redistributed more efficiently using Classless InterDomain Routing (CIDR). This eliminates the partitioning into three types of address and supports the more flexible apportionment of networks of a size more closely adapted to the needs of each group of users. Thus, CIDR reduces the rate of increase of the routing tables.

In the longer term, the IP protocol will have to evolve. This is the objective of IPng (IP next generation or IPv6) which is intended to replace IP. But, in addition to extending the addressing capacity of the network layer, IPng will also overcome the defects and gaps of IP and be adaptable to new requirements (such as mobility).

Thus, the specifications for IPng should meet a certain number of crucial technical requirements. These correspond to a continuity in the evolution of IP, to the elimination of a number of shortcomings or, primarily, to the support for new capabilities, associated with the current and future size of the Internet, and the new connection modes resulting from recent technical advances.

- The ability to manage at least 10^9 networks and 10^{12} terminal devices (stations) and, preferably, the ability to manage 1000 times these minimum values (for the case of a non-optimized distribution); this can essentially be done using 16-byte addresses.

- Use of conservative routing methods.

- Support for various interconnected network topologies.

- Optimal exploitation of high-performance networks with a simple and strict header structure (accelerated processing with a header without checksum, divided into multiples of four bytes).

- Introduction of a clear and realistic method of migration from IP.

- Provision of a reliable and robust service.

- Independence from the physical network (in addition, the flow label may correspond to the ATM virtual circuits).

- Provision of a datagram-type service (connectionless oriented).

- Support for auto-configuration of addresses (DHCP like).

- Guaranteed security for certain operations (specific mechanisms for authentication or encryption at the network level).

- Unique global addressing for each device (even with topological structuring).

- Based on open, publicly accessible standards (RFC).

- Support for group broadcast (multicast).

- Provision for evolution with extensible headers for the implementation of options (new and additional functions).

- Support for various classes of service (QoS with the flow label).

- Support for the mobility of devices and their connection to the network.

- Incorporation of control protocols similar to those of IP (ping, traceroute).

- Support for encapsulation in various IPng protocols (tunneling).

The new IP protocol is called IPv6. In fact, the Internet Assigned Number Authority (IANA) has assigned version number 6 to IPng, being an evolution of the present IP protocol which has version number 4. It is defined in RFC 1883.

Gateways

Gateways are interconnection devices which carry out their processing on the layers of levels greater than 3 (from 4 to 7). Thus, for a gateway to operate at level N, it must be able to decode the lower layers (from 1 to N) of the communication systems to which it is attached, which will enable it to obtain the level N message by successive decapsulation. It should then be able to transport the data for this message (which it understands) between its two (or more) communication interfaces and execute the encapsulation steps associated with the port on which it is to emit. Thus, the gateway can interlink two different networks at all levels, provided that on either side the packets transport information from the same unique application process.

It can be seen that its function is more complicated than those of the devices discussed up to now, which were limited to a view of the first three layers only. In addition, since the requirement met by the gateway is always special, the machine may be a business computer programmed as a function of the protocols used and the applications to communicate. Since it is generally not a machine whose architecture was developed for this function only, its performance in terms of frames forwarded per second may be noticeably lower than that of routers or bridges.

Conclusion In certain situations, repeaters have been replaced by bridges, which represent more complex interconnection devices supporting the natural filtering function and which can be used to extend Ethernet installations over several networks.

As the technology has evolved, bridges (or switches) have proved able to take on the task of repeaters, with the advantage of achieving a performance close to the maximum physical level speed. Today, routers are also able to segment networks from a logical point of view. However, since these interconnection devices operating at levels 1, 2 and 3 are the only elements which handle routing data (in the broad sense), they will continue to coexist and there is no risk of their being supplanted by another device operating on the higher layers (layer 4 switches being complementary, not competitors).

13.5 Terminal servers

Among the various devices studied so far, the terminal server is slightly separate, since its primary function is not to support the operation of one or more networks, but to use them. The terminal server is a device capable of concentrating several terminal links (mainly of the asynchronous type, with speeds of a few kbps each) and passing these through a network with a sufficiently high speed, such as Ethernet.

On one side the terminal server has an Ethernet port, generally involving a 15-point AUI socket, while on the other side it has a certain number of sockets (often a multiple of eight, up to 128) for passive terminals. The links may be of the RS-232 or RS-423 type with a speed of up to 38.4 kbps per port, and the connector technology is of the 50-point Telco, DB25, RJ12 or Modified Modular Jack (MMJ) form.

Thus, its work is first to transport the packets coming from the terminals on the network to their destination (which, in most cases, is a mainframe or another terminal server) and, second, to switch the packets received from the network towards the terminals for which they are destined. To carry out this transport the server encapsulates the messages in Ethernet frames, but it is also obliged to use an additional layer, which will contain the information relating to the exchange (identification of the terminal and the host computer, connection characteristics, see Figure 13.29). Two protocols are used for this, namely DEC's Local Area Transport (LAT) and TCP/IP. Today, almost all terminal servers are capable of working with

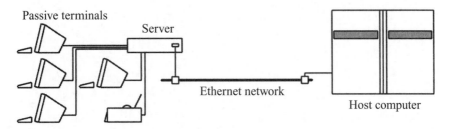

Figure 13.29 Schematic diagram showing the typical use of a terminal server.

both protocols, even simultaneously. As far as LAT is concerned, we note that it is a non-routable protocol, which has to be transported by bridges or requires the activation of the bridging function on the routers.

Terminal servers may themselves use the network to find their configuration or their system software on a server at boot time. For this, they use the TFTP protocol with BOOTP or RARP, or the MOP protocol for remote loading of the files and data vital to their operation.

In addition, these terminal servers may also be used to interlink modems or printers, and sometimes have parallel link type ports (Centronics) for this. Over time, the basic function has been supplemented by other capabilities, such as the possibility of several simultaneous sessions in LAT and/or TCP/IP on each terminal, and terminal servers have acquired an increasingly higher performance.

Chapter 14

Ethernet via ATM

- LAN–ATM interconnection

- LAN_E

- MPOA

14.1 LAN–ATM interconnection

The issues discussed here concern the use of ATM in a remote computing environment, and thus data transmission. The topic will be approached from a realistic viewpoint, that is, reflecting what is currently in use, namely traditional local networks, composed of a MAC layer and a frame format of Ethernet or Token Ring type, and a communication system using one of the current protocol families (TCP/IP, NetWare, DECnet, AppleTalk, NetBIOS, OSI, and so on). The objective is to look at the practical solutions which integrate the description of a mode of communicating computer data on ATM, and also the interconnection with existing LAN networks and environments.

Historically, Classical_IP has been the first solution, followed by LAN_ Emulation 1.0, then by NARP, NHRP, LAN_E 2.0 and MPOA. In the following sections, we will deal with the main ones in order of importance in terms of implementation and/or interdependence. Some emphasis will be put on LAN_E which, although far from being perfect, was the first 'universal' standard solution.

Upward compatibility

The development and introduction of an entirely new technology such as ATM, even though it is a self-contained technology, would be unthinkable without a preliminary phase of soft transition during which it must be possible to continue using existing networks and if possible make them communicate with the new architecture. Thus, several modes of exploiting an ATM infrastructure exist today in remote computing, two of which, although not representing the most direct way of interfacing, do however provide compatibility with traditional LAN technologies, together with support

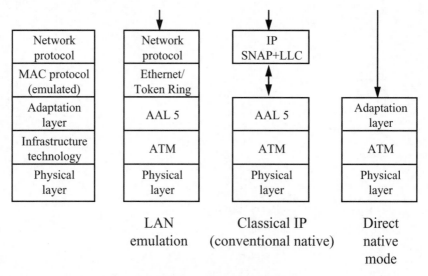

Figure 14.1 Sequence of layers.

for the most widely used network protocol. The modes are LAN Emulation on one side, and Classical IP on the other.

Note, however, that ATM is sufficiently rich (routing protocols included) to be considered as a level 3 technology in its own right, which means that at least in theory it can be used directly with a Transport protocol. The four existing layers 4 would thus interface with ATM services. TUNIC (TCP & UDP) over a nonexistent IP connection propose to interface transport protocols directly in the AAL. We will see this type of setup below when we will be looking at the different models envisaged for TCP/IP on ATM.

One might even envisage removing all communication stacks in favor of exploiting the whole of the capacities of ATM by means of a native API. This would be quite revolutionary, and, although desirable in the end, cannot be conceived without (durable) migration phases in real conditions.

These last two modes have the obvious flaw of not defining simple conversion methods towards existing networks, except for the passage through applicational (thus inevitably specific) gateways.

Moreover, for all modes of exploiting data on ATM. ATM has naturally to be adapted to the legacy computer communication technologies. Thus, there will often be no demand for guarantee of bandwidth and/or delay, definition of quality (as a percentage of lost cells), and handling of retransmission (appropriate for ATM) in case of error.

On the contrary, the use of ATM must show the usual concepts, such as the capacity for carrying out diffusion (multicast and broadcast), the connectionless aspect and the management of MAC or IP addresses.

Usage

LAN

There are two types of ATM usage in LANs, each of which meets several requirements. The first usage of ATM is as a backbone technology, comparable under certain aspects to 100 Mbps switched Ethernet. The second one is the implementation of ATM down to workstation level, for capillary access, this time in competition with shared or switched 10 Mbps Ethernet.

Site connection The main advantage of ATM at the heart of the network is that it is an open technology which allows short-term joint transmission of data, telephone, and even video-conference flows. In this sense, ATM has no competition, and allows companies that intend to merge their remote computing and telephone infrastructures in the medium term to take a first step in this direction.

Another clear advantage will very shortly be the continuity of inter-site WAN technology at the center of every large site. Since ATM on WANs has financial advantages, it is probable that it will become of general use in private and/or public WAN networks. This continuity entails a number of technical capacities, because all ATM signaling and routing could be homogeneous from the LANs through to the WAN.

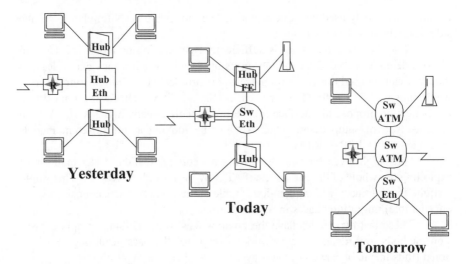

Figure 14.2 Development of connecting and concentrating network technologies.

We will investigate one of the technical advantages of ATM which can be exploited in LAN and WAN connections, namely the intelligent management of network topologies with load sharing, and the associated capacity of automatic redirection.

Finally, a minor advantage lies in the performance of ATM which, being entirely switched and at a relatively high throughput (155 and 622 Mbps full-duplex), provides substantial global bandwidth. But this is also true for the current 10/100/1000 Mbps Ethernet. Even the adaptation of ATM to structured cabling and traditional media (unshielded twisted pair and multi-mode optical fiber), although appreciable, does not allow it to be differentiated from the other LAN technologies.

With regard to the disadvantages of using ATM only in the backbone, and not as a complete technology, we note that this implies that there is always a stage of ATM–LAN conversion towards each network of capillary access, whose devices can only be penalizing in terms of delay and probably even of pure performance, and are often synonymous with an inevitable loss of quality of ATM services. In all cases, it is desirable that servers are connected directly to the ATM connection, so that in client–server exchanges the conversion stage is only gone through once.

Access concentrator   In access concentration, in the same way as a hub the ATM switch acquires another dimension. It is in fact the guarantor of the bandwidth (at 25 or 155 Mbps), better than a switch LAN, but it is above all the secure passage towards the support of multimedia applications accessed by each workstation. It is effectively the only theoretical means of having a technology truly capable of transporting synchronous and asynchronous flows down to every potential user. IP TOS bits or RSVP could offer an equivalent of this type of service on LANs.

This implementation can obviously only be conceived in continuity with the previous backbone technology, and can easily be understood as the second stage

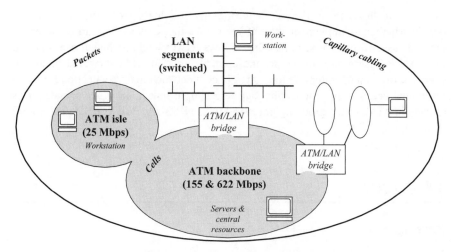

Figure 14.3   LAN and ATM architecture.

towards the generalization of ATM on LANs. During the migration phases, it is possible to envisage the creation of ATM islands in stages that will progressively replace the capillary service LANs.

Finally, we conclude that ATM in capillary service can only be justified by the wish to adopt ATM as a global technology to meet application requirements fully.

WAN

ATM in WANs can be implemented by operators (private environment) and/or enterprises (public environment). Since discussion of the public environment aspects is beyond the aims of this book, we will simply remind the reader that the technological development has been guided by the requirements of the operators, and that ATM meets them particularly well. In fact, ATM basically allows bandwidth usage to be optimized by 'intelligent' dynamic multiplexing enabling operators to sell the maximum of Xbit/s and make their infrastructures profitable. The exploitation of the intrinsic security of network topologies is as accessible in ATM as it was in X.25, for example, with the network topology of connections also providing efficient and profitable load sharing. But we will see that the advantages of this technology can also be applied to private enterprises.

Today, any multi-site enterprise is faced with a choice of WAN interconnection technology. It can opt for X.25, Frame Relay, RNIS, statically multiplexed LS or, finally, ATM. Only ATM will allow this enterprise to realize the dynamic multiplexing that best chains IP, SNA, telephone (MIC inter-PABX link) and potentially video-conference (RNIS in H.320) flows. Since ATM identifies the requirements of each flow, the constraints will be respected, but the concurrent use of bandwidth will always be optimized. This financially profitable aspect of ATM should allow it to establish itself in the same way as TDM multiplexers became established in the past.

Note that choice of a WAN technology still leaves it to the enterprise to decide whether to implement it itself or to hire the service from an operator. In the first case, the enterprise rents LSs and buys ATM switches which it uses to build its WAN infrastructure. In the second case, it hires an ATM service available at each site from an operator and must merely connect each main connection line with the rented access. This connection can be a simple link if the LAN connection is already in ATM, or the grouping of several links (IP, SNA, PABX, RNIS, and so on) if it is not.

14.2 LAN_E

Introduction

The basic idea of LAN Emulation is to provide a solution for the support of all current traffic flows between computers by emulating a traditional LAN layer on an ATM infrastructure. In fact, if it is possible to simulate the equivalent of the MAC layer of the most widely used LANs, it is by definition possible to transport all traffic flows that use a protocol family which can already be interfaced on Ethernet or Token Ring. Thus, the main advantage of this solution lies in its universality, because it deals with the most common MAC layers (level 2).

Therefore, all existing drivers (such as ODI and NDIS, widely used in office automation) can be easily ported to this semblance of a local network, which still shows the specific features of shared media technologies such as, in particular, the connectionless aspect, the capacity of reaching several or all addressees by means of a single transmission (broadcast frame), the identification of workstations by means of a MAC address and a packet format of variable length (which can be relatively long: up to several thousand bytes).

LAN Emulation is also a means of simulating the local network(s) beyond the LAN concentrators and switches through an ATM infrastructure (AAL 5), obviously authorizing communications between the devices connected on either side (LANs and ATM). Thus, from its very origin, LAN_Emulation does more than define a simple connection technology (as done before by FDDI with its encapsulation bridges), by also specifying how ATM and LAN workstations can communicate with each other.

By placing itself at MAC level, LAN Emulation implicitly allows all Network protocols to be supported, including the non-routable protocols (such as LAT, SNA or NetBIOS). This represents an undeniable advantage in terms of uniformity, but does not allow the specific features of ATM to be exploited in detail. In fact, LAN Emulation hides the potential requirements of the Network layer (and the higher layers) and therefore does not offer to put them into relation with the parameters specific to ATM and available to meet the criteria of the connections to be established.

LAN Emulation is defined by the ATM Forum; the first standard, version 1.0, appeared in January 1995. This document is seen as an important step, but was

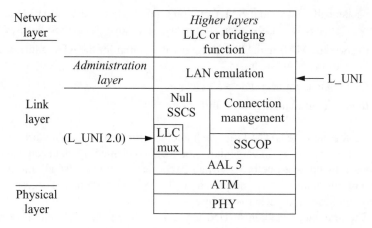

Figure 14.4 Division into layers.

followed and extended by version 2.0 in 1997 and 1999. Thus, these are not the final specifications.

Two local network technologies can be simulated, namely the most popular ones: Ethernet and Token Ring. A supplement of LAN_E 1.0 proposes indirect support of an FDDI emulated by using the IEEE and IETF conversion standards at MAC level towards Ethernet or Token Ring, in the same way as in an environment without ATM. Note that the existence of the Ethernet and Token Ring functioning modes does absolutely not imply integration of the communication function between a LAN Emulation Ethernet access and a LAN Emulation Token Ring access, this conversion having always been realized by a complementary (and possibly external) routing or bridging function.

Note also that, with regard to the efficiency of LAN Emulation, the encapsulation amounts to a duplication of layers 2 (that of ATM and that of LAN) and 3 (that of ATM and the effectively employed Network protocol if there is one). But the most regrettable feature is being able to use ATM only as a simple LAN, without access to the quality of service (bandwidth, delay, error rate).

First, we will concentrate on LAN_Emulation version 1.0.

Principles

In order to be able to simulate a LAN on ATM, the different devices that want to be connected must implement the same functioning mode. For this purpose, the ATM interface cards (NIC) and the traditional network devices (bridges and routers) wanting to take part in an Emulated_LAN (E_LAN) must all work in LAN_Emulation.

It is the task of LAN_Emulation:

- to provide a packet interface (note that LAN_Emulation systematically relies on an AAL 5 layer (ATM Adaptation Layer) which provides the capacity of packet/cell conversion: SAR), and on a minimalistic service: UBR, remembering that AAL 5 is the simplest, but also and above all the most diffused layer;

- to correlate MAC and ATM addresses and search for the ATM address on the basis of the MAC address;
- to emulate a connectionless service;
- to be able to manage packet diffusion.

As for the other ATM-LAN technologies, the last two points are not very obvious, because ATM is fundamentally connection-oriented (no data cell can circulate between two devices before a virtual circuit has been established) and because diffusion of information is less easy than in a LAN (where the shared access method generally implies that a packet is easily visible by all).

The referenced version of UNI is theoretically version 3.1 (the most recent one), but support of version 3.0 (still common today) is also described.

Technology

A LAN_Emulation network consists of clients (stations connected in ATM or ATM–LAN bridge) exchanging frames via the ATM network. However, this emulated LAN network is driven by three functions called servers, indispensable for the activation of this E_LAN.

The servers   Three server functions are needed for the constitution of an E_LAN: LECS, LES and BUS.

- The LECS (LAN_Emulation Configuration Server) has the task of supplying the parameters needed for the configuration of a client station during the initialization of its attachment to an E_LAN. There is at most one LECS per domain. However, the LECS is not completely indispensable.

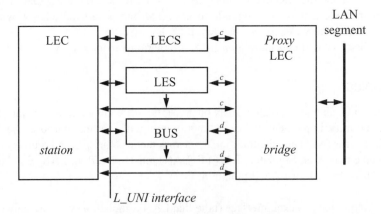

Figure 14.5   L_UNI connections.

- The LES (LAN_Emulation Server) has the task of answering the requests of all clients of an E_LAN searching for the ATM address of an access on the basis of its MAC address (request of type ARP: Address Resolution Protocol). For this purpose, it centralizes a table of ATM/MAC address correlations. There is one LES per E_LAN and thus potentially several LES per administration domain. This corresponds to the declaration of several distinct logical networks (or virtual LANs) in the same ATM infrastructure. During its intialization, the LEC registers with the LES.

- The BUS (Broadcast and Unknown Server) has the task of packet diffusion in multicast or broadcast, together with the handling of packets of unknown destination (when the LES is incapable of supplying the correlation). In practice, the LES and the BUS are systematically implemented together. We will see that an 'intelligent' BUS can partly substitute the function of the LES, which further encourages them to be implemented jointly.

These different server functions, which are nothing more than software, can be localized in any accessible element of the network: edge workstation, (application) server, ATM switch or ATM–LAN bridge. However, this choice might be dictated by constraints of availability, position within the architecture of these resources, or underlying processing capacity.

In fact, with LAN_Emulation, the capacity to convey remote computing data requires two main components on the side of the network: 'physical' transport capacities which are the task of the ATM switches (with UNI, P-NNI, and so on) and 'logical' emulation capacities which are the task of the LAN_E components (server and client functions). Since the two capacities are indispensable for the use of an ATM network in LAN_E, it is relatively logical to associate the crucial elements. Thus, it is frequently proposed to locate the LAN_E servers on the CPU of the principal ATM switch, putting together in one product two capacities which in any case have no *raison d'être* if the availability or accessibility of one of them is lost.

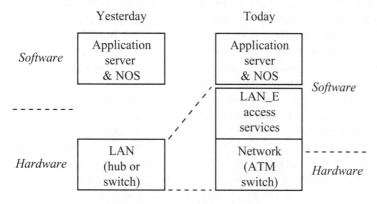

Figure 14.6 Functional changes.

The clients   The LEC (LAN_Emulation Client) is the software layer or driver that allows an ATM interface to be used as a LAN interface. The LEC uses the E_LAN driven by the servers. We can therefore find LECs on stations directly attached to ATM, but also on LAN–ATM bridges, or on routers that have an ATM interface. Only LAN–ATM bridges are a specific type of LEC, whereas routers have a LEC perfectly comparable with that of a workstation natively connected in ATM.

   After the initialization phase, which we will discuss in more detail later, the LEC must use the LES and BUS servers to find its correspondents and broadcast its frames, respectively. Note, however, that in LANs a workstation seldom knows the MAC address of its peer right from the beginning. Therefore, the use of the BUS is relatively frequent for the first frames.

   The ATM–LAN bridges are special LECs because they hide a certain number of MAC addresses placed behind them. They are therefore announced as Proxy LECs during registration, and handled slightly differently during functioning. A TB bridge actually registers only its own MAC address. With regard to spanning tree management, the ATM–LAN bridges appear the same as any other LAN bridge. They output and read the BPDU and follow the phases of learning and retransmission of the IEEE 802.1D standard.

Functioning

Two phases of functioning can be identified in LAN_Emulation, the former being the configuration of a client (LEC) access at initialization, followed by its attachment to and registration with an E_LAN. The latter, during functioning, requests ATM addresses (towards LES and BUS) and transmissions between LECs.

The initialization procedure

Attachment to the LECS   When a client (LEC) initializes its LAN_Emulation connection, it looks for its LECS. Three means are defined to achieve it: the first uses ILMI to find the ATM address of the LECS (Get on the MIB), the second employs the ATM address predefined by the ATM Forum (Well-Known Address: WKA = 4700790...0A03E00000100), and the third uses the predefined PVC (VPI = 0, VCI = 17). The attempts must be carried out in this order. In addition, with some manufacturers, it is possible to connect to the LECS by means of an ATM address manually configured in the client station.

   Finally, it must be remembered that it is also possible to do without the LECS, and to ask the LEC to connect directly to the LES, by means of a preceding manual configuration of the LES ATM address in the LEC.

   The LECS knows all active E_LANs in the domain of administration (and the addresses of the corresponding LESs), together with those that can be used by default.

   After the connection (Configuration Direct VC), the LEC supplies its MAC address and potentially (as an option) the name and type of the E_LAN sought for with its LE_Configure_Request. The LECS responds to the LEC with an

LE_Configure_Response, supplying the ATM address of the LES of the E_LAN it will join, the type of E_LAN (Ethernet/Token Ring), the maximum packet size (MTU), and the symbolic name of the E_LAN. The LECS is thus capable of implementing a certain level of security by refusing an attachment, or by redirecting it towards an E_LAN considered as 'public'. It can complete information supplied by optional counters and timers.

Once the necessary information has been obtained, the LEC-LECS VC is terminated, which frees a circuit (and some resources) which are of no further use (as long as the LAN_E network functions).

Attachment to the LES During its first connection to the LES (automatically, as described above, or possibly via an ATM address or a VC predefined in the absence of a LECS), the LEC outputs an LE_Join_Request. This supplies its ATM address, its MAC address, and the name, type, and MTU of the E_LAN, and specifies whether it is a Proxy. If the LES accepts the LEC, it responds with an LE_Join_Response and registers the pair of ATM/MAC addresses. The response frame gives the LEC its LECID, a unique identifier in this E_LAN which allows the LEC to recognize its own frames when it receives them, as a complement of its MAC address. The LEC can now register the other MAC addresses which it represents and which are necessary.

The LEC and the LES remain connected by a bi-directional point-to-point Control Direct VC plus a mono-directional point-to-multipoint optional Control Distribute VC. Only requests and responses of LE-ARP type (control frames) circulate on these VCs, but no MAC frames.

In the case of a 'closed' E_LAN, the LES (or the LECS) can refuse the insertion of the LEC. In fact, it is possible to implement a simplified security by providing the LES with the capacity to filter and select the requests for connection to an E_LAN. This filtering is *a priori* carried out on the ATM or MAC address of the new arrival, on the name of the E_LAN required, and will be validated on the basis of a predefined table of authorized entries.

The ATM address of the BUS is obtained by making an LE_ARP request to the LES on the MAC address: FF-FF-FF-FF-FF-FF. Again, LEC and BUS remain connected by a bi-directional point-to-point Multicast Send VC and a mono-directional point-to-point or point-to-multipoint Multicast Forward VC. On these VCs, MAC frames circulate that are destined to be diffused.

Note that the data frames can circulate on the point-to-point VC between the LECs, but also via the BUS. LAN_Emulation guarantees, on the one hand, ordering of unicast frames between themselves, and on the other hand, ordering of broadcast and multicast frames between themselves (dealt with by the BUS). Since it occurs frequently that the first exchanges, even if unicast, are directed towards the BUS before the establishment of the point-to-point VC, there is a way to ensure that the last unicast frames that have started their journey to the BUS do not arrive after the first frames sent on the direct VC between LECs. This is the Flush, which must empty the VC towards the BUS. The Flush request sent via the BUS represents the end of the use of the BUS for transmission to a station. Its return response (via the LES) is the indication that the circuit is empty, and that a direct route can thus be employed.

Improvements The LAN_E 1.0 standard leaves a non-negligible leeway for implementing LES and BUS. With regard to LES, there could be two types of point-to-multipoint VC, one towards all 'simple' LECs, the other towards all Proxy LECs (bridges). This would provide a simple means for efficiently passing a request only on to those elements that can 'cache' MAC addresses which are unknown to the LES at a given moment.

In the same way, the LES can follow the traffic circulating via the BUS to extend its own table.

Moreover, LAN_E 1.0 does not impose any constraint on the localization of the LAN_E services, without, however, defining their interaction either. In fact, the relative position of LECS and LES-BUS is of no major importance because they do not work in parallel on the same requests. Since LAN_E 2.0, on the contrary, LES and BUS are considered to be implemented in pairs (to be collocated). Thus, the close coordination between LES and BUS is again left to the manufacturer. Note that it is, however, reasonable to provide LES and BUS with a common knowledge base. This avoids having to perform similar learning processes in parallel and very simply makes the BUS substantially more efficient. In fact, the BUS is not required to have any knowledge base to carry out the diffusion. However, using the LES table, it can probably redirect a good deal of Unknown traffic on its point-to-point VCs when the destination is known and localized.

Address search Every time one workstation tries to communicate with another, it will first verify that it knows the other's ATM address. If this is not the case, it will call the LES on the Control Direct VC to obtain the ATM address of its correspondent on the basis of the MAC address: LE-ARP request. If the LES knows the answer, it returns (or causes the LEC in question to return) the ATM address aimed for, and the 2 LECs establish a point-to-point bi-directional Data Direct VC for the transfer of their data. If the LES does not have this MAC address in its table, it will pass the request on to the Proxy LECs. Finally, if the LES does not respond, the LEC will repeat its request to the BUS, which has the task of broadcasting the MAC frame, the addressee being considered non-localized.

Data format

The LAN_Emulation packets (Ethernet, Token Ring, or control packets, represented on Figures 14.7 & 14.8) are transmitted to the AAL layer 5 (which can accept a data field of 65 536 bytes). Note that the data packet format has no CRC, because the AAL 5 PDU-CPCS already incorporates a CRC of 4 bytes in its postfix.

The LEC_ID is used to identify the emitting LEC, to recognize its own frames coming from the BUS. This identifier allows a guarantee that an ATM–LAN bridge (which cannot use the source MAC address of frames to verify that he sent them on the ATM network) will not reproduce towards the LAN frames in diffusion that come from it.

The op-code field indicates the type of control frame: request/response, configuration/attachment/registration/de-registration/ARP/NARP/Flush, and so on.

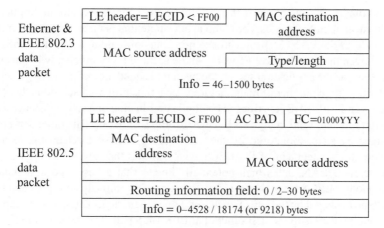

Figure 14.7   LAN_E data frames.

Marker = FF00		Protocol = 1	Version = 1
op-code		Status	
Transaction ID			
Requester LECID		Flags: 1=Remote address 80=Proxy flag 100=Topology change	
LAN source destination: MAC address or Route descriptor			
LAN target destination: MAC address or Route descriptor			
ATM source address			
LAN type	Max frame	# TLVs	Name size
ATM target address			
ELAN name			

Figure 14.8   LAN_E control frame.

Developments

LAN_Emulation 1.0 presents two major flaws: on the one hand, its lack of reliability, because for a given E_LAN there is only one LES–BUS pair activating the E_LAN (and thus a unique point of failure), and on the other hand limited scalability. In fact, if the network receives several hundred LECs, the BUS very rapidly becomes a penalizing bottleneck. We will see below how these two problems can be partly solved.

Redundancy   The insertion of the different server functions into an Application and Physical architecture has brought a new potential source of failure. Yet, in version 1.0 of the LAN_E specifications, no means of reassurance is described.

Given that the Physical network can be secured (very efficiently by means of P-NNI), just as the application server, the need for redundancy of the LAN_E servers is evident. A large number of manufacturers have thus proposed solutions that allow the LECS and LES/BUS functions to be duplicated, having one single instance active at a given moment (and in a given E_LAN for the LES/BUS). The other servers are in a stand-by state, monitored by the active server. These mechanisms resort to requiring an enhancement of the LECS which knows that several LES/BUS pairs can drive an E_LAN, and which potentially knows that it has to go to a stand-by state if another LECS (of higher priority, for example) is already active. Redundancy can also be managed by the LEC which, for a given generic E_LAN, has the capacity of demanding access to the first functional LES-BUS pair. The name of the E_LAN thus comprises a complementary 'number' or identifier.

The redundancy of the LECS can also use the different modes of accessing LECS. It remains, however, important that only one LECS must be active per ATM network (administrative domain).

Limitation of Broadcast   The limitation of frames in diffusion is doubly important in LAN_E. The purpose is to reduce the quantity of multicast and broadcast frames received by each station, in the same way as for a switched LAN, but also particularly for the LAN_Emulation, because the BUS can be a bottleneck and thus limit performance for the whole architecture.

Consequently, it quickly becomes indispensable to implement intelligent BUSes which will deal with different categories of clients (LEC) via different point-to-multipoint VCs. Thus, by understanding certain higher-level protocols, a BUS will be able to differentiate the accesses to stations and (transparent) bridges, to client stations and to servers, and to IP, IPX, or NetBIOS machines, by implementing an intelligent filtering identical to that which might be required from a LAN switch.

This enhancement of the diffusion management function is closely related to the size that can be reached by 'flat' switched networks or broadcast domain (at the MAC level).

Obviously, routing multiple switched logical networks remains a way of overcoming these problems, either with an external router, but preferably with integrated routing (making use of short-cuts), for example of MPOA type.

LAN_E 2.0

The new version of LAN_Emulation appears in the form of separate specifications for the client–server part (L_UNI dealing with LEC ↔ (LECS, LES-BUS) communication) and the inter-server part (L_NNI describing the interaction between multiple instances of LECS and LES-BUS). We can say that LAN_E version 1.0 implicitly corresponded to L_UNI 1.0, without any inter-server communication being described.

The aim of this new version is clearly to allow more populated, more robust, and more powerful emulated networks to be built. Moreover, LAN_E 2.0 also wants to adapt itself better to E_LANs distributed on WANs, and to allow the notion of QoS to be taken into consideration.

Finally, all of these contributions must guarantee upward compatibility (at least for the LECs) and even a natural integration with MPOA.

The specifications of L_UNI (indispensable for an opening up MPOA) were ratified in mid-1997, whereas those of L_NNI should be ratified in early 1999.

L_UNI

LAN_E UNI brings some noticeable improvements, such as ABR support and other qualities of service, but consists principally in the addition of support for a new encapsulation. The LLC/SNAP format has been added to the basic VC-multiplexing to allow an MPOA client to convey datagrams without a MAC header, as required for the MPOA short-cuts.

LLC encapsulation Support of LLC encapsulation is indicated during the connection to the LES. The value of the OUI used to indicate that the frame is an ATM Forum frame is 00-A0-3E. The Type 000C corresponds to an IEEE 802.3/Ethernet LLC-encapsulated frame, and 000D to an IEEE 802.5 frame (Figure 14.9).

A total of 12 bytes is added before the non-multiplexed format.

This new type of encapsulation also allows easy realization of multiplexing by connection (in cases where several logical accesses are available in one station). In fact, in LAN_E 1.0, for a machine implementing N protocol families or N network addresses, having many logical LAN interfaces required many LECs. With LLC encapsulation, the VCs are no longer dedicated, and the LEC can thus appear as just as many distinct interfaces.

1st byte	2nd byte	3rd byte	4th byte
LLC DSAP = 0xAA	LLC SSAP = 0xAA	LLC control = 0x03	OUI
OUI = 0x00-A0-3E		Frame Type = 0x000C	
E_LAN ID			
LE Header (= LECID of the emitter or 0000)		Destination Address	
Destination Address			
Source Address			
Source Address		Type/Length	
Info			
. . .			

Figure 14.9 LLC encapsulation of an Ethernet frame.

QoS   L_UNI 2.0 adds support for UNI 4.0 (always on AAL 5) and thus, as an option, for ABR (of VBR and CBR) and, in addition, for UBR. All parameters belonging to ABR are thus accessible during a connection, as well as the implicit management of TM 4.0 and of RM cells. Note that, contrary to the new type of encapsulation which allows economizing of VCs, it is possible to have several VCs between the same LECs for different QoS requirements.

Multicast   The support of numerous new parameters declared during registration makes it possible to demand to be included or not in a circuit of multicast diffusion. In a manner comparable to what is proposed by IEEE 802.1p, the BUS can thus feed multicast frames only to those LECs that have explicitly asked for it. In this perspective, the BUS can have multiple point-to-multipoint VCs, dedicated to different multicast flows.

L_NNI

LAN_E NNI deals with communications between servers. These specifications, which are relatively ambitious, are meant to provide a solution for LAN_E architectures on LANs and across WANs, to cover the requirements of availability as well as of performance. Finally, L_NNI also wants to define explicit multicast servers.

L_NNI must therefore allow E_LANs driven by several instances of LES-BUS to be built, under the responsibility of a LECS, which can itself have one or more helpers. Thus, the communications LECS-LES, LES-LES and BUS-BUS are defined, where LES and BUS are considered as jointly implemented, on the basis of these specifications. As mentioned above, all this must not change anything for the LEC (whatever its version is), which still only knows one LECS, one LES, and one BUS.

The topology between the services can be of any kind (tree, mesh, and so on); communication between servers is managed by a spanning tree which sees each LES-BUS as a bridge, and each inter-server connection as a LAN. The STA allows an exchange topology without loops to be defined between (LES-Bus).

LECS-LES   Each LES must register with the LECS (the one that is active) and supply the name of the E_LAN it drives.

LES-LES   Sensibly, all LESs know all of the LECs connected. For this purpose, they use an IETF protocol: SCSP, Server Cache Synchronization Protocol. This allows them to inform and to be informed of any newly registered LEC, information which circulates following the logical topology established by the spanning tree. Thus, when a LES receives a request from one of its directly attached LECs, it is able to respond to it or redirect it to the known Proxies.

BUS-BUS   The BUSes share the task of diffusion among them. In the case of a unicast frame, they can limit its diffusion, possibly by making use of the table of the associated LES. In the case of a broadcast frame, each BUS will retransmit it to the LECs it handles and to all other BUSes.

As a complement of the BUS, it is possible to define SMSes (Specific Multi-cast Servers), explicitly charged with the diffusion of frames for a multicast address. The SMS registers as a LEC with the LES and supplies the multicast addresses it can serve, and also with the BUS that will appear in its diffusion circuits. In spite of this, the SMS can relieve the BUS of multicast traffic if the stations can explicitly express their needs at the time of registration.

Thus, L_NNI provides the stepping stones which make LAN_Emulation a robust and effectively powerful solution. In fact, the multiplicity of LES-BUS servers allows the tasks of address search and diffusion to be segmented into as many entities as there are instances of services. If the E_LAN sees a new LES-BUS couple arrive, it will integrate this without interruption of traffic, and will strengthen the global power. If a LES-BUS disappears, only the directly connected LECs must re-establish their connection, by referring to the LECS in the traditional way. The security of functioning is thus real, and the power of processing proportional to the number of servers.

In practice, the LES-BUS to which a newly connected LEC will attach can be determined as a function of several factors. The LECS can circularly subdivide the logical accesses between all LES-BUSes, or oriented the LEC according to another criterion, such as physical proximity, possibly by using an Anycast address, as for the search for the LECS.

Finally, in the draft version of L_NNI, how the LECS is made secure is not made explicit. There is always only one LECS active at any given moment in an administrative domain. The others are in stand-by state and are charged with moni-toring the principal LECS so they can relieve it in case of failure. The LECs are synchronized through a specific VCC. Each LECs may know about the other LECs by, either manual configuration of their ATM addresses, dynamic discovery via ILMI request on local ATM switch or when they connect (with the Alive-Notice).

In practice

Below, we will introduce two ways of approaching LAN_Emulation in a more practical manner, on the one hand, by describing the functionality fulfilled by the access switch, and on the other hand by showing a simplified scenario of connections in LAN_E.

Products

The access switch The access switch (or edge/access device) is the device that joins an ATM network and a LAN network. It can implement a bridging or routing type function.

In the latter case, it is a router with at least one ATM interface equipped with LAN_Emulation. In the former case, instead, it is the equivalent of a bridge in

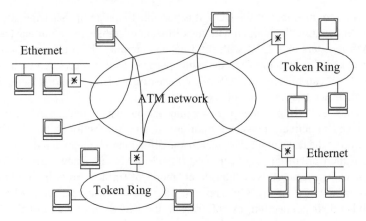

Figure 14.10   LAN edge device.

transparent bridging (and/or source routing) conforming to IS 10038 functioning at MAC level as defined by the LAN_Emulation.

In the case of transparent bridging, where the access switch has only one ATM address (but represents, however, multiple MAC addresses), only one MAC address is transmitted and registered by the LES: first, because this avoids submerging the LES with thousands of MAC addresses (if the LAN segments are effectively densely populated) and second because the access switch has not necessarily learned all the MAC addresses at the time of its attachment. The transparent bridge is seen as a Proxy by the LESs, and must be registered as such during its attachment to the E_LAN.

The Ethernet–ATM bridge implements the spanning tree, thus appearing exactly as a simple Ethernet bridge.

The virtual LANs   As we have seen above, one of the great richnesses of ATM consists in its capability for declaring several logical attachments on the same interface card. Thus, each ATM NIC can connect to several E_LANs (up to 256 with the same MAC address) corresponding to virtual LANs, using different ATM addresses, thanks to the last byte: SELector, managed locally. If connection to more than 256 E_LANs is required, it is always possible to handle more than one ESI (equivalent of the MAC address) on the ATM card.

Let us, however, not forget the practical aspects which limit the logical access number through the number of virtual circuits an interface can manage. Generally, the limitation will come from the disproportion represented by the access to several dozen E_LANs for a workstation and the sum of VCs to be maintained.

The advantage of E_LANs over VLANs lies principally in their capacity for allowing all conceivable intersections. Each ATM access can potentially be integrated into any subset of all E_LANs. There is, however, no E_LAN which as such would be the union or intersection of other E_LANs.

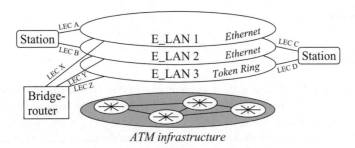

Figure 14.11   Multiple E_LANs.

Examples of exchanges

To illustrate the functioning of MAC frame exchange on LAN_Emulation, we will describe in more detail an example of TCP/IP communication on LAN_E. We will start with a configuration consisting of two stations A and B, where A is already connected to the E_LAN, and B can be either in ATM or on a LAN.

A wishes to reach B, but it only knows the IP address for B. It will therefore use an ARP request to determine the MAC address of its counterpart. Since the ARP frame is a MAC broadcast, it is sent to the BUS.

The BUS diffuses the arriving frame to all accesses, including A, which does not take it into account, having recognized its LECID (and its MAC address).

Even though the ARP response of B is not in diffusion, it is sent to the BUS to save time and thus reaches A, and all the other LECs of the E_LAN.

A now knows the correspondence between the MAC and IP addresses of its interlocutor. It will thus make an LE_ARP request to the LES to obtain its ATM address, with the aim of communicating directly with it.

Since B has correctly registered in the E_LAN, the LES knows its ATM address and in response supplies it to A. If B is behind a LAN–ATM bridge, its MAC address cannot yet be known by the LES. On reception of the LE_ARP request, the LES will forward it to all LEC Proxies. Since B is known to the bridge (it has just answered an (IP) ARP request), this will respond to the LES, and the LES to A.

From this moment, A can establish a direct VC with B to communicate with it.

To respond to the received IP frame, B asks the LES for the ATM address of A (or it can learn it from the frame received on the VC).

Since a VC is already open, B responds to A on this connection.

However, A and B might wish to begin to communicate even before the direct VC is established. In this case, they could exploit the Unknown function of the BUS and make it diffuse their first frames. These flows are, however, limited to at most one frame per second, and should be followed by a Flush before using the direct VC.

After 5 minutes of no activity on a direct VC, it is automatically terminated.

Summary

Synthesis

Although LAN_Emulation 1.0 is currently a perfectly operational solution, it should be noted that it is not an ideal solution because it is not capable of exploiting the ATM infrastructure between distinct logical Networks (in terms of bandwidth and quality of service) and makes it necessary to pass through external routers (such as ClassicalIP, which we will discuss below).

The solution envisaged in the medium term therefore consists in the implementation of level 3 knowledge for ATM switches and servers, such as that offered by MPOA (Multi-Protocol Over ATM), but potentially also in the definition of 'gateways' which allows the requirements of the flows to be understood. Thus the ATM–LAN bridges might be equipped with an understanding of IP TOS bits, RSVP messages and IEEE 802.1Q tagging to enable them to forward the equivalent of the expressed needs from one side to the other.

Limits and flaws

LAN_Emulation 1.0 marks a fundamental stage of data transfer in ATM because it is the first standard solution supporting more or less all existing protocols. Nevertheless, version 1.0 has important intrinsic faults:

- number of LECs limited by the power of the LES and above all of the BUS (of the order of 200);

- no standard mechanisms to secure the LAN_E servers;

- no taking into account of the capacities of ATM (indication of congestion with ABR, QoS, and so on);

- inadequacy with the WAN (LAN_E servers centralized by E_LAN);

- no calling into question of the LAN model, and therefore obligation to 'leave' ATM and LAN_E to bridge or route between two E_LANs.

Version 2.0 has corrected the majority of these faults, and since it is open towards MPOA, it also proposes a level 3 switching solution. The only flaw that persists in spite of everything is the lack of adequacy with the quality of services offered by ATM. In fact, unless applications can remain unchanged, it is likely that the exploitation of QoS will arrive too late.

14.3 MPOA

Introduction

Need

Switching is synonymous with increased bandwidth, flexibility of choice of through-put and simultaneity of communications. This is perfectly true, since it is now common to find switches that operate internally at several Gigabps, links that work in Megabps or in Gigabps, and devices that have the capacity to transport hundreds of cells or frames concurrently.

Alas, all this is practically accessible only, in LANs as in ATM, inside one single logical network. In fact, even if an IP network (for example) has a huge bandwidth, its interconnection with other IP networks (or LIS: Logical IP Subnets) is still carried out via the intermediary of traditional routers. This means that one leaves the Physical network (that is, assembling of cells and MAC decapsulation) to process the header of the datagrams. Since these rather complex operations are at least in part dealt with by software, they inevitably represent a bottleneck of an order of magnitude below the fluidity provided inside Physical networks.

This limitation can be acceptable when the design of all of the networks has allowed the client stations and their principal servers to be grouped inside each LIS, but it imposes a strong constraint of localization and is sometimes difficult to maintain when the application is centralized, which is more and more frequently the case with the intranet. Thus, transverse flows are inevitably penalized vis-à-vis local communications.

Principle

The solution of level 3 switching consists in bringing the performance of the rout-ing function up to the level of switching performance. This is easily feasible if one avoids the routing stage and passes from one logical network to the other without leaving the Physical network.

This is what is proposed by MPOA (Multi-Protocol Over ATM) for ATM cell switching networks, and by several more or less competing proprietary solutions.

MPOA must above all be seen as a means of circumventing (or short-cutting) the router, which (as in NHRP) is a novelty in the world of routing because up to now it has been impossible to pass from one logical network to another without traversing a router.

For this purpose, MPOA offers to convey information directly in the form of datagrams (level 3 units) by getting rid of the MAC encapsulation and the associated LAN context. MPOA can thus potentially process all routable protocols (IP, IPX, CLNP, DECnet, AppleTalk, and so on).

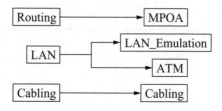

Figure 14.12   MPOA stratification.

Implementation framework

MPOA deals with networks connected by a core in ATM, but also integrating possible peripheral local networks.

MPOA has been developed in the framework of the ATM Forum, and for the benefit of all manufacturers and users wishing to comply with the existing technology. Thus, MPOA uses the mechanisms of LAN_Emulation, but also uses work carried out in parallel by the IETF, principally NHRP (Next Hop Resolution Protocol), as well as SCSP (Server Cache Synchronization Protocol).

This attitude (which is different from the initial MPOA committee's attitude, which was rather inclined to redefine everything) is pragmatic and more efficient, as well as revealing a soundly based desire to connect and unify ATM data technologies (which will certainly be profitable for ATM development). In fact, only the multitude of technical solutions is likely to put a constraint on the possibility that ATM will become widely accepted as tomorrow's solution.

MPOA builds on LAN_Emulation (version 2.0 to incorporate support of indispensable encapsulations of level 3, inspired among others by RFC 1483) for all communications inside a logical network, including communications between MPOA clients (MPC) and MPOA servers (MPS) that allow 'shortcuts' or direct VCs to be established. This means that in this scheme, the equivalent of frame transport that was guaranteed by yesterday's local network is now entirely handled by the LAN_Emulation, and that all MPOA elements have one or more LECs (LAN_Emulation Client, conforming to L_UNI 2.0).

This return to LAN_Emulation also allows upward compatibility with all 1.0 and 2.0 LECs to be guaranteed, providing effective continuity during a phase of migration towards MPOA.

Note that from the moment that LAN_E is used, a LIS can extend from ATM to LANs connected by means of bridge type edge devices where the bridge provides the continuity from the network point of view, because the E_LAN is the prolongation of the LAN.

The model preserves a structure by default based on the router as the interconnection product between LIS. This (multi-protocol) router is enriched by the function of the MPS.

The return to the NHRP specifications is based on the integration of the NHRP server function (NHS) into the MPS (thus the MPS capacity to communicate directly with true NHS). Moreover, the MPC does not take over all characteristics of the NHRP clients (NHC); therefore they need MPS.

Functioning

As mentioned above, MPOA provides important upward compatibility and effectively builds on UNI 3.0, 3.1 or 4.0, LAN_E 2.0 and NHRP. LAN_E 2.0 in turn provides compatibility with LAN_E 1.0.

Client and server

The MPOA client (MPC) is implemented in the drivers of the stations directly connected to ATM (Host), in the LAN–ATM bridges (edge devices), and in the routers (which can also shelter an MPS).

The MPC emitter (Ingress) has the function of detecting the generated flows that could benefit from a direct circuit. It thus has the capacity for forwarding datagrams, but does not manage routing protocols. In reception (Egress), the MPC has the function of re-encaspulating the datagram with a Link header (MAC in practice for a LAN) as indicated by the MPS, before supplying the frame to the superior layer.

The Ingress cache is created by the LEC which demands opening of a direct VC. The Egress cache is supplied by the Egress MPS to the Egress LEC for establishing the direct VC.

Since the MPC is not an NHC, it obviously cannot register with the NHS. MPC and NHC can, however, communicate directly on a short-circuit, under the implicit conditions of not being in the same LIS and of employing only unicast traffic.

Keys			Contents	
ATM MPS control address	Destination network address	ATM destination or VCC address	Encapsulation information	Other info required for control: flow count & holding time, . . .

Figure 14.13 Ingress cache.

Keys			Contents		
Destination network address	ATM source/ destination address	(Tag)	LEC	MAC header	Other info required for control: holding time, . . .

Figure 14.14 Egress cache (with or without tag).

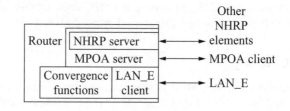

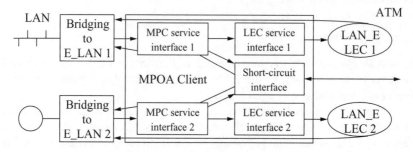

Figure 14.15 MPC and MPS.

The MPS is a logical element of the router, which integrates a complete NHS (plus some extensions). The role of the MPS is to supply the information indispensable to the LECs for establishing a direct VC. For this purpose, the MPS exploits its NHS to localize the addressee and its router to indicate the encapsulation to be reproduced.

One or more MPS can find a place in one router. Each MPS has (*a priori*) several LECs.

Since the MPS incorporates an NHS, it can obviously manage NHC requests, and communicate with a neighboring NHS.

MPC and MPS automatically 'discover' their capacities via extensions to the TLV of LAN_E during their connection to the LECS. Subsequently, each LEC must indicate whether it is MPS, MPC, MPS/MPC or non-MPOA.

Finally, with MPOA, we often find the associated notion of virtual router. This is due to the fact that the functions of routing are effectively separated into two: Route Computation on the MPS and Frame Forwarding, which can be done directly via the ATM network merely by means of the MPCs. Route computation corresponds to routing protocol processing and management of the associated routing tables.

Procedure

Each (host) machine starts by integrating itself into the E_LAN to which it belongs, in the same manner as a local network. Thus, it carries out the process of searching for LECS and then for LES and BUS to be able to integrate a framework of communication with the other devices of its LIS. This allows it to exchange data inside this LIS, in the form of MAC frames in LAN_E.

If the machine needs to communicate with a station which is not in its LIS, it will obviously ask the router charged with reaching the destination network to forward these frames. It uses its (static or dynamic) routing table to select the router to be used. Then the machine establishes a VC with the LEC of the router, by means of a traditional LE_ARP request to its LES. As before, the router is charged with forwarding the packet to the destination network, no matter whether it is a LAN or ATM. Up to here, nothing has changed.

However, the MPC function of the emitting machine requires it to be capable of deciding whether a shorter path must be requested (provided the router has an MPS). This MPOA request is usually triggered by a threshold in pps (10 packets per second by default) or by using a given higher-level protocol. Thus, the MPC asks the MPS of the router if it is possible to establish a direct path towards the destination, and if so, to transmit to the emitting (Ingress) and receiving (Egress) MPC the information needed to be able to perform the equivalent of the datagram routing function. Note that the Ingress MPS can also trigger a request by the Ingress MPC (using the Trigger message).

The search of the addressee between MPSs exploits the mechanisms of NHRP and is carried out in an identical way up to the Egress MPS. The return response passes through the different MPS implicated in its propagation.

Once the direct VC is established and the caches of the Ingress and Egress MPC are filled, the edge machines share the routing functions, knowing that they exchange datagrams (that is, data without MAC encapsulation).

Thus in IP, the emitting machine is charged with decrementing the TTL (time to live), processing the options (if it does not have the capacity of doing so, one

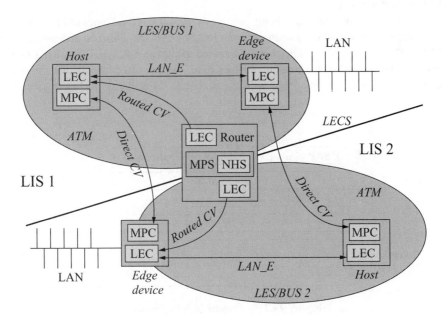

Figure 14.16   Flow between MPOA entities.

contents oneself with transport through the router without shortcuts) and completely managing the ICMP protocol in case of problems (fragmentation, parameters, and so on).

The request generated by the MPC towards the MPS to ask for establishment of the direct circuit is an MPOA Resolution Request. It is translated into an NHRP Resolution Request of the Ingress MPS towards the MPS following on the path. The MPS that serves the destination (Egress MPS) transcribes the NHRP Resolution Request it has received into an MPOA Cache Imposition Request towards the target MPC. We see that the inter-MPS communication mode is effectively taken over in NHRP (with the exception of one type of packet: ar$op.type). The destination MPC (Egress MPC) responds with an MPOA Cache Imposition Reply, which is translated into an NHRP Resolution Reply and circulates from MPS to MPS towards the source. The Ingress MPS in turn translates this response into an MPOA Resolution Request.

Data format

The format of packets of data is by default conformant to the LLC/SNAP encapsulation of RFC 1483. However, MPOA allows negotiation of the format with, as optional alternatives, the Null encapsulation (VC Mux) compatible with LAN_E 1.0 (Figure 14.7) and a specific MPOA tagged format for routed protocols (Figure 14.17).

In MPOA, the MTU is by default 1536 bytes. However, this size can be negotiated up to a maximum of 65 535 bytes. In the case of connection with an access in native IP on ATM, the default size is 9188 bytes (9180 + 8 bytes for the LLC/SNAP header).

Theoretically, the router being capable of handling several types of MAC interface, the facility to route between different technologies must also be accessible via MPOA. In fact, a LAN_E Ethernet flow routed towards a LAN_E Token Ring flow can also be subject to a short-cut. In this case, we must understand that the two edge accesses are not concerned with the problem of translation in heterogeneous

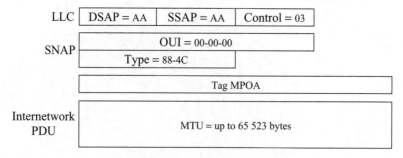

Figure 14.17 Tagged MPOA packet.

environments, because the MPC that will communicate between them on the short-cut only generates datagrams, freed from any MAC header. On the contrary, each station has the task of adding the appropriate header before supplying the received packet to its driver.

Note that concerning the capacity of securization to guarantee the availability of the network functions, MPOA benefits from the mechanisms of LAN_Emulation (2.0) and those of the routers. In fact, the LAN-equivalent part is made secure by the capacities of L_NNI 2.0, and the redundancy of the MPOA servers can take over the same principles they apply to routers. In this case, the existence of multiple routes is managed by the routing protocol (RIP, OSPF, and so on) as such.

MPOA in practice

The fact that the MPC can be a simple ATM–LAN 'bridge' is a noteworthy differ-ence to NHRP. In fact, in this case, the LEC does not necessarily have a Network address. It relies on its MPS to carry out the necessary functions, and communicates by means of MPOA messages. On the other hand, the MPC Edge Device fulfills the functions that the station connected on the LAN cannot fulfill, and accepts or starts, and then manages, the connection by a direct VC to another MPC.

Each bridge can shelter several MPCs, and each MPC can have several LECs. Thus, an ATM/Ethernet/Token Ring bridge has by default two LECs (one in Ether-net and one in Token Ring) and a single MPC. Initially, the traffic is bridged on the LEC consistent with the LAN of origin. If an MPOA short-cut can be established, the MAC header to be removed or added depends on the LAN output port.

Example in IP

In the case of the IP protocol, to handle short-cuts correctly the Ingress MPC (emitter) must be capable of decrementing the TTL and subsequently modifying the checksum of the IP header. It must be capable of reading the IP options expressed in the header, and if it does not support or understand them the MPC must continue to transmit the packets to the MPS (for explicit routing).

In case of problems, the MPC is capable, as a router, of emitting ICMP packets under the following conditions: Destination Unreachable (fragmentation necessary but forbidden by the DF bit), Time Exceeded (during retransmission) and Parameter Problem. If the MPC does not implement the capacity of emitting these ICMP messages, it must forward the packets unchanged to the MPS (outside of the short-cut). Finally, the MPC can fragment a datagram in the case of an MTU which is smaller in output than in input. If it cannot handle the necessary fragmentation, the MPC will not ask for establishment of the short-cut.

The Egress MPC can, from its side, announce a rather large MTU if it is capable of fragmenting in reception.

Example in IPX

The Ingress MPC must increment the TC (Transport Control) before sending the packet on the shortcut. When the counter reaches the maximum value (initially 16, or more with NLSP), it is sent to the MPS.

   If the received packet bears no source network number, the router charged with accepting these packets and indicating the correct Source Network Number continues to forward the packets, and the MPC thus sends these 'incomplete' packets, still to the MPS.

   The Egress MPC simply has the task of giving back a MAC header to the received datagram. This encapsulation is not necessarily the same as that of the Ingress MPC level. Please note that among the four IPX encapsulations on Ethernet, Raw Ethernet can only be recognized by the checksum field set to 0xFFFF (equivalent to a non-filled value), which is therefore indispensable.

Synthesis

The MPOA specifications were ratified in 1997. They are relatively succinct, and integrate *in extenso* the draft RFC of NHRP. Examples of use are given for the IP and IPX protocols, but MPOA is theoretically applicable to all other routed protocols (DECnet, AppleTalk, OSI, XNS, and so on).

   Via NHRP, MPOA benefits from work already carried out by the IETF, such as SCSP which is employed by NHRP. On the other hand, the interaction of MPOA with MARS needs complementary studies to verify the functioning of MARS via several LIS.

   The main limit currently lies in the absence of distinction between applications. Since a short-cut is established between Network entities, all applications will

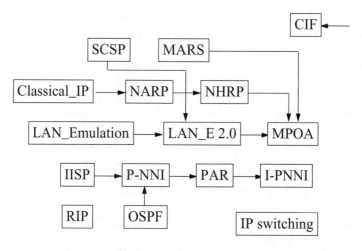

Figure 14.18   Summary.

be able to benefit from this, but without distinction. Once the direct VC is established, no more control is possible at the level of the MPS router. However, the MPC that requests the short-cut has a detailed knowledge of the traffic it conveys and can thus, by means of extensions, handle distinct circuits, with different QoS, for each category of flow. This will become all-important for flows that will have to traverse a WAN on their way.

We can thus imagine that both NHRP and MPOA will in future intelligently interface with IP TOS bits or RSVP and serve as gateway towards the QoS of ATM (with ABR or VBR), but also towards the beginning in solutions in the LAN world proposed by IEEE 802.1p & Q. MPOA could thus become the guarantor of a much better correlation between levels 2 and 3.

MPOA carries with it the hope of soon seeing richer and more powerful data solutions on ATM compared with their equivalents in switched LAN, together with a clear highlighting of the richness of ATM technology, even in the LAN environment.

PART III

Engineering and maintenance of a network

Introduction

At the beginning of the 1980s, Ethernet networks were installed to meet immediate needs, using existing hardware, with no great concern for the installation rules, the possibilities for evolution, access to the cabling or conformance to laying proced-ures. The coaxial cable had to run near the machines, being as accessible as pos-sible so that a tap could be inserted wherever it was desired to feed the newly arrived station (see Figure III.1). Often, security constraints were satisfied simply by ensur-ing that the braid at one end of the cable was grounded.

As Ethernet has evolved, the size of the networks to be installed has increased (see Figure III.2), and laying rules have been issued. Adherence to these major directives has become crucial to the facilitation of large-scale operations, the acquisi-tion of homogeneous installations and the application of re-usable methods. Thus, the lifetime of a local area network, from its design to its obsolescence, has been divided into stages, which has made it possible to divide the work into elementary tasks that are easier to handle and to impose an organization on the activities relating to the installation of a LAN. In addition, as each task corresponds to a simple, well-defined objective, the ideas and documents generated at the time of an implementa-tion are then readily available for use in other studies.

In Part III, we shall touch on the main aspects of each phase, giving examples where necessary (these are sometimes special cases which may not be well adapted to other conditions). The emphasis is on a description of the work to be carried out at each stage and the presentation of a form of solution which readers may choose to follow more or less faithfully.

Practical details will also be presented so that readers can then make their selection from all the techniques currently on the market.

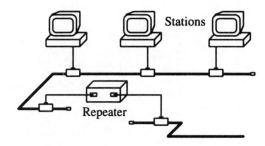

Figure III.1   Small easy-to-install Ethernet network.

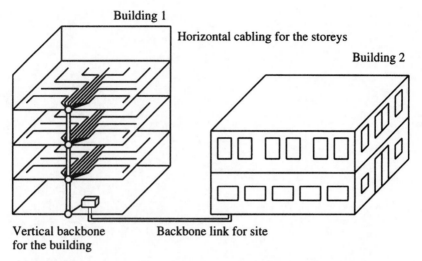

Figure III.2   Network relying on a complete cabling of the buildings on a site.

Chapter 15

Stages

- Study

- Installation

- On-site monitoring

- Acceptance operations

- Evolutions and modifications

- Maintenance operations

- Management and security

- Switched network management

- ATM network management

Global observation of the process of the creation of a local area network from its installation to its death/replacement/obsolescence, rapidly shows that it is possible to distinguish relatively specific tasks. These relate to feasibility and study stages, the description of a real solution, installation and implementation, on-site monitoring and, finally, the validation of the installed network (generally called acceptance).

More precisely, in the case of an important mission, the following phases may be involved:

- The brief preliminary design phase comprising the presentation of various possible solutions, accompanied by a comparative study, the selection of one of these and the technical justification of this choice, a brief description of the solution arrived at, an evaluation of the possible implementation planning and the associated global cost, together with an estimate of the margins of uncertainty at this stage of the project and the basic elements (delays and prices) that have been used in the calculations.

- The detailed preliminary design phase comprising a more complete presentation of the solution chosen and its variants, together with useful details, explanations and justifications (choice of hardware), a more precise evaluation of the delays and costs, covering any additional work required (electricity, masonry) and the availability of the entities involved. The detailed preliminary design also involves the compilation of a technical dossier for the work consisting of useful plans (cable measurements) and assessments of quantities (connectors and patching).

- The production of the detailed technical specifications follows the detailed preliminary design phase; these specifications are intended to provide all the information needed to carry out the work effectively. They cover the fundamental functionality required, the capabilities desired and the choices of hardware. The description of all positions of active elements of the network, the possibilities for drawing cables in the rooms and corridors concerned, the media lengths and the numbers of each useful component are determined at this stage. The overall work may be partitioned into batches so as to distribute the tasks according to their common denominator. Thus, there may be a cabling batch, comprising the laying of the media and involving the laying of cable runs and ducts and the necessary removal of suspended ceilings and raised floors, and so on. A second batch may concern connectors and patching, involving all the tasks of installing sockets and patching modules, together with installation of all the jumper cables. Another batch may be concerned with active elements, including tests of each unit, their installation and attachment. The detailed technical specifications are usually accompanied by functional diagrams and work plans, which include all the diagrams and charts providing an unambiguous description of the work to be carried out.

- The enterprise consultation document is generated as a specific proposal to the enterprises to which it is envisaged the work will be subcontracted. Thus, it covers all the elements of the detailed technical specifications which may help the company to estimate the cost and, ultimately, carry out the work, if it is retained. The first part of the consultation document is thus extracted from the detailed technical specifications and merely covers the technical points relevant to a costing of the installation. The rest of the document consists of financial and administrative clauses governing the project management.

- The overall job control phase, constituting what is commonly called on-site monitoring or follow-up. This task is directly concerned with the problems raised by the installers, which sometimes have repercussions on the technical choices. It includes monitoring the whole cabling operation, quality control for the work, the arrangement of on-site meetings, the preparation of associated minutes and the signing of interim reports. The main aim is to ensure that the network installed is laid in conformance with the security rules and the technical directions established in the detailed technical specifications. It also involves taking informed decisions should practical questions not envisaged in earlier preparative phases arise.

- The acceptance of and detailed accounting for the work correspond to the acceptance of the results of the installation work (signing of the definitive acceptance document) and the release of payment to the contractor. The description in what follows of the acceptance of and detailed accounting for the work is decomposed into several different stages according to the level of observation. A document giving a precise description of the work will be requested from the contractor. This document will include, for example, the cable paths drawn on building plans, the contents of the plant rooms, details of the connector system, an explanation of the labeling used and its contents, the characteristics of the hardware and cables used, and the results of measurements and tests.

- The dossier of work performed constitutes the end of the installation. It may consist of a compilation of all the technical and administrative documents described above, supplemented by the summary of each stage and the inclusion of any elements which may be of relevance later when carrying out repairs or when an extension is required.

We note that certain stages may be superfluous in the case of limited installations. However, these seven phases should primarily serve as a model leaving everyone to establish his or her own personalized process.

Other entities may be involved once the network is in place and operational. These include repair operations, since not all the elements are infallible, and activities relating to modification and extension (which are similar). These last two are generally inevitable once the network becomes several years old.

The operational stage is not really part of the overall activity, since, if all is well, the network should satisfy the users at this stage and require only a small amount of additional activity. It has only been shown in Figure 15.1 to make the diagram more readable.

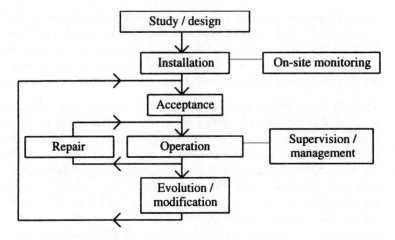

Figure 15.1   Decomposition into various stages.

The term 'management' covers a number of aspects, which it is advisable to distinguish between in order to determine the inherent requirements of an installation and to better judge the capabilities of the products offered. Thus, there may be a management function for the network hardware (configuration, monitoring and maintenance) and for the communication software (version management, consistency checking), a management of the network traffic (choice of interconnection elements, implementation of filters), a management of the invoicing for the network services provided to users, and so on. In the section on management, we shall see how these objectives may be divided into separate tasks.

Since the skills required for installation, acceptance or repairs do not necessarily lie in the same area, it is therefore preferable to dissociate each action from the overall process and to assign it to the group of people who can best handle this matter and resolve any related problems which may arise. Chapter 16, on human resources, deals with this aspect in more detail.

15.1 Study

The first stage naturally involves studying an installation request (Figure 15.2). Care should be taken throughout this work to ensure that the solution envisaged corresponds to the requirements expressed by the future users. Those responsible for the study should seek to restrict themselves to answering the request, even though this may include proposing global solutions which they would like to see as an option.

Given that Part II essentially dealt with technical aspects relating to the operation of an Ethernet network, the knowledge of real installations has not been discussed in detail until now. Thus, specific practical aspects are described which are useful when equipping sites with data communication capabilities. More refined

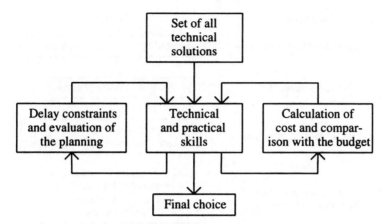

Figure 15.2   The three main components involved in the selection of a solution.

appraisals are then considered, covering, for example, the choice of topology, the medium, the technology, and the type of patching. This will be followed by assessments of the cost and time needed for all these operations.

The information now given relates to hardware aspects of the installations, which are equally linked both to the technology of the local area network envisaged and to the laying rules used by those responsible for the cabling in the buildings.

Design

The design of the network involves the definition of the architecture to be implemented, that is, primarily, the choice of technologies for the physical, MAC and network levels, the schematization of the global network topology and the enumeration and specification of the nodes and interconnection devices (Figure 15.3).

If the architecture consists of several local area networks on distant sites which are to be interconnected, a WAN will be necessary; this will have to be studied in this stage at the earliest. The criteria will be the estimated cost, the bandwidth offered and the flexibility of this (as a function of the type of traffic or of availability criteria), and the degree of privacy and security required. The choice may be from among leased lines (totally dedicated to a user), public or private packet switching networks (X.25 or Frame Relay), ISDN, the public switched telephone network, ATM, or a combination of these technologies which provides greater security or answers a need for additional bandwidth to cope with overflow situations.

The choice of the protocol(s) used will be determined by the set of computers to be attached. Unless the enterprise has decided on progressive homogenization of its network protocols (for example, IP), the applications and computer systems to be connected will determine this choice.

The MAC level technology should be selected from among the most common LANs and MANs. Even though only Ethernet, Token Ring and FDDI may appear to

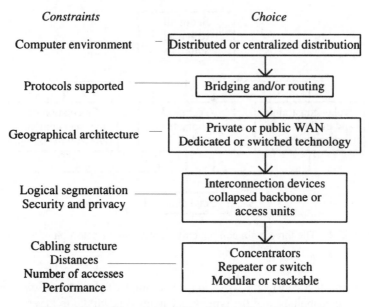

Constraints   *Choice*

Computer environment — Distributed or centralized distribution

Protocols supported ———— Bridging and/or routing

Geographical architecture — Private or public WAN / Dedicated or switched technology

Logical segmentation / Security and privacy ———— Interconnection devices collapsed backbone or access units

Cabling structure / Distances / Number of accesses / Performance ———— Concentrators Repeater or switch Modular or stackable

Figure 15.3 Progression in the design of an architecture.

be in the running (the latter appears to be losing momentum), it remains to define the general network topology and the machines of which it will be composed.

Depending upon the size of the site and the buildings, it is the cabling which will dictate the position of the plant rooms as a function of the realizable cable lengths. In fact, since twisted pair is used almost systematically for all recent capillary services, the distance between a socket in an office and the arrival of the cable in the plant room should be strictly less than 100 meters (a distance of 80 meters is often used, for security; this leaves a margin for the patch cords on either side). The network topology to be implemented at the end of the infrastructure will generally be a LAN (Ethernet or Token Ring) with a broader or narrower bandwidth. For example, in Ethernet 10 or 100 Mbps are shared between all attachments to the plant room, dedicated station by station or even switched between ten or so machines with a minimum share to each port.

The number of these plant rooms and their distance apart will determine the choice of the backbone topology. If the distances require it, (single-mode) optical fiber will be used. Finally, the speed, the redundancy requirement, the number of different logical networks, and the criteria for evolution will favor a given technology. Taken together, the possibilities include LANs (as before: Ethernet and Token Ring, at various speeds, shared or switched, half duplex or full duplex), MANs (principally FDDI), various proprietary solutions, and ATM.

Although the router remains totally indispensable in response to interconnection requirements (including LAN–WAN access) it would be wise not to place a traditional router, or even a 'collapsed backbone', at the center of a homogeneous infra-structure, whose main requirement is only a relatively simple forwarding or high-performance switching function. Powerful layer 3 switch may be preferred when routing is required inside the LAN.

Cabling

The cabling of a local area network, which involves the installation of medium segments in the rooms to be served, comes under the management of the building work, just like electrical cabling and telephone cabling. The Ethernet installation rules should thus be compatible with the working methods used in these areas. However, local area network technologies are much more recent than the supply of electricity or telephony, and therefore a certain number of procedures to which the network will have to conform, unless all the previous choices are to be called in question (paths, ducts), are already in place.

Since the cabling of local area networks could easily be studied and then carried out by the same entities responsible for drawing the electrical cables or telephone pairs, it is natural to think in terms of joint laying operations in which cable runs are installed in parallel routes, wall boxes include electrical, telephone and computer sockets, and plant rooms contain both telephone hardware (for example, PABX) and network hardware (hub, bridge, router) (Figure 15.4).

Since the electrical cabling generally carries much higher voltages than cabling for the telephone and local area networks, it will generally be installed in a separate cable run, but may end in the office in a modular box combining all the types of wall socket needed by the user. The other two types of cabling, for telephone and data communication, have similar characteristics and may thus be laid side by side.

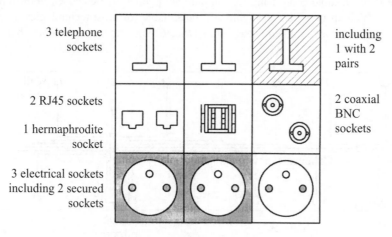

Figure 15.4   Example of a multi-usage wall box.

Prewiring

In the same way as for electrical and telephone networks, cabling for local area networks may be provided in advance with a service distributed homogeneously in all the rooms which are likely to be used as offices at some time. In fact, the number of electrical and telephone sockets in a room or office is generally chosen independently of the precise needs of the future occupants, with provision being made to accommodate the needs in the great majority of cases. However, these desirably universal installations are a preparation for the changes which will take place in the building with removals and the movement of personnel, furniture, and partitions.

Thus, the concept of prewiring had its origins in the need to lay media segments uniformly in the rooms of an enterprise. This cabling can be defined before the need is expressed and may, from its design on, support certain technical advances. Thus, the prewiring is necessarily a homogeneous cabling which usually exceeds the extent or density of the installation required at a given time, with the intention of covering future needs. Despite its cost, which it is difficult to justify at time zero, this concept of prewiring is now quite common, since a simple calculation shows that it is often more expensive to rewire all or part of the local area networks on each removal than to re-use the existing prewiring and, if necessary, move certain active elements from one plant room to another.

Thus, the prewiring involves the definition of a typical installation (sufficient and with a capacity for evolution) that it is hoped to apply everywhere, using as reference unit the surface area occupied by the offices to calculate the number of sockets to be provided. Within each building, the prewiring is defined on a per storey basis. That is, each storey has one or more plant rooms which centralize the links feeding all the accesses in that storey. Except in the case of a very small building, a single plant room will not serve offices on a different floor (Figure 15.5).

The most suitable medium for these diverse uses is often the twisted-pair cable. Thus, a cable comprising several pairs will generally be chosen (four in most cases) which ensures that one cable will be suitable for most technologies. In fact, local area networks implemented using twisted pairs rarely need more than two

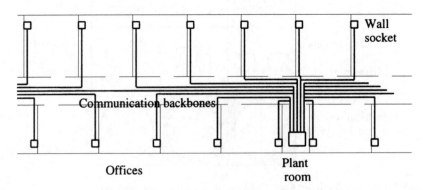

Figure 15.5   Synopsis of the capillary path of the prewiring, ending in a plant room.

pairs (one for emission, one for receipt). Since the physical performance of the cable cannot evolve with future technologies, a compromise is sought in which a cable with a reasonable capacity satisfying the known needs is chosen, in the hope that future technologies will be compatible with this medium (which is quite common). When a coaxial access is needed, a balun is used; this is a small special-purpose element which adapts the impedance of the twisted pair for the desired access (50, 75 or 93 Ohm).

Other media are conceivable, but only optical fiber is used to extend networks beyond the maximum length of a twisted-pair segment (usually 100 meters), or for cable runs near electrical cables. This is reserved as the medium for the main artery or the communication backbones, and is only used to serve station access under exceptional circumstances.

The cables run in cable paths or ducts, which should preferably be metallic for the purposes of electromagnetic shielding. These cable paths leave the plant room for the offices (for the capillary service) and for the other plant rooms (for the communication backbones).

The offices are located around plant rooms, which are placed at the center of the star followed by the cabling topology. This means that when installing prewiring it is vital to find a certain number of plant rooms or, if this is not possible, sites reserved for patch cabinets. Each of these plant rooms should be less than 100 meters from the wall sockets of the offices it services (depending upon the cable path: up into suspended ceilings, down into skirting boards, in a zigzag, and so on) (Figure 15.6).

Each plant room contains the patch cabinets which bring together the entry of all the cables from the offices served by the room the active hardware of the local area network(s), together with the patch cabinets of the communication backbones between the different plant rooms. Note that the communication backbones, which correspond to the artery concept, may be constructed from twisted-pair, coaxial cable or fiber optic links. In fact, one of the three types will be chosen, depending upon the distance criteria, the risks of perturbations, and the requirements for intermediate connections.

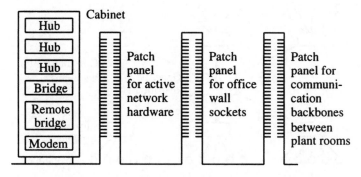

Figure 15.6 Equipment in a typical plant room.

Thus, the plant room can be used to connect all the conductors of the media segments within the building (via the patch panels). In addition, it harbors the active devices attached to the network, since the rack cabinets can accommodate stars and hubs and also the interconnection devices (bridge, router, modem).

For practical purposes, it should have an air vent, or better still, ventilation, if it houses active devices, and it should have a minimum floor area (5 m² is often thought to be an acceptable value). One should not forget that engineers should be able to move freely between the patch panels to work there and that the active elements should be accessible from both sides (front and back), which means that the two doors of the cabinet should be freed.

The telephone

Telephony, which has long since proved the concept of prewiring, with a quasi-systematic service to the offices, and which uses a medium based on twisted pair, can easily be mixed with the computer-related prewiring (Figure 15.7).

In reality, we have seen that the physical medium dedicated to data communication should have capabilities exceeding the simple criterion for voice transport. However, nothing prevents us from passing telephone signals on so-called data grade twisted pairs. At a slightly greater cost, this makes it possible to homogenize the cables laid for the prewiring and obtain a global set of links which can be shared as desired between the telephone and data communication needs. Note that, in fact, the classical unshielded twisted pairs have a characteristic impedance of ~600 Ohm at voice frequencies (1 kHz).

Moreover, the distribution via interlinked plant rooms and the use of a patching system are also traditional as far as telephone installations are concerned. In addition, it is apparent that the different patching methods using connection modules applied to local area networks are generally inspired by elements developed for telephony.

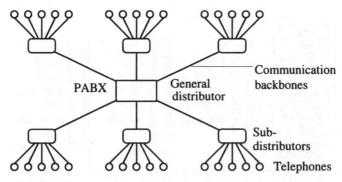

Figure 15.7   Schematic architecture of a telephone installation.

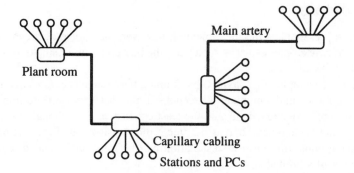

Figure 15.8   Schematic architecture of a data communication installation.

All the telephone links are concentrated in a central point, ending in the PABX, and they may pass through communication-backbone cables based on multiple pairs.

We stress that the association of telephony and data communication within a single prewiring installation is very important and creates few additional constraints. Thus, it is a reasonable solution as far as the implementation of a complete infrastructure is concerned (new rooms or renovation), which has the advantage that it brings together almost all the cable laying operations.

As shown in Figure 15.8, the architecture of data communication networks can easily be matched with the star structure of a telephone installation, since it has fewer constraints at the level of its topology (the communication backbones may form a star, chain or tree).

However, one has to ensure that the patching system (panels of connection modules) is as well suited to data communication manipulations as to those of telephony. In fact, most telephone lines have two wires, which is not the case for local area networks; branching, disconnection, rerouting and test operations take place on a single pair in one case and on two or four pairs in the other case. Note that, in telephony, fax or modem lines may also consist of two pairs.

Conclusion   We note that the main aim of prewiring is to combat the proliferation of all the cable types intended for use with a single technology.

Initially, prewiring was reserved for enterprise sites (offices and computer rooms), then it was applied to other categories of building, such as universities, airports and hospitals. Today it forms part of the infrastructure of these buildings and may be proposed as a fixture when they are fitted out.

Note that buildings which are entirely prewired are sometimes referred to as 'smart buildings' to stress that they can be adapted to many different uses, almost independently of the technologies and topologies desired. This represents a return to the area of home automation, in which a dwelling place is equipped with this same 'intelligence' capable of transporting all types of information (digital data, sound, pictures, video, alarms and detectors, electrical commands).

Other solutions

Prewiring is presented as the ideal method; however, the choice of prewiring with the laying of twisted-pair cables is not always the best solution for small installations (with only a few offices).

In fact, a simple thin coaxial cable running between ten accesses in one room (machine room or small computer center) is still the fastest network to implement, the easiest to modify and extend, and the least expensive. Even though it cannot be adapted to other technologies and its lifetime is directly associated with the presence of the user groups, this form of installation can be tolerated provided it remains temporary or of a limited size.

An industrial, or similar, environment (test chamber) is another case in which the standard coaxial cable retains all its advantages. In fact, it is better protected against electromagnetic perturbations, permits greater distances per segment, is more solid, and has a more robust connector technology than other cables (thin coaxial cable, twisted pair, optical fiber).

In the same spirit, a network served entirely by optical fiber may represent the appropriate solution for an ambitious installation, where there is an overriding desire to adapt to state-of-the-art technologies such as FDDI (initially). When a decision is taken to opt for a medium with a very long lifetime, greater prudence is called for, since the technologies are evolving rapidly and it is very difficult to know today what the optimum medium for networks will be twenty years hence. In fact, while 62.5/125 μm graded index silica optical fiber is the almost universal high-quality fiber today, single-mode fiber, which offers a far greater bandwidth, will probably replace it soon. However, the fact is that technical advances may result in developments relating to operational frequencies. Thus, after ten years, a situation may arise in which a building is fully prewired based on optical fiber of a type which is then obsolete.

Here, we stress that one should not seek a cabling or prewiring with an excessively long lifetime. If an installation effectively lasts for ten years without needing a common modification (laying of new media, change of lengths, modification of patch panels) it will probably have reached the end of its life after that time. Thus, it is wise when evaluating the cabling budget to think in terms of a lifetime of between five and ten years.

The figures in Table 15.1 are only given for indicative purposes, to permit a rapid (and relatively coarse) evaluation and for use in comparative calculations.

Precautions

Whichever cable is chosen, one important criterion that is independent of its electrical characteristics and its transmission capacity is its behavior in case of fire. The cable should not catch fire easily and it should not release toxic gases, thick smoke or high pollutants. These strictures are dictated by safety aspects, since the cables run in occupied buildings, and take environmental considerations into account. For example, cables with PVC insulation may be banned under certain conditions, although PTFE is acceptable.

Table 15.1 Average price of cabling for different LAN technologies.

Medium type	Price of medium (US dollars per meter)	Price of two terminal connectors (US dollars)
Ethernet Standard coaxial cable	3.6	16 Type *N*
Ethernet Thin coaxial cable	1.2	5 BNC
Ethernet Four screened twisted pairs	1	3 RJ45
Ethernet AUI cable	4	48 DB15 with slide latch
Token Ring Two shielded twisted pairs	1.4	21 Hermaphrodite
IBM SNA RG62 coaxial cable	0.8	5 BNC
LocalTalk One twisted pair	0.8	1.6 RJ11
Optical fiber 50/125 62.5/125 100/140μm	5 Bi-fiber cable	30 24 ST SC

Regular efforts are made to improve the safety of those working in rooms in which transmission cables are laid. New materials are being studied and developed as part of a trend to minimize their effect in an accident situation.

Flat cables

It is sometimes said that standard cabling, like prewiring, cannot cover all the user requirements. In fact, delivery to the station may be more-or-less easy.

If the machine to be attached is located by a wall, near a block of sockets, an 'extension cable' (AUI cable, attachment cable, jumper cable) is all that is needed to connect the station to the socket. From the practical point of view, this solution does not present a problem, since the 'extension cable' runs along the wall, possibly behind a table. On the other hand, if the room is large, the station may be located on a table in the middle of the room, far away from the wall blocks. Since the laying of a cable from the table to the wall carries a risk of deterioration for the cable, the machine connectors and the wall block, and is an inconvenience for the occupants of the room, one may consider laying the cables under the carpets.

Recently, a number of companies have produced somewhat specific types of electrical and computer cables which are flat enough that they can be installed under carpets (for convenience, carpet squares should be used). These include shielded and unshielded paired cables (not twisted) with two or four pairs together with coaxial cables and fiber optic cables. This could be thought of as providing a convenient way of extending the prewiring to the site of each machine, since the flat cables are easy to lay in a manner which supports evolution, in that the links can also be moved, extended and shortened.

This section concludes by inviting readers to consider this particular type of solution for requirements which are difficult to meet by the usual methods (large office, small networks in rooms which are difficult to cable, temporary installations). However, this medium should be primarily reserved for short links: capillary cabling.

Connector system

In all cases, whether of a medium based on twisted pair, coaxial cable or optical fiber, the connector system is fundamental as far as reliability is concerned. In fact, it is generally the only part that may be subject to frequent manipulations, of varying degrees of brutality.

This end component should be chosen to be well made if one wishes to avoid problems with the connection quality over time. Of course, the products from the main well-known manufacturers are more expensive, but the materials used are of a higher quality and the connectors are better finished. Consequently, they are more robust and age less rapidly.

For example, one might require the AUI sockets to be cabled according to the standard (five individually shielded pairs, plus a global shielding) and to be mounted in metal covers, and that the pins should be full and soldered. These prescriptions are taken from the recommendations of the IEEE documents, and may be useful to anyone wishing to avoid, as far as possible, operational faults due to the connector system.

It has already been stressed that, in general, a great many of the problems one may meet with a network are associated with the physical medium. Since the cables are generally immobilized and unassailable (overhead ducts, suspended ceiling, raised floor), the only components which can be damaged are the accessible ones: connectors, jumper cables, and attachment cables. Thus, one should ensure that the connectors are not badly made or excessively fragile.

Modular sockets

As far as prewiring is concerned, all the cables arrive in the office at the level of one or more wall-socket boxes. These boxes may combine all the data communication and telephony requirements of a standard user. They may equally well accommodate sockets for local area networks or telephones. However, the adaptability of the prewiring may make it necessary to change the socket type when the occupant changes. In fact, if the cabling is to be re-used to support a new technology without too much difficulty, it is vital to modify the connector system available in the offices so that it corresponds to user needs. The same twisted pair cabling may effectively support the telephone, a serial link, Ethernet 10BaseT, Token Ring or AppleTalk, but

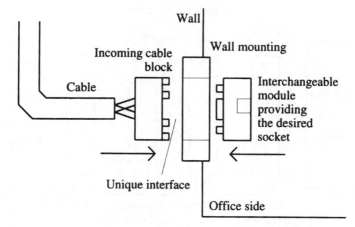

Figure 15.9 Simplified schematic of a connector system using modular wall sockets.

the corresponding sockets are different (T-shaped, DB25, RJ45, hermaphrodite, RJ11).

However, some manufacturers produce modular sockets (consisting of a fixed part housing the end of the cable and an interchangeable part adapted to the technology supported by the prewiring). This second part might be used to distribute the four available pairs across two sockets (as for IEEE 802.3, 10BaseT, which only requires two pairs), and may even incorporate one or two baluns providing coaxial connections at 50, 75 or 93 Ohm, or even twinax (IBM) (Figure 15.9).

This philosophy appears very consistent with the concept of prewiring, in which the installation put in place at a given time has a certain durability in that it can be adapted to the level of the topology (using jumper cables in the patch cabinet), to the level of the technology using the active elements in the plant rooms, and to the level of its access points by providing the requisite type of socket. Of course, the characteristics of twisted pairs (or another medium used) will not evolve easily, and the same applies to the number of links leading to each office.

Modular systems may be used equally well both for wall sockets available in offices and for the patching facilities provided in the plant rooms. This makes it possible to adapt the cabling directly to the active devices using only attachment cables with identical connectors at each end. However, the usefulness of a modular connector technology is primarily reliant on its simplicity as far as the end user is concerned, since generally, patching systems may use a homogeneous connector system for all the cables.

When the cabling includes coaxial cables, coax–twisted pair or even coax–coax baluns may be used to offer an impedance different from that of the actual cables laid at the level of the access points.

It should be stressed that modular sockets extend the adaptability of pre-wiring to the terminal connector technology. This in no way hinders their integration into a standard cabling (laying of the medium as a function of the needs, precisely recorded at a given time).

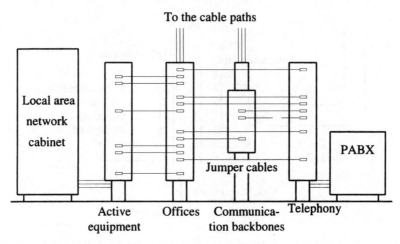

To the cable paths

Local area
network
cabinet

PABX

Jumper cables

| Active | Offices | Communica- | Telephony |
| equipment | | tion backbones | |

Figure 15.10 Example of the arrangement of patch panels.

Patching

The primary function of patching is to permit the modification of the path of a physical link by manipulating the jumper cables located on the desired trajectory. In fact, in the case of prewiring, but also more generally, the cables laid are not linked directly to the active devices (Figure 15.10). If this were the case, it would imply that the physical installation were completely fixed and totally devoid of logical structure. Consequently, it would be very difficult to maintain (repair, modification, extension).

For many years, cables laid have been attached in a group to a distribution panel or patch panel, which presents all the conductors in an accessible manner. This arrangement has become indispensable and, as we shall see, the method used can improve the efficiency of the maintenance teams. Each incoming cable can be given a label on the front face of the modules, making it easy to identify the line one is looking for.

A plant room may include three distribution panels: one concentrates the modules linked to all the cables of the capillary service to the offices which end in this room; the next corresponds to links between this plant room and other similar plant rooms (links by communication backbones); while the last provides access to the active devices located in the plant room. The contacts between the cables leading to these distribution panels are provided by jumper cables (attached lead). If it is desired to separate the cables dedicated to telephony from those dedicated to data communication, another distribution panel has to be added next to the first. On the other hand, if desired, one can opt for a patching system suitable for both types of application. This option has the advantage that there exists a global pool of conductors between the plant room and each office, which can be accessed to meet the telephony and network requirements of each occupant. Since the assignment is

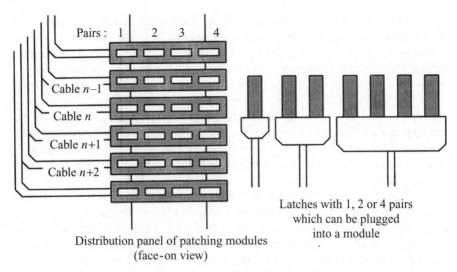

Distribution panel of patching modules
(face-on view)

Latches with 1, 2 or 4 pairs
which can be plugged
into a module

Figure 15.11   Schematic representation of connection modules and associated latches.

not fixed by the technology, it is easy to imagine that the distribution will permit numerous combinations.

The modules connected to each distribution panel may be of different colors according to the function chosen for the panel (Figure 15.11). For example, the modules linked to office sockets may be blue, while those linked to active devices (hub, PABX) will be yellow, those corresponding to communication-backbone links will be green, and those which are cabled entirely to the ground will be black, and so on.

To merge the data communication cabling with the telephone cabling effectively at the patch-panel level, it is important to have a patching system that allows access to a pair as well as to the whole of the cable. In fact, while a cable with four pairs satisfies nearly all the requirements generated by local area networks, a single pair is sufficient to feed a telephone point. However, if the number of attachments increases above that provided for, the greater flexibility obtained will enable full use to be made of all the cables. In this connection, note that an Ethernet 10BaseT link, like Token Ring, only requires two twisted pairs, while LocalTalk only uses a single pair, and 1000BaseT will require the 4 pairs.

By collecting together the maximum number of logical links within each cable, near optimal use of the prewiring can be achieved. Note also that systems with modular wall sockets will carry the greater part of the infrastructure.

Electronic patching

There is a way of avoiding large numbers of jumper cables hanging between the distribution panels, which inevitably involves risks of poor contact and essentially requires documentation of the patching regularly implemented.

This method involves replacing all the distribution panels of a plant room by a high-dimensional switching matrix, the sole purpose of which is to connect an office socket to a port of an active device on request. The matrix will therefore include a large number of inputs and outputs (several hundred), and will be managed by software that can be used to determine the current configuration at any given time.

While this solution is certainly very nice and gives concrete expression to a pleasing concept, it is really only useful when the workload represented by the patching process becomes too heavy. In fact, if the network does evolve greatly, interventions to attach a station or connect a machine which has moved will correspond to a few manipulations per month and will scarcely justify the acquisition of a system with such a potential.

The applications for which this type of product is intended are, on the one hand, installations of large, very dynamic networks (in which the machines move frequently) and, on the other hand, cases where the manager is not on site and has to reconfigure the patching from a distance. In the first case, it is preferable to automate part of the operations to make them less laborious and safer, and at the same time, to ensure the availability of up-to-date documentation describing the current system state. In the second case, if the engineer cannot move around the site rapidly, he or she will also be able to modify the patching instantaneously to meet user needs.

Simulation software

One last tool, whose existence one should be aware of when designing an important local area network, is simulation and modeling software. This type of software is used for virtual operation (on a screen) of a certain number of interconnected networks and their associated technology.

The given items, which are easy to determine at this stage of the project, include the network technologies (Ethernet, Token Ring, FDDI or others), the topologies, the segment lengths, and the number of segments. The capabilities of the interconnection devices are already less easy to determine; for, clearly, evaluations are only of interest if they can be used to validate a solution before the infrastructure is effectively put in place or to evaluate the health of an existing network. Finally, one must also enter as parameters the number of stations it is intended to connect, the quantities of information that it is assumed will cross these networks and the structure of the induced traffic (periodic, regular, slotted, bursty). One should try, for example, to define the servers of other groups of machines explicitly (source of important stream). This may lead one to think that the use of this software, which is sometimes highly instructive, should, above all, be highly precise and meticulous if it is intended to achieve significant results. The presentation of the envisaged network model on which the simulator is to work itself represents a non-trivial task.

Conclusion   To help those responsible for a study, we shall now recall the figures which can be used to evaluate the round-trip delay on an Ethernet network and to validate a configuration on paper.

Table 15.2   Table of crossing delays for all types of media and elements.

Elements crossed on the network	RTD for unit	Total number of elements on path	Total delay due to this type of element	Max. RTD per segment
Standard coaxial cable	8.66 ns/m	m	ns	4 330 ns
Thin coaxial cable	10.27 ns/m	m	ns	1 900 ns
Fiber optic FOIRL	10 ns/m	m	ns	10 000 ns
Fiber optic 10baseFL	10 ns/m	m	ns	20 000 ns
Fiber optic 10baseFB	10 ns/m	m	ns	20 000 ns
Fiber optic 10baseFP	10 ns/m	m	ns	10 000 ns
Twisted pair	11.3 ns/m	m	ns	2 000 ns
AUI cable	10.27 ns/m	m	ns	514 ns
Coaxial transceiver	1525 ns	ns	ns	
FOIRL optical transceiver	700 ns	ns	ns	
Synchronous optical transceiver	300 ns	ns	ns	
Passive optical transceiver	1000 ns	ns	ns	
10baseT transceiver	1400 ns	ns	ns	
FanOut	300 ns	ns	ns	
Internal repeater + transceiver	< 3750 ns	ns	ns	
Repeater	1450 ns	ns	ns	
10BaseT hub	3750 ns	ns	ns	
Synchronous active optical star	1400 ns	ns	ns	

Total delay $< 46\,\mu s$

In Part II it was clearly explained that the time taken to cross a shared Ethernet network must be limited to avoid the danger of being unable to detect all collisions; thus, it is vital to check that the installation envisaged conforms to this RTD criterion. When things are still simple and only coaxial cable and fiber optic FOIRL links are used (the limitations are derived directly from the maximum number of repeaters and segments and the maximum permissible segment length), the arrival of other elements makes the calculation more complex, as explained before.

The round-trip delay for active elements includes the crossing delay for a signal in one direction and that for a collision in the other.

Table 15.2 complements the method of calculation described in Chapter 12.6 (section on repeaters).

15.2 Installation

The installation should adhere to certain rules which ensure that the network will function correctly and will be maintainable. Several of these guidelines are taken from the note IEC 907 (International Electrotechnical Commission), *Local area network CSMA/CD 10 Mbit/s baseband planning and installation guide*. The gist of this technical report is summarized here and advice adapted to the IEEE supplements and to new advances in technology is also given.

Coaxial cable

- The coaxial cable should be grounded by the braid (external conductor) at one end only. The grounding should be implemented using copper wire with a cross section of at least 4 mm^2. This implies that all the other elements of the N or BNC connector system (T, straight connector, terminator) should be protected and insulated (for example, by a plastic sleeve).

- It is always preferable for the cable segment to be constructed from a single production batch so that the sections are more homogeneous (if the cable sections all come from the same manufacturer, this may ensure that the propagation speed will not vary by more than 0.5% between segments).

- The minimum bend radius of the standard coaxial cable is 25 cm once laid and 20 cm during the installation.

- The minimum bend radius of the thin coaxial cable is 5 cm.

- If the cable has to be suspended, it should be tacked down at least every 3 meters.

- It is recommended that the cable should be placed at least 10 m from major sources of radiation (such as lift contactors, electric arc welding sites, generators).

- Pay attention to the damage to which the coaxial cable may be subject during laying: deformation (traction, twisting, torsion, bruising, very short radius), abrasion, severance, cracking. One of the main sources of deterioration during drawing the cables is the presence of sharp edges on the cable path.

- For paths in suspended ceilings, it is advisable to remain less than 3 m from the floor, whenever possible.

- For paths in suspended ceilings or raised floors it is preferable to have a hatch at most 30 cm from the points of possible intervention: on transceivers, connectors, and load adapters.

- The crimping of N or BNC connectors should be finished well (no wires from the braid visible, no crushed sheath, no loose connectors or connectors with play).

- The N connectors should only be tightened by hand.

- Note that, since the useful frequency band for Ethernet is limited to 20 MHz, there is no need to use the connector technology approved for more robust applications (military).

- If the presence of a 30 V AC voltage between the braid and ground is detected after laying, this is an indicator of a fault in the installation and analysis is required before proceeding further.

- In time-domain reflectometry the maximum admissible reflection at a point is 4% (care should be taken to ensure that the transceivers are not emitting during the measurement).

- The maximum admissible reflection at any point is 7%.

- Before grounding, the insulation resistance between the braid (external conductor of the cable) and the ground should be greater than 200 MOhm. This measurement should be carried out using a megger at 500 V with all the transceivers disconnected.

- There should not be a short circuit between the two conductors. However, the loop resistance of a coaxial cable segment should be less than 10 MOhm/m (at 20 °C).

- The loop resistance of the cable with the transceivers should be less than 5 Ohm.

- The transceivers should be installed on reference rings drawn every 2.5 meters on the standard coaxial cable.

- One might suggest that transceivers should not be placed at segment ends. In fact, this would mean that it would be possible not to superpose the variation in impedance due at the attachment point (T or tap) on that of the straight link and the load adapter. Thus, a minimum section (2.5 m in 10Base5, 50 cm in 10Base2) should be left between the last transceiver and the load.

- If the path is such that lightning protection cannot be guaranteed, if the zone is perturbed by electrical noise, if the temperature is too high, if the bend radii extend to 3 cm or if the constraints relating to safe operation of the link are fundamental, then optical fiber should be chosen.

The AUI cable

- It is desirable that the AUI cable should be fixed so as not to pull on the slide-latch lock (reputed to be fragile and unreliable).

The twisted-pair cable

- The wires of each twisted pair of the cable should not be inverted between the patching and the wall socket. Similarly, the pairs should not be inverted among themselves as this might harm the operation.

- The 10BaseT jumper cable in the office should be placed where it is not in the way, to ensure that there is no risk of pulling out the relatively fragile RJ45 sockets.

- It is recommended that the twisted-pair cables should be placed in shielded cable paths dedicated to data communication and, if possible, almost a meter away from high-voltage cables and sources of electromagnetic radiation.

Fiber optic cables

- Optical cables should not be subject to excessive traction when they are laid, and one should ensure that the bend radii indicated by the supplier are respected, otherwise the fibers may be irremediably harmed.

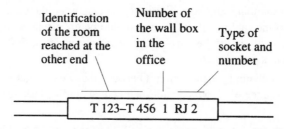

Figure 15.12   Example of a label for a patching module.

The active elements   An equipotential link for the power supply transformers should be provided if network elements are to be installed in zones fed by medium voltage (> 450 V eff).

General   Demand labels on the cables and the patch plates (Figure 15.12). The labeling should be clear and consistent, and the labels should be solidly fixed and have a high physical resistance.

In the case of a twisted-pair cable leading to a plant room, an indication of the plant room may be omitted if it appears superfluous (for example, only one plant room per storey). On the other hand, in the case of a coaxial or fiber optic cable, the technology used might be indicated (Eth for Ethernet, TR for Token Ring, and so on), together with the logical type of the network supported (for example, MN for main network or MgtN for management network).

The more important the network installed is to be, the greater is the attention that should be paid to the quality of implementation, since the network will certainly have to live with this installation for several years. Many problems of a physical level may certainly result from overhasty choices or botched operations.

Finally, to simplify the work of the installer and minimize the choice available to him or her at the last moment, the detailed technical specifications produced should be as precise and consistent as possible. For example, it is not easy to find out that a path cannot be used as specified because it is already full of cables, but one of the tasks of the person responsible for the dossier is to establish realistic specifications, which may call for a number of on-site visits, as necessary, and reference to those who know the site or the building best (the electricians or the works department). Thus, the person responsible should be encouraged to carry out preparative groundwork to avoid being forced to modify his or her plans during the work itself.

15.3 On-site monitoring

This phase has several objectives. The main aim is to ensure that the rules laid down in the schedule of conditions or the detailed technical specifications are adhered to, and that the network installed effectively corresponds to that defined on paper. For this, one has to consider all the technical points where the installer has a margin for maneuver, so that each solution chosen by the latter is appropriate, even when it is a minor detail (position of the distribution panels, color of the connection modules, type of labeling).

The second important aim is to ensure that the laying methods are adhered to, in relation to the security of the operators, the non-degradation of the cables and equipment installed and the global neatness of the whole project.

Finally, monitoring of the progress of the work will enable one to identify any slippage in the planning at the earliest possible time, and to anticipate the consequences of a delay at this stage (ordering of materials, date of payment, call for additional teams).

The first subject is fundamental to subsequent peaceful operation of the network. It is easy to appreciate that any maintenance or extension task may become a real headache if, during the course of the work, it is discovered that the network in question does not conform to the descriptions in the detailed technical specifications. If fact, every action should be preceded by a study to check the actual state of the network. The points requiring vigilance are the choice of the hardware (the cables and their physical characteristics, the cable paths and the associated nuts and bolts, the rack cabinets, the make of the sockets, and the plugs), the effective cabling (in the cabinets, in the sockets, adherence to the patching plan) and the way in which these cables are manipulated during laying operations. One should not forget that a cable (coaxial, twisted pair or fiber optic) may be damaged during installation without the damage being immediately noticeable.

The second subject is concerned more with the person responsible for the security and others dealing with the cabling (telephone, electricity, alarm) that occupies the same paths as those used by the networks. In both cases, it is a matter of integrating the laying of a data communication infrastructure without violating the security rules for the building or the site, and without impeding the other installers or damaging their installations, while even seeking to make use of the existing cabling using the labeling templates or existing routes in the suspended ceilings and ducts. This may provide a better view of the operation of laying the network, which is sometimes seen as an intrusion by those responsible for maintaining the other cabling systems (old and thus understood well).

Finally, the third point is only mentioned here for information, since it adds little to the quality of the implementation, but rather forms part of the project management, in that it provides specific information about the progress of the laying and installation phase.

Here is an example of the great attention that must be paid throughout the on-site monitoring phase. The 10BaseT lines linking the PC interface card to the wall socket should consist of four twisted pairs (two pairs may suffice if they correspond to the pins of the emission pair 1–2 and the reception pair 3–6 of the RJ45 socket). However, if the installer lays flat cable, which is apparently identical (apart from the fact that the cable is slightly thinner since all the conductors are run in parallel), transient problems may then affect the network operation. In fact, above a length of several meters, this type of cable is no longer suitable for communication at 10 Mbps, and intermittently generates errors which may appear as a function of the frame length or the density of transfers. The manifestations of the problem will then be wrongly associated with a particular protocol or type of exchange since this protocol uses longer packets than others. The repair crew then becomes involved in useless and time-consuming research procedures, simply because the cables installed were not those required. A similar thing may occur for other cables and hardware components of the network.

15.4 Acceptance operations

The acceptance operation involves checking an installation, or a meticulous follow-up of the progress of the laying operations, either by tests and subsequent checking or a combination of the two.

Often, the physical acceptance, concerning the transmission medium and the terminal elements (connectors, patch plates), is distinguished from the logical or functional acceptance, which involves ensuring that the network is operating effectively. In fact, the different stages of the acceptance operation correspond to descriptions at various levels in the schedule of conditions. Thus, the functional acceptance which tests the overall capabilities of the network (non-exhaustively in most cases) ensures that the system provides the required global capabilities. The acceptance of each individual unit may qualify the elements as a function of the required characteristics. Careful and continuous on-site monitoring is the best way of monitoring the overall quality of the infrastructure installed. Let us not forget that a major part of the installation will be hidden during the acceptance procedure (in suspended ceilings, raised floors, attachment plates, patch cabinets).

As shown in Figure 15.13, at the time of a large-scale installation, it is best to decompose the acceptance operation into a number of elementary tasks. This decomposition may be carried out logically, proceeding in the opposite direction to the definition. To follow this method, at each stage of the definition a list of the tests that can be used to validate the functionality described has to be drawn up. The more one advances into details of the solution in place, the more the tests or associated checks will concern specific (and generally smaller) elements.

On the other hand, if the test is of a low level, it is realistic to carry out an exhaustive check, although as the level of functionality increases the test will become more global, and thus incomplete, and constitute no more than an indication.

Finally, note that, as far as the progression of time is concerned, the definition stages run from the most general to the most specific, although this order is inverted in the acceptance phases (from the element to the whole).

By way of example, the phases of a typical large installation are now described.

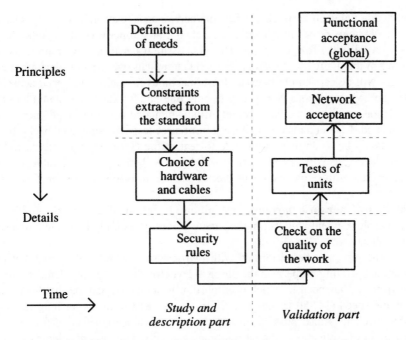

Figure 15.13   Progress of the definition and test stages, by level.

Global operation of the network   The test of the primary operation of the network as a whole will necessarily be at the application level. It may involve:

- Tests of file transfer between workstations (for example, with FTP)
- Opening a session on a remote host
- Emulating a terminal on a remote microcomputer (Telnet in text or terminal mode, X window in graphics mode)
- Access to a server and attempts to share resources (database, peripherals).

If the network includes interconnection devices, attempts may be made to pass traffic through these (bridges, routers, gateways), since these may not have been qualified beforehand on a per unit basis (following the steps described below).

For each test, the framework of the expected results (maximum time taken, admissible number of lost packets, periodicity of measurements, and so on) corresponding to the global acceptance threshold which will permit definitive acceptance should have been established beforehand. Since this preparation requires the implementation of test platforms (from which to deduce the reference measurements), it will facilitate the search for the probable source of any problem which may arise and an appreciation of the importance of this problem, and will allow one to move towards a resolutory approach.

Qualification of each network A network corresponds to a complete entity, such as an Ethernet network or sub-network, or a network or sub-network of any other technology (AppleTalk, Token Ring, FDDI, ATM). The test will involve representative elements of the future set of user machines (PC terminals, workstations, mainframes). Changes will be carried out between these machines to qualify the speed achieved under the best conditions (for example, only one pair of active elements) and the degradation caused by the background traffic, simulated using test equipment, will be evaluated. To obtain maximum benefit from these tests, the simulated background traffic should be as similar as possible to real traffic (variable and irregular). The level of these tests corresponds to the MAC layer. As before, it is preferable to have a precise idea of the expected results before the real tests are undertaken.

Validation of network portions Definition: a portion of a network is either a coaxial cable segment with its transceivers or a point-to-point link, or a hub or a star with its links.

The test may be performed with two test sets, which will verify that the network is operating properly at the physical level (media and active elements) from an AUI port. The speed to which each portion is subjected may be the theoretical maximum speed (14 880 frames/s for short frames, 812 frames/s for long frames). At this level, it is also possible to test the transmission of defective frames, the propagation of collisions or the partitioning capability. The tests may be exhaustive and involve the checking of the operation of each access point on each segment.

Cable and connector characteristics The measurement at this stage involves coaxial or optical reflectometry, which validates the physical characteristics of the medium (measurements of total lengths for confirmation, determination of the attenuation at the operational frequencies for comparison with the figure given by the standard, observation and adaptation of the impedance, localization of perturbations). The optical and twisted-pair jumper cables may also be inspected, to determine a correspondence with the optical-fiber type used in the network infrastructure (diameter, numerical aperture), to monitor the connector technology for the RJ45 sockets (wire color, pin number), and to check that twisted pairs and, if necessary, shielding, are effectively present. At this stage, the measurements are necessarily exhaustive. In fact, if a medium segment were defective, it would be more complicated to repair after the installation of the network was complete (for example, if it were discovered at the time of the final acceptance) than at this stage.

Quality and security of the work, physical details Quality assurance monitoring will take place as the work proceeds. This concerns the crimping of connectors, laying of the medium, cleanliness of the installation and adherence to rules laid down in the schedule of conditions, including the labeling of cables and sockets, the color of connection modules and the position of wiring cabinets and active elements. Care should also be taken to ensure that the quantities of commodities ordered but not installed (jumper cables, 10BaseT transceiver cables) correspond to the schedule of conditions. It is also important to take security aspects into consideration. Finally, the physical details to be reviewed at this stage include the contractor's choice for each element (cable, connector, socket), and accessory equipment (in a cabinet: ventilation, lighting, power supply facilities as a function of the network devices), and so on.

A visual check as part of the on-site monitoring with a regular presence throughout the laying operations will make it possible to provide useful advice at the appropriate time. This will also enable one to ensure that the recommended arrangements are followed and, possibly, to keep a check on the planning. Care should be taken to ensure that methods which are visibly unsuitable should be corrected at the earliest possible time (especially when these may lead to irremediable damage to certain elements).

In the case where the installer himself (herself) tests the physical level (described above), it is wise to monitor the approach he (she) follows when taking the measurements. One's confidence in the results will depend closely upon the test method used. In the same spirit, a measurement performed counter to certain rules or methods may provide unusable results, since it will not give a true or representative numerical indication.

15.5 Evolutions and modifications

The modification phase is generally similar to a small installation task, so it will give rise to the same methods and procedures. Depending upon its importance, care should be taken to produce the preliminary and subsequent documents in the same format as for a typical installation.

It is fundamental that evolutions of the whole network, or of some of its segments, be accompanied by the immediate updating of all documents associated with the network (plans, general and detailed synopses, list of stations, plan of patch cabinets, and so on). Without this, the documentation describing the installations rapidly becomes out of date and loses all its reference value. In fact, the network is 'alive' in the sense that it grows, changes, and evolves as new items reach the market. Thus, even when the dimensions of the cabling were chosen to be sufficient to accommodate all modifications without requiring extension, the set of active access points will alter.

The monitoring of the network thus constitutes a single integral task, responsibility for which should be well defined in order to avoid 'free-for-all' intervention on the network. One natural consequence of this is the need to identify a single spokesperson for the network. He or she will be responsible for following all the procedures relating to intervention (generation of progress reports, updating of cards showing the patching, informing users of outages, and so on). Thus, in parallel with the installation of a network, it is fundamental to define the human structure which will take responsibility for each of its stages. When defining the possible ways of intervention, care should be taken to ensure that this does not lead to any conflict between those involved and that their areas of action do not overlap.

It is clear that a simple intervention in the network is an operation that anyone can undertake. Changing the point at which one is plugged in, modification of the patching by the introduction of jumper cables or the extension of a thin coaxial cable segment are all practical actions that everyone apparently understands and is capable of. However, they may have disastrous consequences for the rest of the network. The machine which is moved without the person responsible having been informed may have unwittingly changed logical networks. Blind manipulation of patching may put a user in the dark, or even cut the access to an element that is crucial to others (router, gateway, server). Extension of an existing cable inevitably leads to a temporary cut on connection and, if one is unaware of the length already laid, may result in transient perturbations (whose probability is a function of the traffic and the frame length) which are difficult to detect when their cause is unknown.

15.6 Maintenance operations

Intervention for maintenance

In the case of breakdown, or where there is doubt about the operation of the network or a particular element of it, the intervention team is called to resolve the problem. The fundamental task of this team is to get the network working again with the minimum delay so that users are not affected for too long a time.

In fact, as networks are now integral parts of the office automation environment, they have become vital to the smooth running of some departments. Thus, the objective is simple: to cure or reduce the problem as rapidly as possible. This implies acting methodically and progressively, carrying out all the stages of the repair process in a proper manner.

On the other hand, the repair team must avoid aggravating the problem, for example, by making it definitive or by interrupting ongoing activities before the results of the intervention have been anticipated. This action should have a simple aim (to test the operation of a single element, replace a component, introduce a partial modification to a configuration). The possible results of this action should be anticipated beforehand, so that a conclusion can be drawn rapidly. The team should also ensure that a backup machine can be introduced at any time, should the tests not be successful. This will avoid the accumulation of several modifications, since explanation of any cure soon becomes laborious. In summary, methodical procedures should be adopted.

As shown in Figure 15.14, it is vital to know just which point the repair procedure has reached at any given time. One needs to know what has been analyzed and ruled out and what has been and may be involved in measurements still to be taken, and to be able to identify the part that remains to be dealt with. Moreover, it is practical to be able to determine, at any time, the time spent in each stage and the time it will still take either to complete the repair or conclude the analysis. This enables one to make a reasonable choice of the tests to be undertaken, or to put in

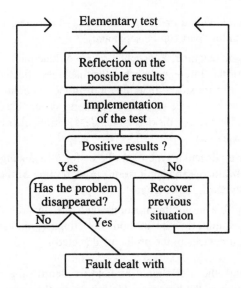

Figure 15.14 Methodical approach to repairs.

place a provisional, degraded but adequate, configuration. In fact, the determination of the area which may be affected may lead the repairer to prefer a partial modification to the network configuration, rather than to risk inconveniencing the users for too long a period.

Repair methods

In a repair operation, the problem detected by the user may be the consequence of a fault of any kind. It may involve a hardware fault, an error in the software parametrization (level 3 and 4 protocols) or a configuration which is ill adapted to the network.

It is vital to be able to determine the type of anomaly rapidly, so that one can work on a broad spectrum of faults. Although there is no substitute for experience as far as this task is concerned, certain arguments may help one to determine the reason for the user's unhappiness.

The first phase involves translating the fault as described by the user into network-technology terms. There are two main categories of fault phenomenon:

- A global or specific decrease in performance, with a noticeable variation in the speed, collision rates or number of errors.

- An intermittent, periodic or continuous, but clear fault (given that certain periods of the day are particularly heavily loaded: 9–11 am and 3–5 pm), where the problem can be reproduced with varying degrees of difficulty. Moreover, this fault may affect all or part of the network, and thus the relationship between the problem and the stations affected should be investigated. Breakdowns may:

- be associated with a machine or a place (which means that the machines and the cabling part can be separated)
- concern one machine, a particular group of machines or all the machines (the link or the difference between the machines affected should be investigated: hardware side – manufacturer, model, attachment type, physical position; software side – network operating system used, communications configuration (server, diskless or dataless station, distributed application), software version)
- occur for a particular type of traffic or for all exchanges (traffic characteristics, protocols and applications used, routing of the exchange, server or gateway used, frame length)
- be perceptible in communications with the outside or only in internal communications, in one or both directions (implication of the interconnection devices in the problems detected).

Thus, discussions with the user should be held to identify the relevant elements, including those relating to the hardware, the protocols, the software (applications), and the configuration. What the user says should be recast to associate the breakdown with as precise a category as possible.

One approach involves taking a logical route and following it as closely as possible. We shall describe two examples of ways in which this may be done.

Method 1   Begin with the element with the least restrictions which is the nearest to the manifestation of the fault (when this is localized). If this element is ruled out, gradually broaden the range of devices and components to be considered. This will give a progressively larger set, which will inevitably lead to questions about the source of the fault. For example, one might follow a sequence implicating the state of the following items of equipment in the order given in Figure 15.16.

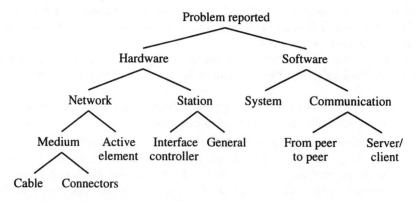

Figure 15.15   Example of the classification of sources of problems which may affect the network.

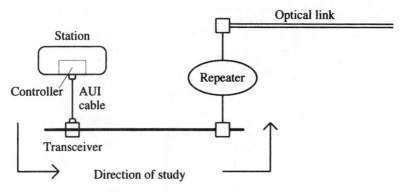

Figure 15.16 Sequence for the case considered.

- The AUI connector technology of the NIC and the NIC itself
- The AUI cable
- The medium segment (its connectors and its grounding)
- The repeater or the hub (its AUI cables and transceivers)
- Other network segments (and their repeaters)
- The local switch or router (and the networks interlinked by these)
- The remote bridge or router
- The modem or the serial line
- The network of the remote site.

Method 2 Begin with the physical layer and move up through the OSI layers at each stage (which implies testing the most elementary things before the most complex). As before, we can give an example of a logical sequence of points to be considered. Investigate whether the problem may reside in (see Figure 15.17):

- The bottom of the physical layer: the AUI, N, BNC, optical or patching connector technology; the medium segments, whatever they may be (adaptation, parasitic reflection, length); the transceivers
- The PLS level (repeaters, hubs, multimedia stars)
- The MAC level (NIC, switch, bridge, and also the configuration authorized)
- Levels 3 and above (router, gateway, protocols used in the exchanges, routing protocols)
- Level 7 (application, software used, server used).

At each stage, one should check that the point in question is operating properly in conformance with the standard. If, at each stage, care is taken to eliminate the element tested, one will finally discover the origin of the fault (see diagram on

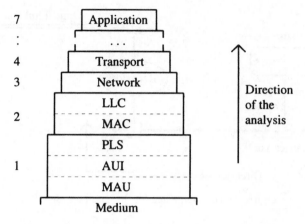

Figure 15.17 Progression through the layers of the OSI reference model.

Figure 15.18). When checking a particular component, it is simplest, when possible, to replace it by a reference element; otherwise, the performance of the component should be quantified in a sequence of tests.

Returning to the scheme described at the beginning of the section, recall that the most complicated breakdowns to resolve are those which combine various causes whose manifestations are similar enough to be confused. It may then be quite difficult to establish operationally that the source of a fault has been effectively identified, while at the same time the problem has apparently not disappeared. However, a methodical approach should help one to progress gradually towards the solution.

Test devices are not always crucial, but they simplify the work considerably, since, apart from the stations and the machines using the network effectively, they can be used to evaluate the elements at the physical level.

The most useful of the devices described in Part II are:

- The coaxial reflectometer for installations in which the cabling is mainly based on coaxial cable
- The twisted-pair tester for infrastructures comprising twisted-pair cables (shielded or unshielded), including prewired sites
- The optical dBmeter and the associated calibrated source, which are simple and practical tools for checking fiber optic links
- The pair of test sets for carrying out tests at the MAC level
- The LAN analyzer to observe the traffic and decode all the protocols (level 1 to 7).

The merits of these devices are reviewed in more detail in Chapter 17 (documents and necessary hardware).

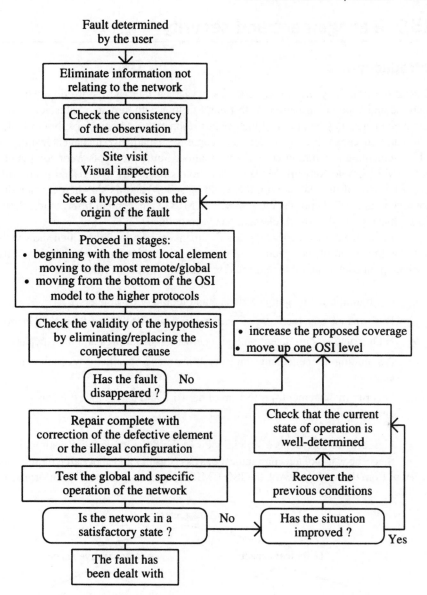

Figure 15.18   Example of a procedural repair method.

15.7 Management and security

Introduction

During the past 15 years, local networks have seen their need for administration increase and become structured with time. Starting with simple, exclusively functional elements, they had to meet the need of resorting to statistics or submit to tele-configuration capabilities in order to become systematically manageable objects all implementing a common core of information. Some protocols were competing, but SNMP (Simple Network Management Protocol) quickly established itself with LANs because of its relation with the world of TCP/IP and its simplicity, which did not require much CPU power. With SNMP, an MIB (Management Information Base) for each category of network element has been defined.

Let us recall that the ISO defines five management domains which show very well the dimension of the spectrum of activities to be encompassed. SNMP and its current applications cannot be expected to cover the whole of these functions:

- Configuration management: device and topology parameters.
- Performance management: measurements, statistics of load, flows, and errors.
- Fault management: detection and localization of failures and their bypass.
- Accounting management: inventory, invoicing, profitability, maintenance contract.
- Security management: protection of network and users against intrusion and aggression.

Figure 15.19 represents a simpler view of the different domains dealt with.

Since the world of telecommunications has a history and above all requirements different from those of the LAN, the ISO CMIP (Common Management Information

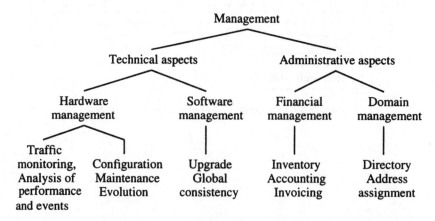

Figure 15.19 Division of the management into sub-domains.

Protocol) appears to be the best solution to the operators' needs because it responds more adequately vis-à-vis the size of the networks and the constraints of security and redundancy.

Other management protocols or solutions must be quoted, such as HLM, which is an implementation of CMIP on LLC employed in IBM environments (CMOL: CMIP Over LLC), the combination of Network and Transport layers of the TCP/IP and ISO world with the management protocol of opposite origin (CMOT: CMIP Over TCP/IP or the inverse). The description model of CMIP, namely GDMO (Guidelines for the Definition of Managed Objects), is still employed by the IEEE to define manageable objects associated with a LAN technology. And finally, we must not forget the purely MAC protocols such as NMT in Token Ring and SMT in FDDI which allow users to resort to highly significant information on the development of communication on the network (PMD, PHY, and MAC layers).

Finally, to conclude this introduction, we insist on the fact that, in contrast with the LAN technologies it supervises, the network administration which encompasses complex and ambitious functions, is currently still under development and has not yet reached a satisfactory state of maturity.

SNMP protocol

The SNMP protocol is designed around elementary commands allowing communication of the counters and variables of a device. For this purpose, each potentially manageable element is equipped with an agent. All agents are controlled by one (or more) management stations. Each agent is charged with acting as a gateway between the information known and manipulated by the device that hosts it, and its exchange via SNMP (on the network) with the master station.

SNMP is defined by three main RFCs (1157, 1213, and 1155). They describe the SNMP protocol, the management information base (MIB), and the structure of the information (SMI). The SNMP protocol consists in the definition of the encapsulation of the messages on UDP (port numbers 161 and 162) and the definition of

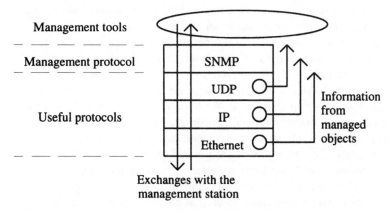

Figure 15.20   Protocol layers vital to a managed node.

such request and response messages. MIB-II is the basic tree-like information structure. It is, however, rather IP-oriented. Finally, SMI describes the usage mode of ASN.1 for the coding of the different types of variables of the MIB. GDMO is the counterpart of SMI for the CMIP world.

Note that SNMP relies on UDP and IP. This has once again the merit of simplicity because it only uses a little power to make an agent function, but it also turns SNMP into a non-reliable protocol, given that good communication is generally guaranteed by writing followed by reading of the value for verification. In case of non-response, the request is simply reiterated.

Insisting once more on the simplicity of SNMP, other (less common) implementations have been defined, one of them on IPX, which avoids the stage of manually configuring the logical address of the agent. Another implementation allows SNMP to rely directly on Ethernet, without the use of Transport and Network protocols. This last encapsulation is rather surprising, given that MIB-II is fundamentally IP, but in spite of everything consistent with the idea that an SNMP agent, such as a hub, may *a priori* have no knowledge at all of level 3 and 4 protocols.

Master station

The master station (NMS: Network Management System) in SNMP has the task of periodically interrogating the agents, and it is also the addressee of the Traps spontaneously generated by the agents. Obviously, the higher the frequency of interrogation, the more detailed the returned information.

However, this makes the SNMP traffic grow in proportion. On a shared network, this problem of management traffic load can be a problem. In fact, if there are a large number of devices to be monitored and the polling frequency is high enough, the SNMP traffic, being additional by definition, can disturb the functioning of the network by putting useless loads on it. There are two solutions to this, the first being to limit the traffic, by reducing the quantity of requests per second or by synthesizing the circulating information (as RMON allows to do), and the second being to dedicate a separate network to the transport of SNMP flows. This second solution may appear demanding, but it usually affords largely superior security, because even if the data network experiences serious problems, it is always possible to monitor it or even to intervene to correct or prevent the dysfunction by remote control.

Thus, in general, the station interrogates the devices via the same network as the one being observed, which is the so-called In-Band communication. There are two other modes of implementation. We have just seen the Side-Band mode which consists in using a similar but parallel network. Finally, the Out-of-Band mode consists in using a WAN infrastructure to communicate with the agents that monitor the LAN segments. This solution is usually based on low-throughput links (telephone line and modem) which connect the station and the agents. It is, however, not ideal because it does not allow *a priori* communication with all agents concurrently (calling each distant device successively), as on a local network. Moreover, this can hamper the open management platform.

Agents

Each agent is responsible for responding to the requests of the master station by returning the value of the sought parameter, by setting a variable to the communicated value, or by spontaneously emitting an alarm in case of a critical event.

The basic commands are:

Get Request	demands the value of the specified variable
Get Next Request	demands the 'next' value in the tree structure
Get Response	sends the requested value
Set Request	configuration of a variable to the specified value
Trap	autonomous indication from the agent

Note that an agent, even if it needs few resources, can only function on a CPU. This obviously implies that devices which do not necessarily need a microprocessor to ensure their network function, such as switches, concentrators, repeaters, and transceivers, must be equipped with an 'excrescence' dedicated to administration. This also explains the paradox that an element that processes a signal at MAC or Physical level is nevertheless capable of communicating in SNMP/UDP/IP. Be careful, though, as this capacity to deal with 'high' level protocols does not change its behavior at all. Thus, a manageable hub will still forward inconsistent frames at levels 2 or 3, while on the other hand it can potentially count them to inform the administrator. Finally, note that the truly simple elements such as transceivers or media converters rarely incorporate an SNMP agent because that little complementary intelligence would represent much more than the basic function itself.

To protect itself from unwanted reading or writing requests, the agent has community names that apply to Get and Set respectively. This community name (public, by default) is in fact the only means of security available to prevent the SNMP agents from becoming the prey of hackers. We must recognize that this obstacle is very limited, all the more so because the community name is conveyed in the frames and can thus be easily pirated.

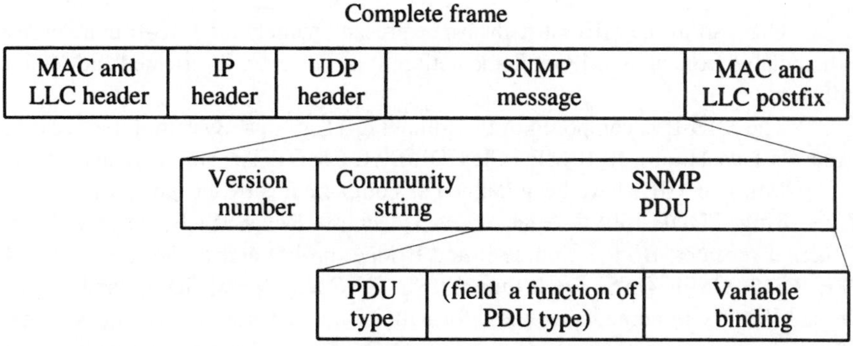

Complete frame

MAC and LLC header	IP header	UDP header	SNMP message	MAC and LLC postfix

Version number	Community string	SNMP PDU

PDU type	(field a function of PDU type)	Variable binding

Figure 15.21   Encapsulation of SNMP information.

MIBs

The management information of an element of the network is stored in a tree structure called an MIB. Via a 'pointer' (sequence of successive selections inside the tree), this MIB gives a unique access to all managed parameters. Note that, moreover, the majority of devices today opt for the set of values constituting their complete configuration to be accessible by SNMP, complementing other possible means (Telnet, console port).

The elements of information stored in the MIB conform to ISO ASN.1 (Abstract Syntax Notation) coding; they can have different formats (integer numbers, bit sequence, byte sequence, null, object identifier, sequence of).

The identifier of the position of a variable can be given as text or as numbers, thus iso.org.dod.internet.mgmt.mib.ip and 1.3.6.1.2.1.4 both correspond to the subtree of the MIB of the IP values of the observed element.

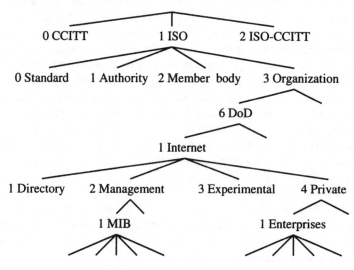

Figure 15.22   Tree structure of the database.

One part of the MIB must always be present, namely the MIB-II more or less indissociable from an SNMP implementation. It is, however, IP-oriented and seldom sufficient.

The MIB-II is composed of the following 11 groups: System, Interfaces, AT (Address Translation), IP, ICMP, TCP, UDP, EGP, CMOT, Transmission, and SNMP.

Multiple MIBs have been defined as complements by technology (Ethernet, Token Ring, FDDI, 100VG-AnyLAN, X.25, Frame Relay, ISDN, E1), by device (Ethernet repeater, Bridge, Source-Route Bridge, probe) and by protocol (BGP-4, PPP, RIP-2, OSPF, DNS, AppleTalk, CLNS, DECnet, DLSw, SDLC, and so on). These MIBs try to homogenize the information obtained from a given device type. The tendency is to implement the standard MIBs, but products develop only slowly towards this envisaged standardization. In the meantime, the devices usually have complementary MIBs that are significantly richer than their standard MIBs, with the majority of the information appearing under the branch identifying the manufacturer and its products.

SNMP V2 & V3

The principal limitation of SNMP comes from its critical lack of security. In fact, since nearly all active elements are manageable today, and the whole of their functions can be remote controlled, potentially everything can be modified in the configuration of a network via SNMP, and this for the better or for the worse. Now, the only protection relies on the community name, which is not very reassuring because in all shared LANs all traffic on all accesses is visible by default.

The second limitation of SNMP V1 lies in its master station–agent functioning model, which does not easily allow the construction of architectures involving several cooperating masters which share the management and interrogation of agents. Thus, the capability is lacking to distribute the function of the master station in a standard way. Note that this is, in spite of everything, possible by means of intermediary elements that at the same time play the role of masters for a certain number of agents, but also the role of agents for the 'superior' or 'cooperating' stations.

Thus, the development of SNMP V2 has been required in response to these limitations. Given the difficulties encountered during the process of elaborating these specifications, SNMP V3, currently in draft, should be the final solution.

RMON

Among the different MIB standards defined by the IETF, the RMON MIB (Remote Monitoring Network Management: RFC 1757) has acquired a great importance during the past few years. Its *raison d'être* was to homogenize the values that the different probes could send back, based on manufacturer MIBs up to then.

The probe is a perfectly passive element of the network, placed in observation on a significant segment. Its function is to count as many of the items it sees passing by as possible, and subsequently to respond to interrogations of a station wishing to bring this information back home. As opposed to an analyzer, which is placed because of an urgent need during some intervention, the probe is present all the time to supply the performance indicators periodically.

The underlying issue here is to provide the observation devices with a measure of intelligence to enable them to carry out a minimum of smart processing locally and to convey only a synthesis of the most significant information between probe and management station.

The RMON MIB thus defines nine (all) optional groups for Ethernet, each of which processes a given type of statistics. A tenth group has been defined for Token Ring with RFC 1513.

- Statistics
- History

- Alarms
- Hosts
- Host Top N
- Traffic Matrix
- Filters
- Packet Capture
- Events.

The statistics of the segment are the generic counters regarding the different frames, the number of bytes and the types of errors perceived on the network. These counters can be supplied in cumulative or instant values.

The History group takes the same counters as the Statistics group, but is able to display them on curves representative of the past. For this, a buffer size is defined (in number of samples). The recommended tendencies are to keep 50 samples, each representing an average of 30 seconds (total observation time: 25 minutes) or an average of 30 minutes each, giving a total time of 25 hours. Obviously, the number of samples depends on the memory size of the probe and other activated RMON groups.

The Host Table supplies the elementary counters of reception and emission of each MAC address seen on the network.

The Host Top N supplies a table of the first N stations classified according to the quantity of traffic they transmit or their emission error rate.

The Traffic Matrix supplies an indication of the quantity of traffic circulating between each pair of MAC addresses known to the probe. This is a particularly significant table because it shows the exchanges in a unitary way on the whole of the network. This group is sometimes represented graphically with the groups placed on a circle and the exchanges shown by rays of thickness or color proportional to the traffic.

The alarms allow parameters to be set for the levels that trigger automatic emission of traps (see Events group). The thresholds are defined for upward or downward crossing, and with a range value preventing hysteresis. The tested values are all counters known by the probe (including those of the Filters group), both absolute and relative.

The filters are used to trigger the beginning and/or the end of the capture of traffic which will be locally stored with the Capture group. Obviously, the filters can also be used to limit the quantity of saved frames only to the monitored flows. The filters can also be combined by logical operators.

The capture of packets is closely related to the previous group, and the parameters of this group only allow definition of size and type of buffer (circular or not), together with the stored part of each frame (the first bytes corresponding to the header, or the whole frame).

The Events group allows generation of traps under various conditions, as a function of locally managed counters (alarms), filters or changes of state: link up, link down, warm start, cold start, rising threshold, falling threshold, and packet match.

The fact that all groups are optional has left a vagueness in the manufacturers' offers in the first implementations. Today, the majority of implementations are complete (9 or 10 groups depending on the LAN), but not all groups are necessarily active at the same time.

RMON 2   The concept of RMON, which was centered on the MAC level has been brought up to the higher protocols with RMON 2 (RFC 2021). In fact, on the one hand, manipulation of MAC addresses is not easy, and on the other hand, the global statistics where frames are only distinguished by being in diffusion or by their length are not always very representative. Thus, RMON2 proposes to go into more detail of observed flows. The nine groups defined are protocol directory, protocol distribution, address mapping, network layer host, network layer matrix, application layer host, application layer matrix, user history, and probe configuration.

We can see that this MIB is applicable *a priori* to each protocol family, and that it can even have several protocols at the same time.

The clear advantage is that from now on one observes flows between logical entities and their applications (which is significantly better than what was offered by RMON behind a router) and that the consumption of bandwidth can be detailed by protocol families.

It cannot be denied that this is a substantial improvement, but it obviously requires even more processing capacity from the probe, because more intelligence is required from the agent, allowing it to convey only a synthesized and highly significant flow between agent and Manager. This surplus of traffic also has a tendency to require a dedicated device or one whose CPU is normally hardly occupied with other useful tasks.

Obviously, given the wide application spectrum, the RMON2 groups are optional, which requires a comparative study of the proposed solutions.

Monitoring software

Monitoring software is called open-platform when it can take several management software systems at a time and make them function in parallel. This is the case with OpenView by Hewlett-Packard, NetView/6000 by IBM, and Solstice by SunSoft, and also ISM by Bull, Spectrum by Cabletron, and other tools available in the telecommunications domain.

The homogenization of these solutions is making progress, to the benefit of the end user who will in the end have a connection platform on which all management products will interface with the same degree of compatibility.

Thus, the task of this software is to implement all generic mechanisms around SNMP: multi-queue logs with various filtering and event-driven action triggering (Trap received), discovery of the network at IP (and potentially IPX) level, and maintenance of a database of the discovered elements (MAC address, IP address, device type, and so on), minimum surveillance of the presence of these elements (periodical polling), help with the construction of graphs by interrogation of specific variables (or even insertion of formulae), and capacity for implementing scripts combining polling, conditions, and actions. Finally, these platforms must handle manufacturers' software capable of displaying the real configuration of a system and allowing its remote fine-tuning. The finalization of the presentation of the statistics of a device is usually supplied by the manufacturer in the form of complementary software.

Autodiscovery   The management platform should be able to discover the surrounding network by itself. For this purpose, it will listen to all network addresses it sees communicate, but it will also interrogate potential addresses. Note that the auto-discovery supplied by an open platform relies on IP addressing, and potentially on IPX addressing. The task is not to localize the machines physically, but to find out about their existence.

Thus, in addition to passive listening, which supplies a first level of information (feeble, if the management station is behind a switch), the autodiscovery process scans the range of network addresses to which the station belongs to discover all present and active elements. This interrogation is a simple ping in IP, as a function of the subnet mask.

If an element responds to the ping, the management station tries to find out if this element is an SNMP device by carrying out a Get on an elementary value of the MIB II (for example, sysObjectID in System). If this responds, the management station tries to find out if it is a terminal or a network device (repeater, hub, bridge, router). This allows a first level of classification, which is very useful for the construction of an IP cartography of the network.

If the device is a router, and if the station has the task of discovering the network beyond the routers, it interrogates the router to obtain the set of its IP addresses. Then it can go on with the same process as previously on remote networks. In order to gain efficiency, the station can also retrieve the ARP tables of the router, relieving it of part of the discovery work. In general, resorting to a rich IP device (such as a router) at an early stage of the procedure can help save time in the discovery process.

In the best case, this process runs continuously as a background task, constantly updating its knowledge of the network with the dynamic appearance of new nodes, but also the (temporary or otherwise) disappearance of certain nodes (signaled by an alarm).

MIB Browser   The MIB Browser is a simple but very useful tool. On the basis of a compiled MIB, it allows interrogation of whichever value is filled in for an SNMP agent of the network. Thus, outside the ergonomic dressing offered by manufacturers' management software, the Browser makes it possible to search for all the variables out of which the menus and windows of the final software are constructed. This capacity may appear rudimentary, but it allows not only a unitary search for certain para-meters, but also the reading of those counters that are normally not taken up and exploited. These values potentially allow one to go into more detail of the functioning of manageable devices. Associated with each counter, the comments included in the MIB are supplied for explanation. Obviously, all this is present in a simple text format which makes search and manipulation sometimes a bit unrewarding and tedious.

Finally, associated with a Browser, one often finds tools allowing the construction of graphs by periodically polling one or more values of importance for the administrator. This allows easy customizing of statistics by completing them with combinations of particular importance in this or that case.

Physical topology   The software just mentioned systematically offers a capacity of autodiscovery and automatic generation of cartography at level 3 (IP and sometimes IPX). But it cannot easily determine the Physical topology of connectivity, that is, knowledge of the exact positions of the links that connect the elements constituting each logical network: repeaters, hubs, bridges, and switches. This level of information cannot, moreover, be deduced from knowledge at the network level; it can only result from a specific dialog between the above elements.

Consequently, as a complement to the capacities of open platforms, manufacturers often supply optional software capable of returning this Physical topology, but which is really efficient in a homogeneous environment. The function relies on the remote guidance of a set of dialogs between the SNMP agents of the network devices and the correlation of all elementary pieces of information obtained.

For example, each agent of a repeater, hub, or switch emits information frames on all of its ports (simultaneously or successively, according to the capacity). In these frames in diffusion, it specifies its MAC address and, if possible, certain elements regarding the emission: number of the backplane bus (in the case of static switching), VLAN (dynamic switching), number of module and/or port, and so on. The agent possibly sends frames to itself to check the presence of third-party MAC bridges on a path.

The receipts (which have approximately the following format: device X communicates that a message coming from Y has been received on port A, module B) are sent home to the management station. In addition, since the SNMP agents generally know the MAC addresses present on each of their ports, their learning tables are also collected centrally. The fine correlation of all this information allows reconstruction of the physical topology of the connectivity, placing the different network devices inside each IP network in a way which is consistent with their real arrangement. The intelligent interpretation of the responses is clearly the core of the technology, but, because at the moment these communications are proprietary, we should understand that a heterogeneous environment would yield only a very partial result.

The exploitation of the database obtained can be carried out by displaying a general or partial physical cartography of the network, including all inter-switch, switch–hub, and inter-hub links, and possibly the MAC addresses of all stations connected to these elements. Moreover, it is usually interesting to find the effective path traveled by the frames circulating between two points. Thus, in a shared or switched environment, it is very instructive, in the event of problems on a client station, to find the path taken by the frames towards the server, since this display incorporates the repeaters, hubs, bridges, and switches traversed to link the two points. It is therefore a precious tool to help with possible troubleshooting interventions.

Others

In the following paragraphs, we will give a very brief summary of the alternatives to SNMP or complementary protocols for management and maintenance functions.

Web

Recently, the tendency of the market, initially for the management of small networks, has been to use a Web Browser as an interrogation tool for management stations, rather than an SNMP software product, which is less common and sometimes quite complicated in its use.

This technique builds on the capacity that a management agent must have to respond to an HTTP (HyperText Transport Protocol) request instead of an SNMP Get. Generally, the agents support both modes. The main difference is that the agent will be asked to make up for part of the functions of laying out the information, because the Web Browser is much simpler than an open platform completed with construction software. Thus, the SNMP agent that has become an HTTP server must know how to present the curves or events by integrating the appropriate graphics. HTML (HyperText Markup Language) serves as a format in the same way as SMI (or GDMO).

For this purpose, a slightly better suited protocol than HTTP must be developed, namely HMMP (HyperMedia Management Protocol), which must, among other things, manage security-related aspects in a more complete way.

The underlying philosophy of this technology is the desire to shift part of the synthesis and presentation work over to the agents, which must be capable of directly supplying graphical information. This new tendency should allow the involved agents to become more autonomous (mini Web servers), making better use of the local data and their own processing capacity. But it does not seem very consistent with the need to obtain 'intelligent' information from the network, assuming that it is desirable that a management system, after a minimal learning phase, should establish elaborate correlations between the events perceived to deduce the most significant information without human aid.

Downloading

The majority of network devices can receive a new version of their latest software by downloading. This allows a product to evolve by enriching its functionality, but also previous faults to be corrected dynamically. The transfer is traditionally carried out under TFTP (because by implementing SNMP, the agent does not necessarily handle the TCP protocol), where the agent places itself as a TFTP Client or Server.

Certain products also propose the FTP protocol which, as opposed to TFTP, is reliable.

Note that this transfer is generally mono-directional, most agents not being able to supply their software via the network.

A second approach of downloading concerns the configuration of devices. This means recovering the existing configuration of a product or setting all the parameters of a device in a single operation. This transfer too is carried out under TFTP. The administrator can thus save the complete configurations of all critical network components, ready to download them to virgin replacement devices in the case of failure of one of them.

Moreover, since the configuration file can be presented in text form, it is easily possible to modify and duplicate it on a workstation before sending it to a network device.

Telnet

Telnet is the virtual terminal protocol of the TCP/IP world. It allows the user to connect to any Unix workstation and many other workstations in text mode and, if the access rights are set accordingly, to carry out remotely any command whatsoever, exactly as in local mode.

Since the majority of intelligent network devices (such as routers and gateways) have a CPU and potentially a Unix kernel, they can communicate in Telnet. If all commands and variable readings (the MIB ones *a priori*) are accessible in Telnet, then, except for the unrewarding aspect of text mode, the entire device management can be realized in Telnet. The presentation of information usually follows a pull-down menu structure.

Despite the rudimentary human interface, Telnet has the advantages of universality and simplicity.

15.8 Switched network management

Introduction

Switching undeniably contributes much to local networks, but also substantially modifies their way of functioning. Consequently, certain management methods must also evolve.

The most important modification lies in the fact that, with switching, there is no longer a unifying network on which one could place oneself to observe and follow the transverse traffic, as was previously possible with coaxial Ethernet arteries, vertical Token Rings or, more recently, FDDI backbones. From now on, the core of the network resides in a box, or several boxes connected at high throughput, and the only means of finding visibility similar to that offered by an RMON probe on the connecting segment will be to place comparable, but proportionally more powerful, capacities inside the switch (the collapsed backbone) itself. Obviously, this problem mainly concerns the central switch (or switches).

As in a traditional LAN, the need for statistics is more crucial at the center of the network, and these statistics generally have greater significance.

Moreover, exactly as in a shared network, the need to know the physical topology corresponds to a tool helping with intervention and trouble-shooting. The representation of the network must integrate the switches, as well as hubs and bridges.

Statistics

Two approaches can be identified in the domain of collecting and processing statistics in a switched environment.

By port

A first, relatively conservative, approach consists in placing RMON probes on each port of the switch, either simultaneously active on all ports, or in an alternating way (so-called roving probes that can be moved virtually). Depending on the CPU capacity of the switch, it will be capable of driving several probes or only a limited number. This solution has the obvious advantage of respect for the standard, and thus provides excellent integration into heterogeneous environments, because the probes of the switch can be interrogated and exploited by every RMON management station or software.

The interest of complete respect of the standard is still more evident when the RMON probes are capable of implementing the entirety of RMON groups, including filters and captures. The latter allow frames to be analyzed in the same way as with an analyzer, but without having to move any material. But beware, capture, and redirection of traffic quickly become unrealistic with higher throughputs: 100 Mbps, full duplex, and 1 Gbps tomorrow.

Global

We must, however, note that the solution consisting of (virtual) probes on each port lacks the capacity of having a global view of all of the switched traffic. The ambition is that, in the same way that a probe placed on the connecting LAN of shared and bridges architectures initially allowed monitoring of all transverse traffic flows, there is a level of global observation per switch. This type of display could subsequently be applied to sets of ports. The display of all flows switched by a switch, or the decomposition of these traffic flows per virtual LAN, represents a particularly important notion, difficult to obtain by correlation of unitary information per port. This hierarchical level can also be used to return statistics indexed by MAC or network addresses, but once again, on the basis of the whole of the running traffic.

The advantage of these statistics also lies in the level of abstraction it supplies vis-à-vis the physical structure of the switch, since the counters of global traffic are mostly independent of the mode of functioning of the switch.

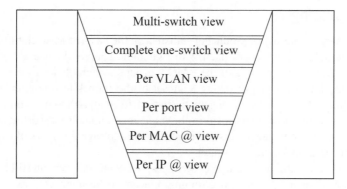

Figure 15.23   Zoom of statistics.

At an even higher level, we could also require a multi-switch view, giving the relative quantities of traffic flows for the principal switches of the infrastructure. Ideally, these counters could be capable of simply distinguishing, for each switch, their own flows and those coming from a neighboring switch. This capacity of decorrelating the flows should avoid counting several times a flow that transits multiple nodes.

In the same way that it is understandable that global statistics should be required, with even more detailed statistics at MAC level, it is reasonable that one would want to see the same thing at Network or higher level. Thus, it is desirable to have a statistics capacity comparable to RMON 2 in the heart of the switch. However, this requires substantial observation power and a level of knowledge of the protocol stacks near to that of an analyzer or a router. The monitoring component will therefore be extremely powerful in order to supply reliable counters independently of the level of decoding, closely associated with a forwarding function (high-throughput router), and thus appear as a control panel of the above-mentioned interconnection devices.

Note that, with regard to the capacity of capturing traffic to analyze it at a later time, this is only possible for a limited part of the global traffic. In fact, it is unrealistic to want to capture and temporarily store traffic that can total several Gigabps. If, on the other hand, one is only interested in traffic coming from one port, this can be realized via Port Mirroring.

Performance

In any case, it is more than desirable that measuring these statistics, whatever their richness, should have little or no influence at all on the performance of the switch, either, in the best case, because they are implemented by specific components that are independent of the transport function (ASIC and/or CPU), or because well-dimensioned thresholds do not authorize activation of more operations than can be executed without altering the proper functioning of the switch.

Port mirroring

Apart from the capability of producing statistics on the basis of network traffic, there is a second problem that poses itself with switching, namely the capture of part of the traffic. This is, in fact, one of the RMON groups, which obviously corresponds to a real need, namely that of taking a subset of the frames having circulated at a given moment back to the management station to analyze them in more detail, decoding them protocol by protocol in the manner of an analyzer. Historically, this is indeed the task of the analyzers one moved around to save the traces of exchanges that might reveal the source of a fault.

However, with the insertion of switches, while an analyzer can still be placed on a switched segment whose functioning appears to be incorrect, observing the traffic emitted and received by a machine in port switching, such as a server, has become very difficult. In order to avoid having to move systematically to change the port of the analyzer or probe (in the case of a segment), a relatively common function currently consists in providing the switch with the capability of duplicating all traffic circulating on a given port towards an observation port. Without influencing communication in any way at all, the switch is thus capable of reproducing all emitted and received frames on an observation port. This is port mirroring. This capability can be implemented in a more or less elaborate way: the switch can replicate the incoming, the outgoing, or the incoming and outgoing traffic, or the traffic of one port or several ports at a time, towards a fixed port or any port of the switch, and finally, it can do this at 10 or 100 Mbps, in half or full duplex, with the copy port similar to the port being copied or with a different speed, and so on.

Anyway, this is a functionality which is practically indispensable when troubleshooting, and it can also be used in preventive maintenance, with the full-time attachment of an analyzer on the principal switch.

Finally, the capability of copying can also be enriched by allowing the traffic to be copied on the basis of other criteria than the simple mirroring of a port, for example, by giving it the possibility to replicate a part of the global switched traffic as a function of the source or destination MAC address, or any other higher-level parameter (IP address, IP network, application, and so on).

VLAN automation

We have seen that the ideal way of constructing a VLAN was the most automatic one possible. In reality, the switch can share this function with the management station, which may have a more complete knowledge of the stations and can possibly integrate notions of security.

Thus, the switch can rely on the management station for all decisions about attaching a machine to a VLAN by simply indicating the event of mobility or appearance. From this moment on, the station can try to get to know the new station better by interrogating it directly, and decide to integrate it into that VLAN.

The station guiding the switches can be responsible for two types of function, either the completely automatic construction on the basis of a virgin situation, which seems a bit ambitious in complex environments, or the monitoring of the network, with a decision-making aid regarding each significant event: change of geographical position, change of network address, MAC address, or appearance/disappearance of a station. The software can function autonomously and report later, or may need an acknowledgment by the administrator for every action to be taken on network devices. In this case, the management station is just the guarantor of a rigorous level of supervision and observation for dynamically developing virtual LANs, and of the maintenance of an automatically updated knowledge database.

The configuration where the management station strongly interacts with the switches has the advantage of being able to make the construction criteria of a VLAN evolve almost dynamically according to the needs of the site, the structure of the network, and the protocols used.

15.9 ATM network management

As opposed to previous LAN technologies, the designers of ATM have from the very beginning provided each elementary technology with an associated MIB. This means that there are numerous standard MIBs for interrogating practically any value whatsoever involved in the functioning of an ATM component, but also that the number of MIBs to implement and manage is quite large. Thus, in addition to MIB II, we find MIB ILMI, AToM, Sonet, LAN_E, and finally ATM-RMON MIBs.

MIBS

The AToM MIB (RFC 1695) is the principal and most common MIB. Its main groups are:

- ATM interface configuration;
- ATM interface DS3 PLCP;
- ATM interface TC Sublayer;
- ATM virtual link (VPL/VCL);
- ATM VP/VC cross-connect;
- AAL5 connection performance statistics.

This MIB thus gives all the necessary information regarding VC and VP (point-to-point, point-to-multipoint, and multipoint-to-multipoint) in an interface or in a switch, and the cells circulating there. In addition, some variables are given at AAL 5 packet level.

However, one of the most significant MIBs is the ATM-RMON MIB (IETF draft and ATM Forum specifications). In fact, it mostly deals with frames and not

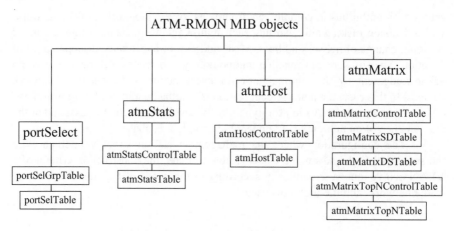

Figure 15.24 ATM-RMON MIB structure.

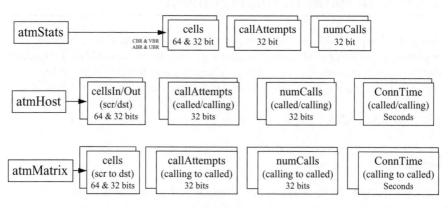

Figure 15.25 ATM-RMON MIB counters.

with cells. Now, the most easily understandable notion in remote data processing is traditionally that of a packet. Moreover, if the management tool has the capability to return information using a unit of frames, it can *a fortiori* go up another level, towards the higher protocols. This is what ATM-RMON is supposed to allow, by opening itself towards RMON 2 (Figure 15.24).

ATM-RMON takes from RMON the philosophy of presentation and remote configuration of counters, thresholds, and filters, with the ATM-RMON agent still having its own local processing and storage capacity (Figure 15.25).

Global visibility of the traffic, as is presented for the management of switched LANs, is also envisaged in ATM. A SMON MIB similar to that described in Figure 15.23 is perfectly conceivable for an ATM switch. The aim is to achieve visibility comparable to what an ATM-RMON MIB can supply, but starting from the level of a switch as a whole, before detailing the traffic flows by E_LAN, by port, and then by ATM address.

Topology

Knowledge of the topology is obviously more important the more the network relies on a narrow meshing or a multitude of elements.

Physical cartography

In the same way that construction software can return the physical topology of a (shared or switched) network, it is interesting to automatically obtain the ATM cartography of a network. This allows work to be carried out on information returned by the network instead of having to establish the layout of the network manually and keep it updated periodically. Most of the useful information can be found in the signaling tables.

We can thus imagine that in an ATM network that is at least partially P-NNI, the set of data indispensable for discovery and elaboration of the topology can be supplied by any node capable of understanding the P-NNI messages that circulate. It is nevertheless necessary that the switches carry out a translation between ATM routing protocols if there remain zones managed by IISP. The advantage of this solution lies in the use of a standard communication protocol, in a way comparable to the use one could make of SMT in FDDI.

VC Tracing

Another particularly useful monitoring tool from the point of view of maintenance and intervention is what is commonly called VC Tracing. This is software which, given two edge devices, finds out the (one or more) VC linking them, and traces their course across the network.

This operation consists in interrogating the two edge devices or the switches to which they are connected to find the circuit(s) leading from one to the other. It should also be remembered that since a VPI/VCI couple has only local significance, the software is forced to search all necessary correspondences in the signalization tables of the transit switches.

Thus, this is the typical tool to be used when perceiving degradation or anomalous functioning between two points (client station, server, LAN–ATM bridge, router). Visualization of the entire route allows one to determine immediately which active links and devices (ATM switches) could be involved.

LAN_E cartography

Some tools on the market propose a cartography specific to LAN_E elements, which we consider at 'MAC' level, vis-à-vis the physical cartography of level 1. This logical topology must allow E_LANs to be arranged as an equal number of independent networks, each E_LAN comprising one or more LES-BUS, active (and/or in load sharing) or in stand-by, and multiple LECs. All E_LANs are under coordination of an active LECS (with possible presence of emergency LECS).

The visibility of the E_LANs provides a level of abstraction more easily understandable to the administrator, because one probably gets nearer to networks of level 3 or entities managed distinctly (network for each department, and so on). In the same way, it is possible to follow the evolution of the effective population of each E_LAN, and to monitor the migrations from one network to the other.

This 'logical' topology can be obtained on the basis of the LAN_E MIBs of the different elements, potentially in a completely multivendor environment.

Port mirroring

Once again, as for a LAN switch, one can require the ATM switch to be able to replicate all cells of a port towards an observation port to which an analyzer will be connected. Since ATM is always full-duplex, part of the visibility is lost with the mirroring if the replication is only carried out in one sense (most often that of incoming traffic). Traffic in both senses is thus practically indispensable.

Moreover, since not all signalization cells are necessarily duplicated with the mirroring, it can be particularly difficult to interpret data exchanges without the signalization exchanges preceding them.

Note, however, that, as opposed to the LAN environment, the majority of ATM analyzers are capable of functioning in series on a link (they are then equipped with two ports). In this case, port mirroring is not entirely indispensable, but it avoids having to move systematically, physically handle the connectors on the switch (to insert an analyzer temporarily), and interrupt communication.

Chapter 16

Human resources

- Useful knowledge

- Day-to-day procedures

It will have become apparent that the main aim of this book is to teach about the technical and practical elements which will be useful to those confronted with the world of local area networks (and, in particular, Ethernet). However, some notes about the individuals involved in this capacity are also in order.

16.1 Useful knowledge

As shown, each stage requires different skills. While the study and design stages require a knowledge of the existing standards to retranscribe the needs expressed by the requesting entity, practical experience acquired during previous implementations is a *sine qua non* for on-site monitoring.

Thus, the principal components of each stage and the skills brought to bear by those responsible are reviewed briefly (see Table 16.1). Each step is described in slightly greater detail to show the qualities needed and the essential aptitudes.

16.2 Day-to-day procedures

Each phase in the processing can be schematized using a certain number of procedures, where it is most important to proceed methodically at all times. Although it is not easy to describe the attitude to be adopted to a question or general problem relating to local area networks, certain indications can be given.

The study stage

This stage is marked by the great freedom available to the person responsible for the study, since he or she is relatively free to move towards any particular type of technology. The only constraints are that a solution should be provided which meets all the needs expressed. In fact, in each case, several more-or-less appropriate answers may be found.

When a new file is opened, it is important that the person responsible for the network design should not start from scratch by reinventing procedures and working methods. It is thus advisable that he or she should ensure that the study phase is essentially repetitive, even if it thereby loses part of its attraction. The resulting organization will inevitably bring a speed-up in the processing and make the set of networks installed more homogeneous. Continuing in this way, one might go so far as to define an in-house doctrine which advocates the topology, the technologies, the media, the connectors, the quantities, the suppliers, and so on. This will make the study work almost automatic, once the structure of the rooms and buildings has been matched with the possibilities offered by the doctrine.

Thus, it is clear that one fundamental aspect of the work carried out during any study or analysis of a network configuration is use of the documentation. One

Table 16.1 Components and skills required.

Stage	Main actions	Useful knowledge and skills	Suitable profile
Study (description of the project)	Understanding of the needs expressed, translation into terms of real solutions	Relevant LAN standards, inherent technical constraints, association between the theory and specifics	Engineer or manager responsible
Definition (editing of the schedule of conditions)	Selection of the topology and the medium, choice of hardware	Knowledge of what is on the market, validation of the chosen solution	Engineer or manager responsible
Installation (on-site monitoring)	Verification of the quality of the installation	Practical details, professional experience (cabler)	Specialist worker
Acceptance operations	Qualification of an installation	Real operation of the network equipments	Engineer or manager responsible
Evolution and modification	Small implementation, brief acceptance	Standards/ documents, predefined procedures	Technician
Maintenance	Repairs	Mastery of existing facilities, and study method	Technician for level 1 and MAC level, engineer for overall views
Administration	Monitoring, supervision, management, parametrization	Capabilities of hardware installed, configuration of the whole network	Technician for the monitoring, engineer for the configurations

needs to know how to use the existing dossiers, and all the evolutionary stages which the project design will pass through must be laid down in practical and clear documents, which, in turn, should be easy to consult and re-use in the future.

The installation stage

This stage consists of precise specification work, which should be implementable without modification, if possible, and work to follow-up and monitor the operation.

The first point requires rigor together with a good knowledge of the problems which may be caused by the buildings or structures that will house the cables and connectors. This means that editing the detailed technical specifications is only of value if one can be almost certain that all the potential obstacles have been listed and that the solution determined has been adapted to this context.

The second point is the counterpart of the first, in other words, if the study work and the work to list the difficulties due to the surroundings noted during visits is successful, it should be sufficient to monitor the progress from a distance, ensuring only that the directions in the schedule of conditions are properly taken into account. Conversely, if the level of detail and realism of the detailed technical specifications is inadequate, it will be necessary to maintain a regular presence on the site in order to be able to answer the questions which the installers will not fail to ask when faced with unforeseen complications.

In both cases, a practical nature is called for, with rapid but rational reaction to potential pitfalls which may arise at any time. In this way, the more skilful personnel will be able to save time and materials during the laying.

The acceptance stage

The acceptance operation is carried out to ensure that the installation conforms with its description in the schedule of tasks. If one has total confidence in the subcontractor, the acceptance may be reduced to something very minor (counting of the equipment, visual check). But this also means that one is certain that the network installed will be capable of meeting the needs, despite the fact that it has not even been tested. In reality, it is always sensible to check the operation of the network before signing the agreement.

However, while the low-level (physical, MAC) tests are simple, the higher-level trials should be developed as a function of the configuration of the network and of future uses.

At the physical level, the test of all the media should be performed using an appropriate tool (coaxial or optical reflectometer, twisted-pair tester). At the MAC level, the tests should also be exhaustive and should validate the wall sockets and the media segments, and then the networks and their active elements, by an exchange of several tens of thousands of frames. Thus, it should be possible to compose the list of trials completed in a relatively systematic way.

At levels three and above the tests should prove that the network actually provides the required communication capabilities. This now involves a quantification of quality which did not exist for the lower levels, whose results are generally of the form accepted/rejected. Thus, one has to know how to judge the validity of a transmission from the delay it entails and be able to interpret the gravity of a fault reported by layer 3 or 4, and distinguish between problems due to the computer system and those due to the network. All this knowledge can only be acquired through experience and practical use of communication systems. It is imperative that the person responsible for defining the acceptance test suite should be familiar with both the computer environment which will use the network, and with the communication software which forms the interface with Ethernet.

The repair stage

Recall that the main aim of this stage is to restore the normal communications functions to the users as soon as possible, even though the repair may be provisional.

As for acceptance, there are two aspects to maintenance, depending on the OSI level investigated. The low levels can be tested and eliminated once and for all by a few simple manipulations (including a test of the medium and the replacement of a number of active elements). These interventions fall wholly within the competence of a team of technicians.

On the other hand, complex breakdowns, such as the degradation of the communication quality (if, for example, equipment is still communicating with each other, but less well than before), may occur at all levels, even at the application level (above the actual communication system). Then, global skill is needed to work towards the origin of the fault. If no-one possesses these skills, the problem will have to be studied by a number of individuals whose areas of competence are partially overlapping and complement one another.

In summary, it may be said that the knowledge required for maintenance ranges from the characteristics of the cables installed to the facilities provided by the communications software and, at the same time, covers a command of the topology and configuration of the interconnection devices. If the network is effectively very extensive, several people will be required to contribute according to the area involved as the research progresses.

Chapter 17

Documents and materials

- Documentation
- Test equipment

Up to here, procedures which permit a methodical approach from the design of a network to its installation have been described. However, studies must be prepared with the usage of reference documents, designing decisions should be made with writing of related files, and tests or acceptance operations should be conducted using suitable measurement apparatus.

Thus, certain documents and materials must be brought together in order to carry out a complete installation operation under the best conditions.

17.1 Documentation

Several types of document are useful when dealing with and monitoring local area networks. These include the purely technical documentation:

- Norms, standards and drafts describing the technologies used or envisaged
- Reviews, notes and specialized works explaining particular aspects which concern us
- Catalogs of the hardware offered by manufacturers, giving the precise characteristics and capabilities of the elements studied,

and the documentation associated with the installation:

- The original request, the schedule of conditions, the complete description of the whole installation, the acceptance schedule (when the laying of the network is complete)
- Evolutions, summaries of extensions and modifications
- A compilation of all the repairs carried out, giving, in each instance, the symptoms and the cause detected or the result of the analysis.

All these documents are useful and may be used to facilitate and improve proceedings. It is advisable to make them accessible to those likely to have to use them, whether to re-use them to refer to or to find information about the existing installation. In all cases, it is preferable that this documentation should circulate and be used profitably rather than lie dormant in a cupboard until it becomes obsolescent.

Reference documents

This category of document covers the official standards (such as those of the ISO), the standards of (generally national) research bodies (such as the IEEE), the drafts which usually precede these standards and the *de facto* standards defined by one or more manufacturers (IBM, DEC, Apple, and so on) or by a state organization (such as the DoD).

During the study and design phase, this type of work should be used to ensure that the edicts of the standard are adhered to. In this way, one can ratify the principal broad outlines of the installation prepared (topology, lengths, number of attachment points, and so on).

During the phases of industrial consultation and installation acceptance, these documents will be used to validate the work carried out (protection, insulation, quality of the grounding) and to check the conformance of the cables and hardware used (sizes of the conductors, attenuation of the segments at the operational frequency).

Books and reviews

In addition to the reference documents, there are also popularizing publications which analyze or explain a system or a protocol. These commercially available books are of variable quality, but generally have the advantage of not drowning the reader in a mass of detail of no concern to him/her, as is the case with a standard in which no points can be poorly defined. There are also complete, well-written books which can be used as an introduction to a technology. However, a search for rigor should preponderate if one is to rely on this type of written support.

In large companies, notes for internal use may provide an analogous source of knowledge, by introducing the reader to a particular technical area and providing useful explanations.

Note that these works, unlike norms and standards, may become obsolete after a few years, since the technologies implemented for a given use may have evolved considerably during this period.

Reviews have an even shorter lifetime and are only really instructive at the time of their appearance. However, the more a magazine is oriented towards a particular area of research, the longer the information remains significant. Conversely, the more the magazine focuses on the technologies, products and materials reaching the market, the more its durability will be reduced.

Reviews have the advantage that they follow the evolution of devices most closely and have an overall, essentially impartial view. Articles contrasting different solutions will encourage readers to ask themselves questions and answer with a personal opinion based on various sources of information. On this subject, it is advisable to obtain more than one magazine, and not to hesitate to buy foreign issues (American in particular).

Manuals and instructions for use

Every piece of hardware is sold with documentation of some sort. Unless this is totally devoid of interest, one should try to keep it as long as the hardware is in place.

If the element concerned is relatively simple (for example, a transceiver or a rudimentary repeater) and the manufacturer did not think it appropriate to include figures characterizing the hardware in the document, the manual will be of no use whatsoever. In all other cases, some information at least will be useful, and it is advisable to archive a copy of the manual.

In fact, it is in these documents that you will find estimates of the crossing delay for the hardware (particularly if this is better than that required by the standard), the lengths of media that can be attached and the manufacturer's recommendations for using the hardware under the best conditions (cable type, connector type, need for external ventilation, electromagnetic environment). One might also look for global characteristics such as the dimensions, the power consumption and the operating temperatures.

The instructions for use or the manufacturer's catalog may also provide information about the options available for this hardware, and the date at which it is intended to modify or update it (additional software option, module for other types of access, change of backplane). Finally, if it is a relatively complicated device (manageable hub, programmable bridge, router) the technical documentation will serve as a reference, since the configuration system and command language are nonstandard and the manufacturer's documents are the main sources in this area. This will include how to become connected (parameters of the VT100 console or definition of the management PC), the list of commands and their action, the accessible counters and their meaning, and so on. Even when the hardware can be managed via SNMP it generally has a direct access mode (serial socket) with a special dialog mode. Moreover, private MIB extensions can only be understood and used with the manufacturer's notes and descriptions. Thus, it is best for the person responsible for the monitoring, maintenance or configuration of the hardware to have read all the documentation thoroughly at least once. The web site of each vendor being a potential source of complementary or updated information.

Monitoring documents

From the original expression of requirements prior to the study to the final acceptance dossier, all the documents accompanying the phases of the network's development should be kept together. Thus, as the project progresses, one accumulates a reference document retracing all the changes made from the original request onwards. Each file contains the level of detail fixed at that stage, the progress of the implementation work or the qualification results obtained. The schedule of conditions provides a complete description of the operation, the acceptance schedule (whole network laid) confirms the required functionality, and so on.

There are two uses for this document. The first corresponds to a search for precise information on what was provided for or implemented (and which must, of necessity, be described there). This information may be useful in a repair operation (precise location of a cable or transceiver in a suspended ceiling, existence of a backup link), when an extension is required (knowledge of the exact length of a segment, position of the ends) or when studying a transformation (re-usable sections, free capacity in the patch panels). The other function this document may have is to serve as a basis for similar implementations in other buildings or on other sites. Then, if the needs of the occupants are similar, it is sufficient to take the existing documents and adapt them to the case in hand. The task will thus be less arduous and better structured from the beginning, but care should be taken to ensure that the work remains perfectly consistent with the new conditions.

Some of these documents will gain from being computerized (placed in a word processor coupled with graphics software). Thus, modules or the whole structure of important documents can be re-used and adapted to handle other similar matters, thereby saving a significant portion of the work. On the other hand, the cabling schemes and network summary will be easier to modify, and will be able to follow the real evolution of the network with regular updating. In fact, the advantage of computer support is quite clear when one needs to duplicate or manipulate the information.

Evolution cards

Once acceptance has been confirmed, so that the life of the network with its modifications and extensions can be followed, a trace of each action should be kept, together with a note of its consequences on the network monitoring documents (discussed above). This is crucial if the documents and plans are not to become obsolete and unusable within a few years. In fact, if they do not include all the changes that have taken place, they no longer represent reality and can no longer be trusted.

This concept of an up-to-date document is very important as far as the work of network maintenance teams is concerned. The value of such a scheme depends closely upon the quality of its updates. Like the documents produced at the time of the installation, modification cards can be computerized. It is most important to keep all the general documents up to date.

For minor matters (extension by a few access points, change of an active element or replacement of an interconnection device), the card may consist of a single sheet summarizing all the stages and the actions undertaken. It should include the following data:

- The entity requesting the modification (name and coordinates of the interlocutor)
- The date the request was transmitted to the relevant operational team
- Information identifying the network uniquely (technology, position, category, number)
- Description of the actions required (quantity, location)
- Person or team effectively responsible for the modification
- Sequence of actions undertaken
- List of hardware installed (type, serial number, location)
- Tests and acceptance methods and results
- Test tools used (type, serial number)
- Dates of the end of the work and completion of the intervention (signature of receipt)
- (Possibly) sub-contractor used.

In all cases, it is best to give the matter an identifier, for example, by assigning a card number.

Collation of these extension or modification cards allows one to finalize the original documentation for the network, update it and to ensure that it retains its value, which is vital to its durability.

Maintenance cards

The maintenance card is intended to provide a clear trace of each repair operation. These cards may then be used to analyze a particular type of breakdown, to improve the procedures for searching for faults or to assess the quality of the work performed by the maintenance teams. In all cases, this written trace, which can easily be archived, can be used to follow the behavior and evolution of a data communications installation.

This amounts to a formalization of the repair work, which slightly increases the work involved in dealing with incidents by making all interventions official, but which is totally indispensable for large installations (more than a few tens of workstations). The maintenance card should, preferably, consist of a single sheet and include the following main items:

Information relating to the discovery of the problem

- The date the problem was detected (and possibly the time)
- Identification of the user or group that noted the fault (allegiance, hierarchical position, phone number, office, building)
- A description of the breakdown or fault (manifestation, repetitiveness, machine concerned, network used, network technology)
- The initial surmises and deductions, whether the user has tried to solve the problem (description of attempts, results, and comments) or reference to a previous defect dealt with in the past.

Information about how the incident was dealt with by the entity responsible for the maintenance

- Date and time responsibility for the repair was assumed
- List of actions performed and tests carried out, showing the repair method used
- Conclusion and explanation of the results obtained, leading to the source of the fault or the reason for the malfunctioning (hardware responsible, incorrect parametrization, illegal configuration, over-demanding application)
- Identification of person(s) carrying out the repair (phone number), list of test equipment used (type, serial number)
- Date and time the intervention was completed.

Note that it is preferable to be able to identify each breakdown by a unique number, which can be assigned when the user requests assistance.

An example of an intervention card for an incident or a repair is shown below.

Repair no:	**Intervention card**	Maintenance contract no:	Date of commencement
Symptoms of the problem:			
Interlocutor:		Department:	
Service:	Building:	Office:	Phone:
Precise location of the network		Network identification	
Technology used	Ethernet Token Ring	LocalTalk FDDI	SNA (IBM) ATM
Type of connection to the medium	Coaxial cable Twisted pair Fiber optic	Connection device used	Repeater Bridge Switch Router
Maintenance team:			Date and time:
Description of the stages in the repair and the method used	1 2 3 4 5 6 7		
Test equiment used	type: SN:	type: SN:	type: SN:
Result of the fault		Determined origin of the fault	
Fault code:		Total time spent:	

In addition, a fault code (bottom left) may be assigned, after examination, for every breakdown; this will simplify the processing of incident cards, for example for a statistical analysis. For information, there now follows a list of codes indicating the causes of breakdowns on an Ethernet network. The code consists of a letter describing the symptoms of the fault and a number identifying the defective element:

A   Clear and definitive hardware fault
B   Clear, but non-definitive hardware fault (blocked state)

C   Transient repetitive hardware fault
D   Transient momentary hardware fault
F   Hardware wrongly configured or parametrized
G   Equipment unsuitable for function
0   No element identified (that is, the problem did not recur or unsuccessful intervention)

1X   Fault linked to the medium
     10   Standard coaxial cable (thick)
     11   Thin coaxial cable RG58
     12   AUI cable (drop)
     13   Twisted-pair cable 10/100BaseT
     14   Fiber optic cable
     15   Patch cord

3X   Fault linked to the connectors
     30   Type N connector
     31   BNC connector
     32   DB15 AUI connector
     33   RJ45 connector
     34   Optical connector (ST, SMA, SC)
     34   Patch panel

5X   Fault due to an active device
     50   NIC card
     51   Coaxial transceiver (N and BNC)
     52   10BaseT transceiver
     53   Optical transceiver
     54   Multiport transceiver
     55   FanOut
     56   Biport repeater
     57   10BaseT hub
     58   Multimedia star
     59   Passive optical star
     60   100BaseT Phy
     61   100BaseT hub

7X   Fault in interconnection device
     70   Local bridge
     71   LAN switch
     72   Layer 3 switch
     73   Remote bridge
     74   Local router
     75   Remote router
     76   Gateway
     77   Modem (and dedicated line)
     78   Repair beyond the competences of the maintenance team

Note that mostly numbers beginning with an odd digit have been used, so as to leave the manager the freedom to introduce additional codes relevant to his/her installation (if this includes networks other than Ethernet, FDDI, Token Ring, LocalTalk, and so on). For example, the following codes might be used:

60 FDDI concentrator
61 FDDI by-pass
62 FDDI concentrator
63 FDDI by-pass
80 Ethernet–FDDI bridge
81 FDDI–FDDI bridge

The clear aim of this coding scheme is to represent the progress of the complete repair in as synthetic and concise a way as possible. If need be, it could be associated with additional documents describing each action of the procedure.

Finally, precise and thorough editing of the intervention reports may help one to implement a form of preventative maintenance, simply through an analysis of the figures for recent months. Simple statistical calculations will bring to light the least reliable elements, the most fragile types of network and any hardware configurations which have disastrous repercussions on the traffic flow. Capture of the report information in a database, together with the use of automatic processing tools capable of providing a periodic synthesis of the actions and their assumed cause, may rapidly become highly efficient methods of investigation.

Thus, in parallel with the network management, intelligent use of the incident cards may provide all the pertinent information about the quality of each device and its operation. This requires the collation of the incident cards for all breakdowns that have occurred, making evident the symptoms together with the cause determined or the result of the analysis.

17.2 Test equipment

The various items of test equipment and the measurement tools were described in the last part of Chapter 12. Some of these are almost indispensable and their purchase should be provided for from the start; others are useful at certain times and should be associated with a category of well-defined tests.

Indispensable tools

Depending on the types of medium used and the extent of the network, certain pieces of equipment soon become indispensable to the maintenance of the network and to the monitoring of its operation.

The twisted-pair tester

If the network is based on building prewiring, and thus primarily uses the twisted pair, the twisted-pair tester will serve as a universal tool. It can in fact be used to qualify each pair (length, attenuation, crosstalk), to follow the cable path in wiring

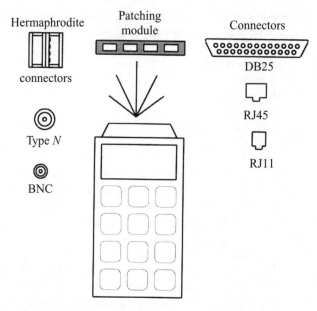

Figure 17.1 Illustration of the capabilities of a tester.

ducts and suspended ceilings, to test the ports of a 10BaseT hub, and even to measure the traffic on a network (see Figure 17.1).

It can be adapted to different types of twisted pair using various connectors (RJ45, RJ11, hermaphrodite, DB25, latch of patching module) and also to different types of coaxial cable (BNC, type N). It can output its measurement results on a printer and communicate with a PC.

This small portable and practical device is still being actively developed and regularly acquires new functions, such as the execution of all the tests adapted to the chosen medium type, with automatic comparison with the values recommended by the standard. Unfortunately, this means that its use may become somewhat complicated, given the number of menus available.

Finally, it is advisable to master the initiation of each test and the choice of parameters (medium propagation speed, test frequency, pin number, sensitivity of the measurements) before the actual operations, so that the desired characteristic can be studied effectively.

The coaxial reflectometer

If the network being maintained is based on coaxial cable (standard or thin), the coaxial reflectometer is the ideal tool for monitoring the quality of the cable impedance along its whole length (Figure 17.2).

The coaxial reflectometer is a very common dedicated device whose function is to determine the impedance curve along the medium. This curve can be used to locate points of variation, such as transceivers, straight connectors or defects

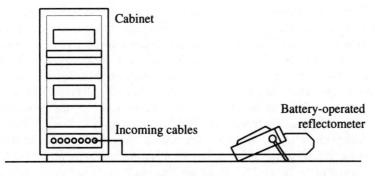

Figure 17.2   Practical measurement arrangement.

(damaged cable, bend radius too small). The coaxial reflectometer can also be used to check the terminator and that its value is correct. Note that, for the measurement of distances to be reliable, the zero must be set exactly and the signal propagation speed on the medium (which is not the same on standard and thin coaxial cables) must be entered.

Finally, to avoid deterioration of the reflectometer's receiver, it is always advisable to use a reflectometer after all the machines have been disconnected from their transceiver on the segment.

The twisted-pair tester described above can also be used to carry out a reflectometry test, but it can only give its distance from a short circuit or an open circuit. In general, it is only capable of displaying the impedance curve with low accuracy, if at all. In this case, it is said to be used as a fault locator.

The test set

If it is required to test the network above the simple physical level, the test set is the simplest tool for this function. It is easy to handle and can be used to perform elementary actions such as counting frames, errors, and collisions circulating on a network, to emit well-defined traffic (regular, consisting of identical frames), or to initiate echo mode between two sets (one master, one slave) (see Figure 17.3). These measurements rapidly provide information about the operation of the access point(s) tested, and can be used to check the transceivers, cable segments, and repeaters. While all this is being carried out it is impossible to obtain information about the contents of the frame MAC field (addresses, type, protocol or even length).

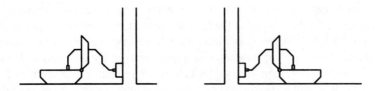

Figure 17.3   Echo mode between two network sockets.

This type of instrument is intended for use in the acceptance of virgin networks, since then the echo mode can be used without hindrance from other traffic. Conversely, when using a test set on an operational network (involving real useful traffic), care should be taken to ensure that the users are not disturbed, since its emission capabilities are relatively large. Great attention should also be paid to the function of systematic collision creation, which can easily block a network.

One way of connecting the test set without disturbing the networking too much involves linking the former to a FanOut which has previously been inserted between an existing transceiver and a station's NIC. However, one should check that one is not at the end of the network, since the FanOut has a non-negligible delay.

Furthermore, recall that certain test sets can be used in pairs to measure the Round-Trip Delay (RTD) over the whole network or between two particular points. This test is less precise than that which can be performed with a reflectometer on a coaxial-cable segment, but it has the undeniable advantage that it can be carried out on a whole network which is ready to use (or even operational, if one is not concerned about blocking the traffic for a few fractions of a second). In fact, since the test involves determining the delay between the emission of a frame and the receipt of the collision caused at the other end, the measurement effectively relates to the passage through the receivers and the multimedia stars crossed. Moreover, in reality, it corresponds to simulation of the worst case (a frame sent from one end, whose collision must reach the originating station before the latter has completed its transmission).

The optical dBmeter

This comprises a pair of devices which can be used to take a rapid measurement on an optical link. They provide unique information, namely, the total end-to-end attenuation on a link.

Fitted with a suitable source, the dBmeter can be used to emit a calibrated signal at the operational frequency (850 nm for 10BaseF) in a fiber (possibly passing through jumper cables) to ensure that the power budget authorized by the technology used is adhered to (9 dB for FOIRL, 12.5 dB for 10BaseFB).

This type of equipment is now common, because it is simple to use, robust and very practical. However, care should be taken to ensure that the jumper cables used to adapt between connectors consist of a fiber identical (diameters, numerical aperture) to that measured. If this is not the case, differences in diameter may give erroneous results, such as an increase in the power received after having crossed the fiber. Generally, it is always advisable to follow the direction of increasing diameters (which means that rays are not lost if the numerical aperture also increases every time). However, for the 'filling' of the fiber to stabilize, it is best if the jumper cables are not too short. In the other case (decreasing diameters), a portion of the luminous power is lost in each pair of connectors, independently of the attenuation due to the trajectories in the fibers themselves. In all cases, the reference measurement (which gives the 0 dB) should be performed by placing the jumper cables to be used during the trials between the source and the dBmeter.

Note the following figures:

Power budget for a link in	FOIRL	9 dB
(always at 850 nm)	10BaseFB	12.5 dB
	10BaseFP	26 dB
	10BaseFL	12.5 dB
Maximum attenuation due to the fiber	3.75 dB/km	at 850 nm
(and for FDDI	1 dB/km	at 1300 nm)
Decay due to the connectors	0.5 dB	ceramic ST
(typical values)	1 dB	plastic ST
	1.5 dB	SMA
	0.35 dB	MFO
	0.4 dB	FC
Attenuation due to a passive star	16 dB	minimum
	20 dB	maximum

In addition, one should not forget to provide for a safety margin, preferably leaving at least 1 dB, to ensure that as the components age and the connectors foul up, the link will not become unusable too rapidly.

Sophisticated measuring devices

In the case where the installation to be monitored is large or the constraints on the down time are substantial, it is better to use more complex hardware with a higher performance so that a greater range of interventions can be covered.

The network analyzer

The analyzer is the most complete network measuring tool from the MAC layer upwards. In fact, although it cannot test the physical level, it has a knowledge of all the levels from the link layer upwards.

The analyzer can provide precise and complete statistics about the traffic circulating on a network. It can monitor a particular machine, a specific exchange or a given protocol exactly. It can also record the trace of frames and calculate the distribution of traffic according to address. It can also decode the contents of packets as a function of its knowledge base, which extends up to level 7.

Thus, it is the universal tool which, once programmed, can adopt the behavior of a test set or be substituted for a probe (without necessarily providing identical means of interrogation). It may concentrate on the traffic of one station to determine whether its average error rate is acceptable or observe a router to ensure that no illicit configuration is implemented. In terms of the range of its capabilities, the analyzer is truly flexible and open to multiple uses.

However, for peaceful operation, care should be taken to use a really reliable and high-performance analyzer (necessarily expensive). Otherwise, one should first evaluate the capabilities of the analyzer using other tools to determine its limits and behavior in each mode, in case these are violated. In fact, it should be pointed out that certain devices sometimes count the traffic right up to their limiting thresholds and then only count a part, while others lose a small percentage under all conditions, where this percentage increases progressively with the load. Similarly, some devices, when they are unable to count all the frames, indicate this with a warning, although the majority do not inform the user. Finally, there also exist devices with a counter for frames seen even though they could not be captured; the validity of this counter must also be checked.

Some capabilities, such as the maximum number of stations which can be monitored concurrently, the overall size of the buffer holding the trace of the last frames seen or the number of statistical samples that can be held in memory during a long accumulation, are described in the documentation. Here again, care should be taken to parametrize the analyzer as a function of its limits in order to obtain the desired results. Recent improvements have added expert system capabilities to analyzer, giving knowledge of level 3 and 4 for in-depth analysis of all exchanges.

In conclusion, we stress that the analyzer is a very useful complete tool, although for it to be used intelligently and for the operator to obtain the maximum from it, one should be aware of its intrinsic capabilities.

The probe

The probe is a node, whose only task is to accumulate monitoring measurements about the traffic on the network segment in which it is located and to transmit these to a management system. Although similar to those of the analyzer, the capabilities of the probe are sometimes lower, not necessarily in terms of speed, but, more often, in terms of capture, storing and decoding of an arbitrary protocol. We also note that the probe can only emit information packets to the master station and cannot generally generate traffic simply to load the network.

As stated in Chapter 12, the probe became of less interest when most network equipment learnt to handle SNMP. Thus, from repeaters to routers, all devices are capable of playing the role of SNMP agent in addition to their own function. Since these devices are spread throughout the network, whose repeating, bridging and routing nodes they form, they are well placed to provide statistics about the segments on which they are located. In this context, the real probe was only of interest for small networks with no manageable equipment, or in the case where there is an ostensible desire to separate the functions of frame propagation and observation of the resulting traffic. Note that the load generated by the probe during its exchange with the master station is usually negligible, which is almost self evident since this amounts to a synthetic summary of the traffic seen. This can sometimes be a very important advantage.

More recently, the probe function regained its importance with the definition of specific very extensive RMON (remote monitoring) and RMON II MIBs, which require a large, dedicated processing capability (usually a RISC CPU with a few Mbytes of RAM). Thus, these MIBs cover all aspects of monitoring and the accumulation of statistics (with history depending on the traffic type, list of all the stations categorized, classification of the most talkative stations, presentation in the form of an intercommunication table/matrix of exchanges) together with the capture of packets using filters and the definition of thresholds for triggering alarms or operations. Furthermore, so that their hardware base can be better exploited, these probes may have several interfaces, and sometimes even provide the same services as a fixed multiport analyzer, including frame decoding by protocol (with the help of the master station and associated software).

Management hardware

Manufacturer's management systems which recover the data from the probes or other manageable equipment are evolving regularly. The reason for this change is that the quantity and level of detail of information is increasing noticeably with every new equipment release.

At present, management systems are still limited to certain areas of monitoring and to areas of (remote) configuration which are often more restricted and provide a presentation via a graphical interface over an open platform. Given the colossal development required, there are few of these open platforms on the market and their number will probably not increase. The manufacturer software available for the open platforms enriches the knowledge base by the addition of a private MIB and brings a graphical view, configuration capability and monitoring tools.

However, one should not forget that some of the devices still installed were designed outside the specifications of SNMP and all other management standards, and correspond solely to proprietary requests; this is especially true outside the LAN field. Although they do not fall in this category, SNA devices supporting NetView present the same difficulties as far as SNMP is concerned.

If one wishes to retain otherwise thoroughly satisfactory equipment of this type for a few more years, one must either use a proxy agent to act as a gateway or converter for requests and responses or find a commercially available management system which, in addition to being able to interrogate recent elements interfacing with SNMP, is also able to communicate with certain rather older devices. In some cases, the solution will be a proprietary management system which has evolved with the inclusion of new capabilities (for example, processing of packets in the SNMP format); in other cases, it will comprise recent software which also takes account of part of already existing systems.

The optical reflectometer

The optical reflectometer is a very expensive tool; thus it will be reserved for the particular needs of a team which is either involved in multiple measurement interventions on fiber optic cables, or which is responsible for qualifying active devices operating on optical fiber. Its purchase is justified in these two cases because other instruments (for example, the dBmeter and the associated source) are incapable of providing the same information. The handling of the optical reflectometer is subject to a number of constraints. The first requires a mastery of the device's operation with an understanding of the importance of all the modifiable parameters. The second is linked to the fact that measurements can only be used for reference if they are performed under reproducible conditions.

Two categories of option can be distinguished, namely, those arising during measurement and those corresponding to a logical processing applied to the curve obtained. The first category includes the power of the emitted peaks, which should be chosen as a function of the length of the fiber to be measured and the desired resolution. It also includes the limit for the length scale (distance from which the reflectometer does not retain a trace) and the number of samples used and averaged by the device to produce the curve. The second category corresponds more to display criteria or to calculations performed on the picture obtained from the reflectometry. One might estimate the attenuation due to a pair of connectors or the attenuation per kilometer of a section, change the vertical scale or record the measurement on disk. Of course, the parameters of the first category are the more important, since only they influence and modify the measurement at the time it is acquired.

As far as the measurement conditions are concerned, it is vital to have perfectly reliable adaptation jumper cables. In fact, since the reflectometer has a fixed connector, it is sometimes necessary to adapt it to that of the fiber to be measured. For this, one uses a jumper cable with one connector corresponding to that of the reflectometer and the other to that of the fiber to be tested. This implies the insertion of a length of fiber which is not necessarily identical to that which is to be measured. Here, the important thing is not so much that it should be adapted (diameters and numerical aperture), but that its quality should be such as not to attenuate or perturb the pulses emitted and the reflections returned. Nowadays, some reflectometers have a removable, interchangeable connector on the source. This simplifies matters considerably, but extreme care must be taken not to dirty the end of the fiber leading from the emitter.

The TCP/IP station

The TCP/IP station, chosen here by way of example, represents a real machine with a common stack of higher protocols. For convenience, it is assumed that it is portable (for example, notebook, with appropriate software).

As a test tool, the TCP/IP station is used to check that real traffic can circulate effectively between two access points, generally separated by at least one interconnection device (see Figure 17.4). It has the advantage over other tools in that it implements communication processes very similar to those of future end user machines.

In the case of a file transfer, the quality of the transmission is thus measured as a rate (volume in bits/total time for the operation) or in terms of the number of packets lost or the number of errors. These last two quantities may be given by a function such as *netstat* or *Etherfind* under Unix, or by reading the report from an analyzer placed in parallel on the network during the exchange. For the measurement to be sufficiently representative, it must last for a certain time. Thus, one should choose a file of at least 1 Mbyte for the transfer, to ensure that the measurement does

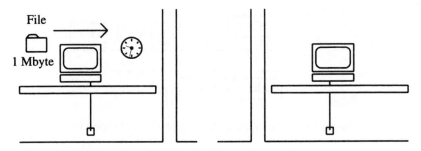

Figure 17.4 Measurement of the time taken to transmit a file over the network.

not depend upon the conditions at a single moment, but is a proper estimate of the normal capabilities of the network. The result of the test using FTP will be judged as a function of reference measurements, which can be used to determine the rate under optimal conditions (on a short, empty segment). Note that if the two stations are placed side by side, alone on a small network or on a fictitious network, the number obtained for the rate (number of bits sent divided by the transfer delay) will most certainly depend upon the capabilities of the NIC used and not on the bandwidth available on Ethernet (almost 10 Mbps under such conditions). Moreover, one needs to know the margin tolerated around the ideal element in order to decide whether the test is conclusive or proves the existence of a defect.

Another type of test may be performed using the command *telnet*, which can be used to obtain locally a connection equivalent to that of a terminal. This checks, first, that the connection is possible and, second, that the transit delays are not a hindrance, since all the screens received pass over the network. If it is desired to subject the network to a severe test, the connections may be tested under the X Window system (using an X terminal) by replacing the pages of text by graphical windows which are much more greedy in terms of bandwidth.

A simpler function that is faster to implement is the simple *ping*, which corresponds to the exchange of a packet (under the ICMP protocol) in each direction between two machines. This command is used to try to access a machine from a connection point being tested.

In the three cases, using a TCP/IP station, it is possible to pass through routers and thus reach all accessible networks. However, this means that the configuration of the test machine which moves should be updated in a consistent manner. Thus, care should be taken to ensure that the software configuration of the machine includes an IP address belonging to the sub-network in which one is situated, and that the declaration of the routers also follows.

Here, we see an advantage of the *telnet* command, which, when a remote machine cannot be reached using a *ping*, enables one to move from machine to machine or from router to router and to continually check the routing tables until the blockage point is found.

There now follows a short aside on the ARP protocol to explain the fact that, during the first interrogation attempt using the *ping* command the first packet may

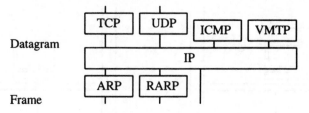

Datagram

Frame

Figure 17.5   Relationship between some DoD protocols.

normally be lost. In fact, it should come as no surprise that the first frame emitted with a view to an exchange is unanswered, if it is the only frame which does not receive an echo.

The ARP protocol has the task of finding the physical address from the logical address (which the user generally uses to denote his/ her correspondents). It is called whenever the IP layer of a machine receives data from higher protocols to be emitted to a station whose Ethernet address it does not know (see Figure 17.5). At the request of IP, ARP emits a broadcast frame at the MAC level, including the IP address sought and the coordinates of the machine which originated the interrogation. However, when IP calls ARP, it loses the packet to be transmitted and only retains the IP address sought. Thus, if this is the first frame of the *ping*, it will never receive an echo. Then, if the machine concerned is effectively accessible, it will recognize its logical address and answer the ARP address placing information in the empty fields. On receipt of this information, the enquiring machine will store the correspondence between the IP and Ethernet addresses in its ARP table; IP will be able to send the following packets without difficulty, requiring at most one access to this table.

Discussion of the TCP/IP station concludes with the remark that a simple portable PC with a standard Ethernet interface and appropriate emulation software can be used to perform various types of level 3 tests, and to measure the network performance in a mode almost identical to that of the real working environment of the users.

The optical set

Assembly equipment for optical connectors, which can be used both to assemble and also test connectors, falls slightly outsides the measuring-device area.

Since the crimping operation for optical connectors is relatively delicate, one might seek to form an in-house skill center or opt to sub-contract this type of intervention to specialist teams with long experience of the manipulations required. It is only sensible to choose the first solution if the specialists are regularly called in to carry out this kind of specific operation (much more than ten times a year).

Qualification hardware

The qualification and validation of hardware is slightly outside the area of test and measurement. This activity should be undertaken from the study stage for a network, in order to develop the global solution as a function of the equipment which will be involved.

In fact, even though all devices claim to meet the standard, not all devices have the same capabilities, whether in terms of performance or of the capacity for evolution. Thus, it is often useful to examine the products on the market before making one's choice. This becomes all the more important as the investment becomes larger.

Selection of equipment

Whether for active network devices (repeaters, hubs, stars), interconnection devices (bridges, routers) or, more simply, cabling components (plug, socket, cable, duct, patching system, jumper cable), the best choice of a specific element, a manufacturer or a particular source will follow a serious comparative evaluation of the qualities of the element. Prior to the establishment of the detailed technical specifications, the results of qualification tests will determine the products upon which an effective implementation of the network will depend.

This test and validation function for hardware for local area networks may be undertaken by a specialist team centralizing all the qualification needs of the enterprise; otherwise, if no such structure exists, responsibility for it may fall to the editor of the detailed technical specifications.

Test platforms may be installed during a large project, with a view to reproducing realistic conditions for the operation of the future network using a representative model of the whole communication chain envisaged.

Often, the experimenter will have to compare devices in order to select one, without having access to an appropriate qualification method. In this case he/she will have to develop test procedures adapted to his/her objective and to the equipment to be validated. Here is some general advice which may help in this task.

First, he/she must identify the essential characteristics of the device; attempts should be made to restrict these to, for example, ten points. He/she will then be able to rank these in order of importance (bearing in mind the possible real conditions under which the element may be used). He/she will then have to construct the trial configurations which will enable him/her to carry out the measurements successfully and to evaluate the desired capability effectively (see Figure 17.6). He/she will have

Table 17.1 Classification of equipment according to two criteria: OSI level and number of ports.

	Monoport device	Biport device	Multiport device
Physical level	Transceiver	Repeater	Hub Multimedia star
MAC level	Test set	Bridge	Bridge/Switch
Network level and above	Analyzer probe	Router gateway	Router Layer 3 switch

to ensure that he/she is actually measuring the desired characteristic and that the latter is not hidden by the performance of another element of the chain or by the test device itself. The more test equipment he/she has, the easier he/she will find it to develop the assembly; however, rigorous qualification does not necessarily depend upon an abundance of devices. It is often the method that determines the quality of the measurement, and one should not forget that it is vital to be fully aware of the capabilities of the measuring devices and their limitations.

Although each category of equipment is quite different, the test and evaluation methods do have points in common. These may be classified as follows. The set of tests will be put together based on two criteria. Very globally, monoport devices will be assessed using incoming or outgoing traffic, biport devices will be subjected to transfers, which may be bidirectional, and multiport devices will be subjected to multiple simultaneous transfers. The physical-level elements will be qualified according to their respect for the characteristics described in the standard, MAC-level devices will be judged according to their performance, and equipment at level 3 or above will be evaluated according to the richness of the capabilities offered.

For example, to evaluate local Ethernet bridges or routers, one should first try to verify the filtering and retransmission rates given in the manufacturer's documentation. For this category of test, the following points may be measured:

- Initialization time when switched on
  Variation of this delay as a function of the network load.

- Observation of the traffic emitted by the isolated bridge or router (STP, ARP, RIP frames).

- Crossing delay
  Minimum crossing delay (regular low load)
  Crossing delay under heavy load (at the limiting threshold)
  Regularity of the crossing delay for heterogeneous traffic.

- Curve of maximum transfer (homogeneous frames, fixed-length frames)
  Abscissa: frame length of the traffic to which the bridge is subjected
  Ordinate: maximum load supported without loss (in frames/s) (usually the upper limit on the performance of a bridge is given in frames/s, almost independently of the frame lengths: from 64 to 1518 bytes).
  Measurement of the percentage of the traffic lost when the load crosses the threshold.

- Study of the variations in the maximum transfer rate for heterogeneous traffic
  Bursty traffic, with a mean value below the loss threshold
  Traffic consisting of frames with multiple destination addresses
  Traffic partially intended for a local destination.

- Measurement of the transfer rate for bidirectional traffic.

- Validation of the 'natural' filtering
  Number of frames used in bridge learning (0 or 1)
  Reaction to a frame with broadcast source address (meaningless)
  Effect of changing from one side of an emitting machine to another.

Readers will naturally appreciate that the most important of these criteria is the maximum retransmission rate and its stability under arbitrary traffic (heterogeneous, irregular). A bridge which collapses when subjected to an excessively heavy load (percentage of losses increasing considerably after the threshold is crossed) should be avoided.

Finally, for a programmable device, one might also test:

- The accuracy of the counters and the difference from reality
  for a weak or average load (supported)
  for traffic including defective frames
  for the maximum load before the threshold is crossed
  for a load above the threshold
  for heavy traffic with a local destination (no retransmission).

- Changes in the performance after implantation of filters (evaluation of the new limiting threshold for short-frame traffic)
  for a single loaded filter (various types of filter to be tested)
  for the maximal combination of filters.

The diversity of measurements envisaged is such that it is left to the reader to develop the series of tests best adapted to his/her needs and environment, based on the few ideas presented above.

If no test method can be implemented, one should rely on reviews and evaluations given in the specialist technical press. The fact that test methods are generally described in parallel with the results means that one should only believe measurements performed consistently and rigorously. However, note that the most common products are generally of high quality, since they have passed the selection process of several large clients to achieve top positions in the market place. Moreover, the size of the manufacturer ensures that its products and their follow-up have a minimum durability. Conversely, the cheapest products rarely lack faults.

Those wishing to test and qualify network equipment should be aware that some trials require particular measuring devices in addition to the test tools discussed above. The main ones are discussed below.

The oscilloscope

The oscilloscope is a basic device for measuring the time taken to cross an arbitrary element; it can be fitted on a coaxial cable segment, a drop cable or a twisted pair. Thus, it is indispensable for the qualification of physical-level equipment (transceivers, FanOut or repeater) whose emission levels and reception thresholds have to be checked. In fact, it conveniently gives signal voltages, displays the rise and fall times and shows their regularity. All these parameters should respect the figures given in the standard. Moreover, it is essential for measuring the crossing delay of most equipment and can be used to monitor the regularity of retransmissions by equipment using visual comparison of the traffic entering and leaving it. To detect

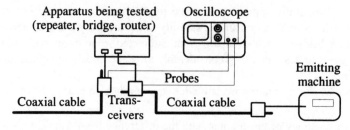

Figure 17.6   Configuration for measurement of the crossing delay.

frames and identify them on input and output, it is advisable to use traffic consisting of frames with slightly different lengths or data field pattern.

The oscilloscope can also be used to sample the electrical signals of optical devices (transceiver, repeater) just before the stages of emission or receipt. In this case, one has to be enterprising and competent enough to open the box and work directly on the electronic circuits without risk of causing their deterioration.

The multiport analyzer

Several multiport analyzers are now available commercially. These generally have an Ethernet and a Token Ring port (see Figure 17.7). However, some also have an FDDI, 100BaseT, ARCnet or LocalTalk interface and/or a serial V.24, V.35, ISDN, Frame Relay, X.25 or (more recently) ATM link. If the ports listed above are numerous, the device will have a modular construction (for example, on a PC base) such that each attach-ment card can be purchased separately.

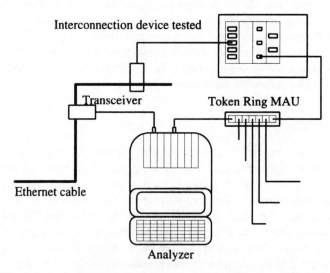

Figure 17.7   Schematic illustration of a biport modular Ethernet–Token Ring analyzer.

The main advantage of this device lies in the fact that the software processing the protocol suite is unique and, hence, the user interface always remains the same whatever type of connection is used. Moreover, if one invests in supplementary decoding modules or in proprietary add-ons to interpret the contents of the packets, this will be executable independently of the NIC. Thus, the tool can be viewed as an almost universal analyzer, in which only one piece has to be changed to adapt to current needs.

Finally, there also exist top-of-the-range analyzers which can activate two of their physical ports simultaneously and operate on the two interfaces in parallel (acquisition of traffic, emission of frames, statistics for each network). This function is typically used to check the work carried out by an interconnection device (repeater, local bridge, router, gateway). In fact, it is easy to monitor the retransmission of each packet by observing the data present on input to and output from the device. When these devices accept interface cards for different technologies, they can be used to test the operation of all the interconnection equipment (remote bridge, bridge between two types of LAN, multimedia router) and to qualify these in a practical and rigorous manner. One other use may be to employ the two connections on a single network to load it in one area with the frames one desires and to observe its behavior under this emission by another access point.

The optical attenuator

There is a tool for testing the transmissions on optical lines by artificial simulation of a decay, namely the optical attenuator. This relatively simple instrument can be used to establish a predefined attenuation between two connectors and so to measure the level of decay up to which active equipment placed at the ends can continue to communicate. This kind of apparatus is ultimately intended mainly to check that the devices operating on optical links are able to read their respective signals correctly when the maximum attenuation is inserted between them.

Conclusion

Whatever test devices the intervention or qualification team has at its disposal, it should also have a set of small items of equipment which will always be useful. These include:

- A pair of reliable IEEE 802.3 transceivers (tested beforehand) with removable and, if possible, interchangeable PMA (BNC, double BNC, double type *N* or tapped).
- 10BaseT transceivers and, if necessary, optical transceivers.
- A few 2.5 m sections of standard coaxial cable with connectors at each end, plus a long section to insert a decay if required.
- A few sections of thin coaxial cable with connectors at each end.
- Straight RJ45–RJ45 lines and a few crossed lines (12–36 for 10BaseT).

- A few AUI cables (preferably of different lengths, from 2 to 30 meters), consisting of five twisted pairs.

- A few smaller connector elements of type *N*, BNC and RJ45: T, straight male–male connector, straight female–female connector, *N*–BNC adapter, crossed connector.

- One or two biport or quadriport transceivers or a small FanOut (using the power supply from the AUI cables, if possible) to connect a test set, analyzer or probe without difficulty.

- Material for cleaning optical connectors if the site has optical cables.

- Coaxial and RJ connectors for crimping with the appropriate pliers (if the skills of the team cover this aspect).

Generally speaking, it is always possible to keep a stock of either the most vulnerable (jumper cables, transceivers) or the most common (balun, coaxial connectors) basic elements. If adaptation leads may be needed between different interfaces (RJ11, RJ45, hermaphrodite, DB9, BNC, type *N* and various patching panels) it is best to carry at least one sample of each type, or even the whole range if this is not too large.

Bibliography

Albert, Bernhard and Jayasumana, Anura P. (1994). *FDDI and FDDI-II, Architecture, Protocols and Performance*. Artech House.

Comer, Douglas E. (1995). *Internetworking with TCP/IP, Volume 1, Principles, Protocols, and Architecture*. Prentice Hall.

De Pricker, Martin (1995). *Asynchronous Transfer Mode, Solution for Broadband ISDN*. Prentice Hall.

Ferréro, Alexis (1996). *The Evolving Ethernet*. Addison-Wesley.

Lynch, Daniel C. and Rose, Marshall T. (1993). *Internet System Handbook*. Addison-Wesley.

Macchi, César and Guilbert, Jean-François (1987). *Téléinformatique, Transport et traitement de l'information dans les réseaux et systèmes téléinformatiques et télématiques*. Dunod.

Malamud, Carl (1992). *Stacks, Interoperability in Today's Computer Networks*. Prentice Hall.

Miller, Mark A. (1992). *LAN Protocol Handbook*. M&T Books.

Perlman, Radia (1992). *Interconnections, Bridges and Routers*. Addison-Wesley.

Stalling, William (1993). *Local and Metropolitan Area Networks*. Macmillan.

Stalling, William (1993). *Networking Standards, A Guide to OSI, ISDN, LAN and MAN Standards*. Addison-Wesley.

Standards

Listed below are the main documents, ordered by organization, and therefore by technology.

IEEE

IEEE Std 802-1990 – Local and Metropolitan Area Networks – 802 – Overview and Architecture

P802/D25-Feb1998 – Draft Standard 802: Overview and Architecture

IEEE Std 802.1B-1992 – Local and Metropolitan Area Networks – 802.1B – LAN/MAN Management

P802.1D-May1998 – Draft Standard for Media Access Control (MAC) Bridges (Common Base Text for revisions detailed in P802.1d and P802.1p)

IEEE Std 802.1E-1990 – Local and Metropolitan Area Networks – 802.1E – System Load Protocol

P802.1G-May1995 – Draft Standard for Remote MAC Bridges

IEEE Std 802.1H-1995 – Local and Metropolitan Area Networks – 802.1H – Recommended Practice for Media Access Control (MAC) Bridging of Ethernet V2.0 in IEEE 802 Local Area Networks

P802.1p-Mar1998 – Draft Standard for Local and Metropolitan Area Networks – Supplement to Media Access Control (MAC) Bridges: Traffic Class Expediting and Dynamic Multicast Filtering (integrated in P802.1D)

P802.1Q-Jul1998 – Draft Standard for Local and Metropolitan Area Networks: Virtual Bridged Local Area Networks

IEEE Std 802.3u-1995 – Local and Metropolitan Area Networks – 802.3u – Supplement to Carrier Sense Multiple Access with Collision Detection (CSMA/CD) Access Method and Physical Layer Specifications – Media Access Control (MAC) Parameters, Physical Layer, Medium Attachment Units, and Repeater for 100 Mb/s Operation, Type 100Base-T

P802.3x-Mar1996 – Local and Metropolitan Area Networks – 802.3x – Supplement to Carrier Sense Multiple Access with Collision Detection (CSMA/CD) Access Method and Physical Layer Specifications – Specification for 802.3 Full Duplex Operation

P802.3z-May1998 – Local and Metropolitan Area Networks – 802.3z – Supplement to Carrier Sense Multiple Access with Collision Detection (CSMA/CD) Access Method and Physical Layer Specifications – Media Access Control (MAC) Parameters, Physical Layer, Repeater and Management Parameters for 1000 Mb/s Operation

P802.3ab-Jun1998 – Local and Metropolitan Area Networks – 802.3ab – Supplement to Carrier Sense Multiple Access with Collision Detection (CSMA/CD) Access Method and Physical Layer Specifications – Physical layer specification for 1000 Mb/s operation on four pairs of Category 5 or better balanced twisted pair cable (1000Base-T)

P802.3ac-Feb1998 – Local and Metropolitan Area Networks – 802.3ac – Supplement to Carrier Sense Multiple Access with Collision Detection (CSMA/CD) Access Method and

Physical Layer Specifications – Frame Extensions for Virtual Bridged Local Area Networks (VLAN) Tagging on 802.3 Networks

IEEE Std 802.5c-1991 – Local and Metropolitan Area Networks – 802.5 Supplements – Recommended Practice for Dual Ring Operation with Wrapback Reconfiguration

P802.5r-Nov1996 – Supplement to – Information technology – Telecommunications and information exchange between systems – Local and metropolitan area networks – Specific requirements – Part 5: Token Ring Access Method and Physical Layer Specifications – Dedicated Token Ring Operation

P802.5t-Mar1998 – Supplement to – Information technology – Telecommunications and information exchange between systems – Local and metropolitan area networks – Specific requirements – Part 5: Token Ring Access Method and Physical Layer Specifications – 100 Mbit/s Dedicated Token Ring Operation Over 2-Pair Cabling and Optical Fiber

IEEE Std 802.9-1994 – Local and Metropolitan Area Networks – 802.9 – Integrated Services (IS) LAN Interface at the Medium Access Control (MAC) and Physical (PHY) Layers

IEEE Std 802.9a-1995 – Local and Metropolitan Area Networks – 802.9 Supplements – Integrated Services (IS) LAN Interface at the Medium Access Control (MAC) and Physical (PHY) Layers – Specification of ISLAN16-T

IEEE Std 802.10e-1993 & IEEE Std 802.10f-1993 – Local and Metropolitan Area Networks – 802.10 Supplements Secure Data Exchange (SDE) Sublayer Management & Recommended Practice for SDE on Ethernet V2.0 in IEEE 802 LANs

IEEE Std 802.10-1992 (includes IEEE Std 802.10b-1992) – Local and Metropolitan Area Networks – 802.10 – Interoperable LAN/MAN Security (SILS)

P802.11D2.0-Jul1995 – Local and Metropolitan Area Networks – 802.11 – Wireless LAN Medium Access Control (MAC) and Physical Layer (PHY) Specifications

IEEE Std 802.12-1995 – Local and Metropolitan Area Networks – 802.12 – Demand Priority Access Method, Physical Layer and Repeater Specification for 100 Mb/s Operation

IETF

RFC 826 – 1982-11 – Ethernet Address Resolution Protocol: Or converting network protocol address to 48 bit Ethernet address for transmission on Ethernet hardware

RFC 894 – 1984-04 – Standard for the transmission of IP datagrams over Ethernet networks

RFC 1042 – 1988-02 – Standard for the transmission of IP datagrams over IEEE 802 networks

RFC 1155 – 1990-05 – Structure and identification of management information for TCP/IP-based internets

RFC 1157 – 1990-05 – Simple Network Management Protocol (SNMP)

RFC 1188 – 1990-10 – Proposed standard for the transmission of IP datagrams over FDDI networks

RFC 1213 – 1991-03 – Management Information Base for network management of TCP/IP-based internets: MIB-II

RFC 1390 – 1993-01 – Transmission of IP and ARP over FDDI Networks

RFC 1483 – 1993-07 – Multiprotocol Encapsulation over ATM Adaptation Layer 5

RFC 1513 – 1993-09 – Token Ring Extensions to the Remote Network Monitoring MIB

RFC 1695 – 1994-08 – Definition of Managed Objects for ATM Management Version 8.0 using SMIv2

RFC 1700 – 1994-10 – Assigned Numbers

RFC 1735 – 1994-12 – NBMA Address Resolution Protocol (NARP)

RFC 1754 – 1995-01 – IP over ATM Working Group's Recommendations for the ATM Forum's Multiprotocol BOF Version 1

RFC 1755 – 1995-02 – ATM Signaling Support for IP over ATM

RFC 1757 – 1995-02 – Remote Network Monitoring Management Information Base

RFC 1932 – 1996-04 – IP over ATM: A Framework Document

RFC 1953 – 1996-05 – Ipsilon Flow Management Protocol Specification for IPv4 Version 1.0

RFC 1954 – 1996-05 – Transmission of Flow Labelled IPv4 on ATM Data Links Ipsilon Version 1.0

RFC 1987 – 1996-08 – Ipsilon's General Switch Management Protocol Specification Version 1.1

RFC 2021 – 1997-01 – Remote Network Monitoring Management Information Base Version 2 using SMIv2

RFC 2022 – 1996-11 – Support for Multicast over UNI 3.0/3.1 based ATM Networks

RFC 2205 – 1997-09 – Resource ReServation Protocol (RSVP) – Version 1 Functional Specification

RFC 2226 – 1997-10 – IP Broadcast over ATM Networks

RFC 2297 – 1998-03 – Ipsilon's General Switch Management Protocol Specification Version 2.0

RFC 2400 – 1998-09 – Internet Official Protocol Standards

RFC 2331 – 1998-04 – ATM Signalling Support for IP over ATM

RFC 2332 – 1998-04 – NBMA Next Hop Resolution Protocol (NHRP)

RFC 2334 – 1998-04 – Sever Cache Synchronization Protocol (SCSP)

RFC 2362 – 1998-06 – Protocol Independent Multicast-Sparse Mode (PIM-SM): Protocol Specification

draft-ietf-rmonmib-smon-04.txt – 1997-10 – Remote Network Monitoring MIB Extensions for Switched Networks Version 1.0

draft-ietf-snmpv3-next-gen-arch-05.txt – 1997-09 – An Architecture for Describing SNMP Management Frameworks

ANSI

ANSI X3.139-1987 – for information systems – Fiber Distributed Data Interface (FDDI) – Token Ring Media Access Control (MAC)

ANSI X3T9.5: 88 – 139 – 1992-12 – for information systems – Fiber Distributed Data Interface (FDDI) – Media Access Control (MAC-2)

ANSI X3T9.5: 88 – 148 – 1992-06 – for information systems – Fiber Distributed Data Interface (FDDI) – Physical Layer Protocol (PHY-2)

ANSI X3T9.5: 88 – 155 – 1989-06 – for information systems – Fiber Distributed Data Interface (FDDI) – Single-Mode Fiber Physical Layer Medium Dependent (SMF-PMD)

ANSI X3.186 – 1991-05 – for information systems – Fiber Distributed Data Interface (FDDI) – Hybrid Ring Control (HRC)

ANSI X3.263 – 1995-03 – for information systems – Fiber Distributed Data Interface (FDDI) – Twisted Pair Physical Layer Medium Dependent (TP-PMD)

ANSI X3T9.5/84-49 – 1992-12 – for information systems – Fiber Distributed Data Interface (FDDI) – Station Management (SMT)

ANSI X3.237 – 1995-01 – for information systems – Fiber Distributed Data Interface (FDDI) – Token ring low-cost Fiber Physical Layer Medium Dependent (LCF-PMD)

ATM Forum

AF-LANE-0021.000 – 1995-01 – LAN Emulation Over ATM, Version 1.0

AF-LANE-0084.000 – 1997-07 – LAN Emulation Over ATM, Version 2 – LUNI Specification

BTD-LANE-LNNI-02.12 – 1998-05 – LAN Emulation Over ATM, Version 2 – LNNI Specification – Draft 12

AF-MPOA-0087.000 – 1997-07 – Multi-Protocol Over ATM, Version 1.0

AF-NM-TEST-0080.000 – 1997-05 – Remote Monitoring MIB Extensions for ATM Networks

AF-PNNI-0055.000 – 1996-03 – Private Network-Network Interface, Specification Version 1.0

BTD-PNNI-02.00 – 1997-09 – Private Network-Network Interface, Specification Version 2.0

BTD-PNNI-PAR-01.02 – 1997-12 – PNNI Augmented Routing (PAR) Version 1.0

BTD-PNNI-IPNNI-01.00 – 1996-12 – Integrated PNNI (I-PNNI) v1.0 specification

AF-UNI-0010.001 – 1993-09 – ATM User-Network Interface (UNI) Specification, Version 3.0

AF-UNI-0010.002 – 1994-09 – ATM User-Network Interface (UNI) Specification, Version 3.1

AF-SIG-0061.000 – 1996-07 – ATM User-Network Interface (UNI) Signalling Specification, Version 4.0

AF-ILMI-0065.000 – 1996-09 – Integrated Layer Management Interface (ILMI) Specification, Version 4.0

AF-TM-0056.000 – 1996-04 – Traffic Management Specification, Version 4.0

AF-PHY-0015.000 – 1994-09 – ATM Physical Medium Dependent Interface Specification for 155 Mb/s over Twisted Pair Cable

AF-PHY-0018.000 – 1994-09 – Mid-range Physical Layer Specification for Category 3 Unshielded Twisted Pair

AF-PHY-0040.000 – 1995-11 – Physical Interface Specification for 25.6 Mb/s over Twisted Pair Cable

AF-PHY-0046.000 – 1996-01 – 622.08 Mbps Physical Layer Specification

AF-PHY-0047.000 – 1994-09 – 155.52 Mbps Physical Layer Specification for Category 3 UTP

AF-PHY-0079.000 – 1997-05 – 155 Mbps Plastic Optical Fiber and Hard Polymer Claf Fiber PMD Specification

AF-VTOA-0078.000 – 1997-01 – Circuit Emulation Service, Interoperability Specification, Version 2.0

AF-VTOA-0083.000 – 1997-05 – Voice and Telephony Over ATM at the Desktop Specification

AF-VTOA-0089.000 – 1997-07 – Voice and Telephony Over ATM, ATM Trunking Using AAL1 for Narrow Band Services, Version 1.0

ISO

ISO 8802-2 – 1994-12 – Information technology – Telecommunications and information exchange between systems – Local and metropolitan area networks – Specific requirements – Part 2: Logical Link Control

ISO 8802-3 – 1996-07 – Information technology – Telecommunications and information exchange between systems – Local and metropolitan area networks – Specific requirements – Part 3: Carrier Sense Multiple Access with Collision Detection (CSMA/CD) Access Method and Physical Layer Specifications

ISO 8802-4 – 1990-07 – Information technology – Telecommunications and information exchange between systems – Local and metropolitan area networks – Specific requirements – Part 4: Token-passing Bus Access Method and Physical Layer Specifications

ISO 8802-5 – 1995-12 – Information technology – Telecommunications and information exchange between systems – Local and metropolitan area networks – Specific requirements – Part 5: Token Ring Access Method and Physical Layer Specifications

ISO 8802-6 – 1994-03 – Information technology – Telecommunications and information exchange between systems – Local and metropolitan area networks – Specific requirements – Part 6: Distributed Queue Dual Bus (DQDB) Access Method and Physical Layer Specifications

ISO 9314-1 – 1989-04 – Information processing systems – Fiber Distributed Data Interface (FDDI) – Part 1: Token Ring Physical Layer Protocol (PHY)

ISO 9314-2 – 1989-05 – Information processing systems – Fiber Distributed Data Interface (FDDI) – Part 1: Token Ring Media Access Control (MAC)

ISO DIS 9314-3 – 1988-04 – Information processing systems – Fiber Distributed Data Interface (FDDI) – Part 3: Physical Layer Medium Dependent (PMD) requirements

ISO DIS 11801 – 1994-01 – Information technology – Generic cabling for customer premise cabling

Others

AMD/Chipcom/DEC/Motorola/SynOptics – 1991-05 – An Interoperable Solution For FDDI Signaling Over Shielded Twisted Pair

Cornell University – 1996-10 – Cells in Frames Version 1.0: Specification, Analysis, and Discussion

Digital/Intel/Xerox – 1982-11 – The Ethernet – A Local Area Network – Data Link Layer and Physical Layer Specifications, Version 2.0

IBM – 1989-09 – Token-Ring Network – Architecture Reference

IBM – 1992-04 – Token-Ring Network – Supplement for Operation with Unshielded Twisted-Pair Lobes

IBM – 1996-11 – HPR Extensions for ATM Networks

IEC 907 – 1989-04 – Local Area Networks CSMA/CD 10 Mbit/s Baseband Planning and Installation Guide

WinSock – 1996-05 – Windows Sockets 2, Protocol-Specific Annex, Revision 2.0.3

Glossary

Access procedure Procedure or protocol used to obtain access to a shared resource. In a local area network, the shared resource is the medium.

Acknowledgment Positive acknowledgment in a transmission procedure.

ACSE Association Common Service Element, lower part of layer 7, standardized by ISO 8649 (service) and 8850 (protocol) or CCITT X.227. This service element is used to enable applications (such as FTAM) to establish and break logical connections with similar entities. Its position is shown in Figure G.1.

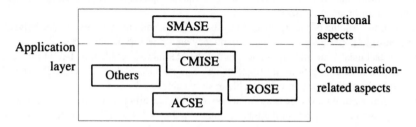

Figure G.1 Cross section of level 7 and positions of several blocks.

Address Sequence of bits (six bytes for Ethernet) which identifies the source or the destination of a data packet.

AFNOR Association Française de Normalisation. French standardization body, member of the ISO.

Analyzer Device for monitoring and measuring the signal or the information exchanged on a transmission channel. In telecommunications, the different types of analyzer check the structure of the data in addition to the signal itself and are able to decode the contents of the packets.

ANSI American National Standards Institute. US standardization body, member of the ISO.

AppleTalk Communication protocol covering layers 3 to 5 defined by Apple for its networks, based on LocalTalk, Ethernet (EtherTalk) or Token Ring (TokenTalk). The AppleTalk address, represented in decimal, consists of 24 bits, 16 for the network number and 8 for the node number. The corresponding Ethernet type field is 809B.

APPN Advanced Peer-to-Peer Networking. Architecture implemented by IBM to interlink its small and medium-size system (AS/400, PS/2) within the SNA framework.

ARCnet Attached Resources Computer Network is a non-standardized local area network with the DATAPOINT Token Bus. It operates at 2.5 Mbps in the standard version (20 Mbps in the latest version) with less than 256 machines on coaxial cable (RG-62, 93 Ohm), twisted pair, and optical fiber. Reliable and inexpensive, it was very common in the USA.

ARP Address Resolution Protocol. Protocol used to find the correspondence between IP and Ethernet addresses, defined by RFC 826 and 925. The corresponding Ethernet type field for an ARP frame is 0806.

ASCII American Standard Code for Information Interchange. The code, which has seven bits plus the parity bit, was established to obtain compatibility of services in data exchange. Very common.

ASN.1 Abstract Syntax Notation 1, CCITT recommendation of 1984, standardized by ISO 8824 and 8825 (CCITT X.208 and 209). Specification language which can be used to give a complete and unambiguous description of all types of data or information circulating at the level of the application-level protocols. ASN.1 has also been used to specify application protocols which have now been standardized.

Asynchronous Data transmission mode in which each character or block of characters has its own synchronization (no prior synchronization between the emitter and receiver). In start–stop operation start and stop bits are used to indicate the beginning and end of each character or group of characters transmitted.

ATM Asynchronous Transfer Mode. Fast cell-switching technique which decomposes the input data into fixed-length packets (the cells) multiplexed on the same circuit so that the use of the bandwidth of high-rate channels can be optimized. This technology will be retained for broadband ISDN.

Attenuation Fading of the signal as it travels along the medium, measured in decibels (dB). Increases in importance as the signal frequency and trajectory length increase.

AUI Attachment Unit Interface cable linking the Medium Access Unit (MAU) to the computer NIC. The connections are made using 15 point sockets with a slide latch. The AUI cable is also called the transceiver cable or drop cable.

AWG American Wire Gauge is an American unit for measuring the diameter of a conductor. The conversion formula is of the type: diameter in mm $= A \times \text{coeff}^{AWG}$, where $A \sim 8.28$ and coeff ~ 0.89.

Backbone Represents the main artery of a network.

Backoff Algorithm used by the Ethernet MAC interface to restart the emission of a frame in the case where a collision has occurred during the previous attempt to emit this frame on the network.

Balun Comes from BALanced–UNbalanced, impedance adaptation element for connecting two different media.

Bandwidth Interval of frequencies dedicated to the channel or data communication system.

Baseband Transmission of an unmodulated data signal such as that generated by the digital circuit in its original frequency band.

Baud From Baudot, inventor of the telegraphic code. Unit to quantify the rate of transfer of symbols. Number of symbols (not necessarily bits) transmitted per second.

BBN Bolt, Beranek, and Newman, Inc. Company responsible for the development of the ARPANET.

BCD Binary Coded Decimal, four-bit coding scheme for decimal numbers (0–9).

BCS Bull Cabling System, cabling system offered by the French computer manufacturer Bull, which is based on various types of cable (including Bull A 2 with four pairs) and a specific patching system (BCS 1 and 2).

BERT Bit Error Ratio Test used to evaluate the quality of a data transmission line, defined by the CCITT.

Big-endian Order of transmission for bytes or bits in serial mode, beginning with the Most-Significant Bit (MSB) and ending with the Least-Significant Bit (LSB). Similarly, the inverse order (LSB first, MSB last) is called little-endian.

Bit   Abbreviation for BInary digiT. The smallest unit of information in the binary system of notation (0 or 1).

Bit rate   Number of bits transiting per second between corresponding entities via a data network. There exist classes of 'bit rate' which differ according to country. For example, for high rates, we have the levels 1.544, 6.312 and 44.736 Mbps in the USA, 2.048, 8.448, 34.368 and 139.264 Mbps in Europe, and 1.544, 6.132, 32.064 and 97.728 Mbps in Japan.

Bit time   Time taken to emit a bit, that is, 0.1 μs, in the case of Ethernet at 10 Mbps.

BNC   Comes from Bayonet-Neil Concelman, bayonet connector for thin coaxial cable, which is also used or optical fibers (ST connectors).

BootP   Bootstrap Protocol. Protocol based on UDP, used by a node (for example, diskless client) to determine the IP address of its Ethernet interface (function inverse to ARP), the address of a server and the name of a file to load into memory and execute. Defined by RFC 951.

Bridge   Device for interconnecting local area networks using identical protocols at the MAC level.

Broadband   Network for which the use of the links is shared between different frequency bands. The data signals are modulated.

Broadcast   Frame emitted by a station to all the other stations of the local area network capable of receiving.

Buffer   Element used in reception or transmission for temporary storage of data units, when the communication between units does not permit constant flow (for example, different rates).

Bus   Topology in which all the stations are connected in parallel on the medium and can simultaneously receive a signal transmitted by the other stations connected to the medium.

Byte   Sequence of successive bits. Generally eight bits (when the term octet is sometimes also used), unless otherwise stated.

Cable   One or more electrical or optical conductors placed inside a protective sheath.

CCITT   Comité Consultatif International Télégraphique et Téléphonique. International Telegraph and Telephone Consultative Committee, being the body responsible for standard-ization of the interconnection of telecommunications equipment on the international scale, via its recommendations. Was created in 1956 as part of the ITU, disbanded in 1992.

Channel   Logical or physical path permitting data transmission.

Circuit switching   Transmission technique which permits the establishment of a temporary physical link between two elements of a network.

CLNS/CLNP   Connectionless Network Service/Protocol. Level 3 ISO protocol (IS 8473) which does not require the establishment of a circuit before transmission. It constitutes one of the two options for the network layer, the other being CONS.

CMIS/CMIP   Common Management Information Services/Protocol. Level 7 ISO service and protocol for network management and administration. It is associated with a database holding the information obtained by observation of the traffic. Standards ISO 9595 and 9596.

CMOT/CMOL   CMIP over TCP/IP and CMIP over LLC correspond to implementations of the CMIP protocol in the DARPA and ISO worlds.

Coaxial   Cable consisting of an asymmetric pair: a central conductor (core) and a concentric external conductor (braiding), characterized by its lower attenuation, its bandwidth and its high immunity to interference.

Code   Set of rules defining a one-to-one correspondence between the data and its representa-tion by symbols or characters.

Collision   Conflict of access, provoked when at least two nodes of the network are simultaneously in an emission state on the same medium.

Compatibility   Ability of two devices to intercommunicate in a meaningful way, that is, to transmit and receive data without software or hardware modifications to either of the two devices.

Conflict   Problem which arises when two (or more) data sources simultaneous try to emit data on the same medium. The resulting superposition will result in data loss, if it is not detected. In the worst case, this may lead to damage to the emitter and the receiver if they are not designed to support the voltage and current levels which may result.

Cord   Relatively short cable with a connector at at least one of its two ends.

CRC   Cyclic Redundancy Check. Field determined using an error detection algorithm, included in the frame before transmission by the emitting station. The receiving station recalculates the CRC and compares it with that which it received. In the case of Ethernet, this sequence of four bytes is also called the Frame Check Sequence (FCS).

Crosstalk (or Xtalk)   Measure of the level of perturbation between two pairs of a single cable, where the emitter and the receiver are at the same end (NEXT). NEXT is an abbreviation for Near End Crosstalk. Corresponds to an imperfection in the transmission caused when part of the signal energy passes from one circuit to a neighboring circuit.
Telediaphonic fading is a measure of the level of perturbation between two pairs of a single cable, where the emitter and the receiver are at opposite ends.

CSMA/CA   Carrier Sense Multiple Access with Collision Avoidance. Access method avoiding collisions by means of an acknowledgment procedure prior to emission of the frame.

CSMA/CD   Carrier Sense Multiple Access with Collision Detection is a conflict-managing access protocol in which the machines share the same communication line.

DARPA   Defense Advanced Research Project Agency, previously known as ARPA, is the (US) government agency responsible for research and development for the ARPANET, and subsequently the DARPA Internet.

Data communication   Exchange of data messages between points on communication channels.

Data link   This is the second layer of the Open Systems Interconnection basic reference model which provides the functional and procedural means to establish, maintain and release data link transmissions between network entities. This layer is involved in the establishment of an active link between stations, the control of the synchronization byte, the insertion of the data in frames, error detection and correction, and the regulation of the data stream on the link.

Data transmission   Emission of data at one point for receipt elsewhere. Telecommunications forms the major part of this sector.

DCE   Data Communication Equipment, providing the functions needed to establish, maintain and break a transmission connection (for example, modem). Forwards the data, but does not manage it.

DDN   (Defense Data Network), improperly used to refer to MILNET, ARPANET and the TCP/IP protocols they use. In fact, it refers to MILNET and the associated parts of the Internet which link the American military installations.

DECnet   Protocol suite developed and supported by Digital Equipment Corporation for its DNA architecture. The last version Phase V is ISO-compatible.

Degradation   Deterioration of the data transmission quality or speed caused by an increasing load or number of users accessing the system.

DNS   Domain Name System. Protocol of the Internet world defined by RFC 1035, 1155 and 2308. It automatically generates the correspondence between the symbolic name and the IP address of the network machines. The IP addresses are structured in tree-like name spaces managed by the name servers. Thus, DNS allows machines which are connected to the Internet to have a documented name of this type.

DoD   Department of Defense of the United States of America.

DQDB   Distributed Queue Dual Bus is a MAN derived from QPSX which was standardized by IEEE 802.6. It operates with a double unidirectional bus at 34 Mbps, 45 Mbps (ANSI DS3) or 140 Mbps (CCITT G.703) using an access method with distributed queues and a protocol for dividing the packets into cells similar to ATM. The two buses are unidirectional and may even be looped. Fair distribution of the accesses depends upon a relatively complex cell reservation procedure.

Driver   Software which manages the exchanges of data between a physical communication port and the programs which use it.

DS   Digital Signal, defines the rates within the hierarchy of carriers in the USA. DS0 = 64 kbps (elementary signal), DS1 = 1544 kbps, DS3 = 445 Mbps.

DTE   Data Terminal Equipment represents the computer and/or the terminal, in contrast to the communication devices. Equipment generating or receiving data.

EBCDIC   Extended Binary Coded Decimal Interchange Code, 8-bit alphanumeric code used by IBM.

EDI   Electronic Data Interchange. Electronic transfer of data and documents between heterogeneous equipment (word processing system, PC, fax, telex) providing services for storage, delayed delivery, multicast, conversion, and processing of message contents.

EGP   Exterior Gateway Protocol. Old protocol for communication between gateways (or routers) linking 'autonomous' systems, used to exchange access and routing information. Defined by RFC 888 and 904.

EIA   Electronic Industries Association. American standardization organization specializing in the electrical and functional characteristics of device interfaces. Recently changed its name to the TIA (Telecommunications Industries Association).

Empty slot   Access method in which an empty slot circulates between the machines and can be filled by data under certain conditions.

Emulation   Substitution of the conventions constituting a protocol, used to simulate a different protocol.

Encapsulation   While the data to transmit are passed (downward) through all applicable layers of the communication model, each level will add relevant information in a header or trailer, and encapsulate this way the $N + 1$ units of information in a slightly larger level N unit of information (or PDU Protocol Data Unit). Even though the OSI model is the standard reference, multiple solutions are still used, as is illustrated in Figure G.2 with the IP protocol over Ethernet.

ES–IS   End System to Intermediate System. Routing exchange protocol defined by the standard ISO 9542. The End System is a non-router host, while the Intermediate System is a router. The ES always belongs to an area and can re-locate the level 1 IS by capturing the ES–IS packets. It will then use the IS to communicate within its area. This will also enable it to leave its area via communication with other ISs.

Ethernet   Local area baseband network with a bus topology and CSMA/CD access method, developed jointly by Digital Equipment Corporation (DEC), Intel Corporation and Xerox Corporation (or DIX), standardized by the IEEE under 802.3 10Base5, then by the ISO. It uses coaxial cable as the medium (optical fiber and twisted pair were added by the IEEE) at a rate of 10 Mbps; the coding is of Manchester type with LSB first. Implementations at 1 and 100 Mbps and 1 Gbps have also been defined.

FACTOR   Industrial local area network developed by APTOR.

Fading per unit length   Fading per unit length of the cable in question.

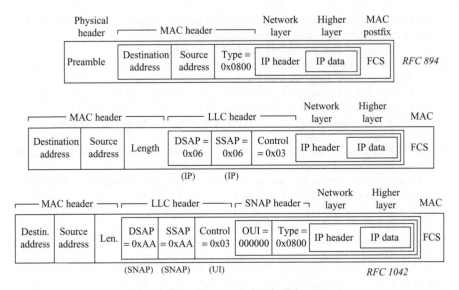

Figure G.2 Encapsulation in Ethernet.

FDDI Fiber Distributed Data Interface. Fiber optic network with a dual ring topology which uses a timed token passing method and operates at 100 Mbps. Standardization of the ANSI X3T.5 standard in ISO 9314 is still under way for the SMT (station management) administrative part and other new sublayers.

FOIRL Fiber Optic Inter Repeater Link. Supplement e of the IEEE 802.3 standard dating from 1987. The characteristics introduced here are explicitly intended to permit the point-to-point interconnection of Ethernet devices (repeater) from different manufacturers over optical fiber. These specifications have been replaced by 10BaseFL, which extends their capabilities, but ensures upwards compatibility.

FOMAU Fiber Optic Medium Attachment Unit, that is, fiber optic transceiver generally with a 15-point socket and two ST optical connectors (one for emission, one for receipt).

Frame Group of characters transmitted as a unit according to a predefined format (including, for example, synchronization and/or error control fields). The frame is subject to an encoding procedure prior to emission (physical level).

Frame Relay New WAN packet-switching technology offering a connection-oriented point-to-point service (CCITT Blue Book I.122). This method, based on the use of permanent virtual circuits, uses an adapted version of the HDLC protocol and involves multiplexing at level 2. It became a very common standard for interfacing to WAN packet services.

Front-end processor (FEP) Peripheral equipment of a central computer, responsible for controlling the communications of the latter.

FTAM File Transfer Access and Management, ISO standard 8571 developed at level 7 (upper part) of the OSI model for exchanges of files between the nodes of a network and administration. Can be used to establish and break a connection and to select, create, delete, read or write to a file. Similar in its objectives to the DAP protocol of DNA.

FTP File Transfer Protocol. Standard high-level protocol for file transfer between nodes under TCP/IP. Defined by RFC 959 and the standard MIL-STD 1780.

Full duplex Denotes a circuit capable of supporting simultaneous transmissions in both directions.

Gateway   A gateway is a specific machine linked to two (or more) networks which routes the packets of one to the other. The term is quite general, but represents, more specifically, the interconnection devices operating on data at level 4 (transport layer) or above.

GOSIP   Government Open Systems Interconnection Profile. Specifications in conformance with OSI imposed by certain governments (USA, EU) for all public purchases.

Half duplex   Denotes a circuit capable of supporting transmissions in both directions, but not simultaneously (which corresponds to alternating communication).

HDLC   High Level Data Link Control is a bit-oriented link-level protocol operating in a bidirectional synchronous mode, standardized by ISO 3309, 4335, 6159 and 6256. CCITT has adapted it for its Link Access Protocol (LAP-B) used in X.25 networks.

HELLO   Routing protocol based on measurement of the delay to determine the minimum path. Defined by RFC 891.

Host   Host machine. Entity which receives or emits information on a network but is not responsible for its transfer.

HPFS   High Performance File System for the OS/2 operating system. Microsoft's LAN Manager and IBM's LAN Server are based on this.

Hub   Concentrator located at the heart of a network star topology (Ethernet, Token Ring, ARCnet). For Ethernet, multiport repeater with attachment to twisted pair according to the IEEE 802.3 10BaseT standard.

Hyperchannel   High-speed network developed by Network Systems Corporation for the interconnection of large systems. Based on a CSMA/CD access method with priority, with a coaxial cable of the 75 Ohm CATV type as medium. Achieves a speed of 50 Mbps per channel (four channels can be combined per link) and at most 16 ports.

IAB   Internet Activities Board. Coordinating committee (composed of researchers) responsible for the architecture, engineering and management of the Internet. The IAB's decisions are public and give rise to RFCs which serve as standards. The IAB is divided into the IETF and the IRTF.

ICMP   Internet Control Message Protocol. Integral part of the IP which manages error and control messages. Defined by RFC 792. Echo Request and Echo Reply packets are used by the command *ping*.

ICS   IBM Cabling System. Cabling system developed by the American computer manufacturer IBM, which is based on hermaphrodite connectors and nine different types of cable, including:

type 1: two shielded twisted pairs, 22 AWG

type 2: two shielded twisted pairs plus four telephone pairs, 22 AWG

type 3: four twisted telephone pairs, 22 or 24 AWG

type 5: two optical fibers (diameters 50/125, 62.5/125 or 100/140 μm)

Idle   State in which a medium or a device is not busy (unoccupied).

IEEE   The Institute of Electrical and Electronic Engineers is a scientific organization which publishes magazines of a high technical level together with standards in different areas associated with its activities. These activities cover the description of local area networks (for layers 1 and 2) and, for example, the binary encoding format for floating point numbers on a computer and the standardization of the Pascal programming language.

IEEE 802   Committee created in 1980, which establishes the standards for the interconnection of computer equipment. IEEE standards 802.3, 802.4, and 802.5 describe the physical and link layers (MAC) of ISO's OSI reference model. These different physical media may interface with the IEEE 802.2 standard which describes the upper part of the link layer (LLC). Here is a list of the IEEE 802 working groups and the result of their studies:

DIS = Draft International Standard

PDAD = Proposed Draft Technical Report

IEEE 802 (Standard) Overview and Architecture

IEEE 802.0 Operating Rules Review Group (ORRG)

IEEE 802.1 Glossary, Network Management and Internetworking

The group determines the global relationships between the 802.X. standards.

Supplement B (Standard): LAN/MAN Management, architecture, and protocol for the management of IEEE 802 local area networks.

Supplement C: MAC service provided by all IEEE 802 local area networks

Supplement D (Standard): Medium Access Control Bridges, architecture and protocol for the interconnection of IEEE 802 local area networks below the MAC layer. Definition of the Spanning Tree algorithm. Taken up by ISO in the standard IS 10038.

Supplement E (Standard): System Load Protocol, services and protocol permitting the loading of core images in a data processing device linked to an IEEE 802 network, using the group addressing concept.

Supplement H (Standard): Bridging for Ethernet V2.0.

Supplement G: Remote MAC bridging

Supplement P: Traffic Class Expediting & Dynamic Multicast Filtering

Supplement Q: Virtual Bridged LAN

IEEE 802.2 (Standard): Logical Link Control (LLC), type 1: Connectionless, type 2: Connection oriented, type 3: Acknowledged datagram.

IEEE 802.3 (Standard): CSMA/CD Access Method and Physical Layer Specifications (taking over Ethernet from Xerox) 10Base5 on coaxial cable, 500 m.

Supplement a: 10Base2, on thin coaxial cable RG-58, 185 m

Supplement b: 10Broad36, on coaxial cable 75 Ohm, 3.6 km

Supplement c and d: repeater and FOIRL

Supplement e: 1Base5, known as StarLAN, on twisted pair, 250 m

Supplement g: method and implementation of conformance tests for AUI cables

Supplement h: relationship between CSMA/CD layers and administrative capabilities

Supplement i: 10BaseT on twisted pair, 100 m

Supplement j: 10BaseF with stars on optical fiber

Supplement k: specifications of repeaters in baseband

Supplement l: PICS for 10BaseT transceivers

Supplement p and q: Managed objects and management layer

Supplement u: 100BaseT, or fast Ethernet, at 100 Mbps

Supplement x & y: full-duplex operation & 100BaseT2

Supplement z: 1000BaseX operation (GigaEthernet)

Supplement ab: 1000BaseT (GigaEthernet over twisted pair)

Supplement ac: MAC Frame extension for VLAN Tagging

IEEE 802.3 10BaseF: Supplement j to the IEEE 802.3 standard concerning the use of a medium based on optical fiber (whence F for fiber) instead of coaxial cable. This involves extending the standardization of Ethernet devices on fiber optics previously limited to FOIRL. Topology changes from the bus to the star (as for the twisted pair). Several types of star are included in the standard: active synchronous stars, asynchronous stars (for compatibility with FOIRL), and passive stars.

IEEE 802.3 10BaseT: Supplement i to the IEEE 802.3 standard, concerning the use of a medium based on twisted pairs (whence the T, for twisted pair) instead of coaxial cable. This supplement describes the functionality of the hubs (concenctrators or stars) and the transceivers attached to them. Note that the topology is no longer that of a bus but that of a star, where all the links between the Ethernet stations and the hub are established as point to point.

IEEE 802.4 (Standard) Token passing bus access method and physical layer specifications (covering MAP)

IEEE 802.5 (Standard) Token passing ring access method and physical layer specifications (covering IBM's Token Ring)

IEEE 802.6 (Standard) Distributed queue dual bus (DQDB) sub-network (metropolitan area network)

IEEE 802.7 (Standard) Broadband LAN (technical advisory and physical layer topics, recommended practices)

IEEE 802.8 Fiber optic technical advisory and physical layer topics

IEEE 802.9 Integrated services LAN (ISLAN or IsoEthenet)

IEEE 802.10 Security and privacy access method and physical layer specifications (standard for interoperable LAN security: SILS)

IEEE 802.11 Wireless access method and physical layer specifications

IEEE 802.12 Demand priority access method (100VG-AnyLAN)

IEEE 802.14 Cable TV set-top box working group

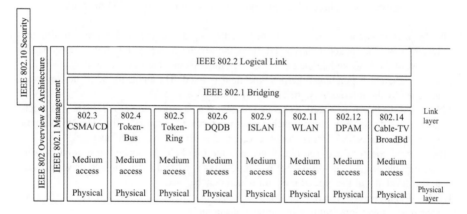

Figure G.3

IETF   Internet Engineering Task Force, forms part of the IAB. This group of researchers is responsible for proposing and specifying protocols and standards for the Internet network. In addition, it is also responsible for guaranteeing its operation.

Interface   Link shared by two adjacent entities. The set of wires linking two adjacent entities corresponds to a physical interface.

Interface protocol   Complete set of rules applicable to the communication between one entity and the next. The use of physical wires interlinking two adjacent entities corresponds to their physical interface. The set of logical messages sent between adjacent layers corresponds to their logical interface.

Internet   The collection of networks and gateways (including ARPANET, MILNET and NSFnet) which use the TCP/IP protocol suite and operate as a unique and cooperative virtual network (same name space) which serves numerous public research laboratories, universities, and military installations (more than 50 countries, 5000 networks, and 7 million machines). The Internet provides universal connectivity and three levels of network service: unreliable (connectionless routing of packets), reliable (routing in full duplex stream), and application-level services (for example, electronic mail), built on the first two levels.

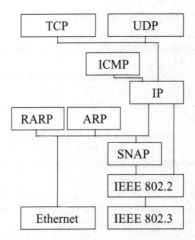

Figure G.4   Three IP encapsulation modes on a CSMA/CD network.

IP   Internet Protocol is a level-3 protocol containing addressing and control information which allows the packets to be routed. IPv4, the version currently in use, was developed by request of the DoD and defined by RFC 791 and 1009 and the standard MIL-STD-1777.

   The corresponding Ethernet type field is 0800. The numbers of IP networks are assigned by the Internet Assigned Numbers Authority (IANA).

IPX   Novell's Internet Packet eXchange protocol is a variation of Xerox's XNS. It is a connectionless datagram protocol (each packet is processed independently). The IPX address is similar to the XNS address, but is represented entirely in hexadecimal.

IRL   Inter-Repeater Link. The IRL appears in the ISO 8802-3 standard as a point-to-point link capable of interconnecting two half repeaters for coaxial cable. No details were given, at that level, about the type of medium which may be used.

IRTF   The Internet Research Task Force forms part of the IAB and is responsible for research and development relating to new technologies.

IS–IS   Intermediate System to Intermediate System is an ANSI routing protocol currently at the stage of Draft Proposal 10589. It defines the exchanges between intermediate systems (routers). Several networks interconnected by routers constitute an area, the lowest level in the routing hierarchy. Several interlinked areas (interlinked by level-2 routers) form routing domains. The concept of routing domain is similar to that of an autonomous system in TCP/IP, and refers to a separately administered region.

ISDN   Integrated Services Digital Network represents a CCITT standard covering several areas of telecommunication, including primarily the integration of voice and data.

ISO   The International Organization for Standardization has defined, among other things, the OSI model (Open System Interconnection) which divides the architecture of a telecommunication system into seven layers.

Isochronous   Signal in which the time interval separating any two important times is always a multiple of some unit time interval.

ITU   International Telecommunications Union. This standardization body, which dates from the days of telegraphy (1865), is attached to the UN. It is responsible for supervising the general organization of telecommunications, their general standardization, and the assignment of radio frequencies. CCITT was part of the ITU before it was disbanded in 1992.

Jabber   Abnormally long Ethernet frame, longer than the maximum length imposed by the standard (1518 bytes, or 1522 for VLAN Tagged frame).

Jam   Sequence of 32 bits emitted when a collision is detected to ensure that the stations concerned have time to detect the problem which has occurred with their frames.

Jitter   Distortion of a signal caused by the variation of one of its characteristics, for example, the frequency.

Jumper cable   Short attachment cord, used by the patching system between patch panels or to change the connector type (case in which two different sockets have to be interconnected).

Layer   Subdivision of the OSI architecture, consisting of subsystems of the same level, responding to requests from the level above using services from the level below.

LAN_Manager   System for sharing the resources of a server (software, disks, printers, streamer, messaging) in the microcomputer world. Used to be a common product developed by Microsoft and 3Com (3 + Open) under OS/2.

LAT   Local Area Transport, developed by Digital Equipment Corporation, identified by the Ethernet type field 6004. This protocol cannot be routed, thus it must be bridged.

LLC   Logical Link Control is the upper half of the second layer of the OSI model. It interfaces downwards with the MAC and upwards with the network layer. IEEE 802.2 is the standardized ISO LLC (IS 8802-2).

Local area network (LAN)   Communication network with a teleinformatic purpose, of limited size (building or site, 1 to 20 km), having a potentially high throughput (1 to 20 Mbps) with low transmission delays and error rates. There are two categories: enterprise local area networks and industrial local area networks.

LocalTalk   Elementary local area network developed by Apple, which operates at 230.4 kbps on twisted pair. The topologies are the daisy chain, the bus and the star, and the distances extend to 1200 meters (PhoneNet). Zilog 8530 is a specialized integrated circuit for this technology.

Loopback   Test facility built into communication equipment. The transmission output is connected internally to the receiving input, thereby activating all the circuits, without necessitating real communication with a second similar device. This type of test was integrated in Ethernet V2.0 specifications, with a frame type of 9000.

LU 6.2   Particular type of logic unit (high-level entity of IBM's SNA architecture) permitting symmetrical exchanges between programs.

MAC   Media Access Control. Method of obtaining access to a network medium via a station. Forms part of the second layer of the OSI model.

MAN   A Metropolitan Area Network has communication capabilities covering geographical areas with a size the order of that of a town (intermediate between the LAN and the WAN).

MAP   The Manufacturing Automation Protocol is an industrial local area network which was originally designed (in 1980) by General Motors. Layers 1 and 2 (MAC) are standardized in IEEE 802.4.

MAU   The Multiple Access Unit for a Token Ring network is the effective heart of the ring network, to which each machine is linked by two twisted pairs, one for emission and the other for receipt. It is also called the MSAU, for MultiStation Access Unit. See under 'transceiver' for an MAU for Ethernet.

Medium   Transmission material allowing signals to pass from one data communication device to another.

Message switching   Transmission technique which can route a message as a function of the address transported, without necessarily establishing a permanent circuit between the two elements of the network: copper, biber, air, etc.

MIB Management Information Base. Database for the SNMP management protocol, with a tree-like structure. Thus, it corresponds to the information gathered by the managed entity available to the master station.

MIC Medium Interface Connector for Token Ring and FDDI. This denotes the standardized connector with the technology.

MIC Message Integrity Check, or sequence of data associated with the message to control its integrity (one example is the FCS).

Modem Comes from MOdulator–DEModulator and denotes a device capable of emitting and receiving digital data on telephone lines or on leased lines. Depending on the requirements, it may operate in half or full duplex, on two or four wires and at from 300 bps to 56 kbps, and more, on leased lines.

Modulation Temporal variation of a physical characteristic (amplitude, frequency, phase) of a signal as a function of the message to be transmitted.

MOP Maintenance Operation Protocol developed by Digital Equipment Corporation, identified by the type fields 6001 and 6002. This protocol cannot be routed and must therefore be bridged.

Multicast Frame emitted by a station to a specific group of stations of the local area network.

Named pipe Virtual communication channels.

NDIS Network Driver Interface Specification developed by Microsoft and 3Com provides a standard driver under DOS or OS/2 for users of the LAN_Manager. NDIS allows several protocol stacks to use the same driver interface, the only limitation being the memory available.

NetBIOS (Network Basic Input Output System) is the standard network session interface for microcomputers, IBM PCs, and compatibles. It enables a client program to find a server process and communicate with it, like named pipes.

NetWare System for sharing the resources of a server (software, disks, printers, streamer, messaging) in the microcomputer world. This product, which is widely spread, was developed by Novell and is based on a proprietary system. The NetWare protocol relies on NFSP (NetWare File Service Protocol, level 6 functionality), NCP (NetWare Core Protocol, level 4), IDP (Internetwork Datagram Protocol) and, finally, on IEEE 802.2 or Ethernet.

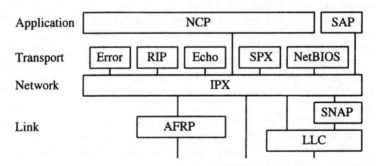

Figure G.5 Protocol architecture used by NetWare.

In Figure G.5, SPX stands for Sequence Packet eXchange. The Ethernet type field corresponding to NetWare frames is 8137.

Network A set of hardware and software elements which permits data transfer locally or over a large distance.

NFS Network File System is a software architecture developed by Sun Microsystems, which is based on IP, and allows one to use shared resources in a transparent manner on a network of stations under Unix (also PCs and Macintoshes). Widely used file and data sharing system defined by RFC 1813.

NIS Network Information Services is a set of services in the Sun environment which propagates information from the master to the recipients. It is used to maintain system files on important networks.

Node Interface unit or station, possessing logic capable of interpreting the network traffic stream passing through it. A node is generally connected to more than one communication network.

NOS Network Operating System denotes the software for bringing together and sharing the overall resources of a set of microcomputers connected to a single network. Such managers include MS-Windows' NT, NetWare, LAN_Server, LAN_Manager and Vines.

NSAP Network Service Access Point (ISO 8348/Ad2) is the address corresponding to the point at which the network service is accessible to the level 4 entity of the OSI model. The structure of a conformant NSAP is shown in Figure G.6.

Initial domain part		Domain specific part		
Authority and format identifier	Initial domain identifier	Area	Station ID	Selector
1 byte	Variable	2 bytes	6 bytes	1 byte

Figure G.6 Decomposition of the NSAP into elementary fields.

The selector byte of the NSAP has a similar function to the port number of TCP and UDP.

ODI Open Data Link Interface represents the driver specifications introduced by Novell in the microcomputer world to allow several protocol stacks (such as TCP/IP or AppleTalk) to use IPX concurrently.

OSI Open Systems Interconnection reference model defined by ISO standard IS 7498. It establishes an architectural model of data communication for networks with seven layers (from the bottom up):

Physical: electrical, mechanical, and functional characteristics of the medium transporting the binary signals

Link: establishes, maintains and releases a connection between two network entities

Network: responsible for relaying, routing, and sorting the data units of a transmission through several nodes

Transport: responsible for flow and error control, fragmentation, re-assembly, and sequencing of the messages of a communication

Session: responsible for organizing and synchronizing a communication

Presentation: provides the syntax and the structure of the data communicated (code and format)

Application: provides the interfaces which can be used by user applications (semantic processing).

OTDR Optical Time Domain Reflectometry measures the attenuation at all points of a fiber. It is carried out from one end. The reflectometer emits light pulses and analyzes the signal received (level of reflection and delay) to produce its result in the form of a curve in dB per meter.

PABX   A Private Automatic Branch eXchange is an automatic switch managing telephone calls, generally called the telephone exchange; it may be public or private.

Packet switching   Transmission technique in which the data is divided into blocks of a controlled size which may use various physical paths in the network during their routing to their destination. Technique standardized by Frame Relay X.25 for WANs.

Patching   Interconnection of lines entering a sub-distributor. Patching is used to modify the physical links by moving jumper cables.

PCM   Pulse Code Modulation.

PDN   Public Data Network refers to public data transmission networks such as X.25 networks provided by national service providers.

PDU   Protocol Data Unit. Data unit exchanged at the level of a protocol, sometimes equivalent to a packet.

Physical   The lowest of the seven layers defined by the ISO Open Systems Interconnection reference model. This layer is responsible for the interface with the medium, the detection and generalization of signals on the medium and the conversion and processing of signals received from the medium and from the link layer.

Ping   Packet InterNet Groper, program which manages the exchange of ICMP Echo request and Echo reply messages, and can be used to test the active and reachable state of a station.

Polling   Method of access by selective calling with centralized control. The central node interrogates each station and, when it judges it necessary, assigns a station the right to emit.

Port   Physical access point on a device, where the signal can be provided, obtained or measured.

Preamble   Series of bits sent by the physical layer at the start of a frame to synchronize the receiving transceiver, consisting of the sequence 1010 (at frequency 5 MHz) for 7 bytes (0×55) and ending with the byte 10101011 ($0 \times D5$).

Prewiring   Cabling infrastructure, implemented before the use to which it will be put has been fully defined. Thus, prewiring is an expression of the wish to put in place a structured cabling which is potentially capable of meeting the majority of current and future uses.

Protocol   A formal set of rules and conventions governing the format, duration and error control applicable when computers communicate.

PSTN   The Public Switched Telephone Network is the system underlying the telephone service provided by the national carrier. Rates of 14.4 or 28.8 kbps full-duplex can be obtained with V.32bis and V.34 standards, which can also be associated with compression algorithms that can be used to increase this speed further.

PUP   Xerox PARC (Palo Alto Research Center) Universal Packet. Fundamental transfer unit of the protocol developed by Xerox Corp. The corresponding Ethernet type field is 0A00 (formerly 0200).

QPSX   Queued Packet and Synchronous eXchange is the description of a MAN of Australian origin, from which in DQDB was derived by the IEEE 802.6 committee.

Recommendation
Standards document relating to telecommunications, published by the CCITT. Recommendation V for analog network interfaces, X for data networks.

Reflectometer   Measuring device which can be used to check that a transmission line impedance is not disturbed (as a result of a connection error, breaking or crushing of the wires, absence of terminal resistors, and so on). The operation is based on the principle that any perturbation gives rise to reflections.

Repeater   Device which propagates the signal from one coaxial cable to another, used to increase the distance and the topology imposed by a single transmission segment (for example, to exceed 500 meters of coaxial cable). For this, it is able to recover the amplitude, shape and frequency of the important data and of collision signals.

RFC Request for Comments. Documents produced by the IAB dealing with the protocols of the TCP/IP suite, characteristics, measurements, and observations of which they describe. These Internet network 'standards' are available from the DDN Network Information Center and via the Internet. They are described by a number, a status, and a state.

RFS Remote File Sharing is another product for distributed file management which is a competitor for NFS promoted by AT&T.

RIP The Routing Information Protocol is used to exchange routing information between machines. It is defined by RFC 1053.

RJ Registered Jack. This is a small modular socket such as RJ9, 11, 12, 45.

RMON Remote Monitoring is based on a standard SNMP MIB which should be enriched by the probe implementing it. Nine groups are available (but optional), dealing with: statistics, history, alarms, hosts, hosts top N, traffic matrix, filters, packet capture, and events. The new RFC 1757 allows us to standardize the probe operation and gain a generic access to all monitoring agents in the network. With all RMON capabilities, a probe can deliver the same service as a fixed network analyzer. A complementary MIB has been defined for Token Ring: RFC 1513.

ROSE Remote Operation Service Element. Set of application level services standardized by ISO 9072 or CCITT X.229. Provides the means of transfer for requests made by CMISE.

Route Denotes the path followed by the network traffic from its source to its destination. This path may cross several gateways and networks.

RouteD Route Daemon is a routing program under Unix using RIP which learns and propagates the routes (paths) between the machines of a local area network.

Router Device interconnecting two networks based on an identical network layer (level 3 of the OSI model), but which are able to use different physical and link levels for each port. The router can also choose between various possible routes for transit.

RPC Remote Procedure Call. Interconnection mode in which procedures are called from different machines on the network. Originally defined by Sun Microsystems, covered by RFC 1831.

RS Recommended Standard of the EIA, for example RS-232, 422, 423, 449.

RS-232C EIA definition of an electrical, functional and mechanical interface for interconnecting terminal and communication equipment. Equivalent to the CCITT Advice V.24 and V.28 and ISO DIS-2110. Exchanges of digital data take place in serial mode, at up to 20 kbps theoretically, over distances of 15 m, using unbalanced circuits and DB25 connectors.

RTD/RTT The Round Trip Delay/Time is the usual measure of the communication delay between two access points.

Runt Abnormally short Ethernet frame, which is shorter than the minimum length imposed by the standard for satisfactory operation (64 bytes) and may result from collision on a normal frame or malfunctioning of a device connected to the network.

SAA System Application Architecture represents the set of rules defining a common architecture for communications support and programming for all IBM systems, providing a compatibility independent of the machines and operating systems.

SAP The Service Access Point is the point at which the services of a layer (or sublayer) are provided to the layer immediately above.

SDH Synchronous Digital Hierarchy is the European counterpart of SONET, which defines STS-N (Synchronous Transport Signal at level N) units as multiples of 155.52 Mbps.

SDLC Synchronous Data Link Control is a protocol for a network of IBM computers associated with SNA, the predecessor of HDLC. The protocol provides the control for a single

communication line or link, manages a certain number of facilities, and operates in half-
or full-duplex mode on private or switched networks.

Server Process executed on a machine which offers access to its resources: peripherals, files
or programs. The latter may be distributed or executed on remote machines.

SFD Starting Frame Delimiter ends the synchronization sequence of the Ethernet preamble
with two bits set to 1.

Shielding Metallic cladding suppressing electromagnetic and radio interference.

Slot time Defined by the standard IS 8802-3 as a time interval of 512 bit times, considered
to be the smallest readable unit on the medium at 10 and 100 Mbps.

SMB Server Message Block. Presentation layer of communications modes of IBM, Microsoft and 3Com adapted to the microcomputer network manager.

SMDS Switched Multimegabit Data Services. MAC-level interface defined by Bell Communication Research (Bellcore) offering connections of the type any-to-any. Based on high-
speed technologies (physical level: DS-1, DS-3, SONET or EDH), this service has no
theoretical limitations on distance. The SMDS Interface Protocol (SIP) is a subset of the
MAC part of DQDB.

SNA System Network Architecture. Layered communication system allowing data transfer
in IBM networks (from mainframes down to passive terminals).

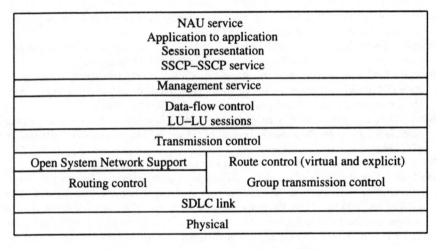

Figure G.7 Layered representation of SNA.

SNMP Simple Network Management Protocol. Network management protocol of the TCP/
IP world, successor to Simple Gateway Monitoring Protocol (SGMP). Built above UDP/IP,
it uses a subset of ASN.1 to encode the MIB data. Defined by RFC 1155, 1157 and 1213
for the MIB-II. SNMPv1 should be followed by SNMPv3 defined by RFC in draft.

Socket Abstraction provided by BSD Unix which enables a process to access Internet
Protocol by opening a connection, specifying the services desired (stream, datagram),
association with the destination (bind), and data emission and receipt.

SONET Synchronous Optical Network. Proposed physical-level protocol for broadband
synchronous services on optical fiber. SONET is one of the first specifications of a standard
for an optical connection interface in the telecommunications world. Moreover, SONET has

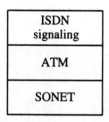

Figure G.8   Example of a stack based on SONET.

taken pains to meet future advances by providing for evolutions in speeds. The bit rate OC-
M (Optical Carrier at level M) is a multiple of 51.84 Mbps and can go up to 48 Gbps.

Space-division switching   Technique in which a physical path is established between two
points, by electromechanical or electronic physical switching.

SQE   The Signal Quality Error is the signal transmitted by the receiver to the NIC when it
detects a signal of poor quality on the medium, such as a collision.

SQE test   SQE test or Heart beat is the short signal transmitted to the NIC by the transceiver following a correct emission in order to validate the collision pair of the drop cable
interlinking them.

Star   Topology in which all the stations are connected to a single concentrator which
manages all the communications. Topologies based on several local stars linked in a
hierarchical manner (high-level tree-like topology) can be derived from this structure.

StarLAN   Local area network derived from Ethernet. It operates at 1 Mbps on a star
topology (whose heart is the hub) with two unshielded twisted pairs per link, and allows
distances of 250 meters per segment. StarLAN was standardized by Supplement e of IEEE
802.3.

Subnet   Corresponds to the ability to partition a TCP/IP network logically by dividing the
local part of the IP address into a field identifying the physical network and a field identifying the machine. RFC 950 and 1219 describe the standard procedure for Internet subnetting.

Switch   In the LAN arena, a product that is able to retransmit multiples frames, datagrams
or flow simultaneously is commonly referred to as a switch. For the end-user, its internal
performances should allow the accumulation of traffic without degradation. But the technologies used are quite diverse, and the scope, which was mainly to bridge MAC frames
between many ports a few years ago, has now become the domain of routers, firewalls and
gateways. Switches try to be the ultimate solution by integrating the most significant
functions of complex (and eventually relatively slow) products in hardware to boost performance, hiding the complexity of the processes. Figure G.9 shows the intermediate
positioning of a layer 2 switch (the most common type).

Switching mode   As described previously, there are many switching modes, of which a
classification is given in Figure G.10.

Synchronous   Data transmission mode for which the clocks of the emitter and receiver are
synchronized using a periodic signal.

TCP   Transmission Control Protocol. OSI level-4 protocol. Provides reliable, full-duplex
data transmission in stream mode. It is connection oriented and uses the IP protocol.
Defined by RFC 793 and the standard MIL-STD 1778.

TDR   Time Domain Reflectometry measures the variation in impedance along a cable, from
a cable end. The reflectometer emits electrical pulses and analyzes the signal received
(reflection level and delay) to produce its result in the form of a curve.

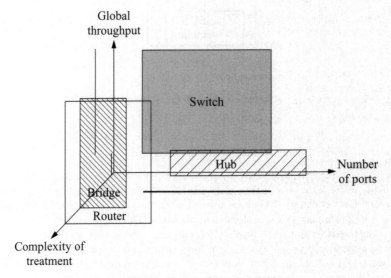

Figure G.9 Positioning of switching.

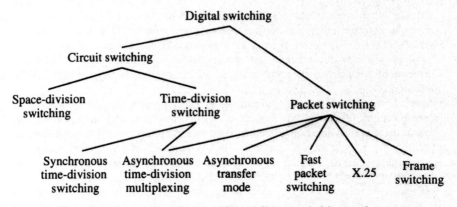

Figure G.10 Classification of the different switching modes.

Telnet Protocol used to simulate a remote terminal, based on the TCP/IP protocol suite. Defined by RFC 854, 855 and 856 and the standard MIL-STD 1782.

Terminator Connector with a resistance placed at the end of a cable. By impedance adaptation avoids signal reflections which could create interference.

Test set Rudimentary portable test device capable of simulating the operation of a station by the emission of Ethernet frames, counting receipts or tracking an echo mode between two sets located in the same network.

Thin cable (RG-58) Thin Ethernet coaxial cable of the 10Base2 type, conforming to the standard IEEE 802.3a (known as Cheapernet), which is less expensive than the thick cable and can only be used to implement segments of a maximum length 185 meters. The connectors are of type BNC.

Time-division switching Technique in which a path is reconstituted by means of multiplexing, demultiplexing and storage in intermediate buffers.

Token A token is a frame without a data field which circulates on the network and gives access rights to the medium. If its priority is sufficiently high, a device driver can capture the token and thus acquire the right to emit. There are at least three well-known token-based techniques for sharing the channel: Token Ring (on a ring, circular transmission) Token Bus (on a bus, linear transmission) and FDDI.

Token Ring Local area network with a ring topology and a token-based access method, originally developed by IBM and standardized (in part) by IEEE 802.5. It principally uses individually shielded twisted pairs and optical fiber for media, at speeds of 1, 4 or 16 MBps, the encoding is of the Manchester differential type with MSB first.

TOP Technical Office Protocol is a suite of protocols based on Ethernet at the low levels, whose definition was sponsored by Boeing Computer Services.

Topology The topology of networks may be centralized or distributed. Centralized (or star) networks have all their nodes connected to a single element. One alternative is a distributed topology, in which each node is connected to all the other nodes. Typical topologies include the bus, the ring, the star, the tree, and the mesh.

Traffic Measurement of the passage of data (in terms of volume) on a communications medium.

Transceiver Comes from the beginning of 'transmitter' and the end of 'receiver'. Following IEEE 802.3 the transceiver is referred to as an MAU for Medium Attachment Unit. This component is directly connected to the physical medium (generally twisted pair or optical fiber) of the local area network system and performs coupling, emission and transmission functions on the transmission medium. This component may be connected by a drop cable to the computer interface circuit.

Translation Translation bridging consists of transparently changing the type of frame or encapsulation without intervening in the bridging type itself. This will typically be used to connect Ethernet and FDDI networks, Ethernet and Token Ring (as long as all networks use TB) or even Ethernet V 2.0 and IEEE 802.3 networks. Although the MAC formats seem quite similar among LAN technologies, translation bridging is not a simple task, and the frame may be corrupt while retransmitting it if MAC addresses are used at a higher layer.

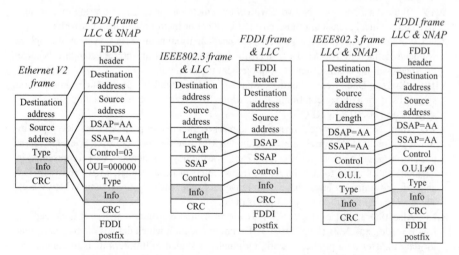

Figure G.11 Translation bridging Ethernet–FDDI

Transport Fourth layer of the OSI model, responsible for managing routing of the data. Standardized by ISO 8072 (service), 8073 (protocol, connection oriented mode) and 8602 (protocol, connectionless mode) or CCITT X.224.

UltraNet Very high speed network (1 Gbps) developed by the company Ultra (acquired by CNT) for connections between large systems and powerful graphics stations. Star topology, medium based on coaxial cables and optical fiber. With the Link Adapter the backbone may extend to 150 meters, links to CRAYs being of the order of 25 m and those to IBM machines of the order of 10 m.

User Datagram Protocol Relying on IP, this protocol permits the exchange of datagrams by associating one port number per application in communication. Defined by RFC 768.

UTP Unshielded Twisted Pair. Characteristic of twisted pairs without shielding, such as that provided AT&T's PDS Systimax cabling. There are various qualities of UTP, the most modest being reserved for voice transport, while the best (data grade UTP) are also suitable for high-speed data communications (10 Mbps and above). UTP should be contrasted with STP (Shielded Twisted Pair) such as IBM's ICS type 1 and with FTP.

UUCP Unix to Unix Copy Program. Application program developed in the 1970s for Unix version 7, allowing a Unix time-sharing system to copy files to and from another via a simple line. Based on Usenet. Improperly used to refer to Unix Mail Transfer.

VAN Value Added Network. Public or private network whose capacity is resold to third parties together with various services. The added value may come in various more-or-less complex forms (protocol conversion, invoicing, storage, database access, electronic messaging).

Vines VIrtual NEtwork System for sharing the resources of a server (software, disks, printers, streamer, messaging) in the microcomputer world. Product developed by Banyan, recognized on the international scale for its directory management facilities. The corresponding Ethernet type field is 0BAD.

VT Virtual Terminal which can be used to work remotely via a network. ISO level 7 service and protocol (upper part), standardized in ISO 9040 (service) and 9041 (protocol).

V.24 Definition of the exchange circuits between data terminal equipment and data communication equipment (EIA RS-232C).

V.35 CCITT standard for transmission at 48 kbps (theoretically) on primary group circuits in the band 60–180 kHz.

WAN Wide Area Network. Network with communication capabilities covering more extensive geographical areas than those covered by local or metropolitan area networks.

X X Window System Protocol Version 11 (hence the usual name X.11). System of graphics windows defined by RFC 1013 (issued for information, not an Internet standard because the specifications are insufficient to implement the protocol).

XDR eXternal Data Representation. Standard machine-independent data representation system used for external communication, which forms part of NFS. Defined by Sun Microsystems and covered by RFC 1832.

XNS Xerox Network Service. Term used to refer to the internet protocol suite developed by Xerox researchers. Although similar to the DARPA Internet protocols, XNS uses different packet formats. The XNS address has 32 bits for the physical network part (represented in decimal) and 48 bits for the host part (represented in hexadecimal, MAC address). The network and transport layers have been reused for other architectures (such as NewWare). The corresponding Ethernet type field is 0600.

X.25 Also ISO 8208 (level 3), ISO 7776 (level 2, frame structure and HDLC procedure, LAPB mode), and X.21 (level 1). CCITT recommendation which defines the packet format for data transfer on a public network. Originally designed to link terminals to computers,

X.25 provides a reliable stream transmission service which supports remote connections. Widely used in Europe.

X.400 Message Handling System (MHS), CCITT advice 1984, electronic messaging standard for the upper part of OSI layer 7. Its two main components are the Message Transfer System (MTS), which represents the ability to transport data between different entities using store and forward methods, and the Messaging System (IPMS), which is built above the former and provides personal multimedia communications.

X.500 Standard directory service, CCITT advice dated 1988. It corresponds to the standardization by ISO 9594 of a directory (or distributed database) of people, organizations, and applications. This type of directory holds information such as telephone numbers and network or electronic mail addresses which facilitates communication between individual and processes. X.500 occupies the upper part of OSI layer 7.

Yellow Pages Commercial name for NIS.

Acronyms

AAL   ATM Adaptation Layer
AARP   AppleTalk ARP
ABR   Available Bit Rate
ACR   Allowed Cell Rate
AEP   AppleTalk Echo Protocol
AFP   AppleTalk Filing Protocol
AFNOR   Association Française de Normalisation
AIS   Alarm Indication Signal
AMP   Active Monitor Present
AN   Auto-Negotiation
ANSI   American National Standards Institute
API   Application Program Interface
APPN   Advanced Peer-to-Peer Networking
ARB   All Route Broadcast
ARP   Address Resolution Protocol
ARPA   Advanced Research Projects Agency
ASCII   American Standard Code for Information Interchange
ASIC   Application Specific Integrated Circuit
ASP   AppleTalk Session Protocol
ATM   Asynchronous Transfer Mode
ATP   AppleTalk Transaction Protocol
AUI   Attachment Unit Interface
AUJA   Accumulated Uncorrelated Jitter Alignment
AURP   AppleTalk Update-based Routing Protocol
AWG   American Wire Gage
BECN   Backward Explicit Congestion Notification
BER   Bit Error Rate
B-ICI   Broadband Inter-Carrier Interface
BISDN   Broadband ISDN
B-ISUP   Broadband Integrated Service User Part
BGP   Border Gateway Protocol
BPDU   Bridge Protocol Data Unit
bps   bits per second
BPSK   Binary PSK
BRI   Basic Rate Interface
BUS   Broadcast & Unknown Server
BSC   Binary Synchronous Communications
CAC   Call Admission Control
CAP   Carrierless Amplitude/Phase modulation
CBR   Constant Bit Rate

CCITT   Comité Consultatif International pour la Télégraphie et Téléphonie
CDV   Cell Delay Variation
CER   Cell Error Ratio
CES   Circuit Emulation Services
CIDR   Classless InterDomain Routing
CIF   Cells In Frames
CIP   Classical IP
CIR   Committed Information Rate
CLNP/S   ConnectionLess Network Protocol/Service
CLP   Cell Loss Priority
CLR   Cell Loss Ratio
CMIP/S   Common Management Information Protocol/Service
CMOL/T   CMIP Over LLC/TCP
CONP/S   Connection Oriented Network Protocol/Service
CPCS   Common Part Convergence Sublayer
CPE   Customer Premises Equipment
CPU   Central Processing Unit
CRC   Cyclic Redundancy Check
CRS   Configuration Report Server
CS   Convergence Sublayer
CSMA   Carrier Sense Multiple Access
CSTA   Computer-Supported Telecommunications Application
CTI   Computer-Telephony Integration
DAC   Dual Attachment Concentrator
DAN   Desktop Area Network
DAS   Dual Attachment Station
DAT   Duplicate Address Test
dB   decibel
DBPSK   Differential Binary Phase Shift Keying
DCE   Data Circuit-terminating Equipment
DDCMP   Digital Data Communication Message Protocol
DDN   Defense Data Network
DDP   Datagram Delivery Protocol
DIX   Digital Intel Xerox
DLCI   Data Link Connection Identifier
DLS   Data Link Switching
DMD   Differential Mode Delay
DNA   Digital Network Architecture
DNS   Domain Name System
DoD   Department of Defense
DQDB   Distributed Queue Bual Bus
DBPSK   Differential Quadrature Phase Shift Keying
DSSS   Direct Sequence Spread Spectrum
DRP   DECnet Routing Protocol
DTE   Data Terminal Equipment
DTR   Dedicated Token Ring
      Data Terminal Ready
DVMRP   Distance Vector Multicast Routing Protocol
DXI   Data Exchange Interface

EIA   Electrical Industries Association
ED   Ending Delimiter
EDI   Electronic Data Interchange
EFCI   Explicit Forward Congestion Indicator
E_LAN   Emulated LAN
EMC   ElectroMagnetic Compatibility
EMI   ElectroMagnetic Interference
EPD   Early Packet Discard
ER   Explicit Rate
ES   End System
FAI   Functional Address Indicator
FCS   Frame Check Sequence
FCA   Fiber Channel Association
FDDI   Fiber Distributed Data Interface
FDM   Frequency Division Multiplexing
FEA   Fast Ethernet Alliance
FECN   Forward Explicit Congestion Notification
FEFI   Far End Fault Indication
FHSS   Frequency Hopping Spread Spectrum
FFOL   FDDI Follow On LAN
FPGA   Field Programable Gate Array
fps   frame per second
FSM   Finite State Machine
FTAM   File Transfer Access & Management
FTP   File Transfer Protocol
        Foil screened Twisted Pair
FRAD   Frame Relay Assembler Disassembler
GARP   Generic Attribute Registration Protocol
GCRA   Generic Cell Rate Algorithm
GDMO   Guidelines for the Definition of Managed Objects
GEA   Gigabit Ethernet Alliance
GFC   Generic Flow Control
GFSK   Gaussian Frequency Shift Keying
GOSIP   Government OSI Profile
GGP   Gateway to Gateway Protocol
HDLC   High level Data Link Control
HEC   Header Error Control
HiPPI   High Performance Parallel Interface
HOL   Head Of Line
HPR   High Performance Routing
HRC   Hybrid Ring Control
HSLAN   High Speed Local Area Network
HSSI   High Speed Serial Interface
HW   HardWare
ICMP   Internet Control Message Protocol
ICR   Initial Cell Rate
IDP   Internetwork Datagram Protocol
IEEE   Institute of Electrical and Electronics Engineers
IEC   International Electrotechnical Commission

IETF Internet Engineering Task Force
IFG Inter Frame Gap
IGMP Internet Group Management Protocol
IISP Interim Interswitch Signalling Protocol
ILMI Interim Local Management Interface
IMA Inverse Multiplexing for ATM
ION Internetworking Over NBMA Networks
IP Internet Protocol (v4)
IPG Inter Packet Gap
I-PNNI Integrated P-NNI
IPX Internetwork Packet eXchange
IS Intermediate System
ISDN Integrated Services Digital Network
IS-IS Intermediate System to Intermediate System
ISM Industrial, Scientific & Medical
ISO International Organization for Standardization
IWF InterWorking Function
LAG Logical Address Group
LAN Local Area Network
LAN_E LAN Emulation
LAPB/D Link Access Protocol Balanced/D channel
LAT Local Area Transport
LCF Low Cost Fiber
LEC LAN_E Client
LECS LAN_E Configuration Server
LED Light Emitting Diode
LES LAN_E Server
LIJ Leaf Initiated Join
LIS Logical IP Subnet
LLC Logical Link Control
LMI Local Management Interface
LMSC LAN/MAN Standard Committee
LOS Loss Of Signal
LU Logical Unit
L_UNI LAN_E UNI
L_NNI LAN_E NNI
MAC Medium Access Control
MAN Metropolitan Area Network
MAP Manufacturing Automation Protocol
MARS Multicast Address Resolution Server
MAU Medium Access Unit
  Multistation Access Unit
MCR Minimum Cell Rate
MCS MultiCast Server
MIB Management Information Base
MIC Media Interface Connector
MII Media Independent Interface
MGT Management
MLT MultiLine Transmission

MMF   Multi-Mode Fiber
MOP   Maintenance Operations Protocol
MPC   MPOA Client
MPOA   MultiProtocol Over ATM
MPS   MPOA Server
NAC   Null Attachment Concentrator
NBP   Name Binding Protocol
NCP   Network Control Program
          NetWare Core Protocol
NEXT   Near End CrossTalk
NARP   NBMA ARP
NAUN   Nearest Active Upstream Neighbor
NBMA   Non-Broadcast Multiple Access
NHC   NHRP Client
NHRP   Next Hop Resolution Protocol
NHS   NHRP Server
NIC   Network Interface Card
NFS   Network File System
NLSP   NetWare Link State Protocol
NMS   Network Management System
NNI   Network-to-Network Interface
NOS   Network Operating System
NRZI   Non Return to Zero Inverted
NSAP   Network Service Access Point
NSP   Network Service Protocol
NSR   Non Source Routed
OAM   Operation And Maintenance
OC   Optical Carrier
OSI   Open Systems Interconnection
PABX   Private Automatic Branch eXchange
PAD   Packet Assembler Disassembler
PAM   Pulse Amplitude Modulation
PAR   P-NNI Augmented Routing
          Project Authorization Request
PBX   Private Branch Exchange
PCM   Pulse Code Modulation
PCR   Peak Cell Rate
PDH   Plesiochronous Digital Hierarchy
PDN   Public Data Network
PDU   Protocol Data Unit
PEP   Packet Exchange Protocol
PHY   Physical Layer
PICS   Protocol Implementation Conformance Statement
PIM   Protocol Independent Multicast
PLCP   Physical Layer Convergence Protocol
PLL   Phase Locked Loop
PLS   Physical Layer Signalling
PMA   Physical Medium Attachment
PMD   Physical Medium Dependent

PMP   Point-to-MultiPoint connection
P-NNI   Private NNI
POF   Plastic Optical Fiber
PPP   Point-to-Point Protocol
pps   packets per second
PRI   Primary Rate Interface
PSK   Phase Shift Keying
PTI   Payload Type Indicator
PU   Physical Unit
PVC   Permanent Virtual Circuit
OSPF   Open Shortest Path First
QLLC   Qualified LLC
QoS   Quality of Service
RARP   Reverse ARP
RDF   Rate Decrease Factor
REM   Ring Error Monitor
RFC   Request For Comments
RI   Ring In
RIF   Routing Information Field
       Rate Increase Factor
RII   Routing Information Indicator
RIJ   Route Initiated Join
RIP   Routing Information Protocol
RJ   Registered Jack
RLE   Réseau Local d'Entreprise
RLI   Réseau Local Industriel
RM   Resource Management (Cell)
RMON   Remote MONitoring
RNIS   Réseau Numérique à Intégration de Service
RO   Ring Out
RPC   Remote Procedure Call
RPS   Ring Parameter Server
RTMP   Routing Table Maintenance Protocol
RSVP   Resource Reservation Protocol
RUA   Reporting station's Upstream neighbor's Address
Rx   Receive
SAAL   Signaling ATM Adaptation Layer
SABME   Set Asynchronous Balanced Mode Extended
SAC   Single Attachment Concentrator
SAP   Service Access Point
       Server Advertising Protocol
SAR   Segmentation And Reassembly
SAS   Single Attachment Station
SC   Subscriber Connector
SCR   Sustainable Cell Rate
SCSI   Small Computer System Interface
SCSP   Server Cache Synchronization Protocol
SDH   Synchronous Data Hierarchy
SDLC   Synchronous Data Link Control

SDU   Service Data Unit
SEAL   Simple and Efficient Adaptation Layer
SGMP   Simple Gateway Management Protocol
SIG   Signaling
SIN   Ships in the Night
SMA   Sub Miniature Assembly connector
SMB   Server Message Block
SMDS   Switched Multimegabit Data Services
SMF   Single Mode Fiber
SMP   Standby Monitor Present
SMT   Station Management
SMTP   Simple Mail Transfer Protocol
SNA   Systems Network Architecture
SNAP   SubNetwork Access Protocol
SNDCP   SubNetwork Dependent Convergence Protocol
SNICP   SubNetwork Independent Convergence Protocol
SNMP   Simple Network Management Protocol
SNR   Signal to Noise Ratio
SONET   Synchronous Optical Network
SPM   Sonet Physical layer Mapping
SPP   Sequenced Packet Protocol
SPVC   Soft PVC
SPX   Sequenced Packet eXchange
SR   Source Routing
SRB   Single Route Broadcast
SRF   Specifically Routed Frame
SRTB   Source Routing Transparent Bridging
SSCOP   Service Specific Convergence Protocol
SSCF   Service Specific Convergence Function
ST   Straight Tip bayonet connector
STA   Spanning Tree Algorithm
STE   Spanning Tree Explorer
STP   Spanning Tree Protocol
          Shielded Twisted Pair
STM   Synchronous Transfer Mode
STS-Xc   Concatenated Synchronous Transport Signal level X
SVC   Switched Virtual Circuit/Channel
SVD   Simultaneous Voice & Data
TAPI   Telephony API
TAU   Trunk Access Unit
TAXI   Transparent Asynchronous Transmitter-receiver Interface
TB   Transparent Bridging
TC   Transmission Convergence
TCP   Transmission Control Protocol
TCU   Trunk Coupling Unit
TDM   Time Division Multiplexing
TFTP   Trivial File Transfer Protocol
THT   Token Holding Timer
TLV   Type Length Value

TM Traffic Management
TOP Technical and Office Protocol
TRT Token Rotation Time
TSAPI Telephony Services API
TTA Technique de Transfert Asynchrone
TTRT Target TRT
Tx Transmit
UBR Unspecified Bit Rate
UDP User Datagram Protocol
UNI User-to-Network Interface
USB Universal Serial Bus
UTP Unshielded Twisted Pair
VBR Variable Bit Rate
VCC Virtual Circuit/Channel Connection
VCI Virtual Circuit/Channel Identifier
VICP VINES Interprocess Communications Protocol
VIP VINES Internet Protocol
VLAN Virtual LAN
VLSI Very Large Scale Integration
VPI Virtual Path Identifier
VTAM Virtual Telecommunications Access Method
VTOA Voice & Telephony Over ATM
WAN Wide Area Network
WBC Wide Band Channek
WinSock Windows Sockets
WLAN Wireless LAN
XID eXchange (Station) Identification
XNS Xerox Network Systems
Xver Transceiver
ZIP Zone Information Protocol

Index